FIFTY YEARS
OF
INDIAN AGRICULTURE

VOLUME – 1 : PRODUCTION AND SELF-SUFFICIENCY

Vol. 1 : Production and Self-Sufficiency
Vol. 2 : Determinants of Production

About the Editors

Prof. Ali Mohammad is a distinguished author and teacher. An M.A. and Ph.D. from Aligarh Muslim University. His field of specialization is Agricultural Geography, Food Security and Nutritional Problems in rural India. He worked as a Senior Research Fellow in Jawaharlal Nehru University, as an Associate Professor at the Centre of West Asian Studies, Aligarh Muslim University, Aligarh, Associate Professor in Egerton University, Kenya, Professor in Asmara University East Africa, Eritea, and at present Professor in the Department of Geography, Aligarh Muslim University, Aligarh, Dr. Ali Mohammad has in his credit numerous research papers and more than one dozen books on Agriculture, Food Security and Nutritional Deficiency.

Prof. Abdul Munir is working as Chairman in the Department of Geography at the Aligarh Muslim University, Aligarh (India). Prof. Munir has a distinguished academic record and stood first at the M.A. examination. Prof. Munir has a wide ranging interest in many branches of Geography but specializes in agricultural Geography, Urban Geography and Quantitative Geography. Prof. Munir has authored a large number of articies which have been published in journals of repute. Besides, he has also authored several books in the field of Geography.

Prof. Hifzur Rehman is working as Professor in the Department of Geography at the Aligarh Muslim University, Aligarh (India). Prof. Rehman has authored many articles which have been published in journals of repute. Besides, he has supervised several research projects and authored several books in Geography.

FIFTY YEARS OF INDIAN AGRICULTURE

VOLUME – 1

PRODUCTION AND SELF-SUFFICIENCY

Edited by
ALI MOHAMMAD
ABDUL MUNIR
HIFZUR REHMAN

CONCEPT PUBLISHING COMPANY, NEW DELHI-110059

Cataloging in Publication Data—DK
Courtesy: D.K. Agencies (P) Ltd. <docinfo@dkagencies.com>

Fifty years of Indian agriculture / edited by Ali Mohammad, Abdul Munir, Hifzur Rehman.
2 v. cm.
Contributed articles.
Vol. 2 has editors: Ali Mohammad, Abdul Munir, Shamsul Haque Siddiqui.
Includes bibliographical references.
Includes indexes.
ISBN 8180693600

1. Agriculture—India—History. 2. Agricultural productivity—India—History. 3. Agriculture and state—India—History. I. Mohammad, Ali. II. Munir, Abdul. III. Rehman, Hifzur.

DDC 338.109 54 22

ISBN : 81-8069-360-0 (Set)
ISBN : 81-8069-361-9 (Vol. I)
ISBN : 81-8069-362-7 (Vol. II)

First Published 2007

Published and Printed by
Ashok Kumar Mittal
Concept Publishing Company
A/15-16, Commercial Block, Mohan Garden
New Delhi-110059 (INDIA)
Phone : 25351460, 25351794
Fax : 091-11-25357103
Email : publishing@conceptpub.com

PREFACE

The idea to complete a book on the performance of Indian agriculture after independence was originated with the discussion by Sompalji (Member Planning Commission) at Nagpur in the National Association of Geographers of India (NAGI) Conference and was decided that such a critical issue and a proper evaluation is possible only through organizing a conference at national level in an interdisciplinary manner. The much cherished aim to develop the agriculture was either fulfilled or remained incomplete was discussed in the conference within various agreement and disagreement. The issue of food self-sufficiency, being the main thrust while the food security as a dependent factor not only on food self-sufficiency, but various issues such as distributional factor at regional level was discussed. Environmental factors were also discussed at great length because during the conference period it was argued that environment was more or less favourable with the period 1989 till 2006 but fluctuation in food grain production was recorded very high in many years. It was also pointed out that during the inception of green revolutionary period wheat belt was highly encouraged while rice region was neglected inspite of that our two-third population is rice eater. A critical evaluation was highly appreciated that irrigation which is a crucial factor in agriculture was neglected as its increase was only 19 to 43 percent after independence till 50 years, while the fertilizer use, mechanization etc. was encouraged in an abnormal manner as compared to irrigation.

Some political aspects were also discussed in the context of the agricultural development after the division of the country. The focus was on rice and wheat production area. Our best land of wheat production and rice region both went to Pakistan as well as the two major dynamic community, i.e., Punjabi and Bengali largely remained with Pakistan which affected the production aspect of the country to such an extent that it was not easy to come out with the production gap created. Various other major issues were discussed in a highly interesting manner.

Among various issues of agricultural development after independence, British period was mentioned in relation to the land involved in food grain production and amount of land involved in commercial crops. The result of the argument was appreciated that instead of devoting 30 percent land in commercial only 10 percent should be given for this purpose. Additional land was responsible for the increase in production. But the argument took the turn that till now only 20 percent land was increased but production increased from 50 million tonnes to 210 million tonnes, the responsibility for such a high increase is thrown on the increase in per hectare productivity, therefore, only one option is left that productivity factors should be discussed and involved for further increase in production. Still the productivity per hectare of Indian agriculture is just half to the developed countries, therefore, this aspect i.e., productivity response factors should be identified at great length. A very optimistic picture emerged that such an agriculturally giant country can keep upper hand in food politics at least in Indian Ocean Countries.

Need is great to acknowledge the help received from various quarters in the preparation of this work. Mention must be made of the Department of Geography as a full cooperation of all the faculty members both teaching and non-teaching; of Mr. Sompalji ex-Minister of Agriculture and Member Planning Commission of India who thoroughly discussed the problem and especially appreciated the idea to evaluate the performance of Indian agriculture after independence; of Dr. K.V. Sundaram who inspired to hold such a conference and gave the direction being as a geographer and planner also was involved in various governments in planning; of Dr. M. Moni, Deputy Director General of Technology and Communication. There is a long list to be mentioned to acknowledge the people of various walks of life but we are especially thankful to all the authors of articles published in these two volumes.

Editors

CONTENTS

INTRODUCTION

Indian Agriculture govern the fortunes of national economy as it contributes about 40 per cent of gross domestic products and employing about two-third of the country's labour force. It is a well-established fact that rapid agricultural growth holds the key to the solution of the endemic socio-economic problems and elevation of rural poverty confronting the country. The much-vaunted trickle down effect of industrial sector has not materialized. Therefore, agriculture will remain as a major source of sustainable livelihood for the two-third of the total population. The Green Revolution has solved the food problem of the country and helped to keep the growth rate of food production ahead of the population growth rate of the country but has created the regional imbalances in agricultural development which is against the basic spirit of the planning objectives, i.e., to remove the regional imbalances and bring the social justice.

It was a challenge to the planners because a depressing picture. How far the objectives achieved after fifty years of independence on a very poor base has been taken into account in this conference. During the British period over 80 per cent of the sown area was under cultivation of foodgrain crops and yet the total output of foodgrains was insufficient for the needs of the country. The large part of the farming was of subsistence nature and average size of holdings was small and uneconomic. About 25 per cent of the total sown area received irrigation and the rest 75 per cent had to depend on rainfall for raising any crop, which created a situation of high level of fluctuations causing food insecurity. The incentives for greater efforts on the part of the farmer for increased production or for the landowner to make investments in permanent improvements of land were practically non-existent. During the end of the British period the peasantry was mired in poverty and heavy indebtedness. These were little institutional credit available and borrowing that was mainly for consumption purposes had to be from the village moneylenders and the urban traders to whom the farmer would pledge to next year's produce. The number of landless labours had been increasing for the last several decades and today it is reached to the level of 17 per cent. Apart from unemployment for more than six months in a year, the wage rate paid to the farm labours during the days of employment were low but after 50 years of independence the situation has taken a bit positive turn, i.e., unemployment period is reduced and wage rate has been changed because of the increased rate of irrigation in many pockets of India as well as development in transportation system which has increased the efficiency in movement of labours to the regions of high productivity area. During the end of the British period scientific agriculture was yet to make its appearance in the country. No doubt the adoption and diffusion of HYV and pesticides as well as irrigation and fertilizer intake the move towards Green Revolution has changed the total scenario in achieving the food self-sufficiency till the end of the century. No doubt lapses are there as there was a great emphasis to develop the wheat belt as compared to the rice belt and pulses production remained stagnant. During the end of the British period lift irrigation and ploughing were based on drought animals but today in larger part of the area it is done with the help of tractors, pumping sets and tubewells. An interesting picture has emerged, i.e., small landholders are hiring these facilities from the large size farmers to plough the land and irrigate the crops. It will not be non-serious to mention that the situation has taken just opposite to the long prevailing system, i.e., small and marginal farmers were being hired to plough, irrigate and harvest the crop but now large size of landholders are being hired for these activities. What are the positive and negative impact of such a system needs further investigation. It is also being observed that big international companies are acquiring the land for agro-based industrial set-up. After an intensive survey of large number of villages, spreading from Punjab to West Bengal (Indo-Gangetic plain), it is observed that scientific agriculture has been adopted in all the regions in different locations in the Indo-Gangetic plain with variations in scale out of 10 locations of the region (Indo-Gangetic) the situation twenty-five years before was negligible in terms of the scientific agriculture except of three location, i.e., Etah, Aligarh, Meerut, Rohtak, Karnal and Patiala-Ludhiana. After 1985 no doubt tube-well irrigation has spread in well-identified locations with great success such as in Eastern U.P. and North Bihar plain. These regions were far behind the level of self-sufficiency but today these were one of the poorest food regions of the country is producing more than 18 per cent in surplus. Farmers may turn their policies to change the cropping pattern replacing with high remunerative value crops. An individual decision may lead the cropping pattern in a wrong direction.

The historical shortcoming either have been removed or still prevailing is a matter of discussion. It is removed either it has taken a wrong direction or helped the farmer in a sustainable manner.

On the whole British period provided a very poor base to achieve the required level of food self-sufficiency because of the overemphasis on non-commercial crops by 30 per cent of gross cultivated area. After independence till 2001 it is reduce upto 10 per cent only and to achieve the self-sufficiency 90 per cent is being devoted to foodgrain crops. After 1965 emphasis was given on two major crops, i.e., Wheat and Rice occupying about 67 per cent of the gross cultivated area. These two crops are characterized as the highest productivity crops and till 1985 the performance is now characterized as self-sufficient in foodgrains production. With the increase of irrigation, fertilizers and HYV, the best pulses growing area was converted under wheat or rice crops. The most required protein rich pulses crops remained stagnant both in terms of area and total production with an insignificant variation from 10.7 million hectare to 12.6 million hectare after independence. With the increase of population per head availability declined from 64 grams to 24 grams per day. The prices of pulses increased very high in the ratio of prices of cereals, and importation became a big liability on the nation. During 1960s it was being considered as a poor man's diet now it is the rich man's diet as compared to the substitutes available such as potato and vegetables.

To what extent these above mentioned shortcomings were removed within the fifty years of independence and national need was fulfilled were discussed during the period of the conference. Basically a set of articles were presented on the total achievements of the fifty years and large number of articles were presented on the existing level of achievements and the results obtained can be related with past situation.

After independence we started the agricultural development planning with the following objectives:

(i) Increase in foodgrain production and protective foods to improve the food security situation through the basic food items and improve the pulses situation because of its value as a protective food.

(ii) To improve the situation of regional imbalances in agriculture performance with the major consideration of social justice.

(iii) Stimulating production of raw materials for industry and exports.

(iv) Securing remunerative prices for the producer and fare wages to agricultural labour.

(v) Ensuring fare distribution of the food produced as it is one of the major components of food security. The situation till now is very critical. Firstly, the storing performance is so poor that trucks used to wait for more than one week to unload the foodgrains and it is stored at various places in the half constructed buildings without roof.[1] Similarly the distribution of foodgrains at critical period of time the region effected by some natural disasters remain untouched with food distribution. A major problem is already existing and likely to take a serious turn in future, i.e., distribution of food production among the most disadvantageous and deprived segment of population. They are identified as population below the poverty line such as urban-slum dwellers with poor purchasing power, landless agricultural labourers, small-marginal farmers etc. The system of the distribution of foodgrains is needed to be improved also among all the sections of population either rural or urban. Any judicious exercise is needed in fixing the sale prices as well as the scale and size of production is to be decided with the increase and change of rural and urban population and change in income. All these is needed to decide the quality and quantity of production in order to check the disbalanced production effecting the fluctuations in prices. A very serious attempt is still needed for the benefit of both producers and consumers.

(vi) Increase in area under foodgrain, non-foodgrain and fodder is needed in a situation of largest share of small and marginal farmers to the total number of landholdings as well as increasing landlessness. It will provide the landownership among these segments of population which will check the unplanned rural out-migration to the big and industrial cities. The attempt during the period of 'fifty years' is going on by establishing the landuse board in various states but it is most unsuccessful in the hilly, mountainous and semi-desert regions. The reclamation of culturable wastelands and its distribution even without reclaiming the land is under plan but not very laudable, though a large share of land is available under this category of land, i.e., about 124 million hectare land is under net cultivated area and 64 million hectare under culturable wasteland in the country. Intensification of cultivated area is still needed as its scope and possibilities is about 300 per cent but today it is only 141 per cent. The

1. A survey result of storage of foodgrains between Aligarh to Moradabad Road on 15th June 2001.

direction of landuse pattern needs special attention, i.e., land capacity analysis is required and share of land under different uses should be scientifically and economically decided. Therefore an intensive analysis of land cover and landuse change at micro level is needed. Similarly the diversification of cropping pattern needs special attention differently among large size and small size landholders with remunerative value of crops. The practice and policy of large-scale foodgrain production is being rejected by some of the regions after achieving the food self-sufficiency because of the low remunerative value as compared to some of the cash and commercial crops. The best example so far available is derived from the most recent agricultural data from seven districts of Western Uttar Pradesh mostly along the border of Haryana where about 70 per cent of the cultivated area is devoted to non-foodgrain crops. It shows that the model presented by the Punjab and Haryana is now no more applicable and useful to the farmers. Only one option is left with the existing system of foodgrain production, i.e., the country is surrounded by some of the chronic food deficit regions with Geographical proximity such as West Asian and Indian ocean coastal African countries. If India compete with the quality in the international foodgrain market it will help in minimizing the deficit trade balance especially with the Middle Eastern countries. However, distribution is one of the best indicators to promote quality, quantity and type of production.

(vii) An assured base of water supply for irrigation will remain a crucial factor in a country like India where about 80 per cent of the cultivated area is depend on natural rainfall while only 20 per cent is free from enviromental influence. The level of irrigation could not increase to a desirable extent because of the low priority as compare to the fertilizer, HYV etc. the increase after fifty years is recorded only from 19 per cent to 47 per cent while during early 1970s Water Commission emphasized that if all the cultivated area is irrigated the nation can produce 450 million metric tonnes of foodgrains. In some of the pockets the identification of the means of irrigation boosted the production after 1980 such as spread of tubewells.

Still the desired level of irrigation is not achieved which needs a special emphasis at regional level to remove the high level of fluctuations in foodgrain production which is still considered as a major threat to food security system. The unequal distribution of irrigation rate is affecting the spread of improved variety of seeds and needed fertilizer intake. The situation is still in the same ratio as it was in the beginning of the Green Revolution.

With the beginning of Green Revolution in 1967-68, there was a dramatic change in the situation. The revolution caused a qualitative change in the food and agriculture situation. The Pearson report described the change as 'one of the authentic marvels of our time'.

In the fourth plan growth with social justice policy was adopted to help the vulnerable section of backward areas. Beside attainment of self-sufficiency in foodgrains, the plan envisaged building-up of a sizeable buffer stock of foodgrains and stoppage of concessional imports of foodgrains.

The fifth plan, while adhering the basic policies of the fourth plan, made some modifications in the programmes for agriculture with a view of increasing their efficiency. It was proposed to cover more food crops under HYV. New programme was to cover not only irrigated agriculture but also dry farming areas in a large scale. A new programme was chalked out particularly for oil seeds and pulses, which were in serious short supply. Drought prone areas to tackle in a systematic way during the plan period. Subsequently in sixth to eighth plans the objective of planning remained more or less the same except of the emphasis on 'growth with social justice'.

The experience upto eighth five year plan seems to be encouraging at cereal front but the situation of pulses is still very poor and availability per head is declining causing heavy imports; on the whole the nation has achieved the food self-sufficiency but the contribution of pulses has gone down just to half after independence. The foodgrains growth from the last many years is recorded more than the population growth but on a very poor base of availability. Still the foodgrains production fluctuation is a serious problem to be tackled causing food insecurity among the small farmers and disadvantageous rural classes.

However, the following are the basic issues to be raised and to be solved :

1. Growth with social justice.
2. Control over the foodgrain fluctuation situation.
3. Scarcity in plenty—the chief characteristic of water resources on irrigation front should be tackled.
4. Regional inequality in agricultural development.
5. Population and food availability should be the basic criteria to identify the agricultural backward areas.
6. After achieving the national goal of food self-sufficiency, a new direction of agricultural development in relation to international

perspective should be the objective as the country is surrounded by the chronic food deficit countries and regions.

7. A diversified cropping pattern is needed and a thorough research and survey is needed at micro-level to introduce the high value crops among the disadvantageous group of small and marginal farmers. Only an integrated approach is needed to prepare a sound plan for this segment of population, which can provide sustainable livelihood in the villages in order to minimize the unplanned movement of population to many of unattractive locations.

The proceeding of the conference is divided into two volumes, i.e., Production and Self-Sufficiency and Determinants of Production.

Swaminathan in his article of Indian agriculture has pin-pointed that the prevention of famines and achieving self-sufficiency in foodgrain has been the outstanding feature of Indian agriculture after independence. Political will and action being the factor responsible for the transformation. Thus, on the threshold of new century and millennium, India is poised to become the flagship of a global movement for an evergreen revolution on the farms rooted in the principles of ecology, economies, social and gender equity, energy conservation and employment generation.

Sundaram in his article of the small farmer development strategies for the next millennium, attempted to synthesize the various operational ways adopted by government in the developing countries of Asia to encourage small farmers' development. During the course of the discussion, the relevance of as well as the inadequacies in the various strategies adopted by government has been critically commented upon. The author points out to certain corrective measures as well as lessons and provide some direction for change. This sufficient indication on the analysis shows that the small farmers have not received the just and equitable share of development benefits from the normal development strategies.

Husain in his study of Green Revolution in India and the performance of major cereal crops has found that the adoption of HYV of major cereal crops like wheat and rice has been considered a significant achievement after the Green Revolution. These varieties of seeds have revolutionized the agricultural landscape of India by enhancing area, production and yield of wheat and rice significantly. The author has emphasized that there are inter and intra-regional variations in the productivity of wheat and rice which is a cause of great concern of the Indian agriculture.

Arora and Mangal in their article of Fifty Years of Vegetable Research in India revealed that in past three decades India has made a quantum jump in vegetable production, securing second position in the world. Vegetable research in India gained momentum after first-half of the century to acquire the present status having moderate infrastructure facilities and research priorities for vegetables in Indian institutions. However, authors pointed out that the amount of vegetable production is much less than our requirement. Thus, the strategy and guidelines may be used for bridging the existing gap between production and requirement.

Tapeshwar Singh in his study of Green Revolution, food security and agricultural sustainability in India revealed that the achievements of the Green Revolution in the context of natural food security and agro-ecological problems play an important role. Sustainability aspects of the current policies and practices of agricultural development is also examined in the present study. Efficient management of natural resources and environment-friendly farm technology may play a pivotal role in crop production and sustainable agricultural development.

Siddiqui in his paper, dimension of agricultural land resource and population pressure in Deoria district of U.P. pointed out that the increasing pressure of human resource on land resources are creating problems in agro-based societies. The author has pointed out that, if these lands are utilized at maximum level the pressure of human resources on land may be minimized. Further, if multi-cropping system is encouraged and current fallow land are brought under cultivation the pressure on land resources and security of food may be reduced.

Asad and Sami in his study of hydrological environment and water resource evolution of an alluvial aquifer in the central Ganga plain found out that the rapid agricultural growth, rising standards of living and changing social structure have in recent years put severe stress on water resources. Because of its stable quality, groundwater has long been reliable source of water for domestic, agricultural and industrial users. Authors have drawn conclusion after investigation that study area has large potential of good quality groundwater.

Ahmad and Rahman in their study of techno-institutional and socio-economic determinants and their correlation with the adoption of agricultural innovations in Upper Ganga-Yamuna Doab, revealed that with the inception of Green Revolution, different forms of agricultural innovations have been introduced in India, which has radically transformed the methods and techniques used in agricultural practices. The variations are among farmers to the adoption of these new methods and techniques due to existing diverse physico-cultural and socio-economic conditions in ecological setting of the region. Study further reveals that all the factors considered in the discussion have positive correlation with the adoption of agricultural innovations.

Khursheed and Jeelani in the hydro-geo-chemical investigation of major springs of Kashmir Valley found that the discharge of the spring responds directly to the melting of snow in the upper reaches. Rock water interaction of the springs has a direct control over the quality of water. Author, classified twenty samples in two classes, i.e. cold (sixteen) and hot (four) springs. Analytical parameters show that the spring water in Anantnag, Kashmir is potable and can be used for irrigation and other purposes.

R. K. Sharma in his article population growth and agricultural change in India since independence discussed that despite the population growth, there is sustainable increase in food production, which has increased significantly after independence. The compound increase in cropping area, irrigation facilities and use of multiple cropping and HYV. Author emphasized that in order to reduce dependency on agriculture, Government should create employment opportunities in the rural areas by developing agro-based industries in rural areas.

Sharma and Tripathi have made the study of assessment of the potential and demand of water resources of Tons basin and found out that the use of water is not limited to drinking, domestic and irrigation purposes, but has multiplied. Contrary to the expanding demand, its supply is limited and can be depleted or made unusable by excessive utilization, inadequate conservation, misutilization, pollution or careless management. Multifaceted approach would be necessary to ensure a balance in the water system. Technical means can also minimize the damage caused by floods, which is a major natural hazard.

Nikhil and Mobin have analyzed the management of irrigation efficiency in Damodar river basin. They observed that the basic problem facing the agriculturists and engineers is how to use the water efficiently so that maximum profit can be obtained. Irrigation efficiency according to them is the percentage of delivered irrigation water that is stored in the soil and available for consumption and use by crops. The proper water management is not simple, especially, for the farmers of developing countries due to lack of modern technology.

Iqbal in his study of scientific approach through local adages in Indian agriculture analyzed that agriculture plays significant role in the economy of India. The Indian peasants have good knowledge of weather and may forecast it. They have also through scientific knowledge of timely irrigation, weeding of crops, application of manures and fertilizers, methods of harvesting etc. although the majority of the peasant population is not literate but they achieved the scientific knowledge for good agriculture harvest through their long practical experience which is really commendable.

Ahmad and Kausar have studied the trend and level of diffusion of irrigation and its impact on the adoption of agricultural innovations in Upper Ganga-Yamuna Doab. They concluded that irrigation is not only essential for the sustenance of agriculture but also its assured and timely supply is prerequisite for diversifying agriculture and to enhance resource efficiency of related inputs. The adoption of certain agricultural innovations like chemical fertilizers, HYV, plant protection chemicals etc, is solely depends upon assured and timely availability of water. Analysis also revealed that new package programmes have a profound influence to bring more and more area under irrigation.

Gill and Yadav in their article, consequences of groundwater depletion in a semi-arid tract of Haryana, attempted to analyze the consequences of depletion of groundwater in Dochana village of Haryana. The village witnessed rapid increase in area under tubewell irrigation during 1975-85 which, in turn, led to depletion of its groundwater resources. Consequently, most of the tubewells had gone dry in the village by early 1990s. The study focuses on the socio-economic impact of the rise and fall in the tubewell irrigated area in this semi-arid tract of Haryana.

Bagchi has discussed the locating data gaps in planning strategies for micro-level development of difficult rained areas of eastern India with particular focus on soil and water resources management. He has elaborated that the participatory resource mapping being supplemented with computer aided tools like GIS can come to our aid not only to identify resource endowment but also to prioritize development steps.

Ahmad and Ghazala in their article of the study of regional imbalances of agricultural productivity have pointed out that in terms of social justice the imbalances in level of agriculture productivity should be minimized to attain an over all self sufficiency at spatial level and not only at national level and a strategy for planning and development should be evolved.

Ala Eldin *et al.*, in their study of assessment of seepage losses from canal in Ganga Kali sub-basin, have analyzed that the irrigated agricultural area in the central Ganga-Plain is dependent mainly on the groundwater resources for sustained growth and prosperity. However, declining water levels and increase in demand for more groundwater exploitation threatened the future development of agriculture that is solely dependent on groundwater. The groundwater balance in study shows that half of the seepage losses from the canals leaves the basin as groundwater effluence to Ganga, Chioyya and Nim rivers.

Surendra in his paper, regional dimensions of agricultural growth potentials, incorporated a normative production function for the analysis of identifying and regionalizing growth potential phenomena for preparing regional investment strategy area development. It is concluded that the lowland areas of main rivers have higher intensity and magnitude of production potentials than the central part of the study area.

Rangi and Sidhu have analyzed the problems and prospects of agriculture in Punjab and pointed out that, the number of factors have made possible the progress in farm sector in Punjab. These include the introduction of HYV, assured price policy and supporting infrastructure for supply of different inputs and dissemination of technical knowledge. To enhance income of the farmers of state, subsidiary enterprises may be encouraged by the policy makers and administrators.

Shafiqullah in his study of pattern of agriculture employment in Uttar Pradesh found that Uttar Pradesh is predominantly agriculture economy, having population pressure on agriculture and reflects the lack of development in other sectors. Study further revealed that agricultural employment is inversely proportional to urbanization, industrialization, vital process, literacy rate and workers in other sectors.

Yasir and Mahfooz in their study of the development of floriculture in India found that floriculture has become a potential money spinner for the developing country like ours. Authors concluded that India has immense potential of floriculture to exploit it commercially in the domestic market as well as for export.

Irfan in his article of principles of pest control of agro-ecosystem pointed out that the ultimate objective of the integrated pest control system is to produce the optimum crop yield of high quality at minimum cost taking into consideration the ecological and sociological constraints in that particular agro-ecosystem and the long-term preservation of the environment.

Yasir and Jamshed have discussed the crisis, constraints and causes in pulses production in Uttar Pradesh since independence. The low productivity of pulses in various parts of the state and country as well are due to non-availability of high yielding disease resistant varieties, cultivation on marginal and sub-marginal lands under deficit moisture, fertility and poor pest management.

Mansoor and Ameenul in their article quality of water for irrigation of Garra River, have emphasized on the suitability of water for irrigation. On the basis of analysis of water quality parameters, authors concluded that quality of water has greater importance than quantity of water.

Mansoor and Mujtaba examined the inter-state pulses situation in India. They analyzed the variation in availability of pulses per capita per day at state level. Study revealed the declining trend of availability of pulses since 1970s. They emphasized the need for enhancing area under pulses production, besides having more attention to formulate the suitable programmes and policies from planners and researchers.

Mansoor, Yasir and Mujtaba in their article foodgrains availability in Indo-Gangetic plain made an elaborate study of foodgrains availability in this physiographic division of India taking it as a whole. Although Indo-Gangetic plain is self-sufficient in foodgrains production but in terms of per capita availability at micro level they are not self-sufficient. They emphasized that there is a need to re-evaluate and re-organize the plan and policies at priority basis to eradicate the imbalances in per capita availability of foodgrains.

LIST OF THE CONTRIBUTORS

Ahmad Mujtabe Siddiqui, Research Scholar, Department of Geography, Aligarh Muslim University, Aligarh

A.K. Chhaukar, Reader, Department of Geography, N.R.E.C. College, Khurja (U.P.)

Ali Ghufran, Ex-Research Scholar, Department of Agricultural, Economics and Business Management, Aligarh Muslim University, Aligarh

Ali Mohammad, Chairman, Department of Geography, Aligarh Muslim University, Aligarh

Anil Kumar, Head, Department of Geography, T.M. Bhagalpur University, Bhagalpur (Bihar)

Dhian Kaur, Department of Geography, Punjab University, Chandigarh

G.S. Chauhan, Department of Geography, Dr. Bhim Rao Ambedkar College, University of Delhi, Delhi

Hon'ble Chaturanan Mishra, Former Union Minister of Agriculture, Government of India

J.L. Mangal, Head, Department of Vegetable Crops, CCS Haryana Agricultural University, Hissar

Jabir Hasan Khan, Lecturer, Department of Geography, Aligarh Muslim University, Aligarh

K.V. Sundaram, Member, State Planning Board, Karnataka

M.S. Sidhu, Department of Economics and Sociology, Punjab Agricultural University, Ludhiana, Punjab

M.S. Swaminathan, Chairman, M.S. Swaminathan Research Foundation, 3rd Cross Road, Taramani Institution Area, Chennai.

Majid Husain, Department of Geography, Jamia Millia Islamia, New Delhi

Mansoor Ali, Research Scholar, Department of Geography, Aligarh Muslim University, Aligarh

Miss Ananya Taraphder, Research Scholar, Burdwan University, Burdwan (W.B.)

Mohammad Siddique, Reader, Department of Geography, Aligarh Muslim University, Aligarh

Mohammad Yusuf, Assistant Librarian, Maulana Azad Library, Aligarh Muslim University, Aligarh

N.K. De, Research Scholar, Burdwan University, Burdwan (W.B.)

Nisar Ahmad Khan, Reader, Department of Economics, Aligarh Muslim University, Aligarh

P.S. Rangi, Senior Economist, Department of Economics and Sociology, Punjab Agricultural University, Ludhiana

R.C. Tyagi, Fellow, Giri Institute of Development Studies, Sector 'O', Aliganj, Lucknow

R.S. Sangwan, Department of Geography, M.D. University, Rohtak (Haryana)

Rais Ahmad, Reader, Department of Agricultural Economics and Business Management, Aligarh Muslim University, Aligarh

Rameshwar Thakur, Reader, Department of Geography, B.R. Ambedkar College, University of Delhi, Delhi

S.K. Arora, Department of Vegetable Crops, CCS Haryana Agricultural University, Hissar

S.M. Waseem, Ex. Dean Faculty of Commerce, Chairman, Department of Commerce, Coordinator DSA Programme, Aligarh Muslim University, Aligarh

S.S.A. Jafri, Senior Fellow, Giri Institute of Development Studies, Sector 'O', Aliganj, Lucknow

Shah Manzoor Alam, Former Vice Chancellor, University of Kashmir (J & K)

Shri Sompal, Member, Planning Commission, Government of India, New Delhi

Surendra Singh, Department of Geography, North-Hill University, Shillong

Y.K. Mittal, Department of Geography, J.V.M.G.R.R. College, Charkhi, Dadri (Haryana)

Yadvinder Singh, Department of Geography, Punjabi University, Patiala

Yasir Sayeed Hanafi, Research Scholar, Department of Geography, Aligarh Muslim University, Aligarh

1

PRESIDENTIAL ADDRESS

HON'BLE SHRI SOMPAL*

Respected Vice-Chancellor Dr. Mahmood-ur-Rahaman Sahib, Pro-Vice-Chancellor Prof. Jafri, Dr. Ali Mohammad Sahib, heading the Department of Geography currently, Prof. Dr. K.V. Sundaram, Prof. Shafi, Dr. G.B. Singh, distinguished delegates from other countries, and our own, distinguished media representatives, Dear Members of alumni, Faculty Members, Ladies and Gentlemen.

I feel highly honoured to have been invited to inaugurate the Golden Jubilee Celebrations of the Department of Geography at the Aligarh Muslim University. As students of History, we know that the Indian polity and society witnessed great changes during the later part of 19th Century and the first half of 20th. A series of reformist movements came up during this period, seeking to change the medieval India into a modern one. The greatest thrust of these was on education. Great personalities like Raja Ram Mohan Roy, Bankim Chandra Chatterji, Rabindranath Tagore, Swami Vivekananda, Swami Dayanand Saraswati, Mahadev Govind Ranade, Bal Gangadhar Tilak, Subhas Chandra Bose, Mahatma Gandhi and many more were in the forefront. A great son belonging to this class was Sir Syed Ahmed Khan, who founded the Mohammadan Anglo-Oriental College, which was raised to the status of university in 1920. The Department of Geography in this University was created in 1924 and thus it happens to be the oldest centre of geographic studies, not only in India, but whole of South Asia. The Department has since then produced a galaxy of geographers. Most of

* Member, Planning Commission in the Inaugural Session of the International Conference on Golden Jubilee Celebrations of the Department of Geography, Aligarh Muslim University, Aligarh.

the Departments of Geography in the universities of India, Pakistan, Bangladesh have been headed by an 'Aligarian', as all products of this great university are fondly called. The first research journal simply named 'the Geographer' too was started here in 1926 by the founder of the Department, Prof. Major E.W. Dann. The journal commands global reputation by now. Having a rich library with 30,000 books and several national and international journals, four lecture theatres, two laboratories, one cartography lab, map and photography sections, survey instruments room, twenty staff rooms and modern computers, the Department must be the best equipped in the country and thus a matter of envy for all other Indian universities. It is, therefore, that late Prof. Dudley Stamp had rightly declared it as the Mecca of Indian Geography, which I am confident and wish it will remain for ever. It is my proud privilege to congratulate you all on this grand occasion when the Department has completed 75 successful years with alround glory.

Friends, may I reveal that geography has been the most fascinating subject for me since my childhood school days. I fondly recall how we were taught to draw, in free hand, maps of district Meerut, U.P. State and then India in our 3rd, 4th and 5th standards in the village primary pathasala and remember by heart, the boundaries, called in Urdu *Hadudarba* and the important geographical features thereof. Fortunately, in those days, we continued with geography studies as a separate subject in our middle classes too. I do not know what is the position today. The monsoons, climates, Himalayas, major rivers, soil types, coastal areas and tides, the reversing direction of day-night breeze thereon, the celestial bodies like earth and moon, the eclipses, the volcanoes, the geographical formations, the hot and cold streams in the ocean, the forests, crops, animals and human races all were studied by us. I must confess that when I came to the Parliament of India and later was appointed Minister of Agriculture and Water Resources, the basic knowledge acquired at primary and middle school stage helped me a lot in my contribution to Parliamentary debates and influence Government decision-making through Parliamentary committees, then in the Ministry and now a Member of the Planning Commission.

Today's function for me is a great co-incidence. I had a chance meeting with Prof. Ali Mohammad, currently heading this Department during the 21st Geographic Congress of India on 2nd January, 2000 at Nagpur. Immediately after the inaugural session of the Congress, Prof. Ali Mohammad informed me of his intention to invite me to today's function. And I readily agreed. I am told that the main thrust of this

Department's studies has been agricultural geography. Though other fields like environmental geography, population geography, rural geography, urban geography, social geography, bio geography, political geography, regional development and planning and mathematical geography too are studied and researched here. Of late, arid zone research and use of remote sensing and aerial photo interpretation too have been added.

Friends, having been born in a very ordinary farmer's family in a small remote village Kakorkalan in Distt. Meerut, now Baghpat, situated on the eastern bank of river Yamuna, fortunately, I have seen and experienced the difficulties and drudgery of farming classes; and more fortunately, with God's grace, I have been able to keep my sensitivity towards these intact so far. Therefore, my agricultural bias is but natural. Even at the cost of being called an heretic, I may allude that I continue to subscribe to the view of French School of Economists, known as Physiocrats, who believed that agriculture is the only productive economic activity. All others, including industry and trade, are nothing but conversions of basic agri-produce. If we view the God's creation in form of all celestial bodies and more so our Mother Planet Earth, all products – natural or man-made – have something or the other to do with natural bio-mass production. Even the sustenance of environment of this planet depends on the green cover in form of forests, orchards, crops, medicinal plants, aromatic plants, etc. Rather the whole life cycle including that of birds, the animals, human beings and micro organisms is derived from and related to green cover. Therefore, I am really delighted to know the emphasis here is on agricultural geography.

Geographically, our country India is really unique. We all know that a great accident of nature, known as the movement of tectonic plates separated the Indian plate from the African continent some millions of years ago. The plate then collided with the Eurasia plate on the southern verge of China. It is held by the scientists that that south-western pressure on the plate still continues to be exerted, pushing one part of India plate under China and the upper part, known as Himalayas, rising by a few inches every year. The great accident turned out to be a boon for us as it is this event that was responsible for creation of the highest and the longest mountains of the world, the Himalayas. The 7,700 km. long shallow coastal zone including Arabian Gulf in the west and the Bay of Bengal in the east, extending up to the Emerald Archipelago, the Andamans and the 200 miles Exclusive Economic Zone throughout this length are of great economic and security value to us. India, perhaps, is the only or one of the few countries in the world, who can boast of having all the 15 major climates of the globe. We have a great diversity in terms of varied rainfalls and sunshine patterns including the 0-50 mm lowest or no rainfall arid areas of Thar Desert in the west and the highest rain point in the world, known as Chirapunji in north-east, receiving about 13,000 mm rains per year; the round-the-year snow clad Himalayas, depicting a polar scenario and the southern tip of Kanyakumari known for high humidity, high temperature, presenting the equatorial climate. We have more than 46 of about 60 major soil types found in world. Commensurate with these, we have a tremendous bio-diversity in form of plants, animals, birds and humans. In has 48,000 plant species, which is about 11 per cent of the world's plant genetic resources. Similarly our domestic and wild animal wealth is 10 per cent of the world, while our geographical area is only 2 per cent. If we have a look at the list of domesticated animals, we find that there are 30 descript breeds of cattle, 20 of goat, 12 of sheep, 6 of horses, 4 of camels and many other animals like donkeys, mules, yaks and so on. Similarly, rich is our wild animal wealth. We, perhaps, have the largest number of fruits, vegetables, foodgrains and commercial crops, legumes, oilseeds, flowers, medicinal and aromatic plants. The International Gene Bank collection of rice at Manila, Philippines, is said to be having 70,000 accessions from all the rice producing countries of the world. More than 20,000 of these have been contributed by India. Our Ayurvedic and Unani systems of medicine have been using thousands of herbs since long to cure human and animals. The culinary habits and cuisines perfected by Indian society over ages are not only magnificently large in numbers but also excellent in taste and relish the human palate world over. India is known to be having a history of agri-practices as old as 10,000 years, as per the Royal Commission on Agriculture, set up by the British in 1936. Based on agriculture, our culture too is equally old and diverse and may be it is therefore that impelled some scholars to remark that India has only one culture, that is, agriculture. Along this great diversity developed our languages, customs, family system and villages and towns making it the richest in the world.

India, thus, has always been an agricultural country and continues to be so even now. Approximately 64 per cent of our population is still directly dependent on agriculture. 28 per cent of our GDP is contributed by the agriculture sector. Thus, it is not only the largest source of production but also the biggest consumer. It provides not only all food needs, but also all the major raw-materials required by industry. The largest industries of our country, i.e. textiles, sugar, food processing and edible oil and vanaspati, are directly dependent on agriculture for their raw materials in form of cotton, silk, jute, mesta, foodgrains, oilseeds, vegetables, fruits, flowers, milk and milk products. Thus, agriculture is the largest employer, biggest producer-supplier and the biggest consumer and, therefore, the widest market of our economy.

We have made tremendous progress in agriculture since independence. There was a time when we were living in a ship-to-mouth regime, as we were importing large quantities of foodgrains to feed our hungry millions. For about two decades, we were getting food aid under PL-480 from America, which was dried up in 1967. The next year, i.e. 1968 happened to be a year of great difficulty. Neither we had enough production nor adequate foreign exchange to buy food in international market. The then Agriculture Minister of India Shri C. Subramanyam was sent abroad to buy food. On his return, the media persons present at the Delhi Airport wanted to know from him about his experience. While responding to them, Mr. Subramanyam virtually broke down and painfully remarked : "Let God never create a situation where once again, I have to go abroad begging for food." It was in the wake of this bitter experience, that the strategy of intensive agriculture based on high irrigation, dwarf high yielding varieties, of rice and wheat particularly, and high direct input use was conceived and put into practice. This has obviously paid high dividends and we are now producing not only enough for our own consumption, but for exporting and you will be pleased to know that every sixth dollar earned by way of exports comes from agri exports. Last year, we have been able to achieve an all-time high of 203 million tonnes of foodgrain production. In milk, India has attained first position in the world by producing more than 74 million tonnes beating America. In production of fruit, vegetable, fish, wheat, cotton, coffee, tea, tobacco, potato, jute and mesta etc., we rank 2nd or the 3rd. This success story of Indian agriculture has been given by the now famous name of Green Revolution. Along with the Green, we area now talking of White, Blue and Yellow Revolutions in the fields of milk, fish and oilseeds. All the countries of the world including the most developed ones have hailed the success. The developing countries have started looking towards India as their role model and trying to emulate.

In addition to factors like irrigation, high yielding varieties, use of direct inputs, availability of credit, storage facilities and remunerative prices based on statutory minimum prices assured to farmers, that have contributed to this success we must not forget that basically it has been possible on account of our natural resources created by geographical situation and features of India. We are aware that agriculture is an economic activity based on bio-mass production with the combined use of three basic natural resources – land, water and genetic material. Even the human resource is genetic one.

The question, which usually crops up at this stage, is where to go beyond this point and how to produce more. Whether Indian agriculture can give us higher production and productivity than the present. There have been apprehensions expressed earlier and as late as mid-70s some prophets of doom predicted that Indian agriculture would collapse. They have been doubting India's capability to produce enough for its consumption, not to say of surpluses to export. We have great satisfaction in saying that these prophets of doom have been proved wrong. At least, I do not have any doubt about raising the levels of production as well as productivity in our country. My assessment is based on the following few facts.

We still have substantial resources in terms of land, water and genetic material, which if properly utilised, can take us to substantially higher levels. The usual impression created that we do not have land beyond 144 million hectares of the present cultivated area is not correct. Fortunately, 56 per cent of our total geographical area of 328.9 million hectares is arable as compared to 11 per cent of the globe. According to the land used survey statistics, we still have about 80 million hectares of unutilised land, which can broadly half at half be utilised for agriculture and afforestation. Unfortunate part is that it is not only lying unutilised, but being subjected to several types of threats of the degradation like erosion, corrosion, desertification, water logging, alkalinity, salinity, etc. If this basic resource could be made available to the people in viable economic sizes, it can prove to be the first and the foremost programme for alleviating poverty and imparting dignity to minimum half the population living below poverty line in rural and tribal areas. The most elementary needs of drinking water, food, clothing, shelter and nutrition can be provided to such a large number of poor people within the shortest possible time.

The geographers are expected to come out with a realistic and reliable survey of such lands and suggest the economically viable sizes according to fertility and location which will help devise a practicable land use programme. Even for undertaking measures like consolidation, which has been mainly responsible for enhancing of production and productivity in the Green Revolution areas, led by Punjab, Haryana,

Rajasthan, U.P., etc., the geographers do have a role. Tackling the menace of stress on soil fertility, caused by water logging, alkalinity, salinity, erosion, etc., the geographers' contribution can be valuable. Green Revolution, though a great success, but has generated its own set of problems, now being called as second or third generation problems. Fertility of soils in the mono-cropped, heavily irrigated high intensity areas is going down on account of depletion of major and micro nutrients. A recent report of ICAR has brought this fact out and suggests that in these areas, diminishing returns not only in economic terms, but also in physical terms, measured by response to nutrient application are observed to be coming down. The only way suggested is to go back to organic farming. Some research based on our ancient practices recorded in some scriptures, give higher hope, as they have scientific formulae on use of organic material in a calibrated manner and the name given to it this science is Bio-Dynamic Farming. Farm residues, urban and rural garbage, animal and bird excreta fermented and decomposted by organisms like earthworms can provide us bio-fertilisers, which have been tested to be containing as many as 16 micro nutrient elements as against only three supplied by the complex fertilisers, i.e. NPK. Such bio-dynamically treated organic matter can take care of depleting nutrients like nitrogen, phosphate, potash, sulphur, zinc, iron and so on. Similarly, eco-friendly alternatives to the chemical insecticides, pesticides, weedicides and fungicides known as bio-controls are being emphasised.

This brings me to the role of cattle in our agriculture. Traditionally, rearing domestic animals including cattle has been an integral part of our agriculture. With the advent of dwarf varieties, the chaff-to-grain ratio has been altered from the usual 70:30 to 50:50. This has given us more grain production from the same soil, but a shortage of fodder has occurred. This coupled with the low prices of milk on account of a policy of providing adequate liquid milk at cheap prices to the local urban population, the economy of rearing cattle and other milch animals has been destroyed. On the one hand, nutrition has been affected adversely, especially in rural areas, and on the other, animal excreta, which has always been the richest source of organic matter required by the soils stands reduced critically. Geographers are expected to undertake scientific studies on this aspect. All our land races of crop cultivars, trees, vegetables, fruits and cattle and other animals are under stress because of cross-breeding and mono-cropping programmes. The whole genetic base is being narrowed down as exotic breeds, which are costly to maintain and difficult to sustain in our environment, are being brought in a big way. The consequence is that several of our native varieties and breeds have got neglected and are on the verge of extinction. We have to have a comprehensive programme of not only preserving and conserving our native land races, but augmenting and upgrading them through selective breeding. Geographers have to come out with tangible information in this regard.

Designing drainage systems, irrigation systems, watershed management techniques and soil and bio-mass conservation also requires assistance from geographers. Modern development based industrialisation and huge infrastructure like roads, railways, airports and ports, power houses, canals, tubewells, is having a heavy toll of our natural resources. Chemicals used in agriculture, industry and houses, effluents from industries and urban habitat are causing immense damage to ecology and environment and thereby to human and animal health. The worst is the case of water. Global concern is being expressed about all these. The geographers have to be part of the effort aimed at finding sustainable practicable solutions to these problems. I do not mean that everything has to be done by the geographers. Obviously, you do not have the resources. But your inputs in all these matters are not only valuable but indispensable. A continuous audit and evaluation of the natural resources should be undertaken by the geographers as they are the best equipped to do so.

With these words, I conclude, and once again, felicitate you all and Prof. Ali Mohammad and his colleagues very specially, on convening the Golden Jubilee Celebrations to mark completion of 75 years of their Department and holding this International Conference on Geography. I also express my heart-felt gratitude to have been invited to participate in this great event.

Thank you, Jai Hind !

2

ROLE OF SCIENCE AND TECHNOLOGY IN INDIAN AGRICULTURE

HON'BLE CHATURANAN MISHRA

I am glad to find myself in participating in the National Conference organized by the Department of Geography, Aligarh Muslim University, Aligarh. A theme on fifty years of Indian Agriculture is most useful for discussion. A symposium on the conditions and directions of agriculture and rural society in the "21st Century" was organized in the last month in Delhi by Kisan trust. Fortunately, I found an occasion to participate in that symposium. When I use the term *agriculture,* it means the inclusion of foodgrains including pulses, oilseeds, livestock, forestry farming, bee farming, pisciculture, flower culture, vegetables, cotton, jute, sugarcane, tea, coffee, rubber, spices and coconuts, etc. Though all these products are not governed by Agricultural Ministry, Government of India. Most of the scholars of national and international repute are expressing distress and disquiet regarding the shortage of foodgrains and subsequent starvation in the 21st century caused by agricultural deterioration and increasing population. I am against to these views. Only thirty per cent of the total cultivated land of India is under Green Revolution and is self-sufficient in foodgrains. If remaining seventy per cent of the land and 19 million hectare of barren (*user*) land are brought under Green Revolution and cultivation respectively, we cannot only feed our growing population, but also we are able to feed to the other regions of the world. As compared to other nations, our crop productivity is very low, as it is evident from Table 2.1.

Table 2.1

Crop	*Rank in Production*	*Rank in Yield*
Rice	2	51
Wheat	2	43
Maize	8	98
Pulses	1	128
Sugarcane	2	35
Rapeseed	3	40
Groundnut	2	70
Cotton	3	62

The great variation in yield is not only found at International level but it exists within the country. Last year there was a hue and cry for onions. The largest onion producer is Maharashtra, but per hectare production of onion in Maharashtra is only 12,451 kg while it is 27,063 kg in Gujarat, 12,928 kg in UP and 7,846 kg in Bihar. It is obvious, if the agricultural productivity to be increased with the help of science and technology certainly India may find its best place in the agricultural market of the world. Our agriculture Research centres are at par with the world. The problem is to use the science and technology in the field, because our land holdings are very small.

But it all depends upon the position of the Himalayas and the monsoon in future. But the question is how far the originality of soil can be saved the effects of El-Nino continues, the position of the environment remains, the change of climate, fertility of the soil may be maintained. How far science may be helpful in drought and efforts to crops in drought affected areas. All these are related to the discipline of geography and the scholars sitting among us. As a common man I wish that the scientists of the world involved in thinking seriously on these subjects may get success in their goals. The success of human being lies in the success of their objectives in many ways. Though the scientists work for the humanity and the world built the capitalist society are much exploiting taking the benefit of their reasonless. If it is not to be tackled, the science has reached to such an extent that it can be able to eradicate the starvation from the planet.

I want to warn only for one thing that multi-national companies and developed nation do not remember the welfare of the human being in the race of gaining more and more income. Multi-national companies and developed nations have their clutch on science, technology and capital. They are engaged in the globalization of trade to increase their income. For this, they have established world trade organization. America was the top benefitter to this globalization of trade (*Herald International Tribune*, May 12, 1998). The country has gained an additional income of 100 billion dollars from 1983 to 1992. Asia-Mexico crisis did not harm American investors because IMF comes at their rescue. Karl Marx has rightly said in his commence declaration that capitalist society is able to demolish the Chinese wall without using gunpowder. Once the meet of globalization of trade is used to be held, why not the arrangement at the conservation of water at international level and their harvesting, to maintain the health of soil, or to restrict the erosion caused by Himalayan rivers be maintained, which covers the benefit of the entire human society. The maximum environmental pollution is caused by developed nations and amongst them America is on top of the list. The countries like China and India constitute more than half of the world population but their share in creating pollution is less than half per cent of the net pollution, why the quelt to protocol compels the developing nations to follow the rules and regulations regarding the pollution? Like WTO they have self-evolved quelt to protocol, and we compelled to accept indiscriminatory agreement. America plays negative role for the growth and development of science and technology in India. For this the country is compelling Russia in numerous ways and is trying to maintain her supremacy by hook and crook. Friends you know how America has tried to show that the cultivation of rice increases the quality of methane gas. They know that if India and other rice producing countries start consuming wheat due to this, their trade will take a boom. So, I request all the scholars of geography to take the work of geographical research in an appropriate way so that the national interest may be defended. It is time to think on the role of climatic change and pollution in the production of mango in North India. During my ministerial tenure I have allotted this work to the agricultural scientists.

Geographical factors cause instability in the agricultural production of our country. One year we record bumper cropping followed by low production in another year. To some extent, this is due to scarcity in assured irrigation. How far the changing climate is responsible for it, is a matter of research for you people? The instability in the agriculture of the developed nations has been lessened and they are controlling world agricultural market by its regular supply. We should follow their pattern.

Cotton, gram and other pulses are prone to insects. Insects are killed by chemical methods. What is the relationship between the genesis of the insects and climate or pollution, and what necessary steps should be taken, is a matter of research and investigation.

The World Bank under the guardianship of FAO has prepared a report on the occurrence of cyclone in the coastal region of Andhra Pradesh. The report discussed much on the recurrence of various storms and the ways and means to minimize these. I enquired him as a minister, why there is recurrence of least storm in Sundarban region as compared to the Andhra coast, Chittagong and Philippines? Do the forest check the storms? They replied to study all these related questions. I didn't know upto what extent, this is a subject of research for your people.

At present situation at one end there is great necessity of change in the progress of agriculture in India while at the other end sustainable agriculture is the need of the hour. Indeed, in our country the agriculture had self-constructed management. For example, growing crops with the help of animals, feeding straws and lands of paddy crops to animals and to maintain the fertility of the soil by animal excreta. People think, does science can provide such a complete management that can persist for a long time. It is bitter experience that new seeds are short lived. Besides, the genesis of terminator seeds has created much crisis. Multinationals that were involved in big industries and chemical industries are now coming in the field of agriculture, seed and food.

Agriculture science with the help of biotechnology, genetic engineering or transgenic and cloning whatever is generating is a signal of far reaching impact.

However, it is necessary to carry over science and technology in the agricultural fields and for that for our farmers need some education. Although they are more experienced and adopt new things fastly. Our very complex problem lies in marginal and small farmers constituting 80 per cent of the farmers population. With the help of science and technology, per hectare yield of the fields may be raised to two-three folds. This will reduce poverty. This will reduce the supply of the public distribution system and subsequently minimize the subsidy. Agriculture provides a great potential to minimize poverty. Farming and livestock has the great potential in employment generation too.

Unfortunately, after first Five-Year Plan, farming has not been given priority resulting in the severe poverty in India. A new crisis has arisen, i.e., the crime of capitalism that has proved fatal in eastern Asia, Latin America and Russia but its worldwide impact is due. I want to give a reference of *London Economist* dated 20th February, 1999. This fresh forecasting is that, at the end of 1999 the difference between the net production and production potential of the global production will be the highest after the decline of 1930s. The world will experience a great decline provided that the economy of Europe and America suddenly tremble down. This will result in the fast decline of cost and production as it had happened 70 years earlier. I recommended all of you to read that write-up.

This will lead to few possibilities in export day by day. Hence, recasting the present budget into agriculture-oriented budget by increasing the purchasing power of the farmers, industrial decline should be competed.

With these words, I declare the inauguration of this seminar and wish its full success.

Thanks

3

KEY-NOTE ADDRESS

PROF. SHAH MANZOOR ALAM

Text of Speech Delivered by the Chief Guest, Prof. Shah Manzoor Alam, Former Vice-Chancellor, University of Kashmir, at the National Conference on Fifty Years of Indian Agriculture, in the Department of Geography, Aligarh Muslim University on 17th March 1999.

I was pleasantly surprised and simply overwhelmed to receive your gracious invitation to be with you all today as your Guest Speaker at this National Conference on Fifty Years of Indian Agriculture. It was with a deep sense of humility and immense pleasure that I accepted it. I feel greatly honoured when I realise that this invitation from Dr. Ali Mohammad, Professor and Chairman of the Department of Geography accords recognition to my humble contribution to Geography in India. I am deeply beholden to the Vice-Chancellor, Dr. Mahmood-ur-Rahman and the Chairman of the Department of Geography and all his colleagues for the honour they have done me. I have never felt more humble, never felt more proud than being present in your midst today. I am most grateful to Allah (SWT) for his great and small mercies.

I am thrilled by the fact that I am addressing you under the auspices of my own department, which is one of the most distinguished departments of the Aligarh Muslim University, our great Almamater. The Geography Department of the Aligarh Muslim University had the unique distinction to initiate first, post-graduate and research studies in geography, among all the universities in India. The diffusion effect of this headstart in geography was tremendous. The Alumni of this department moved across the country with vigour and enthusiasm. They disseminated the culture of academic excellence and intellectual dynamism in other academic institutions as well. The geography graduates of this University, by sheer merit and intellectual ability, contributed significantly in shaping the development and destiny of a large number of geography departments among the universities in India. I state it with pride and pleasure, but in total humility, that we did not disappoint our Almamater. Wherever we worked we made a mark and the impact of our dedicated work is still discernible in the portals of those Universities. It was sheer hard work and dedicated effort, and not coincidence, that the geography departments of the Aligarh Muslim University and of the Osmania University, both headed by Aligarians, were the first two Geography Departments of Indian Universities to be recognised as Centres of Excellence and sanctioned funds under Special Assistance Programme of the University Grants Commission. The incessant search for excellence lends abiding strength to the academic culture of this University and inspires us to strive for still greater excellence.

The Geography Department of the Aligarh Muslim University is known nationally and internationally for its valuable contributions in field of Agricultural Geography. It was in recognition of the work in this field carried out by the Department that it was identified for financial assistance under the Special Assistance Programme of University Grants Commission. It is therefore in the fitness of things that you have taken initiative in convening this National Conference on Fifty Years of Indian Agriculture. I extend my warmest congratulations to the Chairman of the Department and all his colleagues for taking this initiative. Agriculture constitutes a major sector of Indian economy. Nearly 30 per cent of the GDP is contributed by agriculture. It employs 64 per cent of the total labour force and accounts for 18 per cent of the share in exports. It is only through proper development of agriculture that food security for the people of India can be ensured. Agriculture also provides raw material for some important industries and lends stability to the Indian economy. Agriculture during the last fifty years has made phenomenal progress. The Green Revolution in Indian agriculture was brought about by the application of scientific methods and modern technology. Agriculture Geography can contribute significantly in explaining the transformation in Indian agriculture since independence. It can be extremely helpful in formulating meaningful agricultural policy in the right perspective. I do not propose to give a discourse on Agricultural Geography for that would be treading on dangerous ground. I have never dabbled in this field and claim no expertise.

I would however like to draw your attention to the health of the discipline geography about which I am really concerned. Geography is the most down to earth discipline. It is a thoroughly applied discipline since it deals with the interaction of man and environment. It has a significant role to play in explaining regional and economic development of a country, national or international geopolitics, socio-political environment of any region. It also commands some of the most powerful tools of analysis, such as statistical and cartographic techniques, aerial photographs, satellite imagery and Geographical Information System (GIS), yet its impact as a discipline on the policy making issues has been minimal. It has therefore failed to attract the attention of the policy makers. They are thus totally ignorant of the fact that geographical inputs can provide appropriate perspectives to the understanding of policy issues and in formulating policy alternatives. Perhaps the policy input is rather weak in geographical analysis. Geographical researches have therefore received scant recognition at the highest political and administrative level. Consequently geography has thus remained an academic discipline despite being most pragmatic in its approach and outlook.

I submit for your consideration that geographical studies need reorientation in order to take it out of its academic shell and make it more dynamic and policy oriented. Geographical researches should focus on lively issues which concern the society so that the validity of geography as a pragmatic discipline dealing with the problems of the society is well established. We should identify some of the major policy issues on which geography can make a meaningful contribution. As for instance we can systematically analyse the impact of taxation, subsidy on energy and fertilizer, import and export policies, on crop distribution, cropping pattern and overall agricultural development. Similarly the influence of energy policy on consumption pattern of fuels in the household sector can be critically examined. The findings of such a study will be policy-wise most relevant. A number of similar issues of topical importance which are crucial for the development of society can be selected for detailed, close and critical analysis. Let me elaborate it further.

Geographers usually overlook the dynamic elements which usher in change in consumption and production. Policy instruments are critically important to determine the nature of economy one proposes to develop. The annual budget of the Government of India is one such critically important instrument which determines the direction of economic development. The taxation and excise duty incentives have direct bearing on crop pattern. Has any geographer ever examined the impact on cropping pattern and crop productivity due to taxation, pricing and subsidy and import and export policies of the Government of India. It were the policy directions of the Government of India that have made this country self-sufficient in food. The recent onion crisis in India, when the prices of onion shot up to Rs.60 per kilo, was also the consequence of faulty government policy.

You must also be aware of the fact that bio-technology and external environment are going to cause a revolutionary change in crop productivity, crop mix and cropping pattern in India. The students of Agricultural Geography must be thoroughly acquainted with these new developments. Bio-technology will revolutionise the nature and character of crops. In view of the shrinking land resource and in order to sustain growing population the need for more food has to be met through higher yield from less per capita land. Hence besides land, water and climate, researchers in Agricultural Geography must get themselves thoroughly acquainted with "three major revolutions in science and technology which will influence agricultural technology in a fundamental manner. They are the gene revolution, the information and communication and ecotechnology revolutions" (Swaminathan, Survey of Indian Agriculture 1999 – *The Hindu*, p. 11).

There will also be a radical transformation in agricultural development in India because of the fundamental changes in the external environment such as liberalisation of economy, globalisation of international markets, and India joining the World Trade Organisation. This will exert tremendous pressure on Indian agricultural system. Indian agriculture will be exposed to international competition and will have to be competitive globally if it wants to make major gains in export market. Fellow geographers you have to take cognizance of these basic changes in the Indian agricultural environment in order to make teaching and research in Agricultural Geography in perfect harmony with the latest trends, and of great relevance to both the policy makers and society in general.

Power sector is another area with strong policy implications. Power is the key to modern economic development. It provides the motive force for all the sectors of the national economy such as, agriculture, industry, commerce, transport, and domestic (households). Of these, the domestic sector is one of the most important users of both commercial and traditional sources of energy. The contribution of geographers in explaining the use of energy resources by the households is minimal. It may be pointed out that the use of various sources of energy such as fuelwood, kerosene, LPG and electricity is administered and controlled by the government. It is the government policy which determines the transition of energy among households from inferior to superior fuels, i.e. from fuelwood to kerosene, kerosene to LPG. It is the government which controls the supply, distribution and prices of all these fuels. The concept of "energy ladder" in the household sector is equally valid since there is a direct relationship between income and the type of cooking fuel used.

Another major policy issue relating to the energy sector is that of subsidy on all fuels including electricity used by the households. It is because of subsidies that the State Electricity Boards across the country are incurring colossal losses. Subsidies are meant to help the poor in order to improve their quality of life. The irony is that it is the rich who benefit most from these subsidies on fuels. A recent study on energy consumption by the household sector in metropolitan Hyderabad reveal the fact that the annual subsidy on all fuels including electricity amounts to Rs. 800 million. Of this, approximately Rs. 570 million is doled out to the middle and higher income groups. The share of the target group, i.e. the poor is dismally low, a mere 30 per cent of the total subsidy (Hyderabad : World Bank Study, 1997).

Spatial patterns of the consumption of domestic fuels, the fuel-shift (energy transition), the concept of "energy ladder" and the problem of subsidies are relevant areas of research for geographers and are critically important issues. Our research studies and findings in these areas will have great impact and will invite attention of the policy makers. I am stating this from personal experience.

Geopolitics is a very valid area for geographers to delve into. You must be aware that with the collapse of the Soviet Union international geopolitics has radically transformed. The dominance of the United States of America in international politics is complete. There is no longer any serious threat to the security of the industrialized West. They have however played havoc with the human and natural system through the misuse of science and technology and excessive exploitation of resources. This malfunctioning of the global environment is threatening to destroy the whole biosphere. The security of the planet earth itself is threatened by the depletion of the ozone layer, acid rain, global warming and nuclear radiation. Moreover pollution has assumed menacing proportion and has spread globally. It cannot be contained, like communism, and it needs no visa to move across international boundaries. *The world is threatened by acute ecological stresses of transnational character.* Geographical studies with their global approach and integrated outlook can play a crucially important role in evolving a pragmatic policy to resolve this global crisis. This is a challenging task which only geographers can take up competently because of the integrating nature of their discipline. No one understands the planet earth better than geographers do and no discipline is committed to interdependence as geography is. It is only geography which highlights the fact that we are having in a world of interlocking need and total interdependence.

Another fascinating geopolitical concept which has emerged lately is that of Fault Line Wars. It is being advocated by Samuel P. Huntington in his recently published book : *The Clash of Civilizations and Remaking of the World Order* (1997). He has advanced the idea that the future wars will be wars of cultures and civilizations with strong religious overtones. It will be worth examining the validity of this extraordinary concept.

Finally, in the area of geopolitics another interesting idea is being floated around that future wars may be wars for water. In the words of Crispin Tickell one of the organisers of the Rio de Janiero Earth Summit – 1992, "water will be the progenitor of more wars than oil. World demand for water doubles every 21 years, but the volume available is the same as in Roman Times" (*Time Weekly*, Special Issue – Our Precious Planet, November, 1997, p. 18, New York). It is predicted in a Report published by the UN Stockholm Environment Institute that "by the year 2025 two-thirds of the World Population will be affected by water shortages" (*Time Weekly* – Special Issue – November, 1997, p. 17). The global supply of renewable fresh water annually "amounts to 40,000 cubic kilometres, of which about 14,000 cubic kilometres are exploitable each year as stable sources settled in rivers, lakes, glaciers and acquirers. The world actually uses only about 4,000 cubic kilometres annually for human needs" (*Manorama Year Book* 1999, p. 518). The supply of fresh water is very unevenly distributed. Approximately 66 per cent of the total supply of fresh water is locked up in the polar ice caps. The balance of 33 per cent is concentrated largely in the least populated icy lands of Canada, Siberia and Antarctica. The uneven distribution of fresh water both globally and regionally is indeed of grave concern and can act as flash points for future wars. It is a serious problem with grave policy implications and should be of serious concern to geographers for critical and objective analysis.

Fellow geographers I have identified only a few frontier areas of policy oriented research in geography. It is for you to probe deeply and identify other areas of interest for geographical research which will be of great relevance in the 21st Century. We must commit ourselves to make geography a frontline discipline which contribute significantly to the making of socio-economic policies for the benefit of not only Indians but for the entire mankind.

4

INDIAN AGRICULTURE

PROF. M.S. SWAMINATHAN

The great Bengal famine of 1942-43 which resulted in the death due to starvation of over 2 million children, women and men provided the backdrop to India's independence. Mahatma Gandhi, speaking at Noakhali (now in Bangladesh) in 1946 said, "to the hungry, God is bread; the foremost duty of independent India is to ensure that every man and woman is enabled to earn this bread". As we approach a new century and a millennium, it can be said without fear of contradiction that in addition to a steadfast adherence to democratic traditions, the single most significant achievement of India during the last 52 years is the prevention of famines and achievement of food self-sufficiency.

How did this transformation happen? The principal factor was political will and action. The first Prime Minister of India, Jawaharlal Nehru said in 1948, "everything else can wait but not agriculture". Consequently, public action for achieving sustainable food security took the following forms:

- Integrated rural development involving attention to irrigation, rural communication, electrification, education and health care.
- Accelerated mobilisation of science and technology through a chain of national institutes, Agricultural and Veterinary Universities. All-India coordinated research projects, all supported by the Indian Council of Agricultural Research.
- Efficient extension of research results to small farms through a national extension service, Krishi Vigyan Kendras (farm science centres) and "Lab to Land" and "Land to Lab" programmes.

- Organisation of input supply services to ensure that farm families gain access at the right time and place to inputs such as seeds, fertilizer, pesticides and credit. Fertilizer use which was less than 2 kg/ha. in 1950 increased to 84 kg/ha. in 1995.
- Increase in gross irrigated area from 30 million ha. in 1950 to 70 million ha. in 1995. About 42 per cent of irrigated area contributes over 72 per cent of cereal production, since where there is irrigation, high-yield technologies can be introduced.
- Announcement of a support price for important food commodities prior to the sowing season based on the recommendations of an Agricultural Costs and Prices Commission.
- Ensuring that farmers get the prescribed support prices through agencies like the Food Corporation of India and NAFED (National Agricultural Cooperative Marketing Federation of India).
- Promotion of agrarian reform through Acts relating to ceilings on land holdings, security of tenure and distribution of ceiling surplus land to landless families. States which have implemented land reform measures effectively, as for example West Bengal, have witnessed high agricultural growth rates.

The Punjab, which was the earliest to launch the Green Revolution in 1968 had the following prerequisites essential for deriving benefits from high yielding seed varieties and agronomic practices.

- Owner cultivation
- Land levelling and consolidation
- Rural roads
- Rural electrification
- A dynamic Agricultural University and extension service

Above all, it is the Indian farmers who have been the backbone of the Green Revolution. Writing in the *Illustrated Weekly of India* in 1969, I described the role of farmers as follows:

> Brimming with enthusiasm, hard-working, skilled and determined, the Punjab farmer has been the backbone of the revolution. Revolutions are usually associated with the young, but in this revolution, age has been no obstacle to participation. Farmers, young and old, educated and uneducated, have easily

> taken to the new agronomy. It has been heart-warming to see young college graduates, retired officials, ex-armymen, illiterate peasants and small farmers queuing up to get the new seeds. At least in the Punjab, the divorce between intellect and labour, which has been the bane of our agriculture is vanishing.

It is particularly appropriate to pay tribute to Punjab farmers on the occasion of the 300th anniversary of the founding of the Khalsa Panth by Guru Govind Singh. The wheat revolution, which began in the Punjab and north-west India in 1968 soon became a Green Revolution encompassing rice, potato, sugarcane, grapes and a wide variety of crops. The revolution also spread to all irrigated areas. Rainfed farming lagged behind. However, with the launching of a National Movement for Watershed Development and the formation of Water Users' Associations, for which financial provision has been made in the budget of the Government of India for 1999-2000, it should be possible to accelerate and stabilise agricultural production in rainfed and dry farming areas.

India has introduced many innovative programmes in the field of agriculture. Among them, mention may be made of the Technology Missions, which were initiated over ten years ago, first in oilseeds and later in maize, pulses and cotton. A Technology Mission involves an end to end approach, starting with seeds for sowing and ending with the consumers or relevant industry (as in the case of cotton). Such a systems approach to production, processing, marketing and consumption led to a doubling of oilseed production within a span of 6 to 7 years.

Today, India occupies the first or second position in the World not only in crops like wheat and rice (Table 4.1) but also in milk production. The total foodgrain production is likely to exceed over 200 million tonnes during 1999. This marks a four-fold increase since 1947, when the total foodgrain production was about 50 million tonnes. To understand the magnitude of the agricultural transformation brought about by Indian farmers, scientists and policy makers, let me cite the example of wheat.

Wheat cultivation in India began during the Mohanjo Daro civilization, dated over 2000 BC. From that time upto 1947, the Indian farmers developed the capacity to produce 7 million tonnes of wheat. During 1999, the wheat harvest is expected to exceed 70 million tonnes. In fact between 1964 and 1968, wheat production increased by 7 million tonnes. Thus, 4000 years of wheat production history was compressed in 4 years. No wonder, the Government of India issued a special stamp in July 1968, titled "the Wheat Revolution".

Table 4.1 : India's Share in the World Production and Area for Major Crops, 1995-97

Crops	*India's Share*		*India's Rank*	
	Prodn.	*Area*	*Prodn.*	*Area*
Wheat	11.4%	11.2%	2	2
Rice	21.4%	28.5%	2	1
Pulses	26.0%	36.6%	1	1
Groundnut	28.6%	35.2%	1	1
Sugarcane	22.6%	20.0%	2	2
Tea	28.3%	18.5%	1	2
Jute	52.5%	51.5%	1	1
Cotton (Lint)	14.0%	20.7%	3	1

Source: FAO, 1997.

Such progress was possible only because of a symphony approach to agricultural planning and development leading to the introduction of mutually reinforcing packages of technology, services and public policies. While the rate of food production has remained above the rate of population growth during the last 25 years, there are large number of women, children and men who still go to bed undernourished.

The policy of the Government of India since 1970 to maintain substantial grain reserves has saved the country from famines even when there has been failure of the monsoon rainfall. The maintenance of an efficient public distribution system, the introduction of targeted public distribution system to reach the poor, initiation of Food for Work and Employment Guarantee Schemes, provision of nutritious noon meals to all school children and several other steps designed to strengthen the livelihood security of the poor, have helped to reduce substantially the number of persons going to bed hungry. Still inadequate purchasing power resulting from lack of opportunities for non-farm employment, leads to under and malnutrition in families suffering from poverty. Creation of adequate avenues for both on-farm and non-farm employment has thus become a major food security challenge.

To meet this challenge, a new agricultural strategy is now being developed. This strategy will have as its foundation the integrated and sustainable management of natural resources like soil, water, biodiversity and forests. The production techniques will be based on the principles of precision farming leading to a reduction in both the cost of production and enviro*nmental damage. Frontier technologies like biotechnology, space and information technologies and renewable energy will be harnessed. India has one of the world's largest public sector plant breeding enterprise. Knowledge Centres for sustainable livelihoods are being established, using computer technology.

Ecotechnologies based on appropriate blends of traditional and frontier technologies are being developed. Ecological farming methods are being promoted. Thus, on the threshold of a new century and millennium, India is poised to become the flagship of a global movement for an evergreen revolution on the farms rooted in the principles of ecology, economics, social and gender equity, energy conservation and employment generation. Such an evergreen revolution is essential since India has nearly 25 per cent of the world's farming population and since over 60 per cent of India's population, now reaching a billion, depends upon agriculture for their livelihoods.

5

FIFTY YEARS OF INDIAN AGRICULTURE

ALI MOHAMMAD

The basic objective of this paper is to evaluate the performance of agricultural sector after fifty years of Independence as it has been on the top priority during all the Five Year Plans. Indian agriculture presented a depressing picture at the end of the British rule such as:

(i) over 80 per cent of the sown area was under cultivation of food crops and yet the total output of foodgrains was insufficient for the needs of the country.
(ii) the larger part of the farming was of subsistence nature.
(iii) the average size of holdings was small and uneconomic.
(iv) less than 25 per cent of the total sown area received irrigation.
(v) the rest 75 per cent had to depend on rainfall for raising any crop.
(vi) the land system of the country was unconducive to agricultural development specially for food crops.
(vii) incentives for greater efforts on the part of the farmer for increased production or for the land owner to make investments in permanent improvements of land were practically non-existent.
(viii) the peasantry was mired in poverty and heavy indebtedness.
(ix) there was little institutional credit available and borrowing that was mainly for consumption purposes had to be from the village money-lenders and the urban trader to whom the farmer would pledge to next year produce.

(x) the number of landless labourers had been increasing for the last several decades.

(xii) apart from unemployment for more than six months in a year, the wage rate paid to the farmer labourers during the days of employment were low.

(xii) scientific agriculture was yet to make its appearance in the country.

(xiii) lift irrigation and ploughing were still done with the help of drought animals.

(xiv) tubewells and tractors were uncommon.

(xv) yields under circumstances were necessarily low in comparison with international standards.

(xvi) there were only a few bright spots on the agricultural scene, like canal irrigation, colonies in the Punjab and canal irrigated areas of Sind.

On the whole the country, at the time of Independence, was facing two major problems, such as:

(i) total stagnation in agriculture and no trace of dynamism in terms of growth and agricultural infrastructure.

(ii) the more immediate problem was to increase the production of foodgrains to make the country self-sufficient.

How and to what extent these objectives have been achieved in the last fifty years since Independence and what implications the agricultural development of India has over the regional and neighbouring countries. The basic subject matter of the problem is to study the extent of achievement of food self-sufficiency and shortfalls caused by the partition in the supply of two major industrial raw materials, i.e., cotton and jute.

Food Supply Situation during the British Rule

In the year 1880 'Famine Commission' made its estimate of food production and consumption because of a short decline in the availability of food. The situation worsened because of stagnation in production and increasing population. From 1891-1921 there was a net increase of over 12 million population. There was some increase in agricultural production also in the first two decades of the century caused by extension of canal irrigation in Punjab and Sind and improvement in irrigation and agricultural practices. After 1921 the population began to increase fast and at the same time, the momentum of agricultural growth exhausted in the north-west region. Therefore, there was a sharp decline in the output and availability of foodgrains as can be seen from Table 5.1.

Table 5.1 : Population and Food Supply

Period	*Population Index*	*Foodgrains per Capita Index*	*Index of per Capita Land*
1895	100	100	109
1905	101	95	103
1915	107	91	109
1925	109	90	111
1935	120	78	104
1945	138	68	85

It is evident that population increased by 38 per cent over the fifty-year period and availability declined by 32 per cent. Two factors were responsible such as increase in population and decrease in the sown area by 25 per cent. After 1921 the per capita cultivated area started declining from 1.11 acre in 1921 to 0.94 acre in 1941 and 0.84 acre in 1951. Another trend which had come into operation after 1921 was the substitution of commercial crops for foodgrains and cultivation of better quality irrigated lands under commercial crops leaving inferior lands to the raising of foodgrains. As a result foodgrains production suffered further. The area under cultivation of foodgrains and output declined while the population increased rapidly.

The foodgrain supply situation during the World War II was explosive. The food availability was short because of the low level of production, low imports of two million tonnes and low purchasing power. The Foodgrain Policy Committee (1943) came to the conclusion that the country was then in short supply in respect of foodgrains by at least ten million tonnes.

It was also observed before the Independence that there exists a wide spread hunger and under nourishment among the large mass of the country's population. In 1933 it was reported by Sir John Megaws that about 40 per cent of India's population did not get enough food to eat even in a normal and good weather year. Similar reports during this period was presented by various Expert Committees and Commissions ranging between 30 to 40 per cent population suffering from chronic food deficit in the country.

The Bengal Famine of 1943 must be regarded as a landmark in the long history of food shortage and famines in the country. From 1910-1940, there were 18 scarcities but no major famine involving loss of life due to starvation. The famine is best described as a 'tragedy in unpreparedness'. The situation can be compared with the present day scarcity of Kalahandi in Orissa that the people were hurdling together and waiting for the death.

The history of India's food problem and agricultural development of independent India begins with the famine of 1943, which encouraged to more food production. It also marked the beginning of the policy of food control, including control over food prices and distribution of foodgrain, more particularly to the vulnerable sections of the community. Though India attained freedom four years later, the famine of 1943 provides the most suitable starting point for a study of the country's food problem and agricultural development since Independence. A "Grow More Food Campaign" was initiated by the government in wake of that famine.

In contrast to the policy towards production of food crops, the British had actively encouraged the growth of commercial crops. Cultivation of jute, cotton, tea and coffee got encouragement. The price advantage that commercial crops came to enjoy over food crops because of foreign demand also helped in the growth of cultivation of these crops. India was, consequently, relatively better placed in regard to the development of commercial crops than in respect of foodgrains during this period.

After Independence the main goal was to be 'to move the country away from the menace of famine to a new vigour and prosperity'. According to the statement 'the All India policy is to promote the welfare of the people and to secure a progressive improvement of their standard of living. This includes the responsibility of providing enough food for all, sufficient in quality and of requisite quantity for the achievement of these objectives high priority will be given to measures of increasing the food resources of the country to the fullest extent and in particular to measures designed to increase the output per hectare and to diminish dependence on the vagaries of nature but till now we have been able to control the vagaries of nature in twenty per cent of the cultivated area of the country. The major objectives to remove these problems are as follows:

(i) increase in production of foodgrains and protective foods,
(ii) improvement in methods of agricultural production and marketing,

(iii) stimulating production of raw materials for industry and exports,
(iv) securing remunerative prices for the producer and fair wages to agricultural labour,
(v) ensuring fair distribution of the food produced,
(vi) promoting nutritional research and education,
(vii) increase in area under food and fodder crops by bringing new land under cultivation, double cropping and diverting land from non-food crops to food crops,
(viii) increase in the supply of water for irrigation by improving and extending existing irrigation systems,
(ix) increase in the supply of improved seeds, and
(x) increased use of fertilizers.

It is observed that a little progress was recorded at that time because of the various strains on the government. But the food situations became even more critical after Independence. Large number of programmes were started with the objectives to win freedom from foreign bread and achieving self-sufficiency. In 1952 a special inquiry into the working of the campaigns was ordered. For the first time the food problem of the country came to be viewed in a dynamic setting of a continuous increase in food production to meet the growing demand for food in future.

Agriculture under plans was received on top priority treating it as development in the broader perspective of planned growth of the economy as a whole. The basic thing in Indian context was that without the healthy and vigorous agricultural sector the rest of the economy could not grow, therefore, agriculture was given the highest priority.

The overall progress is considered most laudable. Till 1960, foodgrain production increased to 75 million tonnes over 50 million tonnes just after the Independence but fluctuations in production remained the major threat of food security. Third Plan noted that progress in the agricultural field during the Second Plan period had been inadequate not only in terms of increase in production and achievements of production targets but also in implementation of various planned programmes, consequently the plan document declared 'a much larger task in agriculture remains to be accomplished during the Third Plan'. Development of irrigation, soil and conservation programmes, supply of fertilizers, improved seeds and credit and extension services were on top priority. But only the supply of fertilizers and area covered by new variety of seeds were encouraging while irrigation rate was far below the desired goal. The actual achievement in terms of agricultural output was far below the target. The reasons were well known such as: (i) the conflict with China in 1962, (ii) the Indo-Pakistan conflict in 1965, and (iii) the disastrous draught of 1965-66. At the end of the Third Plan the agricultural and food situation in the country presented a gloomier picture than the one at the end of Second Plan.

With the beginning of Green Revolution in 1967-68, there was a dramatic change in the situation. The revolution caused a qualitative change in the food and agricultural situation. The Pearson report described the change as 'one of the authentic marvels of our time'.

In the Fourth Plan growth with social justice policy was adopted to help the vulnerable section of backward areas. Besides attainment of self-sufficiency in foodgrains, the plan envisaged building-up of a sizeable buffer stock of foodgrains and stoppage of concessional imports of foodgrains.

The Fifth Plan, while adhering to the basic policies of the Fourth Plan, made some modifications in the programmes for agriculture with a view of increasing their efficiency. It was proposed to cover more food crops under HYV. New programme was to cover not only irrigated agriculture but also dry farming areas on a large scale. A new programme was chalked out particularly for oil seeds and pulses which were in serious short supply. Draught prone areas to be tackled in a systematic way during the plan period. Subsequently in Sixth to Eighth Plans the objectives of planning remained more or less the same except of the emphasis on 'growth with social justice'.

The experience up to Eight Five Year Plans seems to be encouraging at cereal front but the situation of pulses is very poor and availability per head is declining causing heavy imports on the whole the nation has achieved the food self-sufficiency but the contribution of pulses has gone down just to half after Independence. The foodgrains growth from the last many years is recorded more than the population growth but on a very poor base of availability. But foodgrains production fluctuation is still a serious problem to be tackled causing food insecurity among the small farmers and disadvantageous rural classes.

However, the following are the basic issues to be solved:

1. Growth with social justice;
2. Control over the foodgrain fluctuation situation;

3. Scarcity in plenty – the chief characteristics of water resources on irrigation front should be tackled;
4. Regional inequality in agricultural development;
5. Population and food availability should be the basic criteria to identify the agricultural backward areas; and
6. After achieving the national goal of food self-sufficiency, a new direction of agricultural development in relation to international perspective should be the objective as the country is surrounded by the chronic food deficit countries and regions.

No doubt an impressive development took place in the extension of net cultivated area but it increased from 119 million hectares to 142 million hectares, i.e., 19.76 per cent area increase contributed in the total production while gross cropped area increased from 132 million hectares to 187 million hectares, i.e., about 41.45 per cent which contributed relatively more in total production as compared to the net sown area during the period 1951-97.

In the year 1951 only 21 million hectare land was under irrigation, which increased to 53.51 million hectare in 1996 contributing by 156.6 per cent increase. Gross irrigated area increased from 22.56 million hectare to 71.51 million hectare in 1996 contributing by 247.8 per cent increase.

At current prices production (GDP) increased from Rs. 42,466 crore in 1951 to Rs. 359,586 crore in 1997 contributing about 746 per cent increase.

Aggregate foodgrain production has increase by 5.2 per cent from 192.4 million tonnes to 202.5 million tonnes in 1997-98. This has enabled the economy to sustain the high growth trend in Gross Domestic Product (GDP). Much of the impressive growth rate of agriculture in 1988-89, in fact, was due to lower base in the preceding year, when the production fell by 7 million tonnes over the previous year. In actual terms, foodgrain production increased by only 2.1 million tonnes compared with the previous normal year of 1996-97. As such, the growth rate of foodgrains production has been markedly lower in the nineties compared to the eighties. Aggregate production has increased by about 26 million tonnes since 1990-91 as against 52 million tonnes in the eighties. Apparently, the decline in the growth rate of foodgrain production in the nineties was due to stagnation in the area under cultivation and deceleration in yield rates—total cultivated area under foodgrains increased by just about 3 per cent in eight years between 1991-92 and 1998-99.

Table 5.2 : Availability of Foodrgrains and Pulses per Head per Day (1990-1998) Based on Production not Based on Actual Consumption

Year	*Cereals*	*Pulses*	*Foodgrains*
1990	431.5	41.1	472.6
1991	468.5	41.6	510.1
1992	434.5	34.3	468.8
1993	427.0	36.2	464.1
1994	434.0	37.2	471.2
1995	469.6	38.0	507.7
1996	452.9	32.9	485.8
1997	473.7	38.4	512.1
1998	450.9	33.2	484.1
Average	449.2	37.0	486.3

The availability of 33.2 grams of pulses in 1998 is much lower as compared to the 1990, i.e., 41.1 gram per head/day. The declining trend of pulses follows the increasing trend of population because the production remained the same during this period. On the whole availability of foodgrains, which has many ups and down remained more or less the same. The slight variation is caused by the climatic change. The average of the decade, i.e. 449.2 is not much lower than the highest and the lowest production and it is up to the level of standard requirement. Keeping in view the total foodgrains availability the situation is quite normal because all the years are above the standard requirement of foodgrains.

It is evident from Table 5.3 that in spite of the normal weather since 1991 to 1999 production fluctuation in some of the years was recorded highly negative, i.e., 11.08 and 7.01 million metric tonnes in the year 1995-96 and 1997-98 respectively. It shows that weather based on rainfall is not the only factor but a temporal change in climate seems to be most effective. Similarly an increase of 19.02 million metric tonnes of production does not mean a very high increase it is only because of a very low base but definitely production of 199.44 million over 191.50 million tonnes is a healthy increase for the nation. Again production of 202.54 million metric tonnes is closely associated with the production of 199.44 million metric tonnes though the production of 192.43 million metric tonnes is far below the 1998-99 production.

It is evident from Table 5.4 foodgrain share and annual variations that Punjab, Haryana, Assam, Tamil Nadu and Karnataka recorded negligible variations in production during this period while the state of Rajasthan, Maharashtra, Gujarat, Bihar recorded a very high level of

Table 5.3 : Fluctuations in Foodgrain Production and Area in India

Year	*Production (mmt)*	*Fluctuation (mmt)*	*% Fluctuation*	*Area (M.Ha)*	*Fluctuation*	*% Fluctuation*
1991-92	168.38	-	-	121.87	-	-
1992-93	179.48	+11.10	+6.59	123.15	+1.28	+1.04
1993-94	184.26	+4.78	+2.66	122.75	-0.40	-0.40
1994-95	191.50	+7.24	+3.93	123.86	+1.11	+1.01
1995-96	180.42	-11.08	-5.81	121.01	-2.85	-2.01
1996-97	199.44	+19.02	+10.54	123.58	+2.57	+1.02
1997-98	192.43	-7.01	-3.51	124.07	+0.49	+1.00
1998-99	202.54	+10.11	+5.25	125.75	+1.68	+2.01
1991-98-99 (Average)	187.31	34.16	+20.32	3.88	+3.88	3.05

Table 5.4 : Percentage Share of Production of Each State of India

States	*97-98*	*96-97*	*95-96*	*94-95*	*93-94*	*92-93*	*91-92*	*90-91*
U.P.	21.75	21.25	21.27	20.48	20.18	20.18	21.10	20.22
Punjab	10.99	10.80	10.98	11.38	11.71	11.15	11.65	10.91
Madhya Pradesh	9.06	9.77	10.02	10.16	10.38	9.41	9.21	10.20
West Bengal	7.46	6.90	7.14	6.93	7.11	6.90	7.64	6.39
Rajasthan	7.29	6.43	5.30	6.12	3.83	6.40	4.74	6.20
Bihar	6.70	7.23	7.18	6.77	6.93	5.06	6.32	6.95
Haryana	5.89	5.74	5.62	5.74	5.57	5.71	5.40	5.42
Andhra Pradesh	5.69	6.86	6.47	6.15	6.65	6.50	6.95	6.99
Maharashtra	5.05	7.32	6.43	6.02	7.37	7.83	4.97	6.91
Karnataka	4.57	4.62	4.79	4.32	4.70	4.74	4.71	3.63
Tamil Nadu	4.41	3.47	3.55	4.75	4.48	4.66	4.90	4.22
Orissa	3.45	2.42	3.77	3.60	3.95	3.29	4.91	3.94
Gujarat	2.97	2.61	2.27	2.74	2.05	3.01	2.02	2.75
Assam	1.86	1.77	1.97	1.82	1.92	1.92	2.01	1.95
Himachal Pradesh	0.69	0.65	0.76	0.73	0.67	0.78	0.80	0.81
J&K	0.76	0.67	0.82	0.75	0.79	0.77	0.83	0.76
Kerala	0.35	0.43	0.54	0.52	0.57	0.62	0.64	0.63
Manipur	0.19	0.20	0.19	0.26	0.19	0.15	0.21	0.16
Tripura	0.28	0.28	0.26	0.23	0.28	0.25	0.29	0.29
Nagaland	0.12	0.11	0.13	0.11	0.12	0.13	0.12	0.11
Meghalaya	0.10	0.09	0.08	0.07	0.08	0.08	0.09	0.09
Mizoram	0.07	0.07	0.07	0.07	0.07	0.07	0.05	0.05
Arunachal Pradesh	0.11	0.10	0.11	0.10	0.13	0.11	0.13	0.12
Goa	0.08	0.08	0.08	0.07	0.08	0.08	0.09	0.08
Union Territories	0.08	0.08	0.14	0.14	0.13	0.15	0.16	0.15
Sikkim	0.05	0.05	0.06	0.06	0.05	0.06	0.06	0.07
TOTAL	100.0	100.0	100.0	100.0	100.0	100.0	100.0	100.0

variations in production. For example Rajasthan recorded a very high level of percentage share by 7.29 in the year 92-93 while in 96-97 it recorded only 3.82 per cent because production achieved was just half to the year 1992-93. In Indian context a change of 19.02 million metric tonnes was recorded over the previous year while a highest positive change was recorded by 11 million in the year 1995-96.

However, the impressive performance of 1990s has enabled the economy to achieve an increase in the GDP with the growth being over 7 per cent in 1994-97 with a rise to 7.8 per cent in 1994-95 from 6.2 per cent in 1993-94 and 7.2 per cent in 1995-96 and 7.5 per cent in 1996-97. In these years the contribution of the agricultural sector was commendable with its growth being higher at 5.2 per cent in 1995-96 and 7.3 per cent in 1996-97.

As the demand for fine cereals will be growing steadily, the yield of both wheat and rice will have to increase to 180 million tonnes by 2001-2002. Coarse cereals too may be in greater demand because they are also used for certain industrial purposes and the output will have to be atleast 40 million tonnes against the earlier peak of 36.6 million tonnes in 1992-93. It was only 26 million tonnes in 1991-92.

The situation of pulses has not been improving at the desired rate for various reasons and the shortage was 1.5 million tonnes in 1997-98 with an output of 13.1 million tonnes in 1991-92. If there has to be self-sufficiency in pulses in the face of the rising consumption the output will have to be higher at 20 million tonnes by 2001-2002.

Therefore, the total production of foodgrains (cereals and pulses) will thus have to be 240 million tonnes in 1998-99 with an increase of 30 million tonnes in 1992-97, the target of 240 million tonnes in the Ninth Plan cannot be considered ambitious.

The target production can be obtained only with the increase of productivity. A greater attention is needed in some of the potential regions at present backward agriculturally, there must be an increase in area under High Yielding Variety seeds and improvement in agricultural practices by using more fertilizer, irrigation and other green revolutionary measures. A heavy investment in agricultural sector is already visualized by the Planning Commission in more potential area where productivity level is very low. The target can be achieved by improving productivity and redressing regional imbalances in outputs and yields per hectare.

The nation has to go ahead to feed the increasing population. Increasing urbanization and increasing income along with the population increase is going to be a major threat to the food security. These problems

Table 5.5 : State Level Share and Annual Change in Foodgrain Production (Million M. Tonnes)
(Figures in parenthesis indicate the % share)

States	*92-93*	*93-94*	*94-95*	*95-96*	*96-97*	*97-98*
Andhra Pradesh	11.68	12.25	11.78	11.67	13.67	10.84 (6.03)
Arunachal Pradesh	2.98	2.58	2.04	1.93	2.32 (7.14)	1.90
Assam	3.58	3.53	3.56	3.49	3.54	3.45 (1.92)
Bihar	12.90	14.42	12.95	12.97	12.78	9.08 (5.06)
Gujarat	5.71 (7.17)	5.21 (7.20)	4.10 (7.17)	5.25 (7.17)	3.78 (7.15)	5.41 (3.01)
Goa	0.16	0.16	0.14	0.14	0.15	0.15
Haryana	11.33	11.44	10.13	11.00	10.25	10.20 (5.68)
Himachal Pradesh	1.33	1.29	1.36	1.41	1.23	1.40
Jammu & Kashmir	1.45	1.33	1.47	1.44	1.45	1.30
Karnataka	8.80	9.21	8.65	8.11	8.66	8.50 (4.73)
Kerala	0.68	0.85	0.97	1.00	1.04	1.01
Madhya Pradesh	17.41	19.49	18.07	19.43	19.13	16.80 (9.35)
Maharashtra	9.71	14.60	11.60	11.52	13.68 (10.38)	14.04 (7.82)
Manipur	0.36 (5.05)	0.39	0.34	0.49	0.36	0.20
Meghalaya	0.19	0.18	0.14	0.14	0.15	0.14
Mizoram	0.13	0.13	0.12	0.12	0.12	0.10
Nagaland	0.24	0.21	0.24	0.22	0.23	0.23
Orissa	6.64	4.83	6.80	6.90	7.21	5.91 (3.29)
Punjab	21.15	21.55	19.81	21.82	21.60 (4.02)	20.01 (11.15)
Rajasthan	14.03 (7.29)	12.82	9.57	11.71	7.05 (3.82)	11.40 (6.35)
Sikkim	0.10	0.11	0.11	0.11	0.10	0.10
Tamil Nadu	8.48	6.93	6.40	9.10	8.25	8.30 (4.62)
Tripura	0.55	0.56	0.48	0.44	0.51	0.40
U.P.	41.83	42.39	38.37	39.21	37.20	36.20 (20.17)
West Bengal	14.35 (7.45)	13.76	12.88	13.28	13.10	12.30 (6.89)
Union Territories	0.16	0.16	0.26	0.26	0.24	0.20
ALL INDIA	192.43	199.44	180.42	191.50	184.26	179.50
Change Over Previous Year	—	+6.97	-19.02	+11.08	-7.24	-4.76

Table 5.6 : Foodgrain Production Per cent Change Over the Previous Year

States	*93-94*	*94-95*	*95-96*	*96-97*	*97-98*
Andhra Pradesh	5.1	-3.8	-1.0	17.2	-20.0
Arunachal Pradesh	19.3	-16.7	5.3	1.1	1.9
Assam	2.6	-1.3	2.1	-0.8	1.3
Bihar	10.5	11.3	-0.1	1.5	40.7
Gujarat	9.6	26.9	-21.8	38.8	-30.2
Goa	-1.9	17.1	-3.0	4.0	1.9
Haryana	-1.0	12.9	-7.8	7.2	0.1
Himachal Pradesh	3.3	-5.4	-3.1	14.4	-12.4
Jammu & Kashmir	9.3	-9.6	2.1	-0.8	5.1
Karnataka	-4.5	6.6	6.6	6.4	1.9
Kerala	-20.0	-12.5	-2.6	4.3	5.9
Madhya Pradesh	-10.7	7.8	-7.0	1.6	13.2
Maharashtra	-33.5	25.8	0.7	-15.1	3.3
Manipur	-6.6	15.3	-30.7	37.0	28.6
Meghalaya	7.7	24.8	-0.1	4.3	2.9
Mizoram	-3.9	8.2	-0.9	3.4	15.2
Nagaland	12.7	-11.1	8.8	3.7	0.3
Orissa	37.4	-29.0	-1.4	5.4	23.4
Punjab	-1.9	8.8	-9.2	1.1	7.8
Rajasthan	9.5	34.0	-18.3	66.0	-38.5
Sikkim	-2.3	0.0	0.7	4.2	0.3
Tamil Nadu	22.5	8.2	-29.6	10.1	-1.2
Tripura	-1.7	16.6	9.3	-14.3	11.8
U.P.	-1.3	10.5	-2.1	5.4	2.7
West Bengal	4.3	6.8	-3.0	1.4	5.7
Union Territories	-0.9	-38.8	0.3	6.3	8.9
ALL INDIA	-3.5	10.5	-5.8	3.9	2.7

must be calculated in advance to meet the increasing demand. Another important issue, i.e., small and marginal farmers is also going to be another threat. In most of the state about 75 per cent household (size and holding) is not going to support the mass level of population (agricultural household) in the next sub-division of land within twenty years. If the administrators and government are not well prepared and aware, a serious social consequence is quite ahead and near to the public chaos.

The following precautions must be undertaken:

1. Irrigation rate must be improved on top priority as only 38 per cent of the gross cultivated area is under irrigation.
2. The existing share of HYV area (38%) is not enough, though it is increasing at a faster rate.

Table 5.7 : All India Area, Production and Yield of Foodgrains

Year	*Area (million hectares)*	*Increase %*	*Production (million hectares)*	*Fluctution %*	*Yield (kgs / hbct)*	*Increase %*	*% coverage under irrigation*
(1)	(2)	(3)	(4)	(5)	(6)	(7)	(8)
1949-50	99.28		54.92		553		17.8
1950-51	97.32	-1.97	50.62	-8.06	522	-5.61	18.1
1951-52	96.96	-0.37	51.99	+2.25	536	+2.68	18.1
1952-53	102.09	+5.30	59.20	+12.18	580	+8.21	18.1
1953-54	109.07	+6.84	69.82	+15.21	640	+10.34	18.1
1954-55	107.86	-1.11	68.03	-2.63	631	-1.41	18.4
1955-56	110.56	+2.50	66.85	-1.76	605	-5.47	18.5
1956-57	111.14	+0.52	69.86	+4.31	629	+3.97	18.2
1957-58	109.48	-1.49	64.31	-8.63	587	-6.65	19.3
1958-59	114.76	+4.82	77.14	+16.63	672	+14.48	18.7
1959-60	115.82	+0.92	76.67	-0.61	662	-1.48	18.8
1960-61	115.58	-0.21	82.02	+6.52	710	+7.25	19.1
1961-62	117.23	+1.43	82.71	+0.83	705	-0.70	19.1
1962-63	117.84	+0.52	80.15	-3.19	680	-3.54	19.8
1963-64	117.42	-0.35	80.64	-0.61	687	+1.02	19.8
1964-65	116.11	+0.59	89.36	+9.76	757	+7.57	20.2
1965-66	115.10	-2.55	72.35	-23.51	629	-16.91	20.9
1966-67	115.30	+0.17	74.23	+2.53	644	+2.38	22.2
1967-68	121.42	+5.31	95.05	-21.90	783	+21.58	21.6
1968-69	120.43	-0.81	94.01	-1.10	781	-0.25	23.6
1969-70	123.57	+2.61	99.50	+5.52	805	+3.07	23.7
1970-71	124.32	+0.61	108.42	+8.23	872	+8.32	24.1
1971-72	122.62	-1.37	105.17	-3.09	858	-1.60	24.5
1972-73	119.28	-2.72	97.03	-8.40	813	-5.24	25.4
1973-74	126.54	+6.09	104.67	+7.03	827	+72.00	24.5
1974-75	121.08	-4.31	99.83	-4.85	824	-0.36	26.5
1975-76	128.18	+5.86	121.03	+17.52	944	+14.56	26.5
1976-77	124.36	-2.98	111.17	-8.87	894	-5.30	27.4
1977-78	127.52	+2.54	126.41	+12.06	991	+10.85	27.7
1978-79	129.01	+1.17	131.90	+4.16	1022	+3.13	28.8
1979-80	125.21	-2.59	109.70	-20.24	876	-14.30	30.3
1980-81	126.67	+1.16	129.59	+15.35	1023	+16.78	29.7
1981-82	129.14	+1.95	133.30	+2.78	1032	+0.88	29.6
1982-83	125.10	-3.13	129.52	-2.92	1035	+0.29	30.8
1983-84	131.16	+4.84	152.37	+15.00	1162	+12.27	30.9

(Contd.)

Table 5.7 (*Contd.*)

(1)	(2)	(3)	(4)	(5)	(6)	(7)	(8)
1984-85	126.67	-3.42	145.54	-4.70	1149	-1.12	31.9
1985-86	128.02	+1.06	150.44	+3.26	1175	+2.26	31.4
1986-87	127.20	-0.64	143.42	-1.05	1128	-4.00	32.6
1987-88	119.69	-5.90	140.35	-2.19	1173	+4.00	33.5
1988-89	127.67	+6.67	169.92	+17.40	1331	+13.47	34.4
1989-90	126.77	-0.70	171.04	+0.65	1349	-1.35	35.0
1990-91	127.84	+0.84	176.39	+3.03	1380	+3.00	35.1
1991-92	121.87	-4.66	168.38	+4.76	1382	+0.14	36.7
1992-93	123.15	+1.05	179.48	+6.18	1457	+5.43	37.4
1993-94	122.75	-0.32	184.26	+2.59	1501	+3.02	38.7
1994-95	123.86	+0.90	191.50	+3.78	1546	+3.00	39.6
1995-96	121.01	-2.30	180.42	-6.14	1491	-8.37	40.5
1996-97	123.58	+2.12	199.44	-9.54	1614	-1.54	
1997-98	124.07	+0.40	192.43	-3.64	1551	-3.90	

Table 5.8 : All India Area, Production and Yield of Total Pulses

Year	*Area (m. hect)*	*Average*	*Production*	*Increase*	*Yield*	*Average*	*Irrigation %*
(1)	(2)	(3)	(4)	(5)	(6)	(7)	(8)
1949-50	20.17		8.16	-	405		7.8
1950-51	19.09		8.41	+2.97	441		9.4
1951-52	18.78	19.92	8.42	+0.12	448	449.2	9.7
1952-53	19.84		9.19	+8.38	463		9.8
1953-54	21.73		10.62	+13.46	489		9.2
1954-55	21.91		10.95	+3.01	500		8.8
1955-56	23.22		11.04	+0.81	476		8.4
1956-57	23.32	23.06	11.55	+4.41	495	487.2	7.3
1957-58	22.54		9.56	-20.81	424		9.1
1958-59	24.31		13.15	+27.30	541		8.4
1959-60	24.83		11.80	-11.44	475		8.5
1960-61	23.56		12.70	+7.08	539		8.0
1961-62	24.24	24.22	11.76	-7.99	485	478.0	8.1
1962-63	24.27		11.53	-1.99	475		8.9
1963-64	24.18		10.07	-14.50	416		8.9
1964-65	23.88		12.42	+18.92	520		9.2
1965-66	22.72		9.94	-24.94	438		9.4
1966-67	22.12	22.52	8.35	-19.04	377	471.6	10.9
1967-68	22.65		12.10	+30.99	534		8.7
1968-69	21.26		10.42	-16.12	490		9.8

(*Contd.*)

Table 5.8 (Contd.)

(1)	(2)	(3)	(4)	(5)	(6)	(7)	(8)
1969-70	22.02		11.69	+10.86	531		9.4
1970-71	22.54		11.82	+1.10	524		8.8
1971-72	22.15	22.21	11.09	-6.58	501	491.4	8.8
1972-73	20.92		9.91	-11.90	474		8.1
1973-74	23.43		10.01	+0.09	427		7.9
1974-75	22.03		10.02	+0.10	455		8.1
1975-76	24.45		13.04	+23.16	533		7.9
1976-77	22.98	22.32	11.36	-14.79	494	501.4	7.5
1977-78	23.50		11.97	+5.09	510		7.1
1978-79	23.66		12.18	+1.72	515		7.9
1979-80	22.26		8.57	-42.12	385		8.8
1980-81	22.46		10.63	+19.38	473		9.0
1981-82	23.84	22.98	11.51	+7.64	483	481.6	8.5
1982-83	22.83		11.86	+2.95	519		8.2
1983-84	23.54		12.89	+7.99	548		7.5
1984-85	22.74		11.96	-7.77	526		7.9
1985-86	24.42		13.36	+10.48	547		8.5
1986-87	23.16	22.95	11.71	-14.09	506	538.0	9.6
1987-88	21.27		10.96	-6.84	515		9.4
1988-89	23.15		13.85	+20.86	598		9.3
1989-90	23.41		12.86	-7.69	549		10.0
1990-91	24.66		14.26	+9.82	578		10.5
1991-92	22.54	22.05	12.02	-18.63	533	566.0	10.7
1992-93	22.36		12.82	+6.24	573		10.5
1993-94	22.25		13.30	+3.60	598		11.2
1994-95	22.03		14.04	+5.27	610		12.7
1995-96	22.28	22.65	12.31	-14.05	652	592.0	13.0
1996-97	22.45		17.24	+28.59	635		
1997-98	22.85		13.07	-8.95	572		

3. A special attention is needed for the small and marginal farmers and if possible a new system of agriculture should be introduced to minimize the total dependence on agricultural land and income.

Table 5.9 : All India Area, Production and Yield of Wheat

Year	*Area (m. hect)*	*Increase average*	*Increase production*	*Increase average*	*Increase yield*	*Increase average*	*% Irrigation*
(1)	(2)	(3)	(4)	(5)	(6)	(7)	(8)
1949-50	9.76		6.39		655		31.5
1950-51	9.75		6.46		663		34.0
1951-52	9.47	9.94	6.18	6.91	653	696.8	35.8
1952-53	9.83		7.50		763		37.2
1953-54	10.68		8.02		750		36.2
		—		—		—	
1954-55	11.26		9.04		303		35.0
1955-56	12.37		8.76		708		32.7
1956-57	13.52	12.30	9.40	9.03	695	735.4	29.4
1957-58	11.73		7.99		682		33.3
1958-59	12.62		9.96		789		31.8
		23.74%		30.68%		5.54%	
1959-60	13.38		10.32		772		31.8
1960-61	12.93		11.00		851		32.7
1961-62	13.57	13.41	12.07	10.80	890	807.2	31.9
1962-63	13.59		10.78		793		33.8
1963-64	13.50		9.85		730		34.9
		9.02%		19.68%		9.76%	
1964-65	13.42		12.26		913		36.8
1965-66	12.57		10.40		827		43.1
1966-67	12.84	13.95	11.39	13.85	887	979.8	48.0
1967-68	14.99		16.54		1103		43.4
1968-69	15.96		18.65		1169		49.8
		4.03%		28.24%		21.35%	
1969-70	16.63		20.09		1209		51.1
1970-71	18.24		23.83		1307		54.3
1971-72	19.14	18.41	26.41	23.36	1380	1267.8	54.5
1972-73	19.46		24.74		1271		57.6
1973-74	18.58		21.78		1172		57.7
		31.97%		68.66%		29.39%	
1974-75	18.01		24.10		1338		61.8
1975-76	20.45		28.84		1410		61.8
1976-77	20.92	20.70	29.01	27.84	1387	1436.6	65.1
1977-78	21.46		31.75		1480		64.6
1978-79	22.64		35.51		1568		66.0
		12.44%		19.18%		13.31%	
1979-80	22.17		31.83		1436		68.3
1980-81	22.28		36.31		1630		76.5
1981-82	22.14	22.97	37.45	38.77	1691	1683.2	70.7
1982-83	23.57		42.79		1810		72.5
1983-84	24.67		45.48		1843		73.0
		10.96%		39.68%		17.15%	
1984-85	23.56		44.07		1870		74.5
1985-86	23.00		47.05		2046		74.6
1986-87	23.13	23.37	44.32	47.14	1916	2015.6	76.3
1987-88	23.06		46.17		2002		76.8
1988-89	24.11		54.11		2244		79.2
		1.74%		21.75%		19.75%	
1989-90	23.50		49.85		2121		80.3

(Contd.)

Table 5.9 (*Contd.*)

(1)	(2)	(3)	(4)	(5)	(6)	(7)	(8)
1988-89	24.11		54.11		2244		79.2
		1.74%		21.75%		19.75%	
1989-90	23.50		49.85		2121		80.3
1990-91	24.17		55.14		2281		81.1
1991-92	23.26	24.13	55.69	55.54	2394	2300.6	83.7
1992-93	24.59		57.21		2327		84.2
1993-94	25.15		59.84		2380		85.1
		3.25%		17.82%		14.14%	
1994-95	25.70		65.77		2559		85.2
1995-96	25.01	25.82	62.10	65.78	2483		86.8
1996-97	25.89		69.35		2679	2547.7	
1997-98	26.69		65.91		2470		
		7.00%		18.43%		10.74%	

Table 5.10 : All India Area, Production and Yield of Rice

Year	*Avg.*	*Area (m. hect)*	*Incr-ease*	*Production (m. tonnes)*	*Incr-ease*	*Yield (kgs/hect)*	*Incr-ease*	*% coverage under irrigation*
(1)	(2)	(3)	(4)	(5)	(6)	(7)	(8)	(9)
1949-50		30.52		23.54		771		32.3
1950-51		30.81		20.58		668		31.7
1951-52	30.48	29.83		21.30		714		31.7
1952-53		29.97		22.90		764		32.3
1953-54		31.29		28.21		902		33.6
			—		—		—	
1954-55		30.77		25.22		820		34.4
1955-56		31.52		27.56		874		34.9
1956-57	32.01	32.28		29.04		900		35.4
1957-58		32.30		25.53		790		36.4
1958-59		33.17		30.85		930		36.3
					18.63		13.11	
1959-60		33.82		31.68		937		35.8
1960-61		34.13		34.58		1013		36.8
1961-62	34.83	34.69	8.02	35.66		1028		37.5
1962-63		34.69		33.21		931		37.4
1963-64		35.81		37.00		1033		37.1
					24.56		14.48	
1964-65		36.46		39.31		1078		37.3
1965-66		35.47		30.59		862		36.5
1966-67	36.10	35.25		30.44		863		37.9
1967-68		36.44		37.61		1032		38.6
1968-69		36.97		39.76		1076		38.4
					3.22		0.61	
1969-70		37.68		40.43		1073		38.2
1970-71		37.59		42.22		1123		38.4
1971-72	37.60	37.76	4.10	43.07		1141		37.2
1972-73		36.69		39.24		1070		39.1

(*Contd.*)

Table 5.10 (*Contd.*)

(1)	(2)	(3)	(4)	(5)	(6)	(7)	(8)	(9)
1971-72	37.60	37.76	4.10	43.07		1141		37.2
1972-73		36.69		39.24		1070		39.1
1973-74		38.29		44.05		1151		38.4
					17.61		13.24	
1974-75		37.89		39.58		1045		38.8
1975-76		39.43		48.74		1235		38.7
1976-77	39.33	38.51	4.60	41.92		1088		38.4
1977-78		40.28		52.67		1308		40.2
1978-79		40.48		53.77		1328		41.6
					13.25		22.20	
1979-80		39.42		42.33		1074		42.8
1980-81		40.15		53.63		1336		40.7
1981-82	39.96	40.71	0.84	53.25		1308		41.5
1982-83		38.26		47.12		1231		42.0
1983-84		41.24		60.10		1457		42.7
					8.34		6.75	
1984-85		41.16		58.34		1417		43.7
1985-86		41.14		63.83		1552		42.9
1986-87	40.80	41.17	2.10	60.56		1471		44.1
1987-88		38.81		56.86		1465		43.6
1988-89		41.73		70.49		1689		45.8
					20.92		18.57	
1989-90		42.17		73.57		1745		46.1
1990-91		42.69		74.29		1740		45.5
1991-92	42.36	42.65	3.82	74.68		1751		47.3
1992-93		41.78		72.86		1744		48.0
1993-94		42.54		80.30		1888		48.6
					21.15		16.78	
1994-95		42.81		81.81		1911		49.8
1995-96	43.12	42.84	1.79	76.98		1797		50.1
1996-97		43.43		81.74		1882		
1997-98		43.42		82.30		1895		
					7.40		5.46	

References

Data Source : Directorate of Economics and Statistics, Krishi Bhavan, New Delhi.

Report of Famine Commission, 1880, Para 158.

Burns, W., (1935), Technological Possibilities of Agricultural Development in India.

Thomas, P.J., (1935), Population and Production 1920, 1931, *Indian Journal of Economics*, Vol. XV, p. 745.

Government of India, Planning Commission, Fourth Five Year Plan, 1969-74, p. 149.

Dantwala, M.L., (1979), Agricultural Policy in India since Independence, C.H. Shah and C.W. Vakil (Eds), *Agricultural Development in India. Policies and Problems,* Orient Longman, p. 17.

Noor, Mohammad (1980), *Perspective in Agricultural Geography* (Eds), Concept Publishing Company, New Delhi.

Bhatia, B.M., (1988), *Indian Agriculture: A Policy Perspective*, Sage Publications, New Delhi, .

Rao, Y.V. Krishna, (eds), (1993), *Technology and Social Change in Agriculture*, People's Publishing House, New Delhi.

Shah, C.H., Vimal Shah and Sudarshan Iyengar (1991), *Agricultural Growth and Equity: A Micro Level Experience*, Concept Publishing Company, New Delhi.

Govind, Nalini, (1986), *Regional Perspectives in Agricultural Development*, Concept Publishing Company, New Delhi.

Bhagat, L.N., (1989), *Supply Responses in Backward Agriculture*, Concept Publishing Company, New Delhi.

Alagh, Y.K. and Bhalla, G.S., (1979), *Performance of Indian Agriculture*, Sterling Publications, New Delhi.

Khusro, A.M., (1973), *Economics of Land Reforms and Farm Size in India*, Delhi, Macmillan.

6

THE SMALL FARMER DEVELOPMENT STRATEGIES FOR THE NEXT MILLENNIUM

K.V. SUNDARAM

The Problem in its Setting

A central issue in Agricultural Development is the necessity to increase productivity, employment and income of poor segments of the agricultural population. Among the rural poor, the small farmers constitute a sizeable portion in the developing countries. Studies by FAO have shown that small farms constitute between 60-70 per cent of total farms in these countries and contribute around 30-35 per cent to total agricultural output (Randhawa and Sundaram, FAO, 1990). The inequality in landholding distribution is high in most Asian countries, except China and the Republic of Korea. Small farms generally predominate in several countries in the region. Bangladesh, India, Indonesia and the Republic of Korea have a particularly large number of small holdings below 1 ha, while Pakistan, Thailand and the Philippines have relatively few extremely small holdings. Looking at the countries by farm size, large farms seem to control a disproportionate amount of land. The largest 10 per cent of farms control about 40 percent of land in Pakistan, 50 per cent in India and 35 per cent of rice land in Indonesia. On the other hand, in the Republic of Korea and Japan, the distribution of farms is less inequitable (FAO, 1990). These percentages underline the inequitable concentration of ownership and operational land use in these countries. The size of a small farm varies from country to country. In India, a small farm is one which is below 2 ha in size. Those cultivating farms below one hectare in size are classified as marginal farmers. The cultivable land per capita declined in India from 0.48 hectares in 1951 to 0.26 hectares in 1981. It is expected to be 0.11 hectares in 2000 (Swaminathan, 1990). FAO's study of Agriculture at 2000 shows that in most developing countries, the average size of an operation holding will continue to decline (FAO, 1988). This policy analysis paper addresses the several problems involved in designing an efficient agricultural strategy, that has an appropriate focus on small farmers, and identifies the configuration of policies needed in the next millennium, to restructure the agricultural sector in order to achieve growth with equity. The policy analysis attempted here is based mainly on two sources:

1. A study of small farmer development in the Asia and the Pacific Region undertaken by this author (with N.S. Randhawa) in FAO, of seven countries, viz. India, Indonesia, Malaysia, Bangladesh, Sri Lanka, the Philippines and Thailand (Randhawa and Sundaram, FAO, 1990).
2. A review of Rural Development activities in 12 countries in the South and South-East Asia region, undertaken by this author for the Centre on Integrated Rural Development for Asia and the Pacific (Sundaram, CIRDAP, 1996).

Characteristics of the Small Farmers

Basic to the formulation of strategies for the small farmer development, is an understanding of their behavioural characteristics and the various constraints they face in the real world context. Several farm management studies in India and other countries have brought out the salient characteristics of small farms, some of which may be highlighted. In the small farms, agricultural work is carried out mostly by family labour and a large part of family subsistence requirements are met directly from farm production. This would mean that they have a small hired labour component. At the same time, a number of small farmers also participate in labour markets as wage earners. Thus, they are both producers and workers at the same time. Small farms have a high proportion of land devoted to food crops, which is necessary in order to meet the family subsistence needs, i.e., for their "use value". Small farmers also cultivate other crops for their "exchange value".

Crop-mix and intercropping are the characteristics of small-farm agriculture, particularly in rainfed areas. A high proportion of their output is retained for home consumption, that is, they have a lower ratio of marketed surplus to output. Small farms grow a diverse mixture of crops, that allow them to hedge rationally against uncertainties (e.g., agro-climatic conditions and weather fluctuations) and risks (e.g., variation in output prices). Crops are often interplanted. There is ample evidence to show that small farmers generally have higher cropping intensities, more area proportionately under irrigation, and use their resources more efficiently.

In the small-farm household, special emphasis is given to the generation of scarce cash resources, risk avoidance and food security, and in particular to all those activities that will yield fair returns to their most limiting factor of production (land). What is practiced in this context is a complex system of activities—crops, livestock and off-farm activities—in which members allocate the factors of production to each activity in a manner which, given their knowledge, maximizes the goals they strive to reach. Small farms are generally characterized by very low operating capital turnover in production, coupled often with a higher debt burden in relation to resources. This contradiction is due to their need to borrow heavily for consumption purposes, in order to sustain the family from one production cycle to another.

Small farmers are usually unable to make heavy on-farm investments, and in this sense, they are technologically constrained. The small farms are also usually characterized by weak forward and backward linkages except some, which are engaged in commercial enterprises. In regard to the adoption of new technologies by small farmers, three critical lessons emerge from a wide array of studies and approaches. These are:

(i) Small farm families are receptive to change and small farm systems are dynamic. The concept that "traditional" agriculture is static is misleading.

(ii) Small-farm families are selective and adaptive in their adoption and use of recommended practices and technologies.

(iii) No single attitude, trait, factor or farming condition explains the pattern of small-farm adoption of all new innovations (FAO, 1986).

Constrains of the Small Farmers

The constraints of small farmers may be broadly classified as structural, technological, institutional and operational. In reality, many constraints are inter-related and inter-dependent. Because of small size of land, small farmers are compelled to augment their operational area through leasing land. The terms and conditions they face in tenancy market are unfavourable. Although seed-fertilizer technology is supposed to be scale-neutral, in practice, various factors like the community's power structure, uneven access to agricultural extension and information services, inability to obtain adequate irrigation water and unavailability of credit act as deterrents, giving large farmers a clear edge over small farmers. Among institutional constraints, special mention must be made of the unequal access to credit that exists between small and large farmers, and the fact that large farmers manage to corner a higher proportion of institutional credit provided by cooperative credit societies, etc. Small farmers' economic constraints stem mainly from their limited land area, low levels of farm output and income, very little net surplus, and consequently, extremely limited possibility for farm investment out of their own resources. The rural markets in these countries are also functioning in a way unfavourable to small farmers. They do not receive timely market information and experience considerable difficulties in obtaining access to government services, such as extension. The locational inaccessibility of small-farms (with respect to irrigation, roads, extension services, etc.) has been cited especially as a constraint in some studies. Policies and programmes pursued for the development of small farmers: A cross-country analysis. The critical policies and programmes affecting small farmers, by and large, fall in seven major areas. These are:

- (i) Agrarian Reforms;
- (ii) Institutional Credit;
- (iii) Infrastructure and Input Policies;
- (iv) Special Programmes;
- (v) Extension and Research;
- (vi) Organization and Administrative Strategies; and
- (vii) Training.

We may briefly analyse the above policies hitting at some high spots of the evaluation across countries.

Agrarian Reforms

Studies show that in India, agrarian reforms, on the whole, have not made a desired impact on the small and marginal farmers. Their position in the land-lease market remains vulnerable. On the whole, the ownership status of marginal/small farmers has not improved beyond a point, whether due to the failure of tenancy laws or ceiling laws or both (Chadha, 1986). In Indonesia, it is reported that the Land Reform Law (1960) has not been effectively implemented owing to the unholy alliance between land reform officials and the large land owners. In the Philippines, the Agricultural Land Reform Code (1963 as amended in 1971) is reported to be a moderate success (Sirirugsa, 1986). In Thailand, the Land Reform Act (1975) only partially succeeded in achieving the targets. In the South Asian countries, where any substantial expansion of holding size is ruled out by land expansion, the re-distribution of land through agrarian reforms seems to be the only potential solution.

Institutional Credit

Since the late 70s, profound changes have taken place in many countries in regard to agricultural credit policies and programmes. These changes include several policy steps on simplification of lending procedures, interest rates, refinance measures, expansion of the banking network, introduction of supervised credit and in some cases, the doing away with collateral security-based credit system for small farmers and landless labourers. Many country studies reveal, that while informal credit sources still continue to hold sway in different degrees, the availability of institutional credit to farmers has grown in volume tremendously over the years. The provision of concessional loans to farmers has been adopted as a major policy instrument for inducing the adoption of improved farm technology. In some countries, it exists as a general policy applicable to all farmers alike, while in certain others, special programmes of credit for small farmers have been devised. More and more countries seem to be veering round to target-group orientation in the matter of disbursement of agricultural credit.

Price Policies: The weight of evidence thrown by the country experiences points to the conclusion, that the price support policies have, by and large, achieved some success. Fluctuation in prices between the peak and lean seasons have considerably narrowed in most of the countries. There is no evidence to suggest that the small farmers are discriminated against in the matter of prices received by them. The concept of 'weak bargaining power' of such farmers is disappearing fast. Some policy measures, which might greatly benefit the small farmer from the government support price may be noted. These are:

1. Purchases being made directly from the farmer than through intermediaries;
2. Ensuring that "procurement centres" and "buying points" are located within easy access of the farms; and
3. Price support being geared to the nature of crops grown by the farmer, bearing a favourable relation to input prices.

Infrastructure and Input Policies

There is, no doubt, that the provision of subsidy, e.g. for fertilizers has encouraged the small farmers to increasingly adopt the new technology and enhance their productivity. Evidence from Bangladesh shows that any withdrawal of the subsidy will have an adverse effect on the small farmers. Since subsidies are always related to the fulfillment of certain objectives, they need to be gradually withdrawn once those objectives are fulfilled. However, in many countries, this has proved to be difficult. An equally important aspect is the working of the public distribution system. Country experiences have underlined the importance of targeting the supplies and the use of stronger cooperative management to ensure a coordinated and timely delivery of inputs.

Special Programmes

Special programmes for small farmers have been functioning in many countries, e.g. India, Bangladesh, Indonesia, Nepal, the Philippines and Thailand. The major problem about such programmes is their inadequate coverage. Further, they have been confined to the delivery of one or two inputs only, e.g. delivery of credit inputs and subsidies. They have been essentially piecemeal interventions and have tended to function as "isolated" or "disembodied" programmes.

Extension and Research

Many evaluation studies have emphasized that the extension functions cannot be effectively performed by paid professional workers alone. For better spread effect and effective impact, they have to be organized through the trained leaders elected by the farming community itself. In this context, it is necessary to encourage the process of training the villagers themselves, so that they become the effective torch-bearers of essential knowledge to their farming community. On the research side, it should be emphasized that the single crop focused research system must be matched to a far higher degree, by farm management research, dealing with the small farm enterprise as a whole. This will be replacing research "by product" by "research by agricultural system", which will have more pay-off for small farmers. Research has also to focus more and more on the problems of rainfed agriculture and of poor farmers in their environmental setting. This is because, more poor farmers live in rainfed areas and research has, so far, tended to pay less attention to their specific needs.

Organisational and Administrative Strategies

Country studies indicate that numerous organizations are involved in providing services to the agricultural system. They range from local government institutions, extension network, cooperative organizations, commercial banks, to autonomous bodies set up for specific purposes and a host of private and voluntary agencies. In making appropriate choices of organizational arrangements to help the small farmer, it is necessary that the problem has to be addressed at both ends, i.e. at the delivering end, through several governmental/parastatal agencies, and at the receiving or utilizing end, through beneficiary groups and/or local organizations. The latter arrangement is necessary to ensure that the benefits do reach the intended target groups. Apart from constituting specific "receiving mechanisms", it is also necessary to provide for the active participation of small farmers in all elected local bodies by powering them, so that their voices could be heard in the appropriate forums and that they derive due share of benefit from the general and specific programmes of development. This will be best served by encouraging the formation of "small farmer groups", to increase the bargaining strength of small farmers.

Training

In a small farmer development strategy, both the government functionaries as well as the small farmers themselves have to be trained.

Government functionaries need training so as to become more responsive to the needs of the small farmers. For the small farmers, the training is necessary to make them aware of the government programmes/projects that have been intended for their benefit and to enable them to shed their shyness and reluctance for approaching development functionaries. In the case of small farmers, since the target group is very large, training is to be imparted in a "cascading" mode, by first training those who have leadership qualities and through them the larger community of small farmers, on the principle of "one candle lights the other".

Past Strategies and Their Impact

In the past, agricultural development philosophy, strategy and practice have all contributed to the relative neglect of agricultural development in general and of small farmer development in particular. With the current emphasis in development theory being "growth-with-equity", "adjustment with a human face" and "sustainable development", it is being increasingly recognized that small farmer development is not only ethical, but also economically efficient for creating a broad-based and long-term agricultural development. The small farmer development has suffered on three accounts: first, from the low priority accorded to the agricultural sector in development; second from several insidious myths, such as the small farmers being tradition-bound, irrational and fatalistic; and three, from a widespread belief that economies of scale are extremely important. In the past, all these notions led to relatively greater emphasis on large and medium farmer development. Modernization and technological development have, however, brought some changes in productivity relations of small farm *vis-à-vis* large farms. According to farm management studies conducted in India, an inverse relationship between farm size and output per acre was discernible in the 1950s. That is, small farms had higher productivity per unit of land due to more intensive cultivation and greater use of traditional inputs, particularly human and animal labour power. In the early 1970s, the inverse relationship weakened. The analysis of extensive 1974-75 farm data indicated that the marginal and small farmers of the Punjab, despite their limited land base, had been able to record as much total crop output and farm business income per acre as their larger counterparts (Bhalla and Chadha, 1983). Thus the small farmers have demonstrated that they are equally as efficient or are indeed more so than even large farmers, given an appropriate environment and suitable technologies. The economies of scale argument, to deprive small farmers of appropriate attention in development, is thus challengeable. In the past, the general Agricultural Development strategy was mostly growth-oriented and has had a built-in bias in favour of large farmers over small farmers. This bias has operated at almost every stage, in each component of planning, investment allocation, policies, programmes and projects. It has ultimately determined the pattern of growth as well as the distribution of its benefits. Eventhough special programmes have been undertaken in several countries to correct these deficiencies, their impact has been limited. Correcting the bias: The bias in the current policies has to be corrected by a conscious restructuring of the agricultural development strategy and planning, which would accord appropriate weight to the development of small farmers, leading to well-balanced agricultural growth, that embodies growth-with-equity and has a decisive poverty-reducing impact. The implications of this restructuring are manifold and extensive. It has to keep in view several dimensions, such as the economic reforms and liberalization, the globalization of the economy, the technological developments, economic viability and the role and attitudes of government and NGO's.

Facing the New Millennium: The Agenda for Small Farm Reforms

As we are entering the new millennium, three factors must be recognized for understanding the directions of change and to provide a framework to assess the development of small farms. These are:

1. Economic reforms and liberalization;
2. Globalization of the economy; and
3. Technological progress.

The reforms initiated in June 1991, sought to make the Indian economy a fast growing one. Despite the good performance of the economy (7.5% growth rate recorded during three years in succession, 1994-96), our hopes of a sustained higher growth path for the economy were belied and the economy slowed down. However, the present growth is still at over 5 per cent. Inflation is under reasonable control. Exports seem to be turning around. Many new initiatives are underway for the infrastructure sector. The incidence of hunger has been considerably reduced. The ushering in of the information technology has led to the growth of a new breed of skills in the areas of technology and management, which holds out great possibilities for increasing the standards of efficiency and competitiveness among India's firms (Kirit Parikh, 1999). The process of economic reforms and the gradual opening up of Indian agriculture to world markets would create a better incentive environment for agriculture. To fully exploit this opportunity, a major reform in supply-side factors i.e. technology, fertilizers, irrigation infrastructure and credit is needed as well as a total dismantling of all export controls (Hanumantha Rao and Ashok Gulati, 1994). The other factor to be reckoned with is globalization, which is now a fact, not an option. The highly inequitous nature of the on-going processes of globalization—both among nations and among social classes in most nations—has been focused in the recent Human Development Report (HDR) 1999, brought out by UNDP. Both the technologies (Information and communications technology and bio-technology), which are the "drivers" of globalization with their complementarities of liberalization, privatization and tighter intellectual property rights, are bound to create new risks of marginalisation and vulnerability. The HDR admits that "elite groups and other interest groups benefit from the present nature and structure of globalization" (HDR 1999, p.95). Although the report calls for "globalization with a human face", it does not spell out the new "humane" rules that will make capitalist globalization serve human development. The reforms of the 1990s have undoubtedly generated better terms of trade for agriculture by the increase in food prices. But the rural poor, including the small farmers, are not going to be benefited by the higher food prices. Both in the short run as well as in the long run, they will be greatly hurt by higher food prices, if real wages do not rise as fast as relative food prices. Hence the problems of the small farmers are bound to persist in the next millennium. How can they be helped to improve their yield and income in an ecologically sustainable manner and face the new challenges of the millennium is an intriguing question. In this context, two scenarios of change may be visualized. It may be noted that the scenarios depicted here not mutually exclusive. As may be seen in our later discussion, the one may gradually merge into the other. But the changes themselves will traumatic, as far as the small farmers are concerned.

SCENARIO I

The decline and disappearance of small farms

Economic reforms and liberalization of agriculture with their implications of open market operations, will enhance competition in marketing of agricultural production. The small and marginal farmers who have limited staying power, will no doubt find the competition stiff and are bound to suffer to some extent. If economic reforms also imply a reduction in or elimination of subsidies and the government support price programme, they will be affected all the more. If the modern on-going slogans on Population Control like:

1. "*Hum Do, Hamare Do*" (We are two. Our kids are two).
2. "*Paanch Ped, Ek Baccha Yahi Desh Ka Nara Sachcha*" (Five trees, one kid. This is the country's real slogan) become a reality, then the small farmer's, family labour will also considerably decline. Thus unable to face the challenges of liberalization and globalization and unable to benefit by the higher food prices, the small farmers will be forced to "distress sales" of their land and find employment in non-farm activities or join the ranks of the urban poor. Ultimately, many of them may be reduced to wage earners in large agri-business firms, conducting agricultural operations over extensive areas.

SCENARIO II

Adaptations and Innovations

Globalization should translate itself into increased prices for agricultural products and increased employment avenues. However, since these cannot benefit the small farmers they will be compelled to adapt their operations to achieve self-sufficiency and an export surplus in farm production. They may achieve this in various ways by making new adaptations and innovations.

The struggle to face the severe competition may lead them to invent new institutional innovations leading to mutual cooperation and collective self-reliance among themselves. They may be compelled to adopt group cooperation in areas such as, land and water management, integrated pest management, integrated nutrient supply, improved post-harvest technology and organize themselves into local level groups (poly-centric groups) for the maintenance and management of beneficiary programmes, for planning and for conducting evolution exercises. In extreme cases, they may resort to pooling of their lands into viable large "farming estates", avail of all latest technologies and compete effectively in the global export market. However in this case, they will require a lot of technical financial and managerial assistance from various sources, including the government, to improve the productivity, profitability, stability and sustainability of their farming systems. The nature of the packages of technology, services and public policies, as well as the desirable forms of research effort necessary in this context have to be worked out meticulously by public institutions, like the Indian Council of Agricultural Research (ICAR) and agricultural universities. Information technology, bio-technology and genetic engineering will be the driving forces of change. The information technology will be able to produce a penetrating and clinical mapping of the land, encompassing the physical, chemical and biological features, underground water resources and forecast of climatic conditions in a focused manner, that even small geographical segments—the small farms—can be benefited through the guidance provided by the ways in which natural and human resources can be optimally combined with appropriate technologies, inputs and options to enhance and diversify production. Technology, in and of itself, is not sufficient to bring about significant changes in the current economic and social situation of small farmers. It is important to recognize that the adoption of technology calls for the convergence at the small farm level, not only of appropriate and adequate technology, but also of markets, prices, availability of inputs, adequate credit and everything else that fuels the operation and growth of the production system (Pineiro, 1989). Bio-technology and genetic engineering will help develop seeds to meet specific ecological and biological constraints. The positive features of the local environment can be programmed to be exploited. Tissue culture will help in developing new plant varieties to suit the land and climatic factors. Genetic engineering would make it possible to introduce genes for DNA or to manipulate plant tolerance for salinity (Pineiro, 1989). The emergence of the second Green Revolution founded on commercialization of agriculture and introduction of bio-technology for commercial use, the development of transgenic crops that will allow greater flexibility in crop management, reduce dependence on conventional insecticides and herbicides, increase yields and produce cleaner and higher grade of products, are all parts of the grand vision projected for the next millennium by the Scientists. Undoubtedly there are some dissenting voices here about the possible scientific risks in genetic engineering. Notwithstanding these dissensions, one development that is sure to occur is greater and more diversified production through commercialization of agriculture. Small farmers cannot remain aloof when these developments occur. They will be forced to consolidate their holdings, organize themselves into commercial enterprises adopting the most appropriate form of organization, i.e. the company or the cooperative. The former, i.e. the company has worked extremely well in industry and can give similar results in agriculture too. On the working of the cooperatives too, we have the example of the Anand Milk Cooperatives.

If these possibilities can be realized, and if Indian agriculture can be protected from the negative fall out of globalisation and on the other hand take full advantage of the opportunities afforded by it, then the picture afforded by the new millennium will be truly exciting. The countryside will be buzzing with economic activities, rooted in the soil, with the small farmer sharing the benefits equitably and with a greater degree of technological awareness, with village clusters that are alive and prosperous, but not in splendid isolation but with a greater sense of community and fellowship in an interdependent frame work of Rurban settlements constituting a micropolitan environment. The restructuring implied here entails a greater emphasis on multilevel (decentralized) planning, which will be a major departure from the overall top-down planning. With its devolution of political, administrative and fiscal powers, it will bring in its wake a climate conducive to increased economic activity at the local levels away from urban conglomerates. Small farmers empowered and organized into politically active, local and regional associations and fora, will be transmitting their felt needs forcefully:

(i) for technology to research stations;
(ii) for suitable organizational and administrative structures to administrators; and
(iii) for incentives to policy-makers (Sundaram, 1994). The whole chain of transformation will bring about a symbiotic linkage between agriculture and technology and also between agriculture and rural industry, completing a "virtuous circle" of sustainable growth.

Summing Up

In this paper, we have attempted to synthesise the various operational ways adopted by governments in the developing countries of Asia to encourage small farmer development. During the course of the discussion, the relevance of as well as the inadequacies in the various strategies adopted by governments have been critically commented upon. They point to certain correctives as well as lessons and provide some directions for change. There is sufficient indication in our analysis to show that the small farmer has not received the just and equitable share of development benefits from the normal development strategies.

As we are entering the new century, some major challenges as well as transformation are in the offing for the small farmers. There are three major driving forces that will determine these changes. They are liberalization and economic reforms; globalization and technological progress. How these will affect the small farmers is depicted through two plausible scenarios of change, which however, are not mutually exclusive. The emphasizes in the wake of these developments, the small farmer development strategy should make full use of frontier technologies, including bio-technology and ensure the linkages between research, technology and production on the one hand, and effectiveness of the delivery system and extension network to carry the fruits of science and technology to the farmer on the other.

References

Alexandratos Nikos (Ed.), (1988), "World Agriculture Toward 2000—An F.A.O. study", F.A.O./U.N. 1988, Belhaven Press, London.

Bhalla, G.S. and Chadha, G.K., (1983), *Green Revolution and the Small Peasant: A study of income distribution among Punjab Cultivators*, New Delhi; Concept Publishing Company.

Bhalla, G.S. (Ed.), (1994), Economic Liberalization and Indian Agriculture, Institute for Studies in Industrial Development, New Delhi.

Chadha, G.K., (1986), "Impact of Agricultural Policies and Programmes of Small Farmers in India". Report prepared for F.A.O. Regional Workshop on "Impact of Policies and Programmes for increased Agricultural Production, particularly Food by the Small Farmers; RAPA, Bangkok, 11-15 November.

FAO/UN, (1989), "Sustainable Agricultural Production–Implications for international agricultural research", FAO Research and Technology paper No. 4, Rome.

Hanumantha Rao, C.H. and Gulati, Ashok, (1994), *Indian Agriculture: Emerging Perspectives and Policy Issues.* International Food Policy Research Institute.

Kessaba Abbas, M., (1989), *Technology Systems for Small Farmers – Issues and options*, Westview Press, London.

Kirit S. Parikh (Ed.) (1999), *India Development Report, 1999-2000*, Oxford University Press, New Delhi.

Pineiro, M.E., (1989), "Generation and transfer of technology for poor small farmers" in Kessaba, M. (Ed), *Technology systems for small farmers – Issues and options*, Westview Press, London.

Sands, Deborah Merrill, (1986), The technology applications gap: Overcoming constraints to small-farm development" – F.A.O., Research and Technology paper 1, F.A.O./U.N. Rome.

Sirirugsa, C., (1986), "Impact of Agricultural Policies and Programmes on Increased Agricultural Production especially Food by Small Farmers – "The Case of Thailand", F.A.O. Regional Workshop on Impact of Policies and Programmes on Increased Agricultural Production particularly Food by the Small Farmers, RAPA, Bangkok, 11-15 November.

Sundaram, K.V., (1996), "Report on Rural Development in CIRDAP Member Countries 1994-95", *CIRDAP Series No. 171*, CIRDAP, Dhaka.

Sundaram, K.V., (1994), "Decentralised Planning for Agricultural and Rural Development" in Velayudham, T.K. (Ed.), *Challenges Facing Agriculture and Rural Development*, Oxford and IBH Publishing Co. Pvt. Ltd., New Delhi.

Swaminathan, M.S., (1990), "Small Farms and Sustainable Agriculture" in *Sustainable Agriculture in India*, (Ed.) Pradeep Chaturvedi, published by Indian Association for the Advancement of Science and Food and Agriculture Organisation, New Delhi.

Randhawa, N.S. and Sundaram, K.V., (1990), "Small Farmer Development in Asia and the Pacific: Some lessons for strategy formulation and planning", FAO Economic and Social Development paper No. 87, FAO/UN Rome.

7

FIFTY YEARS OF INDIAN AGRICULTURE
An Analysis

S.M. WASEEM

While considering the story of success and failure of Indian agriculture in the last fifty years, we find reasons to rejoice and also the reasons for gloom: What has been achieved is impressive what could not be achieved, when viewed against the backdrop of potentials and the opportunities lost, is significant.

"The agriculture sector, today, provides livelihood to about 64 per cent of the labour force, contributes nearly 26 per cent of Gross Domestic Product and accounts for about 18 per cent share of the total value of the country's exports. It supplies bulk of wage goods required by the non-agricultural sector and raw material for a large section of industry. Per capita net availability of foodgrains went up to a level of 484.1 grammes per day in 1998-99 as compared to that of 395 grammes in the early fifties. In terms of gross fertilizer consumption India ranks fourth in the world after USA the erstwhile USSR, and China. The country has the largest area under pulse crops while in the field of cotton, (she) is the first to evolve a cotton hybrid."[1]

The country today is self-sufficient in food; though the total output of foodgrains during 1997-98 is said to have declined by 3.66 per cent to around 192.3 million tonnes from 199.4 million tonnes in 1996-97. Foodgrains output which stood at 203.0 million tonnes in 1998-99, is estimated to have come down to 199.1 million tonnes in 1999-2000.

The output of foodgrains which increased by 3.22 per cent annually during the 50s, was made possible due to the expansion of the foodgrain sowing area, which remains almost stagnant now since 1970-71.[2] The

1960s were marked by a low annual growth (1.72%), resulting in large scale imports of foodgrains. The decade of 1970s showed an improvement with an annual growth of 2.08 per cent ..... the lumping point in India's foodgrain economy and the path to self-sufficiency was marked by the revolutionary changes in the seed technology that pushed up productivity levels first in wheat and later in rice in the eighties."

"An annual growth of 3.5 per cent in foodgrains in eighties is the hallmark of the Green Revolution that enabled India to become self-sufficient in foodgrains and even a marginal exporter. The decade of nineties could not maintain this pace,"[3] and the "overall growth rate decelerated to 1.80 per cent per annum during the decade of nineties which is just about equal to annual population growth and therefore, is a matter of concern. Annual growth in wheat continues to be robust but in rice it tapered off in nineties after fairly high growth in eighties".[4] The raising of productivity and intensity of cropping pattern continue to be our concern.

The data below give Index-based annual growth rates of production of foodgrain.

Table 7.1: Annual Growth Rates of Production of Foodgrains (Index-based)
(Base : Triennium Ending 1981-82 = 100)

(Per cent per Annum)

Crop	*1950-51 to 1959-60*	*1960-61 to 1969-70*	*1969-70 to 1979-80*	*1979-80 to 1989-90*	*1989-90 to 1998-99**
Rice	3.28	-8.05	1.99	4.29	1.60
Wheat	4.51	5.90	5.68	4.24	3.62
Coarse Cereals	2.75	1.48	0.67	0.74	-0.48
Total Cereals	3.00	2.51	2.47	3.63	1.88
Pulses	2.72	1.35	0.44	2.78	1.19
Foodgrains	3.22	1.72	2.02	3.54	1.80

* Provisional.

Source: Economic Survey 1998-99 and 1999-2000.

It may be discerned that while wheat maintained its growth rate higher than the population growth in the country, rice failed to register its progress. It rather registered a down trend when its rate of growth during the period 1989-90 to 1998-99 slipped to 1.60 per cent per annum from 4.29 per cent per annum during 1979-80 to 1989-90. Decline in the rate of growth of coarse cereals may, however, be due to substitution effect caused by rise in incomes and migration to urban centres inducing change in preferences and also due to the tendency to catch with the Jones. Pulses must attract attention of planners and agricultural experts requiring studies of price and area shifting effects.

The output of commercial crops presents a mixed-picture : While the production of nine major oilseeds (groundnut, castor seed, sesamum, nigerseed, soyabean, sunflower, rapeseed, mustard, linseed and safflower) showed a decline of 14.3 per cent from 25.2 million tonnes in 1998-99 to 21.6 million tonnes in 1999-2000 (Estd.), the output of sugarcane which stood at 277.6 million tonnes in 1996-97, and at 279.5 million tonnes and 296.7 million tonnes in 1997-98 and 1998-99 respectively, is estimated to have reached to 315.1 million tonnes in 1999-2000, thus showing an increase of 27.9 per cent over 1996-97. The production of cotton at 12.1 million bales in 1999-2000 (Estd.), continues to remain almost the same as in 1998-99 (12.2 million bales). "Production of jute and mesta has been fluctuating between 8 to 12 million bales. In 1998-99, the combined production of jute and mesta was 9.7 million bales which is likely to increase to 10.6 million bales...."[5]

The data given in Table 7.2, give area, production and yield of principal crops. Increase in yield (1997-98) over 1950-51, has also been given. Percentage increase in rice production at 183.68 has been lower than wheat (272.55). It speaks of the effects of Green Revolution which was very positive indeed on wheat production.

The existing agricultural output and its productivity as compared to worlds' largest producers of rice, wheat and rapeseed (China), Jowar, Maize and Soybean (USA), etc. after fifty years of planning and private and public investment, continue to be matters of concern. Any lapses, pitfalls and setback in output are continually being ascribed to 'excessive monsoon rains', 'long spells of cloudy weather' and 'pest attacks' (the reasons given for fall by 4.7 per cent in rabi foodgrains output to 90.4 million tonnes in 1997-98 as against 0.7 per cent for kharif foodgrains at 103.7 million tonnes); 'lower yield levels resulting from, inclement weather conditions', (describing the output of wheat at 66.4 million tonnes in 1997-98 which is lower by 4.2 per cent of 69.3 million tonnes during 1996-97), 'absence of technological breakthrough and stagnant irrigated areas' (probable reason for slow down in productivity growth of oilseeds); 'wide cyclical movements primarily due to cane arrears payment mechanism' (while giving the output of sugarcane which is estimated at 260.2 million tonnes in 1997-98 as against 277.3 million

Table 7.2: Area, Production and Yield of Principal Crops – All India India

Area in lakh hectares
Production in lakh tonnes
Yield in kg. per hectare

Crop	*Area*		*Production*		*Yield*		*Increase in Yield**	
	1950-51	*1997-98*	*1950-51*	*1997-98*	*1950-51*	*1997-98*	*Increase (1997-98) over 1950-51*	*Percent age Increase*
Rice	308.10	439.20	205.76	823.00	668	1895	1227	183.68
Wheat	97.46	266.86	64.62	659.07	663	2470	1807	272.55
Jowar	155.71	109.85	54.95	76.82	353	727	374	105.95
Bajra	90.23	97.12	25.95	76.89	288	792	504	175.00
Maize	31.59	63.05	17.29	108.52	547	1721	1174	214.63
Total Cereals	782.30	1012.21	424.14	1793.64	542	1772	1230	226.94
Total Pulses	190.91	228.47	84.11	130.70	441	572	131	29.71
Total Food-grains	97.21	1240.68	508.25	1924.34	552	1551	1029	197.13
Total Nine Oil-seeds[1]	107.07	262.14	51.58	220.15	48	840	729	1650.00
Sugar cane	17.07	39.67	570.51	2762.54	33422	69647	36225	108.39
Cotton (Lint)[2]	58.82	89.04	30.44	11.41	88	213	125	142.05
Jute[3]	5.71	920	33.09	100.11	1043	1960	917	87.92
Mesta[3]	2741[+]	1.95	11.29	1104	742	1019	277	37.33

* Calculated by the author.
1. Nine oilseeds, viz., Groundnut, Castorseed, Sesamum, Nigerseed, Soyabean, Sunflower, Rapeseed & Mustard, Linseed and Safflower.
2. Production in lakh bales of 170 kg. each.
3. Production in lakh bales of 180 kg. each.

\+ Data pertain to 1960-61.

Source: India 2000, pp. 409-10.

tonnes in 1996-97); 'untimely rains and pest attacks' (estimating decline of cotton output to 11.4 million bales in 1997-98 from 14.3 million bales in 1996-97). Further, elsewhere no reasons are often given (viz., despite successive normal measures, the momentum of growth has been weak as compared to higher growth witnessed during 1990s.[6]

Thus, what was described by Knowles and Thompson, Indian agriculture continues to be a gamble in rain and is affected intermittently with floods and draughts. Thus, fifty years' efforts to rescue Indian agriculture from its weak base and to help place it at a high pedestal has not yielded dependable results on a sustained basis.

The country is growing cash crops and has attained a higher level of use of chemical fertilizers[7] and irrigational facilities as compared to the situation prevailing in the 1950s. Due to increase in the irrigation facilities and ensuing agro-rural prosperity the farmers, particularly those having means and resources, are shifting to cash crops. This particularly holds good for the 1990s. With a view to encourage balanced fertilizer use, the Central Government has been providing subsidy (on DAP and MOP), and maintaining the administered price (Rs. 4000 per tonne of Urea since 19-01-99). What irks, is the continuously increasing import of NOK [which stood at 3094 thousand tonnes in 1999-2000 (upto October, 1999) as against 419 million tonnes in 1960-61]. Appropriate pricing measure for fertilizers and the creation and maintenance of rural infrastructure, are also the matters deserving policy decisions for devising a long-term agricultural development strategy. As regards irrigation, the official pronouncements speak of a high priority in planning. From 22.6 million hectares of irrigation potential in 1950, the country's created irrigation potential was 89.6 million hectares by 1996-97 comprising 33 million hectares under major and medium projects and 56.6 million hectares under minor irrigation potential. Mention may be made here of a tardy utilization of major, medium and minor irrigation facilities alike. The 1998-99 data which are provisional, reveal major and medium irrigation potentials' utilization at 30.12 million hectares against a potential of 34.68 million hectares. The data for minor irrigation stood at 53.54 million hectares against a potential of 58.11 million hectares; thus bringing the utilization total to 83.66 million hectares against the potential of 92.79 million hectares. Needless to say that the administrative bottlenecks and financial constraints deserve consideration, and policy and implementation reforms.

Indian agriculture in the wake of a growing population even with a falling compound annual growth rate of 1.90 per cent (during 1991-98) has to play an important role, providing for food and non-food requirements of the Indian economy. What is of concern, is the shifting of acreage in the wake of price movements of different agricultural outputs differently. Agricultural infrastructure and level of capital formation in agriculture are to take to increasing trends to help develop and sustain (Indian) agriculture at the level required of a country like India having almost all the wherewithals. For achieving results we have to consider among other points the following :

(a) Identification and support to 'Lead Villages' with a number of peripheral villages attached to each such village to provide inputs/consultancy, etc. Lead villages are to be identified on the basis of their economic prosperity and financial viability. Consideration is to be given to other variables also such as agricultural productivity, education, health and hygiene, availability of warehousing facility, school/colleges, roads and transport facilities, availability of repair services/mechanics for agricultural machinery, credit institutions, marketing organization, and postal facilities, etc. (Decades ago, the author suggested identification of such villages and linking of peripheral and less-developed villages with these to help develop them, and then to give them independent status).

(b) We committed mistakes in hurriedly taking to bold industrial plans just because of the successful working of our First Five Year Plan. The difficulties witnessed during the Second, Third and Fourth Five Year Plans are well known. The root-causes were particularly a weak and languishing agriculture and lack of required quantum of resource generation. It is, therefore, suggested that "... we must try to create such agricultural conditions which may assure a self-sustained agriculture-led growth...."[8] Agriculture-led growth in areas where agricultural productivity and growth are higher, will lead to resource generation leading to prosperity, higher income and employment, savings and investments, both in agricultural and non-agricultural sectors. A well coordinated plan may be devised for the purpose.

(c) Development and application of indigenous rural technology must be pursued on a concerted basis. Villages should be adopted by Universities and Colleges, more particularly by their relevant Departments including their various Engineering, Commerce and Management Departments.

(d) Functional reorganization of the credit institutions, viz., for provision of credit for marketing and purchase of inputs etc. should be made. Multiplicity of credit agencies and financial institutions must go by assigning them area-wise (geographical) or functional responsibilities. RRBs have been asked to assume an urban role also. It is a pointer to our clarity of views on the judicious use and utilization of our resources.

(e) Any schemes for agro-rural development must give priority to the use of indigenous resources. As suggested by the author for Uttar Pradesh, "A comprehensive survey of local indigenous resources... must be taken up with a view to suggest their utilization in an agro-rural framework, rather than high sounding surveys for massive industrialization possibilities. For example, the agro-based industries must receive active consideration so that they may be knitted into the whole gamut of ....(the) economy."[9]

(f) Cooperatives should be strengthened to play their role at least in the remote village/rural economy lacking in the bank branches and other institutional facilities.

(g) As occasional floods[10] and droughts destroy the national wealth including the damages caused to the standing crops, much needed for India's people, prosperity and agro-industrial development, the author suggested (1973) concerted action by creating a National Flood Control and Drought Relief Fund, besides the state level permanent Flood Control Boards. It is satisfying to note that a Drought Relief Fund has been launched this year (2000) by the Prime Minister. In fact, the need is to create a combined fund (National Flood Control and Drought Relief Fund) for tackling both, flood and drought.

Notes

1. India 2000, Publications Division, Ministry of Information and Broadcasting, Government of India, p. 393.
2. See, Appendix I for data pertaining to area, output and per hectare output of foodgrains.
3. Economic Survey, 1999-2000, Special Supplement No. 1 of 1999 to JMJ Book Info, February 1999, pp. 116-17.
4. Economic Survey, 1999-2000, Economic Division, Ministry of Finance, Government of India, p. 134.
5. *Ibid.* p. 135.
6. RBI Report, 1997-98.
7. See Appendix II for relevant data.
8. See author's Paper "U.P.: Agricultural-led Growth *sine qua non* for Economic Growth", Problems of Agriculture in U.P., Society for Development of Uttar Pradesh, Kanpur, 1973 (Ed. Arjun Arora), p. 116.
9. *Ibid.* p. 113.
10. See author's Article "Economic Backwardness of Uttar Pradesh and Floods", *National Herald* (Magazine Section), New Delhi, November 28, 1971.

APPENDIX I

FOODGRAINS AREA AND PRODUCTION

Year	*Area (Million Hectares)*	*Production (Million Tonnes)*	*Production per Hectare (kgs)*
1950-51	97.32	50.82	522
1960-61	115.58	82.02	710
1970-71	124.32	108.42	872
1980-81	126.67	129.59	1023
1990-91	127.84	176.39	1380
1997-98	123.85	192.26	1552
1998-99	125.36	203.04	1620
1999-2000*	123.31	199.06	1614

* Anticipated.

Source: Economic Survey, 1999-2000, p. 134.

APPENDIX II

SEASON-WISE CONSUMPTION OF FERTILIZERS

(000 Tonnes of Nutrients)

Year	*Kharif*	*Rabi*	*Total*	*Per Cent Share*	
				Kharif	*Rabi*
1980-81	2138	3378	5516	38.8	61.2
1990-91	5741	6805	12546	45.8	54.2
1996-97	6970	7388	14308	48.4	51.6
1997-98	8092	8096	16188	50.0	50.0
1998-99	7834	8969	16796	46.6	53.4
1999-2000	9304	9841	19145	48.6	51.4

Source: Economic Survey, 1999-2000, p. 134.

8

FIFTY YEARS OF AGRICULTURAL DEVELOPMENT IN INDIA
A Temporal Analysis

G.S. CHAUHAN & R.S. SANGWAN

Introduction

Agriculture is considered to be the backbone of rural Indian economy and is the main source of livelihood for nearly two-third (65.5 per cent) of our population. It has been playing an important role in the socio-economic development of the rural masses. Approximately 29 per cent of the country's national income is derived from the agricultural sector alone. India has achieved a growth of 4.58 per cent in agricultural production of all the crops over the preceding year 1997. In fact, it is remarkable while considering the growth in area of only 2.5 per cent. The Indian agriculture system is not only supporting a huge population of nearly one billion which is about 27.57 per cent of Asia and 16.31 per cent of the world, but also a sizeable livestock population of the country, which is approximately 52.97 per cent buffaloes, 19.42 per cent goats, 14.98 per cent cattle, 8.07 per cent camel and 4.12 per cent sheep etc. of the world total livestock population (1994), is totally dependent and primarily based on the agricultural structure. Moreover, almost all the major problems of the country are closely associated with the agricultural system of the country which are mainly food sufficiency, economic, political, rural unemployment and their social conditions.

In fifty years of Independent India, there has been multi-dimensional progress which has collectively improved the socio-economic conditions of the large masses particularly in rural areas during Green Revolution period (1967). It has brought an appreciable increase in certain food-grains especially in rice and wheat and in some of commercial crops as well. The well known aspect of the said revolution is the development of high yielding varieties of cereal crops. The spectacular rise in production of some of selected foodgrains have been called 'Green Revolution'. Secondly, the 'White Revolution' is also liable for the marked rise of milk production in the country including self-sufficiency in milk production.

Statistical figures reveal that the Indian agriculture has achieved desired goal in the last fifty years (Table 8.3). Although, the country's performance is appreciable in almost all the sectors, viz., agricultural, industrial, poverty alleviation, economic, urban and rural, etc., but it has got a key position especially in agricultural sphere.

In the present agricultural scenario when the modern society is on the threshold of the 21st century, India is known as one of the leading agrarian countries across the globe. In some of the recent years, India has, in fact, achieved the first position in the world not only with regard to the area under various crops especially cereals, paddy, millets, sorghum, pulses, beans dry, chick peas, lentils, groundnut, castor seed, seasmum seed, rape seed, mustard, linseed, safflower seed, cotton seed, etc., but also in relation to the production of agricultural crops lime millets, pulses, beans dry, chickpeas, lentils, castor seed and seasmum seed followed by safflower seed during 1994 (Table 8.1).

Moreover, in case of some of the horticultural crops, India's rank is globally highest and the country has first place in the production of banana, mango, coconut and cashew. Similarly, India is among first ten in citrus, pineapple and apple production. In the same fray, the nation also holds the first position in global production of potato, tomato, onion, and green peas. It is also essential and significant to mention here the share of agricultural export. Furthermore, in the same reference, significant strides have been made by the country in agricultural production towards ensuing food security. There has been a significant improvement in the productivity of various agricultural crops which has helped in reducing the rural poverty. But a unique phenomenon has been felt in those areas in which the agricultural productivity was high especially in Punjab and Haryana, but in the recent years the productivity has declined. In the eastern region, except West Bengal, the productivity has been noticed low, mainly due to weak infrastructure.

In fact, India is a country with diverse and unique physiography as well as wide variety of agro-climatic conditions. The availability of huge

Table 8.1: India's Position in World and Asia, 1994

Crops	*World*		*Asia*	
	Area	*Production*	*Area*	*Production*
A. Total Cereals	I	III	I	II
i) Wheat	III	III	II	II
ii) Rice	I	II	I	II
A-1. Coarse Grains	II	III	II	II
i) Barley	XXI	XXII	VII	VII
ii) Maize	V	VII	II	II
iii) Millets	I	I	I	I
iv) Sorghum	I	II	I	I
B. Total Pulses	I	I	I	I
i) Beans dry	I	I	I	I
ii) Peas dry	V	VI	II	II
iii) Chick peas	I	I	I	I
iv) Lentils	I	I	I	I
C. Oilseeds				
i) Soyabean	V	V	II	II
ii) Ground Nut	I	II	I	II
iii) Castor Seed	I	I	I	I
iv) Sunflower Seed	II	VI	I	I
v) Seasamum Seed	I	I	I	II
vi) Rapeseed	I	III	I	II
vii) Linseed	I	III	I	II
viii) Safflower Seed	I	I	I	I
D. Others				
i) Cotton Seed	I	III	I	II
ii) Sugarcane	II	II	I	I

Source: *FAO Year Book*, Vol. 48, 1994.

natural resources such as land, soil, water and forests, etc. provide enough scope for the growth and development of agriculture and associated various crops including foodgrains. But the accelerating population of both human and livestock, along with widespread poverty has generated enough pressure on the available natural resources and ultimately it led to degradation of environment. It has been estimated that out of 329 million hectares of the total geographical area, about 174 million hectares is degraded by various processes and it consists of agricultural as well as non-agricultural lands and forests.

Study Area

The designated study area, India, is approximately situated between 8°4' and 37°06' North latitude and from 68°07' and 97°25' East longitude with an area of 3,287,782 sq. km. comprising about 2.45 per cent of the world total geographical area and 16.31 per cent population of the globe. Climatically, India is one of the important sub-tropical countries and the existing immense agro-climatic diversities often provide the suitable criteria to grow a large variety of agriculture crops as well as horticultural crops. In the mean time, the country has observed a very rapid and drastic population growth and presents a very complex problem ridden scenario. Virtually, the total population of the country was 361.1 million in 1950-51 which has substantially increased to 915.9 million in 1994-95 and has been projected that it would be more than 1 billion by 2000 A.D.

Simultaneously, the density of population has also increased from 216 to 267 persons per sq. km. during the period 1981 to 1991. Out of the entire population, a small portion of it is fairly well off and a sizeable population (65.5 per cent) is basically engaged in agricultural and its allied activities and suffering from a number of problems viz. poverty, illiteracy, unemployment, diseases, malnutrition and hunger including safe drinking water facilities, etc.

Land Use Dynamics

The existing land use system of the country is very dynamic in nature and it is rather full of challenges and opportunities including many discrepancies in their land use. Certain parts of India are very feasible to raise food crops and some are not suitable for various species and vegetational crops. So, different types of agro-climatic regions offer varied types of land use systems. Before going to assess and to know the agricultural performance in the last fifty years, it is essential to understand the entire land use system and occurrence changes therein to get the overall results of crop production and productivity and the related issues. Land use system of the country presents a very typical and unique picture while dealing with its various categories. It has been evidently found that the land use system has perceptibly changed a lot and has got a new dimension in the last five decades and ultimately it indicates that the area under various classes and sub-classes have increased and on the other hand, in some of the categories the related area has gone down tremendously (Table 8.2).

Table 8.2 indicates that the net sown area has increased from 118.7 million hectares to 142.5 million hectares during 1950-51 to 1992-93 and it has been projected that it will touch nearly 148.5 million hectares

Table 8.2: India: Land Utilisation

(Area in million hectares)

Category	*1950-51*	*1960-61*	*1970-71*	*1980-81*	*1990-91*	*1991-92*	*1992-93*
New sown area	118.7	133.2	140.3	140.0	142.5	141.5	142.5
Area sown more than once	13.2	19.6	25.5	32.6	43.6	40.75	43.0
Total cropped area	131.9	152.8	165.8	172.6	185.9	182.2	185.5
Total irrigated area	20.9	24.7	31.1	38.7	47.8	49.9	50.1

Source: Ministry of Information & Broadcasting, Ministry of Finance, Economic Survey and Department of Agriculture, August, 1997, New Delhi.

by 2000 A.D. Simultaneously, the area sown more than once has also recorded an increase of more than three-times from 13.2 million hectares to 43 million hectares during the period 1950-51 to 1992-93 and estimated to be 48.2 million hectares by the year 2000. Another important category has also observed the same trends of transformation and the total cropped area has increased from 131.9 million hectares to 185.5 million hectares during the same transition period. Moreover, the area under irrigation also got new dimension and has gone through almost the similar phase of transition and the total irrigated area was 20.9 million hectares (1950-51) which has further increased to more than double and it was registered 50.1 million hectares (1992-93) and it has been projected that it would touch the figures around 50.9 million hectares in the new millennium. Hence, the overall result depicts that the area under various categories has observed the rising trends of transformation with few exceptions within the designated time period.

Area Under Major Crops

Table 8.3 reveals that area under major crops has increased during the given time period. In almost all the major crops area under the some crops has gone up. For instance, area under wheat crop was recorded only 9.7 million hectares in 1950-51 which has increased to more than double (25.12 million hectares) in 1995-96. In case of another important crop rice too, the area has increased upto a sizeable mark and it has increased from 30.8 to 42.91 million hectares in the same period. Whereas the area under the other cereals have substantially gone down from 37.7 to 31.49 million hectares. But the area possessed by the

Table 8.3: India: Area Under Major Crops (in million hectares)

Crops	*1950-51*	*1960-61*	*1970-71*	*1980-81*	*1990-91*	*1991-92*	*1992-93*	*1993-94*	*1994-95*	*1995-96*
Cereals Total	58.2	9.21	100.9	104.0	103.16	99.31	100.77	100.49	100.61	99.52
Rice	30.8	34.1	37.6	40.1	42.69	42.65	41.78	42.54	42.81	42.91
Wheat	9.7	12.9	18.2	22.2	24.17	23.26	24.59	25.15	25.70	25.12
Other cereals (Jowar, bajra, maize, ragi, millets, barley)	37.7	45.1	45.1	41.7	36.30	33.40	34.40	32.80	32.10	31.49
Pulses (Gram, tur and others)	19.9	22.5	22.4	22.9	24.6	22.5	22.3	22.25	23.03	23.82
Sugarcane	1.7	2.4	2.7	2.6	3.69	3.84	3.57	3.42	3.87	4.14
Oilseeds (Linseed, rapeseed, seasmum, mustard, castorseed)	10.7	13.8	16.6	17.5	24.15	25.89	25.24	26.9	25.30	26.35
Cotton	5.9	7.6	7.6	7.5	7.44	7.66	7.54	7.32	7.87	9.06
Jute	0.6	0.6	0.7	0.9	NA	NA	NA	1.91	1.94	NA

NA – Data not available.

Sources: (i) India, A Reference Annual, 1990.
(ii) Directorate of Economics and Statistics 1998, Ministry of Agriculture, Government of India.

foodgrains have touched the mark of 123.44 million hectares in 1995-96. The area under cash crops like cotton has also increased from 5.9 to 9.06 million hectares and is followed by sugarcane.

However, the latest agricultural scenario depicts that area under foodgrains has marginally declined from 100.61 million hectares in 1994-95 to 123.44 million hectares in 1995-96. While the area cultivated under rice has marginally increased from 42.81 million hectares in 1994-95 to 42.91 million hectares in 1995-96, but in case of wheat the area has declined from 25.70 million hectares in 1994-95 to 25.12 million hectares in 1995-96. The area under important crops like cotton and sugarcane has also increased. The overall picture related to major crops has generally shown an upward trend with regard to area under major crops.

Production of Major Crops

In the changing agricultural scenario, the major crops have got the new dimension with positive growth during the mentioned transition period. The data related to agricultural production reveals that a steady growth is being maintained (Table 8.4). It is all due to the intensive use of fertilizers, application of irrigational facilities on large scale, tractorisation and use of the latest technological innovations including the use of pesticides and insecticides. Due to development of high yielding varieties, the cultivation of wheat, sugarcane, fibre, etc. has got impetus and their production increased to 9.4 per cent, 12.69 per cent and 18.10 per cent respectively in 1994-95 as compared to their production in 1993-94.

In the present agricultural situation, India has emerged as the world leader in developing hybrids for rabi sorghum/jowar, hybrid CSH 12 R, 6 hybrids of pear millet, 3 varieties of finger millet, and one variety of little millet. Although, the process is still continued for developing the hybrid of rice. Moreover, India has also developed the first cotton hybrid in the world, resultantly self-sufficiency in high-yielding varieties.

Table 8.4 vividly depicts that the production of foodgrains has increased nearly four-times from 50.8 to 185.1 million tonnes during the period 1950-51 to 1995-96. The country's agricultural output and hence, even a marginal production has ripple effect on rest of the economy. Despite a near normal monsoon in 1995, the foodgrains output was recorded 185.1 million tonnes in 1995-96 and was lowered by over 6 million tonnes compared to 191.5 million tonnes in 1994-95.

Out of these selected crops, wheat has achieved the maximum production level, i.e. from 6.5 million tonnes to 65 million tonnes, i.e., ten times from the initial production. Although, the production of other selected crops also increased to the highest mark but not higher than the already recorded wheat crop. Similarly, the oilseeds, too have a substantial jump in their total production which increased from 5.2 million tonnes in 1950-51 to 22.4 million tonnes in 1995-96. The production of rice has been recorded 20.6 million tonnes in 1950-51, where about four-fold increase to the level of 79.6 million tonnes has been registered in 1995-96. Among the commercial crops, the production of sugarcane increased from 51.1 million tonnes in 1950-51 to 282.9 million tonnes in 1995-96.

Productivity/Yield of Major crops

The available agricultural statistics for the last five decades indicate that there is steady rise in the average yield per hectare or rise in agricultural productivity (Table 8.5). Actually, with the introduction of economic planning in 1950-51 and moreover, with the special emphasis of agricultural development particularly after the Green Revolution (1967), the previous trend of stagnant agriculture was reversed and subsequently, there is an increase both in area as well as in yield per hectare.

Table 8.4 depicts the increasing trend regarding the yield of principal crops. For instance, in case of the foodgrains the recorded yield was 522 kg. per hectare in 1950-51 which has tremendously increased to 1499 kg. per hectare in the year 1995-96. The rice has also experienced the same pattern of yield per hectare and it has registered an increase of 1187 kg. per hectare from 668 kg. per hectare in 1950-51 to 1855 kg. per hectare in 1995-96. The wheat has achieved the highest maximum yield in comparison to the other principal crops and it has registered nearly four-times yield per hectare per kg. during the given transition period. In the year 1950-51, the wheat yield was noticed 663 kg. per hectare which has reached a record level of 2493 kg. per hectare in the year 1995-96. In the same way, an increasing trend has been noticed in the yields of oilseeds, millets and sugarcane.

Such a good performance made by principal crops in relation to their yield is due to the extensive use of irrigational facilities and application of intensive methods of cultivation. In fact, all the agricultural situation has changed generally after the introduction of modern agricultural practices including the adoption of hybrid varieties of seeds

Table 8.4: India: Production of Major Crops (in million tonnes)

Crops	*1950-51*	*1960-61*	*1970-71*	*1980-81*	*1990-91*	*1991-92*	*1992-93*	*1993-94*	*1994-95*	*1995-96*
Foodgrains	50.8	82.0	108.4	129.6	176.4	168.4	179.5	184.3	191.5	185.1
Wheat	6.5	11.0	23.8	36.3	55.1	55.7	57.2	59.8	65.8	62.8
Rice	20.6	34.6	42.2	53.6	74.3	74.7	72.9	80.3	81.8	79.6
Oilseeds	5.2	7.0	9.6	9.4	18.6	18.6	20.1	21.5	21.3	22.4
Sugarcane	57.1	110.0	126.4	154.2	241.0	254.0	228.0	229.7	275.5	282.9

Source: Ministry of Information and Broadcasting, Ministry of Finance, Economic Survey and Department of Agriculture, August, 1997, New Delhi.

Table 8.5: India: Yield/Productivity of Major Crops (in kg/ha)

Crops	*1950-51*	*1960-61*	*1970-71*	*1980-81*	*1990-91*	*1991-92*	*1992-93*	*1993-94*	*1994-95*	*1995-96*
Foodgrains	522	710	872	1023	1380	1382	1457	1501	1548	1499
Rice	668	1013	1123	1336	1740	1751	1744	1888	1911	1855
Wheat	663	851	1307	1630	2881	2394	2327	2380	2559	2493
Oilseeds	481	507	579	532	771	719	797	799	843	851
Millets	441	539	524	473	578	533	573	598	610	552
Sugarcane (tonne/ha)	33	46	48	58	65	66	64	67	71	68

Source: Ministry of Information and Broadcasting, Ministry of Finance, Economic Survey and Department of Agriculture, August, 1997, New Delhi.

resulting into a steady and continuous increase in the yield per hectare of all crops.

Consumption of Fertilizers

The fertilizers use in the agricultural operations in the production of various foodgrains have also shown the enthusiastic rising trends and brought the overall positive development in the existing agricultural system. Although, due to the over-doses of fertilizers especially NPK, the production as well as productivity of certain crops have achieved the highest level of growth in some of the recent years, but it is also a hard fact that their maximum use have damaged the productivity and resultantly in those areas which are known as 'bread basket' of the country (Punjab, Haryana and Western U.P.), the productivity of certain crops have either declined or their quality has deteriorated up to the maximum extent. The statistical figures as given in Table 8.6 clearly display that the fertilizers use in the country has got new and multiple dimensions. In the initial period of 1950-51, the NPK consumption was 69 thousand tonnes in the country which has increased to 13877 tonnes in the year 1995-96.

In terms of fertilizers consumption per hectare it was 1.9 kg. per hectare in 1960-61 which has increased to 67.68 kg. per hectare during 1993-94. So, the fertilizer consumption in agricultural practices has, of course, brought appreciable positive growth but it is restricted to certain limits. However, its overuse has indeed shown the declining trends. This is also relevant to mention here that number of tractors has increased manifold in the last five decades. The country had only 5000 tractors in 1950, which increased to 1,80,000 only a couple of years ago and these are now touching the figure of 3 lakhs. Similarly, the country had an installed capacity of 2000 MW electricity power in 1950. Presently, it is 85000 MW, which is used in various agricultural operations.

Conclusion

Agriculture and its allied activities including horticulture has occupied a significant place in the Indian economy. It has undoubtedly played an important role not only in the country's economic development but also to improve the socio-economic conditions of the rural based masses. The development of Indian agriculture in the last fifty years is, no doubt, appreciable and remarkable because India has globally achieved a high

Table 8.6: India: Consumption of Fertilizers

Fertilizers Consumption	*1950-51*	*1960-61*	*1970-71*	*1980-81*	*1990-91*	*1991-92*	*1992-93*	*1993-94*	*1994-95*	*1995-96*
NPK ('000 tonnes)	69	92	2177	5516	12546	12728	12155	12366	13564	13877
Per hectare kg.	NA	1.9	13.13	31.83	67.49	69.66	66.52	67.68	N.A.	N.A.

NA – Data not available.

Source: Ministry of Information and Broadcasting, Ministry of Finance, Economic Survey and Department of Agriculture, August, 1997, New Delhi.

rank with regard to certain agricultural crops. Moreover, the country has also got self-sufficiency in various food crops.

Although, the role of Green Revolution was much significant to raise the agricultural production but a number of other factors which are also liable to get the over all agricultural development in the country are mainly the introduction of improved irrigation facilities, high yielding varieties, use of fertilizers, agricultural development programmes, large scale plant protection measures, pesticides, new methods of farming, introduction of new agricultural policy and new technological innovations, etc. The role of eminent agricultural scientists like Dr. M.S. Swaminathan, C. Subramanyam and Dr. Shivraman is equally important to achieve the overall development in the agriculture sector. Dr. Swaminathan who is a protagonist of sustainable agriculture and a crusader for food security is truly *The father of Green Revolution* that is substantial and relevant to India. So, to maintain the sustainability in foodgrains and other important agricultural crops, it is essential to bring these areas under agricultural operations which are lying waste. A balance approach should be adopted in case of fertilizers to maintain the production and productivity of crops. While what have been achieved is really impressive, prospects ahead are challenging in the new millennium. So, to feed the teeming millions of people, there is need of a judicious approach to get more output by launching certain more agriculture revolutions by sustaining agriculture production.

References

Arakeri, H.R. (1982), *Indian Agriculture*, Oxford and IBH Publishing Co., New Delhi, p. 236.

Azad, K.C. *et al.* (1988), *Horticultural Development in Hill Areas: A Case Study of Himachal Pradesh*, Mittal Publications, Delhi.

Brown, D.D. (1971), *Agricultural Development in India's Districts*, Cambridge, Mass.

Chakravarti, A.K. (1973), "Green Revolution in India", *Annals of the A.A.G.*, Vol. 63, pp. 319-30.

Chaudhari, D.P. *et al.* (1991), Landuse, Sustainability and Agricultural Development in the North-West India, Report prepared for Ministry of Agriculture, Government of India.

Dayal, E. (1979), "A Measure of Cropping Intensity", *Professional Geographer*, Vol. 30, No. 3, pp. 289-96.

Farmer, B.H. (1974), *Agricultural Colonisation in India since Independence*, Oxford & IBH, New Delhi.

Pradhan, S. (1997), "Agricultural Research in India", *Junior Science Refresher*, New Delhi.

Singh, J. (1974), *An Agricultural Atlas of India : A Geographical Analysis*, Vishal Publications, Kurukshetra.

Tirtha, R. (1996), "Agricultural and Rural Development" in Tirtha, R. *et al.* (ed.), *Geography of India,* Rawat Publications, Jaipur, pp. 150-179.

9

GREEN REVOLUTION IN INDIA AND THE PERFORMANCE OF MAJOR CENTRAL CROPS

An Appraisal

MAJID HUSAIN

The term Green Revolution has been used to mean two different things. Some experts of agricultural geography use it for referring to a broad transformation of agricultural sector in the developing countries to reduce food shortages. Others use it when referring to the specific plant improvements, notably the development of High Yielding Varieties (HYV). Whatsoever the meaning of Green Revolution may be taken, the adoption of HYV of wheat and rice has been considered a significant achievement as it offered great optimism. In fact, these varieties of seeds have revolutionised the agricultural landscape of the developing countries, and thereby the problems of poverty, hunger and under-nourishment have been reduced in certain regions of the Third World Countries.

In India, the hybridisation of selected crops, i.e., maize, bajra (bulrush-millet) and millets began in 1960. The maximum dwarf varieties of wheat were tried out on a selected scale in 1963-64. Exotic varieties of paddy such as Taichung Native I were introduced in India in 1966. The diffusion of HYV, however, became fully operational in the country in the Kharif season of 1965-66 in which about 17000 hectares of cultivated land was brought under HYV, especially in the Sutlej-Ganga plain and the Kaveri-delta.

Merits of High Yielding Varieties

The High Yielding Varieties have certain advantages over the traditional varieties of cereals which may be summarised as under:

1. HYV have shorter life cycle and thereby enable the farmers to go for multiple cropping. For example, new seeds of rice and wheat complete their life cycles in 110 and 120 days respectively. The traditional varieties of rice and wheat, on the other hand, take about 130 and 150 days respectively to harvest. The new seeds thus enable the farmers to economise on land.
2. HYV need a lot of water for better yields. They yield per unit area is significantly high. If it is considered in terms of water required per quintal of wheat or rice, the new seeds require less water as compared to that of the traditional varieties. HYV thus economise on water also as the crop remain in the field for a shorter period.
3. HYV under optimal conditions require more labour per unit area, and thus help in generating more employment.
4. HYV are scale neutral which means that other things being remaining the same, the big farmers and the small farmers are likely to get the production and profit in the same proportion. In other words, the new seeds are not biased towards the big or the small farmers.
5. The adoption of HYV do not require any special skill and farmers of various socio-economic and cultural backgrounds can adopt the new seeds easily.

When the package programme and new agricultural strategy were adopted in the mid-sixties, it was expected that the problems of food shortage, poverty, hunger, malnutrition, undernourishment and economic inequalities will be largely solved, but these objectives could not be fully achieved because of certain geoclimatic and socio-economic constraints in the cultivation of HYV.

Socio-economic Constraints in the Adoption of High Yielding Varieties

HYV are undoubtedly land substituting, water economising, more labour using, and employment generating innovation; nevertheless, they are very delicate and therefore require a great deal of care if a successful harvest is to be obtained. For example, the new seeds are less resistant to droughts and floods and need an efficient management of water, chemical fertilizers, insecticides and pesticides. Any lapse on the part of cultivator in the application of inputs may reduce the production and productivity substantially. In order to get a satisfactory agricultural return, the farmer should be in a position to arrange the costly inputs on time for which sufficient surplus capital should be available. In the case of non-availability of capital, the farmer should have an easy access to the credit facilities.

Irrigation

Irrigation is the most important input required for the successful cultivation of HYV. Adoption of new needs and intensification of agriculture in the sub-tropical countries like India (characterised with erratic monsoon) are not possible unless adequate irrigation facilities are available. Better results from HYV depend largely on assured and controlled irrigation. The new seeds require water at specific periods of growth, development and flowering. The associated inputs like chemical fertilizers, insecticides and pesticides also perform satisfactory only if timely irrigation is provided to the crop. It may be emphasised that excessive irrigation and inadequate irrigation are both injurious to HYV of wheat and rice. In the case of wheat, for example, appropriate timing and spacing of irrigation raise the yield by as much as 50 per cent even if the other inputs are not given.

Availability of Chemical Fertilizers

After irrigation, chemical fertilizer is the second most important input required for the successful cultivation of HYV. The recommended dose of chemical fertilizer for the new seeds of wheat and rice in terms of NPK is 90-45-45 kg per hectare. The heavy doses of chemical fertilizers may be beyond the reach of marginal and small farmers.

Plant Protection Chemicals

The new seeds are very delicate and highly susceptible to pests and disease. The irrigated fields enriched with heavy energy input of NPK create a micro climate (hot and humid) in the field which helps in the luxurious growth of plants. The hot and moist environment of the field also becomes conducive for the fast growth and multiplication of insects and pests. These insects and pests seriously attack the plants, hamper their growth and reduce the yield substantially. The danger of pests and insects may be reduced by using plant protection chemicals. The problem may be tackled either by developing the disease resistant seeds or by spraying insecticides and pesticides at the prescribed schedules devised for different crops. The plant protection chemicals are, however, quite expensive.

Capital

Availability of capital is also a vital constraint in the adoption and successful cultivation of HYV. The adopters of HYV must have operational capital for the purchase of seeds, installation of tubewells, drilling of pumping sets, chemical fertilizers, plant protection chemicals, tractors, harvesters, threshers and other accessories. In India, most of the farmers, excepting a few larger ones, have no surplus over consumption, and therefore, no saving or operational capital at their disposal. The agrarian institutions like banks and co-operative credit societies have great responsibilities. They should advance loans to the farmers at a reasonable rate of interest. Unfortunately, the credit agencies in India, generally, serve the larger farmers who are economically well-off and politically well connected

Mechanization

Modern farming tools and technology like tractor, thresher and sprayers are also imperative for the successful cultivation of HYV. These varieties, require elaborate arrangements of canal and tubewell irrigation. Raising of three and four crops from the same field in one year is possible only if modern technology is available to the farmer. The traditional plough and bullockcarts are less efficient to finish the agricultural operations on time.

Transport, Marketing and Storage Facilities

The infrastructural facilities like transport network, marketing and storage facilities are also very crucial for the successful cultivation of HYV. It is the transport network which determines the types of crops grown in an agricultural region. It also helps in the marketing and storage of the agricultural commodities. Once a village is linked with a town by a metalled road, its economy undergoes a remarkable transformation. Cultivation of perishable crops like vegetables, fruits and dairy products can also be done efficiently and profitably if elaborate transport, marketing and storage facilities are available.

Extension Service

For the successful cultivation of HYV, there should be an efficient extension service which may guide the farmers about the various agricultural operations and precautions. In the tradition bound Indian society, the efficiency of extension machinery determines largely the efficiency of the producers. There should, therefore, be a perfect understanding and co-ordination between farmers, extension agents, farm supervisors, researchers and agricultural scientists.

Human Factor

In the adoption and spread of HYV the role of human factor is also very important. As a matter of fact, in many cases, man behind the machine becomes more important than the machine itself. The personal qualities of a farmer, his attitude, beliefs, aspirations, progressiveness, education, lifestyle and family values determine his capacity to adopt an agricultural innovation. In fact, there are innovative and hardworking farmers within a village who perform better than their orthodox neighbours whose efficiency may be comparatively low.

Green Revolution : Performance of Crops

Introduction and diffusion of HYV has substantially increased the production of cereals, especially that of wheat and rice. It is because of the new varieties that India is now exporting wheat and rice to Bangladesh, China, Russia, S.W. Asian countries, Ethiopia, and East European countries. The area under cereal crops has increased appreciably as shown in Table 9.1.

It will be seen from Table 9.1 that in the pre-Green Revolution period (1950-61) there was a steady decline in the percentage of area under food crops, being 74 per cent in 1950-51 and 72 per cent in 1960-61. The farmers during that period were more inclined towards the

Table 9.1 : India:Trend in the Growth of Food and Non-food Crops (1950-51)

(in percentage)

Year	*Food Crops*	*Non-food Crops*
1950-51	74	26
1960-61	72	28
1970-71	78	22
1980-81	80	20
1990-91	81	19

Source: Computed from the data published by the Directorate of Economics and Statistics, Government of India, 1950-1991.

cultivation of non-cereal crops (sugarcane, cotton, oilseeds, etc.) which used to fetch more money to the farmers. During that period the yield per hectare of wheat and rice was very low. The situation, however, got changed after the Green Revolution. In 1970-71, for example, the area under food crops went up as they occupied 78 per cent of the total cropped area in 1970-71 against 72 per cent in 1960-61. The areal strength of food crops further increased being 80 per cent in 1980-81 and 81 per cent in 1990-91. The study increase in the area of cereal crops during the last three decades shows that now the farmers of certain areas like Punjab and Haryana are no longer subsistent. They are growing wheat and rice largely for the market. In other words, the traditional classification of food crops and commercial crops has lost its significance. Now, wheat and rice are produced by the farmers of the region of successful Green Revolution to generate income and to fetch more money to the cultivators and rural workers.

Diffusion of HYV has also changed the areal strength of the different crops. The area under different crops in the pre and post-Green Revolution decades has been given in Table 9.2.

Table 9.2 : India: Changes in Areal Strength of Selected Crops (1950-1991)

(in '000ha)

Crop	*1950-51*	*1960-61*	*1970-71*	*1980-81*	*1990-91*
Rice	308	341	375	401	390
Wheat	97	129	82	223	236
Total Cereals	782	920	17	1042	9715
Pulses	190	235	225	224	218
Sugarcane	17	23	25	27	31
Cotton	59	64	69	78	71

Source : Estimate of area, production and yield, 1950-51 to 1990-91, Directorate of Economics and Statistics, Government of India.

An examination of Table 9.2 shows that area under wheat and rice has increased significantly, while the area under pulses is almost unchanged. In many districts of the country, especially in Punjab and Haryana, the area under millets, maize and pulses has declined substantially. The area under wheat has recorded as increase of about 150 per cent during the last three decades while the area under rice also recorded a significant increase. The major expansion of rice took place in the states of Punjab and Haryana which may be attributed to the adequate expansion of canal network and the drilling of millions of tubewells. Area under rice increased in the states of Uttar Pradesh, Jammu & Kashmir, Himachal Pradesh and Madhya Pradesh, and the Bharatpur, Alwar and Ganganagar districts of Rajasthan.

In order to examine the changes in productivity, the average yields of the important crops for the periods of 1960-61 and 1990-91 have been displayed in Table 9.3.

Table 9.3 : India : Average Yield of the Major Cereal and Non-cereal Crops (1960-61 and 1990-91)

Crop	*Average yield in kg*		*Percentage*
	1960-61	*1990-91*	*increase/ decrease*
Rice	915	1612	76.17
Wheat	757	2100	177.40
Maize	856	1335	55.95
Jowar	495	725	46.46
Bajra	303	507	66.33
Pulses	493	549	11.36
All foodgrains	652	1256	48.09
Sugarcane*	38	62	63.20
Cotton	105	202	92.38
Jute and mesta	1034	1507	45.74

* Yield of sugarcane in tonnes per hectare.

Source :Economic Surveys 1990-91 and 1994-95.

The data presented in Table 9.3 reveal that the yield of wheat has increased by over 177 per cent between 1960-61 and 1990-91. Rice is the staple food which recorded the second highest increase in yield being over 76 per cent, followed by bajra and maize which recorded an increase of 66 per cent and 56 per cent respectively. In the pulses, there was, however, a marginal increase of about 11 per cent only. Pulses, being the main source of protein in the country, need special attention for the enhancement of their yields per unit area. Among the non-cereal crops, cotton recorded an increase of about 92 per cent, followed by sugarcane 63 per cent, while the yield of jute and mesta went up by about 46 per cent.

The total production of wheat was only 11 million tonnes in 1960-61 which went up to 59 million tonnes in 1994-95. The high profitability generated by HYV induced the farmers to divert a substantial proportion of their holdings to wheat crop.

The rice production rose to 80 million tonnes in 1990-91 as against 35 million tonnes in 1960-61. The overall production of foodgrains was 185 millon tonnes in 1994-95. Production of pulses in the country is, however, oscillating about 10-14 million tonnes for the last 35 years.

In general, during the post-Green Revolution period, the annual growth rate of foodgrains was 2.62 per cent, a little above the rate of population growth. The only setback being in the case of pulses which continue to register a lower growth rate. Consequently, the per capita availability of pulses has come down from 69 grams in 1961 to about 38 grams in 1994. A substantial increase in the production of pulses in necessary to meet to protein requirements of the teeming millions. Sluggish growth in the production of pulses is mainly due to the failure in the development of HYV for the different agro-climatic regions of the country. Some successful work has been done in the case of arhar (pegion pea), moong (green gram), gram, and black gram, but its impact on enhancing supplies is not yet visible.

A more realistic picture of the performance of HYV and the success or failure of the Green Revolution may be ascertained by examining the performance of the major cereal and non-cereal crops during the last three decades. In order to achieve this objective, the area, yield and production of rice, wheat, maize, millets and pulses have been briefly discussed in the following paras.

Rice

Rice is the staple food for about 60 per cent of the total population of the country. It is grown under diverse temperature, moisture and soil conditions. Availability of moisture either from rains or from irrigation is, however, the main determinant of its cultivation. Cultivation of rice is carried on all over the country expecting the unirrigated parts of Rajasthan, Kutch, Saurashtra, Malwa and Marathwada. After the introduction of HYV, its cultivation has assumed great significance in the cropping structure of Punjab, Haryana and Western Uttar Pradesh.

The Ganga-Brahmaputra plains, the eastern and western coastal plains, the hill states of North-east India, Chotanagpur Plateau, Madhya Pradesh, the Valley of Kashmir and the irrigated parts of Himachal Pradesh are the main rice growing areas of the country. Traditionally, the States of Uttar Pradesh, West Bengal, Assam, Madhya Pradesh, Bihar, Orissa, Tamil Nadu, Andhra Pradesh and Kerala were the main growers of rice. The percentage change in the area, yield and production of rice have been given in Table 9.4.

Table 9.4 : India : Area, Production and Yield of the Principal Cereal Crops

(area in thousand hectares production in thousand tonnes yield in kg/hectares)

Crop	*Year*	*Area*	*Percent-age change in area*	*Produc-tion*	*Percent-age change in production*	*Yield*	*Percent-age change in yield*
Rice	1964-65	36462	16.77	39038	101.15	1078	50.23
	1994-95	42576		78525		1612	
Wheat	1964-65	13422	85.70	12290	376.28	913	130.12
	1994-95	24925		58535		2101	
Maize	1964-65	4618	30.46	4664	8.16	948	40.82
	1994-95	6025		5045		1335	
Jowar	1964-65	18056	-28.23	9749	18.23	543	33.70
	1994-95	12958		11526		726	
Pulses	1964-65	23875	-5.82	12417	17.24	495	11.11
	1994-95	22485		14550		550	

Source : Directorate of Economics and Statistics, Government of India.

It can be seen from Table 9.4 that the areal strength of rice has increased from 364 thousand hectares in 1964-65 to 425 thousand hectares in 1994-95, thereby recording an increase of over 16 per cent. The new areas in which its cultivation has been diffused substantially in the last three decades are Punjab, Haryana, Western Uttar Pradesh and Himachal Pradesh. The production of rice was about 39 million tonnes in 1964-65 which rose up to 78 million tonnes in 1994-95 registering an increase of over 100 per cent.

Although, the yield and production of rice has gone up in all the rice growing areas of the country, it recorded an unparallel growth in area and production in the States of Punjab and Haryana. In these States, the farmers have installed tubewells and pumping sets in almost all the unirrigated tracts. In the semi-arid parts of Punjab and Haryana, the average annual rainfall is about 60 cm while for the successful cultivation of rice about 100 cm of rainfall is required. The deficiency of moisture in Punjab and Haryana is met by canals and tubewells. The cultivation of rice in the rainfall deficient areas with the help of irrigation is, however, a cause of concern as it is causing numerous ecological problems in the region.

Wheat

After rice, wheat is the most important food crop in India. It contributes more than 35 per cent of the total foodgrains production in the country. Table 9.4 gives the changing patterns of wheat area, production and productivity.

It may be seen from Table 9.4 that wheat is the only cereal in which the Green Revolution is a great success. Its area has expanded substantially and its production and productivity have shown unparallel increase during the last three decades. Between 1964-65 and 1994-95 wheat area has increased from 1.34 million hectares to 2.49 million hectares, thereby registering an increase of about 86 per cent. The total production of wheat in 1964-65 was 12.29 million tonnes which reached up to 58.33 million tonnes in 1994-95. The per hectare yield went up from 913 kg per hectare in 1964-65 to 2101 kg per hectare in 1994-95.

The regional pattern of wheat distribution shows an overall expansion of wheat area from the Ganganagar District of Rajasthan in the west to Dimapur-plain (Nagaland) in the east, and from the Suru and Nubra Valleys (Ladakh) in the north to Karnataka in the south. It is not only that wheat has got diffused in all directions from its traditional heartland of Punjab and Haryana, its production and yield also recorded an increase of about 376 and 130 per cent respectively.

Looking at the spread of wheat from the Ganganagar District of Rajasthan to Dimapur of Nagaland and from Ladakh to Karnataka and its excellent performance in the Ganga-Sutlej plain, it may be said that the Green Revolution is a great success in the case of wheat. Moreover, in Punjab, Haryana and Western Uttar Pradesh, it has become a commercial crop. The prosperity of the large and medium farmers of north-west India may be attributed to the diffusion of HYV of wheat and rice.

It may be ascertained from the above discussion that Punjab, Haryana and Western Uttar Pradesh have emerged as the areas of major concentration of rice, while wheat has been diffused in all the directions from its traditional heart land of the north-west India.

Maize

Maize is a foodgrain which grows well in the well drained alluvial soils and it requires warm and moist geographical conditions. Its cultivation is, however, carried on in most of the States of the country as a kharif (summer season) crop, while in the Kandi (undulating hilly tracts) areas of Kashmir, Ladakh and Himachal Pradesh it is a spring season crop. In 1964-65, just before the diffusion of HYV, maize occupied about 4.6 million hectares, while in 1994-95 its area increased to 6 million hectares. In 1994-95, out of the 6 million hectares, about 2.9 million hectares or 45 per cent of the total area under maize was under HYV. Its area has, however, increased by about 30 per cent during the last three decades, while the corresponding increase in production and yield had been 8 per cent and about 41 per cent respectively (Table 9.4).

Despite the development of HYV of maize, its area has significantly shrinked in the States of Punjab, Haryana and Uttar Pradesh. Rice has encroached upon its area as the farmers are getting more agricultural returns from their fields by doing the cultivation of rice in place of maize during the kharif season. It is not only that the per unit area of the yield of maize is lower in comparison to rice, its price per quintal is also low. The farmers have thus generally excluded maize cultivation from their cropping patterns.

Jowar

Prior to the diffusion of HYV of wheat and rice, jowar was mainly sown for the purpose of fodder in the Ganga-Sutlej plain and for cereals in Maharashtra, Gujarat, Rajasthan and Madhya Pradesh. During the last 30 years, its areal strength has, however, decreased substantially. Its area is now generally devoted to paddy crops in the States of Punjab, Haryana and Western Uttar Pradesh. The tractorization and mechanization of agriculture has reduced the importance of bullocks in the farming operations. Consequently, jowar has lost its significance as a fodder crop.

In 1964-65, the total area under jowar was 18 million hectares which shrinked to 13 million hectares in 1994-95. The introduction of HYV of jowar, however, enhanced its production and productivity by 18 per cent and about 34 per cent respectively (Table 9.4).

In general, the area of jowar has decreased in all the States excepting Gujarat and Jammu & Kashmir. In Punjab, Haryana, Rajasthan, Tamil

Nadu, Uttar Pradesh and Madhya Pradesh, the area under millets has been encroached largely by paddy crops.

Pulses

Pulses are the main source of protein in India. They are grown in all parts of the country both in the kharif and the rabi seasons. Their area, production and yield have, however, not shown any significant increase. Contrary to this, their production declined in the seventies and eighties. Taking the country as a whole, the area under pulses has declined by about 6 per cent in 1994-95 as compared to that of 1964-65. Efforts are being made to develop HYV of various pulses to be diffused in the various agro-climatic regions of the country. The enhancement in the total production of pulses will go a long way in improving the protein quantity in the calorie intake of the Indian masses.

Table 9.5 : India: Area under High Yielding Varieties

(in million hectares)

Crop	*1966-67*	*% of HYV area to the total area under the crops*	*1994-95*	*% of HYV area to the total area under the crops*
Rice	0.9	2.6	32.8	68.8
Wheat	0.5	3.9	23.3	88.4
Jowar	0.2	1.1	7.0	52.7
Maize	0.2	3.9	2.9	45.1
Total	1.9		72.2	

Source: Economic Survey 1994-95, Government of India, Ministry of Finance, Economic Division.

A comparative picture of the area under HYV of the principal cereal crops has been shown in Table 9.5. It may be seen from Table 9.5 that in 1966-67 only about 2 million hectares of the total cropped area under cereals (paddy, wheat, jowar, bajra, maize) was under the HYV and the remaining 98 per cent was under the traditional varieties. The diffusion of HYV has, however, been very fast during the last three decades. It may be corroborated from the fact that in 1994-95 over 72 per cent of the total grain cropped area was under HYV.

An analysis of Table 9.5 makes it clear that at present (1994-95) over 88 per cent of total area devoted to wheat is under the HYV. The well off farmers of the Sutlej-Ganga plain also devote a small hectarage of their wheat area to the traditional (*desi*) varieties. It is a belief among the farmers of northern India that the *desi*-varieties of wheat are superior in taste and are not injurious to health. Contrary to this, the new varieties are considered as largely responsible for some of the dreaded diseases like cancer, liver ailment and blood pressure.

In the case of rice also people have given up the traditional varieties as about 69 per cent of the total rice area was occupied by new seeds in 1994-95. In Punjab, Haryana and Western Uttar Pradesh only the HYV are sown, while in the traditional rice grown areas of Assam, West Bengal, Orissa, Bihar and Andhra Pradesh many of the farmers are still in favour of the traditional varieties.

New varieties of millets, bajra and maize have also been developed and adopted by the farmers, specially that of the irrigated tracts. The new varieties of jowar and bajra occupied about 53 per cent and 54 per cent of the area under these crops respectively, while new varieties of maize were sown in 45 per cent of the area under HYV (Table 9.5).

Thus the introduction of High Yielding Varieties in the Indian agricultural landscape has enhanced the area yield and production of wheat and rice significantly. The area, productivity, and production of maize, millets and pulses are, however, not maintaining an upward trend. There are inter-regional and intra-regional variations in the productivity of wheat and rice which is a cause of great concern and demands an in-depth study at the macro and micro-levels.

References

Brown, L.R., (1971), *Social Impact of Green Revolution,* New York, Carnegie.

Frankel, F.R., (1971), *India's Green Revolution*, Princeton University Press.

Husain, M. (1996), *Systematic Agricultural Geography*, Jaipur, Rawat Publications.

Husain, M., (1993), Emerging Pattern of Crops and Social Tension in India, in *Socio-Economic and Policy Issues for Sustainable Farming System*, edited by Paolette, M.G. and Napier, N., Padova, Italy.

Sen, B., (1974), *The Green Revolution in India : A Perspective*, New Delhi, Wiley Eastern.

Singh, Jasbir, (1979), Commercialisation of Agriculture in Punjab : A Spatial Analysis, *Geographical Review of India*, 41, pp. 1-10.

Singh, Jasbir and Dhillon, S.S., (1994), *Agricultural Geography,* New Delhi, Tata McGraw-Hill Pub. Co.

10

AGRICULTURE IN PUNJAB
Problems and Prospects

P.S. RANGI & M.S. SIDHU

The progress made by the farm sector in the State of Punjab is so well-known that one need not cite any statistics to prove this point. A number of factors have made this possible. These include the introduction of High Yielding Varieties (HYVs) particularly of wheat and paddy, assured price policy and supporting infrastructure for supply of different inputs and dissemination of technical know-how. However, the prime movers in this growth process were the farmers themselves who were quick enough to exploit the new production possibilities. The notable achievements are reflected in about eleven-fold increase in the index of production of cereals during the period 1960-61 to 1997-98. The result is that the State with 1.53 per cent of the geographical area of the country accounted for as much as about 64 per cent of wheat and about 42 per cent of rice procured for the Central Pool of foodgrains during the year 1997-98. However, the future may not hold the production possibilities realised earlier (Rangi and Sidhu, 1996). The growth process is not all permeating and, in fact, there are certain crops where breakthrough has not been possible and in respect of major crops also, the rate of production growth is expected to be rather slow (Rangi and Sidhu, 1996). In this study, we have critically examined the problems faced by the agriculture sector in Punjab and its prospects of further development in the near future.

Declining Size of Operational Holdings

The number of operational holdings in Punjab was 11.17 lakh in 1990-91

(Table 10.1). About 45 per cent of these holdings consisted of small and marginal farmers having less than two hectares and about eight lakh farm operators cultivated less than four hectares of land which is below the estimated economic holding of five hectares. The small and marginal farmers operated about 12 per cent of the land area and 70 per cent of the farm operated about 33 per cent land area. Only six per cent of the farmers had 10 hectares and above land area but operated about 27 per cent of the cultivated land. The last group of farmers is better off economically and their economic status is comparable with the urban businessmen and educated service people (Class I and II). The number of operational holdings has been increasing at the rate of 9032 per annum during the period 1980-81 to 1990-91. As such, the number of operational holdings in the State may cross 12 lakh by the year 2000-01. The maximum increase is in the first category comprising of marginal farmers having less than one hectare. The marginalisation of operational holdings is a serious repercussion of the sub-division of land holdings. The average size of the holdings has declined from 3.79 hectares in 1980-81 to 3.61 hectares in 1990-91. It is further expected to decline to 3.19 hectares up to 2000-01 also due to shift of agricultural land for non-agricultural uses.

It is worthwhile to mention here that in the pre-Green Revolution period in the State, the bachelor farmers used to donate their share of land to their nephews (*Bhatijas*). This prevented the land from being further divided. It is known as the Draupadi system after the wife shared by the Pandava princes in the Mahabharata and there in no stigma attached to it (Mishra, 1999). Due to spread of education and awareness among the farmers, this practice has almost disappeared from the rural Punjab during the last three decades and played its own role, *inter alia*, many other social and economic factors for the increase in the number of operational holdings in Punjab.

Increase in the Number of Workers

The information regarding the number of agricultural workers as cultivators and agricultural workers is given in Table 10.2. The number of cultivators has increased from about 16 lakh in 1960-61 to about 19 lakh in 1990-91 whereas the number of agricultural workers jumped from 3.34 lakh to 14.53 lakh in the corresponding period. The trend of sub-division of land holdings is reflected more evidently in the land operated per cultivator and agricultural workers (taken together) which has declined gradually from 1.93 hectares of net area sown in 1960-61

Table 10.1 : Distribution of Number of Operational Holdings by Size groups in Punjab

Size group (hect.)	*1980-81 (No.)*	*%age of operated area*	*1990-91 (No.)*	*%age of operated area*	*Absolute change in the No. of operational holdings between 1980-81 & 1990-91*	*Annual change*	*Projected No. of holdings in 2000-01*
Less than 1	197323 (19.21)	3.03	296131 (26.50)	4.07	(+) 98808	(+) 9881	394941 (32.70)
1 to 2	199368 (19.41)	7.22	203842 (18.24)	8.13	(+) 4474	(+) 447	208312 (17.25)
2 to 4	287393 (27.99)	20.32	288788 (25.85)	20.87	(+) 1395	(+)140	290188 (24.03)
4 to 10	260072 (26.20)	40.21	261481 (23.40)	40.23	(-) 7591	(-) 759	253891 (21.02)
10 and above	73941 (7.19)	29.22	67172 (6.01)	26.70	(-) 6769	(-) 677	60402 (5.00)
Total	1027097 (100.00)	100.00	1117414 (100.00)	100.00	(+) 90317	(+) 9032	1207734 (100.00)
Total area operated (000 hect)		3890		4033			
Average size of holding (hect)		3.79		3.61			

Table 10.2 : Net and Gross Cropped Area Available to the Cultivators and Agricultural Workers in Punjab

Year	*As cultivators (No.)*	*As agricultural workers (No.)*	*Net area sown per cultivator (Hect.)*	*Net area sown per agricultural worker (Hect.)*	*Cropped area sown per cultivator (Hect.)*	*Cropped area per agricultural worker (Hect.)*	*Net area sown per cultivator and agricultural worker (Hect.)*	*Cropped area per cultivator and agricultural worker (Hect.)*
1960-61	1602666	334610	2.33	1.1.2	2.95	14.1	1.93	2.44
1970-71	1665153	786705	2.43	5.15	3.41	7.22	1.65	2.32
1980-81	1758014	1104821	2.38	3.79	3.85	6.12	1.46	2.36
1990-91	1917210	1452828	2.20	2.90	3.91	5.16	1.25	2.22

to 1.25 hectares in 1990-91. In terms of gross cropped area, this figure has declined from 2.44 hectares to 2.22 hectares during the same period. The facts given above are not statistical figures only but have wider social, economic and political implications for the State as well as the country. The unemployed rural youth particularly from the lower middle class peasantry fell prey to militancy in Punjab during eighties and early nineties (Rangi and Sidhu, 1999). The employment creation for this segment of rural society may be priority area of action for the policy makers, administrators, etc. The State may face serious crisis again in future unless some bold steps are taken in this regard.

LAND USE PATTERN

The land use pattern given in Table 10.3 shows that the net area sown in the State was 4266 thousand hectares during 1997-98 out of a total reporting area of 5033 thousand hectares which means that about 85 per cent of the reporting area was already under cultivation which was the highest in the country. There was only negligible area available under current fallows and other uncultivated land. It is worthwhile to point out here that the agriculture has reached at a saturation level since 97 per cent of the cultivable land in the State is under plough (Economic Advisor to Government of Punjab, 1999). Thus, there is little scope to bring more area under cultivation.

The net area sown has increased from 3886 thousand hectares in 1966-67 to 4266 thousand hectares in 1997-98 which means an average increase of about 12 thousand hectares per annum. On the other hand, the total cropped area has increased by 2699 thousand hectares during this period which gives an average increase of about 87 thousand hectares per annum. As already mentioned, there is very little scope to add to net area sown. The only possibility was to add the cropped area through increase in the cropping intensity. It is already high (185 per cent) as compared to 131 per cent in the country. Even our neighbouring State, i.e., Haryana which is among the agriculturally developed states has 167 per cent cropping intensity. Therefore, there is limit even to increase cropping intensity in this State because 95 per cent of the net area sown is already irrigated. About 61 per cent of this irrigation is through tubewells and the rest 39 per cent by canals.

Shift in Cropping Pattern

The cropping pattern in the State is shown in Table 10.4. The figures

Table 10.3 : Classification of Area in Punjab, 1966-67 to 1997-98

(.000 hectares)

Year	*Reporting area for land utilisation purpose*	*Area under forest*	*Area not available for cultivation*	*Fallow land*	*Other uncultivated land*	*Net area sown*	*Area sown more than once*	*Total cropped area*
1966-67	5026	79	640	247	174	3886	1236	5172
1971-72	5031	127	614	126	88	4076	1643	5724
1976-77	5033	205	537	66	58	4167	2118	6285
1981-82	5033	213	529	36	45	4210	2719	6929
1986-87	5033	220	519	48	43	4202	3015	7217
1991-92	5033	210	454	107	47	4215	3303	7518
1992-93	5033	287	488	86	33	4139	3413	7552
1993-94	5033	290	433	76	20	4214	3499	7623
1994-95	5033	290	484	71	11	4210	3413	7693
1995-96	5033	290	496	69	42	4136	3576	7712
1996-97	5033	290	375	101	33	4234	3514	7818
1997-98	5033	261	402	62	42	4266	3695	7871

Source: Statistical abstracts of Punjab for various years.

show that during 1997-98, about 75 per cent of the area was under foodgrains, about 13 per cent under cash crops, i.e., cotton, sugarcane, oilseeds and potatoes and 1.6 per cent was occupied by fruits and vegetables. Per cent area under cereals has increased from 50.9 in 1966-67 to 73.5 in 1997-98. The area under pulses has declined from 13.4 per cent to only 1.1 per cent, under oilseeds from 6.2 per cent to 1.8 per cent and for sugarcane crop from 3.0 per cent to 1.6 per cent during the corresponding period.

Table 10.4 : Shift in Cropping Pattern in Punjab 1966-67 to 1997-98

(Per cent area under crops)

Years	*Cereals*	*Pulses*	*Foodgrains*	*Oil-seeds*	*Sugar-cane*	*Potato*	*Cotton*	*Fruits & Vegetables*
1966-67	50.9	13.4	64.3	6.2	2.0	0.3	8.4	0.5
1971-72	61.9	6.7	68.6	6.6	1.8	0.8	8.5	0.8
1976-77	64.7	6.3	71.0	4.0	1.5	0.5	8.8	0.7
1981-82	67.5	4.7	72.2	3.2	1.5	0.5	9.9	1.3
1986-87	73.5	3.1	76.6	2.3	1.5	0.4	8.7	1.8
1990-91	73.6	1.9	75.5	1.5	1.3	0.3	9.3	1.6
1991-92	73.8	1.2	75.0	2.8	1.5	0.4	9.6	1.8
1992-93	74.1	1.3	75.4	2.6	1.5	0.4	9.3	1.8
1993-94	75.5	1.4	76.9	2.5	1.0	0.3	7.6	1.7
1994-95	75.8	1.2	76.6	2.0	1.0	0.4	7.9	1.9
1995-96	72.9	1.2	74.2	3.1	1.8	0.5	9.6	1.6
1996-97	71.6	1.2	72.9	3.1	2.2	0.6	9.2	1.5
1997-98	73.5	1.1	74.6	1.8	1.6	0.7	9.2	1.6

Source: Statistical Abstracts of Punjab for various years.

However, the area under fruits and vegetables increased from 0.8 per cent in 1966-67 to 1.6 per cent during 1997-98 giving some evidence of diversification in this direction. The proportion of area under potatoes remained almost the same during the period, i.e. about 0.4-0.5 per cent. However, there were some fluctuations in the area under potatoes during different years. There has been marginal fluctuations in area under cotton during the corresponding period.

The cropping pattern in the State has witnessed a distinct shift in favour of paddy-wheat rotation, creating some serious imbalances in the farm production pattern accompanied by several related problems on production, marketing and input supply fronts (Johl, *et al.*, 1986). It has also brought about many ecological changes (Singh, Grover and Lekhi, 1990). The research data indicate that the yield of wheat grown after paddy starts declining after a few years (Singh, Dhaliwal and Randhawa, 1997). Inclusion of paddy in the rotation had profound influence on the physical properties of the soil. The paddy cultivation increases the bulk density, modulus of rapture and dispersion ratio. It also considerably reduced water intake rate and water storage in 0-180 cm profile (Singh, Dhaliwal and Randhawa, 1997).

The indiscriminate and uncontrolled use of underground water may not also be desirable in several areas of the State from the long-run point of sustained use of this scarce and precious resource. A stage has been reached when the State needs to have a very careful look at the available ground and surface water resources and plan its cropping pattern in a manner which ensures a clear balance between the available surplus of water and its potential demand. The future production strategy should be based on maximisation of output per unit of water used per unit time. This would necessitate the reappraisal of water rates policy along with the strict adherence to the scientific water schedules for different crops. It is, therefore, necessary for the State Government to review its decision of free power supply to the farm sector. This decision has not only made the State Electricity Board in the red but would have far reaching implications for the State economy particularly the farm sector. Competitive populism and economic development cannot go hand to hand.

Stagnation in Agricultural Production

The production of important crops is shown in Table 10.5. The rice and wheat crops have shown remarkable increase in production in the State during the last three decades. Now, there is problem of stagnation in the production of these two principal crops also. Moreover, there were occasional drops in their production. The production of maize, barley, bajra, pulses, etc. has rather declined during the post-Green Revolution period. The production of cotton (A) and cotton (D) increased up to 1992-93 but afterwards has shown downward trend mainly due to attack of American bollworm on the crop and waterlogging problem. Consequently, the production of cotton (A) was 134 thousand tonnes in 1997-98 in comparison to 376 thousand tonnes in 1992-93. It is worthwhile to mention here that because of the failure of cotton crop for the past six consecutive years, farmers of this region of the state are facing a tough time. About 150 farmers in the cotton belt have allegedly committed suicides in the past two years due to financial hardships (Mann, 1999).

Table 10.5 : Production of Important Crops in Punjab, 1966-67 to 1997-98

('000 tonnes)

Year/ Crop	Rice	Wheat	Maize	Barley	Bajra	Pulses	Oilseeds	Sugarcane*	Potato	Cotton (A)**	Cotton (D)**
1966-67	338	2451	614	88	150	532	252	436	195	67	85
1971-72	920	5618	857	55	171	302	272	403	222	99	74
1976-77	1776	6392	619	74	142	333	206	607	618	142	51
1981-82	3750	8544	625	176	61	161	179	601	635	182	34
1986-87	5949	9447	528	80	28	183	140	611	521	264	23
1991-92	6739	12310	345	147	10	75	267	693	517	391	35
1992-93	7026	12997	436	112	9	74	236	688	498	376	24
1993-94	7645	13377	359	99	18	70	180	471	382	247	11
1994-95	7662	13542	322	139	11	85	185	495	603	282	20
1995-96	6843	12510	307	125	6	78	288	888	778	300	27
1996-97	7334	13687	351	110	4	78	336	1027	832	291	26
1997-98	7890	12751	344	111	9	56	145	716	788	134	26

* Production of sugarcane is in terms of gur.

** Production of cotton (A) and cotton (D) is in terms of cleaned cotton.

Source: Statistical Abstracts of Punjab, various issues.

Production Growth Rates

The compound growth rates in respect of area, production and yield for important crops of the State for the period 1971-72 to 1996-97 are shown in Table 10.6. These growth rates for period-I (1971-72 to 1980-81), period-II (1981-82 to 1990-91) and period-III (1991-92 to 1996-97) are also shown in Table 10.6. A perusal of the figures shows that rice production recorded the highest growth, i.e., 8.99 per cent per annum. The contribution of area and yield was 6.96 and 1.89 per cent respectively. Among cereals, wheat was the next crop to record a high production growth rate (4.27 per cent). The contribution of area in this was 2.26 per cent and yield contributed 2.88 per cent.

The sub-period analysis of compound growth rates in respect of area, production and yield of different crops showed that many crops failed to achieve significant production growth rates in period-III (Zeleke *et al.*, 1999). The production growth rates of rice and wheat were 0.99 and 1.64 per cent respectively in period-III. For important cotton crop of the State, it was –5.34 per cent in this period . As already discussed, it was mainly due to attack of American bollworm and waterlogging problem. Unless there is a technological breakthrough, it is not possible to achieve the production growth rates of various crops of period-I and period-II in the near future. It is mainly because scope for increasing cropping intensity is limited. In seventies, the cropping intensity increased at a rate of more than two per cent per annum which has decreased to less than one per cent per annum in the nineties (Punjab Agricultural University, 1998).

It would be in the national interest not to reduce production and availability of foodgrain from the State. Yet from the angle of the State, production of foodgrains should be stabilized through increases in productivity (Johl *et al.,* 1986). The area under wheat and paddy should be reduced in order to introduce an element of diversification into the production pattern. This will not affect the national interest adversely in terms of the availability of foodgrains from the State, but will reduce the overall dependence on these crops and improve the economy of the State Johl, *et al.,* 1986). It will also correct the ecological balance from which the agriculture sector of the State is suffering today.

Problem of Waterlogging

Before the inception of the canal system, the areas in the south-western

Table 10.6 : Compound Growth Rates of Area, Production and Yield of Important Crops in Punjab, 1971-72 through 1996-97

Crop	*Period-I (1971-72 to 1980-81)*			*Period-II (1981-82 to 1990-91)*			*Period-III (1991-92 to 1996-97)*			*Overall period (1971-72 to 1996-97)*		
	Area	*Production*	*Yield*	*Area*	*Production*	*Yield*	*Area*	*Production*	*Yield*	*Area*	*Production*	*Yield*
Rice	12.98**	17.70**	4.16**	4.89**	5.62**	0.73NS	1.18NS	0.99NS	–0.18NS	6.96**	8.99**	1.89**
Wheat	2.55**	5.01**	2.41**	0.97**	3.70**	2.71**	–0.21*	1.64NS	1.86*	1.56**	4.27**	2.67**
Maize	–4.60**	–4.00**	0.83NS	–5.72**	–7.00**	–1.41NS	–2.04NS	–0.03NS	–1.04NS	–5.48**	–4.35**	1.20**
Barley	–4.90NS	0.49NS	5.57NS	–8.79**	–3.32NS	6.08**	–5.47*	–2.20NS	3.46NS	–3.37**	1.48NS	5.04**
Bajra	–10.02**	–8.61*	1.17NS	–19.09**	–19.69**	–1.65NS	–0.17NS	–16.68NS	–0.61NS	–13.33**	13.55**	–0.33NS
Pulses	–1.65NS	3.87NS	—	–6.91**	–3.24NS	—	–13.30*	–2.37NS	—	–6.71**	–6.59	—
Oilseeds	–5.76**	–6.34**	—	–4.75*	–2.51NS	—	11.58*	9.72*	—	–2.57**	–0.45NS	—
Sugarcane	–3.35*	–0.65NS	2.09**	0.92NS	0.78NS	–0.14NS	8.62NS	8.29NS	–0.47NS	0.16NS	1.34**	1.10**
Potato	11.88**	17.72**	5.20**	–3.11NS	–3.02NS	0.52NS	10.34NS	9.65NS	–0.41NS	0.88NS	1.76NS	0.86NS
Cotton	3.43**	1.76*	–1.55**	1.15NS	9.80**	8.04*	0.52NS	–5.34NS	–5.86*	1.13**	3.06**	1.89**

* Significant at five per cent level.

** Significant at one per cent level.

NS : Non-significant.

Source : Zeleke, Siloshi Damte 1999, An Economic Analysis of Change in Costs, Returns and Input Structure of Major Crops in Punjab (India). M.Sc., thesis (Unpublished), Department of Economics and Sociology, PAU, Ludhiana, pp. 1-64.

parts of Punjab were rainfed and desert conditions prevailed with the water table as deep as 40-50 metres (Uppal, 1966). With the introduction of canal system and irrigated agriculture, the water table slowly started rising in the area (Gupta, *et al.,* 1995). At present, 37 per cent area (6.3 lakh hectares) of south-west Punjab is experiencing the problem of rising water table. In 20 per cent area (3.4 lakh hectares), the annual rise in water table is more than 33 cm (Gupta, *et al.* 1995). The affected blocks are Malout, Kot Bhai, Lambi, Sangat, Bathinda, Abohar, Khuyan Sarwar and Talwandi Sabo (Table 10.7).

Table 10.7 : Blocks with Rising Water Table from 1979 to 1989 in South-Western Punjab

Rise in water table (m)	*Name of the block*
5.0	Bathinda
5.5	Khuyan Sarwar
6.5	Talwandi Sabo
6.8	Malout
7.4	Kot Bhai
7.5	Abohar
8.3	Sangat
10.3	Lambi

Source: Water Resources Directorate, Punjab, Chandigarh.

A perusal of Table 10.7 shows that the rise in water table in these areas from 1979 to 1989 was between 5 and 10.3 metres. During the year 1997-98, Malout area has experienced waterlogging and flood like situation. In the near future, waterlogging problem is bound to come in areas adjoining to Malout in the south-west direction such as Khuyan Sarwar, Lambi, Abohar, etc. (Hira, Gupta and Josan, 1998).

In these areas of Punjab, there has been a demand for increasing the canal supplies because of increasing irrigation requirements as the cropping intensity has increased than that envisaged when the canal supplies were allocated. At present, in the south-western region, irrigated area with canal is 69 per cent and 31 per cent through tubewells. Though the geographical area of this belt is 34 per cent of the State yet it has only 19 per cent of the total tubewell in the State (Hira, Gupta and Josan, 1998). There is no doubt that the State Government has taken up this problem on priority basis since 1997 but it will take another 3-4 years to make anti-waterlogging measures more effective and show results.

The waterlogging problem has also its impact on the cropping patterns in this belt. Cotton was the principal kharif crop of this region. Now it is being replaced by paddy at a very fast rate. This problem of waterlogging has its social, economic and political implications in the region. There are press reports from time-to-time that many well off farmers have become daily wage earners in the nearly towns due to the menace of waterlogging.

Above all, the quality of ground water varies a great deal from place to place and location to location in this region (Hira, Thind and Murty, 1985). The water quality ranges from fit to unfit for irrigation. Actually, variations in the ground water quality are to such an extent that even in the same village, zones of fit, marginal and unfit water categories can be observed (Hira and Murty, 1985). It has been observed by the authors of the present study during their field visits to this belt applying excessive unfit water to crops like paddy which has made the fields barren. A typical example is of a farmer of Tapa Khera village of Lambi block (Muktsar district) in this regard. The continuous cultivation of paddy crop by this farmer has made his 25 hectares of land unfit for cultivation. It was mainly because paddy crop require 24 to 32 irrigations within a short span of about four months. Keeping all this in view, the agricultural scientists, policy makers, administrators and farmers may take this problem seriously and any delayed action in this regard will be suicidal for the agrarian economy of the State.

Deterioration in the Economic Condition of Small and Marginal Farmers

As already discussed, about 45 per cent of the operational holdings in the State consist of small and marginal farmers having less than two hectares of land. During 1980-81 to 1990-91, about 1.03 lakh operational holdings were added to this group of small and marginal farmers. The economic conditions of the farmers have deteriorated mainly because of the downward fragmentation of the holdings. The returns of a farmer cultivating two hectares under different system for the year 1995-96 are shown in Table 10.8.

A perusal of Table 10.8 reveals that returns over cash costs for a two hectare farm with the paddy-wheat and dairying farming system were Rs. 42180 per annum. The returns over paid up costs exclusive of dairy income based on the dominant paddy-wheat rotation, which is high yielding and more paying than other crops in the State were

Table 10.8 : Income of the Farmer Cultivating Two Hectares under Different Systems for the Year 1995-96

S.No.	*Particulars*	*Paddy-wheat rotation**	*Paddy-wheat and dairy farming*
I	Gross income	72370	—
II	Cash costs	31630	—
III	Returns over cash costs	40740	34080
IV	Returns over cash costs from dairy farming	—	8100
	Total	40740	42180

* Paddy-wheat rotation occupy about 71 per cent of total cropped area of the State.

Source: Punjab Agricultural University, 1998, Punjab Agriculture 2020—Farmers and Farming in Punjab, Mimeograph, PAU, Ludhiana, pp. 1-22.

Rs. 40740. The yields of the small and marginal farmers are at par with the bigger farmers (PAU, 1998). However, the machine costs of small farmers have been rising and are higher than those of big farmers. It may be mentioned here that the average per capita income in the State is Rs. 16044 which works out to Rs. 96246 for a six member family, which is more than double the income of the hectare farmer (PAU, 1998). Assuming that yield of paddy and wheat can be increased by 10-15 per cent in the near future may not take the small and marginal out of the poverty cycle.

Indebtedness of farmers

The new farm technology adopted by farmers of the State since mid-sixties required heavy infusion of capital in the form of farm machinery, irrigation equipment and other inputs like chemical fertilizers, pesticides/insecticides, etc. There were only 5000 tractors in Punjab during the year 1960-61. This figure has reached at the level of about four lakh in 1997-98. Similarly, the number of tubewells has increased from 1.92 lakh in 1970-71 to 9.25 lakh in 1997-98. The fertilizer use was just 38 kgs per hectare in 1970-71, which further increased to 155 kgs per hectare in 1997-98 compared with the national average of 77 kgs per hectare. The steady growth of farm production in the last three decades was made possible by matching accessibility to rural credit for the farmers of the State.

A recent study has revealed that the total estimated debt of farmers in the State was Rs. 5700.91 crores (Shergill, 1998).

It may be mentioned here that out of the total debt amount of Rs. 5701 crores, about 19 per cent was due to commercial banks, 27 per cent was due to co-operative sector institutions, 46 per cent was due to commission agents and 7 per cent was due to agriculturist mortgage farmers who had mortgaged in land of the indebted farmers (Shergill, 1998). It may be noted that about 53 per cent of the total debt of farmers in the State was due to informal sector credit agencies like commission agents and agricultural mortgages; and the remaining about 47 per cent was due to the formal sector comprising of commercial banks and co-operative institutions. The authors of the present study had discussed this matter informally with a number of farmers all over the State who reported a very high rate of interest, i.e., 2 to 3 per cent per month charged by the commission agents. The farmers have no other alternative except to pay high rate of interest in the hour of need because the official procedure in commercial banks and co-operative institutions is lengthy one. Moreover, corruption is a common phenomenon there.

The extent of indebtedness can be judged from the fact that farmers of cotton belt around Bathinda have now started selling brand new tractors, direct from tractor agencies at throwaway prices (Mann, 1999). Debt-ridden farmers of this cotton region are now resorting to this extreme step to meet their domestic requirements, arranging the marriages of their wards or to pay off heavy interest loans taken from the moneylenders. Farmers find it easy to get a tractor loan advanced by pledging their land. And instead of the tractor, they take some cash by disposing of the new tractor at two-third price. Though, they fulfil their immediate needs with the money, but they still have to return the loan in instalments in a couple of years. This alleged practice has been continuing with the connivance of loan advancing commercial as well as co-operative banks (Mann, 1999). The buyers of tractors in these urderhand deal are not farmers but professional agents and *kabadis* (Junk dealers).

Prospects of Agriculture

It is often talked that Punjab may not be able to add much to its agricultural production since it is already near the saturation point so far as exploitation of new areas is concerned. Besides, water is going to become the most limiting resource in further intensification of agriculture. We are of the opinion that unless the State makes rational use of its irrigation resource, it would be difficult to maintain even the present type of cropping pattern in the long run. Already the State is facing the problem of falling water level over vast areas in the central Punjab. This is coupled with waterlogging problem in some parts of south-western districts whereas underground water is brackish. A study conducted at the Department of Economics and Sociology, PAU, Ludhiana has estimated that the production of wheat would be about 143 lakh tonnes in the State by the year 2000-01 (Rangi and Sidhu, 1996)(These estimates are based on the assumption that area under these two crops will remain constant at 1993-94 level). Similarly, the production of rice will be 82 lakh tonnes. Thus, the potential of increasing the production of these two crops will be about 225 lakh tonnes in the State by 2000-01.

To enhance income of the farmers of the State, subsidiary enterprises like dairy farming, poultry farming, bee-keeping, mushroom farming, fish farming, flower cultivation, fruit and vegetable cultivation may be encouraged by the policy makers and administrators. Since, these are capital-intensive and risky crops/enterprises, the availability of capital and market has to be ensured before these are adopted on large scale. The agro-processing and other marketing facilities including modern infrastructure in terms of cool chains developed and may be provided to the farmers. There is potential of export of these high value products in the Gulf countries. The contract farming for these perishable and semi-perishable products may also be built up in the State. The populist measures like free power supply to the farm sector may be stopped without further delay. In fact, it is a subsidy to the consumers of the deficit states as Punjab is contributing cheap cereals towards the national food security system.

References

Economic Adviser to Government of Punjab, (1999), *Economic Survey of Punjab, 1998-99*, Chandigarh, pp. 1-175.

Gupta, R.D., Mahajan, G. and Goyal, B.R., (1995), Availability and quality of water in Punjab State. In : *Proceedings of Symposium on Water Management*—Need for Public Awareness held at PAU, Ludhiana, pp. 18-42.

Hira, G.S. and Murty, V.V.N. , (1985), An Appraisal of Waterlogging and Drainage Problems in South-West Parts of Punjab, *National Symposium on Drainage and Waterlogged and Salt Affected Lands held at Karnal*, Feb. 11-13, pp. 7.

Hira, G.S., Gupta, P.K. and Josan, A.S., (1998), Waterlogging: Causes and Remedial Measures in South-West Punjab, *Research Bulletin*, Department of Soils, PAU, Ludhiana, pp. 1-64.

Hira, G.S., Thind, S.S. and Murty, V.V.N., (1985), *Irrigation Water Quality Management in Punjab*, Department of Soil and Water Engineering, PAU, Ludhiana, p. 60.

Johl, S.S. *et at.* (1986), Report of the Expert Committee on Diversification of Agriculture in Punjab, submitted to Government of Punjab, Chandigarh, pp. 1-62.

Mann, Kuldeep, (1999), Farmers Selling New Tractors at Throwaway Prices, *The Indian Express*, Chandigarh, Vol. 22 (355), August 2, p. 3.

Mishra, Subhash, (1999), Bachelor Boys, *India Today*, Vol. 24(33), Aug. 10-16, p. 10.

PAU (1998), Punjab Agriculture 2020 : Farmers and Farming in Punjab, Mimeograph, PAU, Ludhiana, pp. 1-22.

Rangi, P.S. and Sidhu, M.S., (1996), A Study of Growth of Agriculture in Punjab, *Research Bulletin*, Department of Economics and Sociology, PAU, Ludhiana, pp. 1-20.

Rangi, P.S. and Sidhu, M.S., (1999), A Study on Contract Farming System in Punjab. Mimeograph, Department of Economics and Sociology, PAU, Ludhiana, pp. 1-48.

Shergill, H.S. (1998), *Rural Credit and Indebtedness in Punjab*, Monograph, Institute for Development and Communication, Chandigarh, pp. 1-95.

Singh, Joginder, Dhaliwal, G.S. and Randhawa, N.S., (1997), *Changing Scenario of Punjab Agriculture – An Ecological Perspective*, Monograph, Indian Ecological Society, PAU, Ludhiana and Centre for Research in Rural and Industrial Development, Chandigarh, pp. 1-63.

Singh, Joginder, Grover, D.K. and Lekhi, R.K., (1990), Emerging Cropping Pattern and its Effects on Environment. In : R.K. Sapru and S. Bhardwaj (Eds), *The New Environmental Age*, Ashish Publishing House, New Delhi, pp. 189-93.

Uppal, H.L. (1966), *Reclamation of Saline and Alkali Soils*, Commission on Irrigation and Drainage, 6th Congress, Vol.1(19), pp. 381-440.

Zeleke, Siloshi, Damte, (1999), An Economic Analysis of Changes in Costs, Returns and Input Structures of Major Crops in Punjab (India), M.Sc., Thesis (Unpublished), Department of Economics and Sociology, PAU, Ludhiana, pp 1-84.

11

FIFTY YEARS OF VEGETABLE RESEARCH IN INDIA

A Brief Background

S.K. ARORA & J.L. MANGAL

Introduction

Vegetable research in India is of very recent origin. Research on vegetable crops was started by ICAR with the sanctioning of a nucleus "Plant Introduction Scheme" at the IARI, New Delhi in 1947-48. Simultaneously, the ICAR also started such *adhoc* schemes in different states like Punjab, Uttar Pradesh, West Bengal, Maharashtra, Himachal Pradesh, Jammu & Kashmir and Tamil Nadu.

Prior to Second World War, entire seeds of temperate vegetables were imported from European countries. When during World War II, supply of vegetable seeds from Europe suffered a serious set back, the Government of India felt the need for production of these seeds within the country. As a result of this, the Government of India established a Vegetable Breeding Station at Katrain in Kullu Valley, Himachal Pradesh in 1949. This station was transferred to Indian Agricultural Research Institute in 1955 to undertake research on improvement of temperate vegetable crops, standardization of their seed production technology and to produce seeds of identified improved varieties of temperate vegetables. This research station is carrying out intensive research on all aspects of temperate vegetables including improvements, production technology and their seed production.

Further, a Division of Horticulture was created at the Indian Agricultural Research Institute, New Delhi in 1956-57. However, vegetable research was organized on sound footing with the establishment of the Indian Institute of Horticultural Research (IIHR) at Bangalore with a full-fledged Division of Vegetable Crops in 1968. The vegetable research in India received a further boost when a separate Division of Vegetable Crops and Floriculture was started at IARI, New Delhi in 1970. Later the floriculture work was separated and the division was then named as Division of Vegetable Crops, which was assigned the research work exclusively on different vegetable crops. In the Sixth Five Year Plan, IIHR, Bangalore started two Central Horticultural Experiment Stations, one each at Ranchi (Bihar) and Godhra (Gujarat) to intensity research on vegetable crops. Establishment of Agricultural Universities and All India Coordinated Vegetable Improvement Project gave further fillip to vegetable research in India. Ever since the start of vegetable research in the country in the post-Independence period, efforts have been made to establish a sound research infrastructure to meet the requirements of vegetable research. This includes research by Central Institutes, 26 State Agricultural Universities, Coordinated Projects and *adhoc* schemes (Chadha, 1998).

India is fortunate to have a variety of agro-climatic conditions which enable us to produce both tropical and temperate vegetables. During the last 50 years after Independence, vegetable production of our country has increased tremendously and thus India is the second largest vegetable producer next to China with an estimated production of about 71 million tonnes from an area of over 6.2 million hectares against a requirement of 100 million tonnes. With this production, the availability of vegetables is 210 g per capita per day which is less than the dietary requirement of 300 g per capita per day.

India's population is growing at the rate of 1.8 per cent and it is expected to be over 1.2 billion by the year 2020. Population growth and urbanization are creating increased demand of food. There is growing concern over malnutrition, especially in rural areas. To meet the full dietary needs of the common man, to eliminate malnutrition, deficiency diseases and to relieve overstress on cereals, there is greater need of enhanced vegetable production.

Present Scenario of Vegetable Production in the Country

According to the state-wise distribution of area under various vegetable crops, the maximum area lies in U.P. (12.6 lakh ha.) followed by Tamil Nadu (8.8 lakh ha.), Bihar (8.4 lakh ha.) and West Bengal (4.5 lakh ha.). U.P. contributes maximum share in country's vegetable production while Bihar and Orissa occupy second and third place, respectively.

Variation in Productivity of Vegetable Crops Among States

There are variations among different States of the country with regard to productivity of vegetable crops. Karnataka recorded the highest productivity of 23.49 t/ha. in the country, while Punjab ranked second. In India one of the major reasons of low production of vegetables is steep variation in productivity of vegetables among states. Andhra Pradesh, Gujarat, Karnataka, Kerala, Madhya Pradesh, Meghalaya, Punjab, Tamil Nadu, U.P. and Delhi are having productivity more than 10 t/ha. while there are certain States, where productivity is even less than 5 t/ha. Our country has witnessed 2.6 per cent increase in vegetable production per year in last 10 years (1983-94), which was at par with the region's growth rate (2.7%) and higher than the world growth rate (1.81%).

Low Productivity of the Vegetables in the Country

Although India is second largest vegetable producing country in the world, yet productivity of different vegetables is comparatively low as compared to other developed countries. The average productivity of tomato in our country is 157.10 q/ha. while its productivity in USA is 587.62 q/ha., in Greece 498.6 q/ha., in Italy 465.55 q/ha. and in Spain 466.29 q/ha. The poor productivity of different vegetables in our country is due to several reasons. In developed countries, maximum production of vegetables is under controlled conditions and production does not suffer from severe weather onslaughts, while in our country area under controlled conditions till date is negligible. Similarly in developed countries, hybrids occupy maximum areas and advanced production and protection technology have been standardized to realize the maximum productivity of vegetable crops. In India, area under hybrid vegetables has increased very considerably in last few years, however, maximum share in production is contributed by open-pollinated varieties with the application of farmer's own thinking and their traditional vision. During the last 50 years, concerted efforts have been made in different directions to boost the vegetable production of the country. These newly developed aspects of vegetable production are mentioned below:

Nursery Management in Vegetable Crops

Young seedlings are raised and nurtured in the nursery beds before planting them into the main field. For raising good crop, it is utmost essential that seedlings should be healthy, vigorous and disease free. Seedlings are susceptible to a number of diseases due to its delicate, succulent and highly tender nature. Further sky-rocketing cost of hybrid seeds warrants attention of the grower to produce the seedlings under protected conditions, because every hybrid seed has its accountability owing to its high cost which is 20 to 50 times higher than open pollinated seeds. Raising the nursery under polyhouse/greenhouse and sowing the individual seed of hybrid in potting plug with artificial culture media is well established practice in developed countries. However, in India most of the nurseries are raised under open conditions and it is one of the main reasons of set back to development of hybrid programme during rainy season in northern India. Therefore, it is essential to standardize the nursery raising programme on scientific lines.

Soil Solarization

Recently soil solarization has been proved as cheapest and eco-friendly approach for soil disinfection of nursery beds. Soil mulching is done with transparent polyethylene of 25-100 cm. Thickness during the period of high temperature and solar radiation. Soil should be kept moist before mulching to increase the latent heat and thermal sensitivity of resting structures of soil borne pathogens, harmful pests and weeds. Following this simple practice, population of soil borne pathogen, nematodes, pests and weeds can be reduced to a substantial level.

Raising Nursery Under Polyhouse/Agronet

Nursery raising of vegetables has become a specialized job with increasing susceptibility of vegetables to biotic and abiotic stresses. The major nursery pests and diseases are white fly, cut worms, borers, nematodes, damping off, fungal and bacterial leaf spots. Besides, high and low temperature, excess rains, drought, hot and cold winds affect nursery raising. It has now become possible to raise the seedlings in low tunnels and low cost polyhouses. Production of early cauliflowers, tomato, capsicum, chillies often poses problems in high temperature and high rainfall areas. Use of transparent plastic sheet as low tunnel provides ideal conditions for successful raising of seedling than conventional methods. The time taken for seed germination and seedling growth is reduced under low tunnels compared to open environment in tomato, brinjal and chilli crops sown in winter months for spring transplanting. The utility of low cost polyhouses for raising of seedlings of cucurbitaceous vegetables in winter months to harvest early summer crops has been very successful and commercially adopted by farmers in Punjab, Haryana and U.P. The seeds sown in polybags shown early germination and make faster growth under protected cover. When outside conditions are favourable, seedlings are transplanted along with earth ball in the open field in early spring, the crops flower and set fruits in very short times. This technique is capable of giving highly remunerative yields in northern plains. Besides, the seedlings of tomato, brinjal and chilli also get ready for planting in spring season in plains. The use of shade and agronets have been found very effective in raising of seedlings during high temperature. Shade reduces temperature by 5 to 10°C and protect the seedlings from sun scorching. Agronet protects the seedlings from insect-pests and reduces the vector borne viruses infestation and damage by other insects.

Improved Vegetable Varieties Developed

Lot of progress has been made in the development of high yielding open pollinated varieties, disease and pest resistant varieties and hybrid varieties. Till date 160 improved varieties in 19 vegetable crops have been identified and recommended for cultivation in various agro-climatic conditions based on multilocation and multidisciplinary testing of vegetable varieties. These varieties are given in Table 11.1.

Table 11.1 : Improved Vegetable Varieties

Vegetable Crop		*Variety(ies)*
Amaranthus	:	Badi Chaulai, Co. 1, Co. 2, Co. 3.
Brinjal (Long)	:	Pusa Purple Long, Pusa Purple Cluster, BB-13, PH-4, S-4, PBR-129-5, Azad Kranti, Arka Sheel, Arka Shirish, ARU-1, ARU-2C, KT-4, Hisar Pragati, NDB-25, BB-26, Punjab Barsati, Sel-4, DBSR-31, Punjab Chamkila, Punjab Sada Bahar Baigan
Brinjal (Round)	:	T3, Sel-1, PBR-91-2, K-202-9, Hisar Shyamal, Pusa Upkar, Pusa Uttam, KS-224, DBR-8, Punjab Bahar, Jamuni Gola, Punjab Neelam, Arka Navneet
Brinjal (Oblong)	:	Hisar Jamuni, BH-1, BH-2
Brinjal (Green)	:	Arka Kusumakar

Table 11.1 (Contd.)

Vegetable Crop	*Variety(ies)*
Brinjal (Small round) :	Aruna, DBSR-44, Punjab Moti, Punjab Bindu, PLR-1
Cabbage :	Sel-8, Pride of India, Golden Acre
Carrot :	Hisar Gairic, Chantenay, Pusa Kesar, Nantes, Pusa Yamdagni, Danvers, Imperator, Selection-233, Selection-21, Sel-5, Pusa Meghali
Capsicum :	California Wonder, Yolo Wonder, King of North Early Giant, Vinedale, Bullnose, Chinese Giant, Ruby King, Punjab-27
Cauliflower :	Pusa Early Synthetic, Pusa Synthetic, Punjab Kunwari, Pusa Deepali, Early Kunwari, 327-14-8-3, 351-4-1, Improved Japanese, Synthetic-1, EC-12012, Sel-1, Pusa Snowball-2, 235-S, K1, 114-S-1, 6-1-2-1, Early Synthetic, Punjab Giant-26, Punjab Giant-35, Pusa Snowball-1
Chilli :	G-4, G-5, JCA-154, K-1, K-2, Kalianpur Selection, NP46-A, Pant C-1, Pant C-2, Pusa Jwala, Pusa Sadabahar, Sindhur, X-197, Hisar Shakti, Hisar Vijay, Sel-1, JCA-283, Phula-5, J-218, X-235, Musalwadi, LCA-206 B, Punjab Lal, Punjab Surukh, Punjab Guchhadar
Cluster bean :	Pardeshi, Pusa Mausami, Pusa Navbahar, Pusa Sadabahar, S-279
Cowpea :	Pusa Barsati, Pusa Dofasli, Pusa Komal, Pusa Phalguni, L-1552, Deepaliwal, Sel 61-B, Sel 2-1, Sel 263
Cucurbits :	
a) Ash gourd :	Co. 1, Co. 2
b) Bitter gourd :	Arkaharit, Coimbatore Long, Pusa Do Mausmi, VK-1, Priya
c) Bottle gourd :	Pusa Naveen, Pusa Summer Prolific Long, Pusa Summer Prolific Round
d) Cucumber :	Balam Khira, Japanese Long Green, Poinsette, Priya
e) Muskmelon :	Arka Jeet, Arka Rajhans, Durgapura Madhu, Hara Madhu, Edisto, Pusa Sarbati, S1 445, Sel-2, Punjab Sunehri, Punjab Hybrid, Punjab Rasila, MH-10
f) Pumpkin :	Arka Suryamukhi, Arka Chandan, Pusa Biswas
g) Ridge gourd :	Co 1, Pusa Nasdar, Satputia, HRG-14
h) Snake gourd :	Co 1
i) Sponge gourd :	Pusa Chikni, Sel-99, Pusa Supriya
j) Summer squash :	Pusa Early Prolific, Early Yellow Prolific, Pusa Alankar
k) Wanga	Punjab Wanga-1
l) Watermelon :	Arka Jyoti, Arka Manik, Durgapura Kesar, Durgapura Meetha, Sugar Baby, Shipper, Congo, Improved Shipper, AHW-19, AHW-65 (Mateera)
Fenugrek :	Pusa Early Bunching, Kasuri, Methi No. 14, Methi No. 47, Hisar Methi-57
French Bean :	VL-Boni-1, Arka Komal, UPF-191
Garlic :	Fawari, G-41, G-1, G-50, Punjab Garlic-1, Rajalle Gaddi
Lablab Bean :	Hisar Kirti, HD-60, T-1, Hebbel Avarez, Hebbel Avare 4, IIHR Sel-1, IIHR Sel-2
Lettuce :	Punjab Lettuce-1

Table 11.1 (Contd.)

Vegetable Crop	*Variety(ies)*
Okra :	Harbhajan, Lucknow Dwarf, Pb 7, Parbhani Kranti, Pusa Makhmali, Punjab No. 13, Pusa Sawani, Varsha Uphar, Punjab-8, Hisar Unnat, Punjab Padmini
Onion :	Pusa Ratnar, Pusa Red, Hisar-2, Punjab Selection Line-181, Line 106, S-4, S-131, N-257-9-1, N-2-4-1, Arka Kalyan, Line 102, Arka Niketan, Agrifound Dark Red, VL-3, Agrifound Light Red, Punjab Red Round, Punjab-48, Punjab Naroya, Punjab White, PBR-5, Early Grano, Punjab-48, Punjab Selection, Pusa White Flat, Pusa White Round, Ratna Red
Pea :	Asauji, Bonneville, Early Badger, Early December, Early Superb, Meteor, Perfection New Line, Sylvia, Arkel, GC-195, GC-141, IP-3, P-88, PM-2, VL-3, Lincoln, VL-7, VL-06, PH-1, Matar Ageta-6, Punjab-87, Punjab-88, Har Bona, Mithi Phali, NDVP-8
Potato :	Kufri, Alankar, K. Bahar, K. Badshah, K. Chamatkar, K. Deva, K. Chandramukhi, K. Himalini, K. Jeevan, K. Jyoti, K. Kisan, K. Kuber, K. Kumar, K. Kundan, K. Lalima, K. Lauvkar, K. Mathu, K. Neela, K. Red, K. Safed, K. Sheetman, K. Sindhuri, K. Sutlek, K. Sherpa, K. Swarna
Radish :	Jaunpuri Giant, Japanese White, Kalyanpur T-1, Punjab Safed, Punjab Pasand, Pusa Chetki, Pusa Desi, Pusa Himani, Pusa Reshmi, White Icicle, HR-1, Punjab Ageti
Spinach beet/Beet leaf: (Palak)	All Green, Banerjee's Giant, HS-23, Jobner Green, Palak No. 51, Pusa Harit, Pusa Jyoti, Pusa Palak, Punjab Green
Sprouting Broccoli :	Punjab Broccoli-1
Sweet potato :	H-41, H-42, H-260, Pusa Red, Pusa Safed, V-35, Verde
Tomato :	Best of All, HS-102, HS-101, HS-110, Marglobe, Punjab Chhuhara, Pusa 120, Pusa Early Dwarf, Pusa Ruby, Pusa Sheetal, Roma, S-12, Sel 152, Sioux, Sweet-72, Pusa Uphar, Hisar Arun, BT-12, Hisar Lalima, Hisar Lalit, Sel-120, T-1, T-3, Rs-2, AC-238, Arka Vikas, Arka Saurabh, Pant T-3, CO-3, Punjab Kesri, La Bonita, Sel-7, Sel-1-6-4, Punjab Tropic, Keck Ruth, Keck Ruth Ageti, Punjab NR-7, Utkal Kumari (BT 10)
Turnip :	Purple Top Milan, Purple Top White Globe, Pusa Chandrima, Pusa Kanchan, Pusa Swarnima, Pusa Sweti, L-1
Winged Bean :	Colombo, GRWB-11, IIHR Selection, Karikari, Puttalam, Tyt-1, 3, 14, WBC-2, UPS 62

Source : *"Vegetable Crops"* ed. by T.K. Bose, M.G. Som and J. Kabir; 1993; Kallo, G., 1993; Anonymous, 1999; Pareek and Samadia, 1999.

Breeding for Disease Resistant Varieties

Breeding disease resistant varieties is a novel option to avoid the excessive use of chemicals and to reduce the growers burden on the cost of production (Kalloo, 1988). In past concentrated efforts were made to develop Fusarium wilt, bacterial wilt, early blight, root knot nematode, tomato leaf curl virus, tomato spotted wilt virus resistant varieties in tomato. Against Fusarium wilt a number of varieties like Columbia, Walter, Floradade, HS-110, Homestead and Sel-28 have been found resistant. BT-1 and BT-10, BWR-1, BWR-5, LE-79 are resistant to bacterial wilt. These varieties can be grown successfully in Karnataka, Kerala, Orissa and other bacterial wilt infested areas. Floradade variety has been found resistant to early blight which is a serious problem in many parts of the country. NT-3, NT-8, NT-12 and Sel-120 have been developed as root knot nematode resistant varieties. Varieties H-24, H-36, H-86, H-88 are resistant to tomato leaf curl virus which have been developed utilizing *L. hirsutum* f. glabratum as source of resistance (Table 11.2). In brinjal, which is highly susceptible to bacterial wilt in certain parts of the country, BB-7, BWR-12 and SM-6-7 have been found resistant to bacterial wilt. There is immediate need to develop variety resistant to Phomopsis and shoot and fruit borer in egg plant. Chilli is susceptible to anthracnose, Fusarium wilt, die back, bacterial wilt, bacterial leaf spot, bacterial blight and leaf curl etc. Punjab Lal, Hisar Shakti and Hisar Vijay are the varieties resistant to TMV, CMV and leaf curl virus and moderately resistant to fruit rot and die back has been developed.

Table 11.2 : Vegetable Varieties Resistant to Diseases and Insect Pests

Crop	*Disease/Insect-pests*	*Varieties*
Brinjal	Bacterial wilt	BB-7, BB-26 (Utkal Keshari), BWR-12, Pant Rituraj, Pusa Purple Cluster, SM-6-7, SM-6-6, BB-44 (Utkal Madhuri)
	Phomopsis blight	Pant Bhairav, Pant Samrat
	Shoot and fruit borer and Jassids	Pant Samrat
	Fusarium wilt	BB-26, BB-44
	Nematode wilt	BB-44
Chilli	Leaf curl	Hisar Shakti, Hisar Vijay, Punjab Lal
	Powdery mildew	- do-
	Mosaic	-do-
	Bacterial wilt	Ujwala
Tomato	Bacterial wilt	BWR-5, BT 10, BT-1, LE-79-5
	Verticillium wilt and Fusarium wilt	Pant Bahar
	Root knot nematode	Sel-120, Hisar Lalit
	Leaf Curl	H-24, H-36

Table 11.2 (contd.)

Capsicum	Bacterial wilt	Arka Gaurav
Cabbage	Black Rot	Pusa Mukta
Cauliflower	Black Rot	Pusa Shubhra, Pusa Snowball K-1
Watermelon	Anthracnose	Arka Manik
	Powdery mildew	- do -
	Downy mildew	- do -
Muskmelon	Downy mildew	Punjab Rasila
Cowpea	Bacterial blight	Pusa Komal
Pea	Powdery mildew	FC-1, JP-83, JP-4, PRS-4, PM-2, NSM-2, NDVP-2
Okra	Yellow vein mosaic virus	Arka Anamika, Arka Abhay, Sel-2, Pusa A-4, P-7, Parbhani Kranti, Varsha Uphar, Hisar Unnat
Cucumber	Powdery mildew	Poinsette
	Downy mildew	- do -
Potato	Early blight	Kufri Pukraj
	Late blight	Kufri Pukraj, Kufri Chipsona, Kufri Chipsona 2
	Tolerant to frost	Kufri Chipsona 2
Onion	Purple blotch	IIHR-56-1

Source : Kalloo, G., 1995; Narendra Singh and Verma, V.K., 1998; Bhatnagar, P.S., 1998; Arora, S.K., 1998; Gopala Krishnan, 1996.

In peas, JP-4, JP-83, FC-1, PRS-4 and NDVP-4 have been recommended as powdery mildew resistant varieties. JM-1, JM-2 and Kala Nagin have been found to be resistant to Fusarium wilt. In many parts of the country pea is susceptible to rust, however, there is no definite source of resistance to this disease. Attempts have been made to develop varieties resistant to multiple diseases and pests in peas and JP-179 resistant to powdery mildew and bruchus have been developed. Cowpea is susceptible to *Pseudocerospora, Anthracnose, Macrophomina*, wilt, cowpea mosaic virus and golden mosaic virus. However, there is no systematic disease resistant breeding programme in the country. Only the sources of resistance to *Pseudocercospora*, cowpea mosaic virus and golden mosaic virus have been identified which are required to be utilized to develop commercially viable resistant variety.

Okra is highly susceptible to yellow vein mosaic virus, Fusarium wilt, *Microphomina, Cercospora* and powdery mildew. Varieties P-7, Parbhani Kranti, Arka Anamika, Arka Abhay, Varsha Uphar have been developed as potential resistant varieties utilizing *Abelmoschus manihot* as donor parent (Table 11.3). These varieties are widely being grown in the country at commercial scale. Sources of resistance to *Fusarium* wilt,

Microphomina and mildew and insect pests have been identified in *Abelmoschus* caillei. There is a need to develop multiple disease and pest resistant, i.e. YVMV, microphomina, *Cercospora* blight, jassid, fruit and shoot borer and root knot nematode resistant variety in okra utilizing wild taxa which are easily accessible in the country.

In cucurbits, muskmelon is highly susceptible to powdery mildew and downy mildew. Source of resistance to both of diseases are available. Arka Rajhans is resistant to powdery mildew. DMDR-1 and DMDR-2 varieties have been developed which are resistant to downy mildew and cucumber green mottle mosaic virus.

Table 11.3 : IIHR Varieties/Hybrids with Biotic and Abiotic Stress Resistance

Vegetable Crop	*Stress*	*Hybrid*
Tomato	Tolerance to fruit cracking	Arka Vishal (F_1 hybrid)
	Resistant to nematode	Arka Vardan
	Resistance to bacterial wilt	Arka Abha and Arka Alok, Arka Shresta (BRH 1) and Arka Abhijit (BRH 2) (Both are hybrids)
	Resistance to powdery mildew	Arka Ashish
	Resistance to moisture stress	Arka Vikas
	Resistance to moisture stress	Arka Meghali
Brinjal	Resistant to bacterial wilt	Arka Nidhi, Arka Keshav and Arka Neelkanth
Watermelon	Resistance to anthracnose, powdery mildew and downy mildew	Arka Manik
Roundmelon	Tolerance to fruit-fly	Arka Tinda
Pumpkin	Resistance to fruit-fly	Arka Suryamukhi
Okra	Resistance to yellow vein mosaic virus	Arka Abhay and Arka Anamika
Onion	Tolerance to purple blotch	Arka Kalyan
Dolichos	Photoinsensitive	Arka Jay and Arka Vijay
Chilli	Tolerance to moisture stress	Arka Lohit
Cucumber	Tolerance to powdery mildew	Swarna Poorna
Pea	Resistance to rust and powdery mildew	Arka Ajit

Source : Yadav, I.S., 1996; Yadav, I.S., 1998.

In watermelon, Arka Manik has been developed which is resistant to anthracnose, downy mildew and powdery mildew and this is one of the ruling variety of watermelon widely grown in the country. In cucumber Poinsette is resistant to downy mildew, powdery mildew, anthracnose and angular leaf spot. Bottle gourd is susceptible to downy mildew and summer squash is susceptible to virus diseases and there is need to undertake research programme to develop varieties resistant to common diseases in a number of cucurbitaceous crops.

Onion and garlic are important bulb crops. Onion is highly susceptible to purple blotch, *Stemphyllium* blight and basal rot caused by *Fusarium oxysporum* sp. cepae. Only one genotype IIHR 56-1 has been identified as resistant to purple blotch which can be used to develop new commercial purple blotch resistant variety in onion (Table 11.2).

Increasing the Area Under Improved Variety/Hybrids

Vegetable production of our country is still dominated by the locally available genotypes or open pollinated varieties. This is mainly due to farmer's ignorance and poor extension activities. Hybrid varieties in India are of recent origin. Hybrid technology has been most successful in tomato resulting in large area coverage. Karnataka, Maharashtra, Gujarat and some parts of Andhra Pradesh were first to adopt hybrid tomato varieties because of longer growing period. Hybrid cabbage is next in area coverage to tomato. The entire cabbage production in southern part of Maharashtra and West Bengal is under F_1 hybrids. In capsicum, brinjal, cucumber and watermelon area under F_1 hybrids is small. With awareness of advantages of cultivation of F_1 hybrids, the area is bound to extend. Data presented in Table 11.4 shows the extent of cultivation of F_1 hybrids, open pollinated and unidentified varieties in India.

Table 11.4 : The Estimated Share of Hybrid, Open Pollinated and Local or Unidentified Varieties in Total Cropped Area in India (1997-98)

Crop	*Total Area (ha)*	*Area under F_1 hybrids (ha)*	*Share of hybrid (%)*	*Share of open polli-nated (%)**	*Share of unidentified varities (%)**
Egg plant	479095	85300	17.80	50.00	32.2
Cabbage	242140	76000	31.39	68.61	—
Cauliflower	304156	10000	3.29	50.00	46.71
Chillies	573529	14000	2.44	37.56	60.00
Gourds	409270	10000	2.44	20.00	77.56
Melons	169350	6800	4.02	25.98	70.00
Okra	371665	20000	5.38	80.00	14.62
Tomato	485520	153000	31.51	50.00	18.49

* Estimated figures.

Source : Seed Association of India.

A well planned strategy is needed to cover all the vegetable growing areas under noted identified varieties/hybrids to boost the vegetable production in the country. It is estimated that under eggplant approximately 32.20 per cent, cauliflower 46.71 per cent, chillies 60 per cent and under tomato 18.49 per cent area are under unidentified or local varieties. Here, great scope exists to replace the local cultivars with the improved cultivars having high quality and other preference of the region (Kirti Singh, 1998).

Availability of Quality Seeds and Hybrid Seed Production Technology

Over the last two decades, India has made significant progress in making available the quality seeds both of temperate and tropical vegetables. Many joint ventures for the production and distribution of vegetable seeds have recently come up as a result of the open seed policy leading to global recognition of Indian seeds industry. However, lack of availability of quality seeds at the right time still continues to be one of the major constraints in increasing the vegetable production and productivity especially when dealing with as many as 180 recommended varieties. No doubt India has achieved self-sufficiency in seeds of temperate vegetables and has even started exporting but still much work is required to be done. Seed production jumped from 1.8 million tonnes to 7 million tonnes in 1991-92 within a short span of time. According to an estimate, value of hybrid seed sold in 1994-95 was Rs.730 million. Seeds of F_1 hybrids in vegetables in India are primarily produced in the private sector (Table 11.8). Seed companies primarily concentrated in South (Karnataka, Andhra Pradesh) and West (Maharashtra) and public institutions like NSC, SFCI have been concentrating on seed production mainly of high volume, low value items like okra and pea. While most of the seeds of cole crops is imported, seeds of other vegetables is produced in India mostly in open except capsicum in which case glasshouse facility is required. Most private companies have trained women in hand emasculation and hand pollination technique. In Punjab, PAU, Ludhiana has trained farmers in utilization of genic male sterility for muskmelon seeds production.

F_1 hybrid seed, mostly of cabbage and capsicum, are imported from Japan, Korea, Holland, Denmark and USA. In recent years, Gherkin seeds have been imported from Netherlands. The imported component in hybrid seed contributes the major share in the cost of hybrid seeds, is not substitute for ever, and can only serve as a catalyst in development of indigenous hybrid seed production technology. The cost effective technology for growing F_1 hybrid variety has to be developed by the use of (a) indigenous parent, (b) indigenously produced hybrid seed, and (c) disease resistant parents to reduce the cost of plant protection cover. The Public Sector Seed Industry has taken commercial hybrid seed production technology (Agrawal, 1997) (Table 11.5 to Table 11.7).

Table 11.5 : IARI Released Vegetable Hybrids for All Over India

Released synthetics and F_1 hybrids				
Crop	*Hybrid*	*Yield (in tonnes/ha)*		*Centre showing potential yield*
		Realized	*Potential*	
Eggplant	Pusa Hybrid-5	51	90	Patnanagar
(Brinjal)	Pusa Hybrid-6	42	62	Kalianpur
	Pusa Hybrid-9	50	148	Jalna
Tomato	Pusa Hybrid-2	55	65	Aurangabad
	Pusa Hybrid-1	32	42	Delhi
	Pusa Hybrid-4	65	112	Rahuri
Capsicum	Pusa Deepti	24	50	Katrain
Cauliflower	Pusa Synthetic	19	24	Ludhiana
	Pusa Early Synthetic	10	12	Coimabatore
	Pusa Hybrid-2	23	35	Delhi
Muskmelon	Pusa Rasraj	17	30	Ludhiana
Bottle gourd	Pusa Meghdoot	19	26	Delhi
	Pusa Manjari	16	25	Delhi
Summer Squash	Pusa Alankar	45	54	Delhi
Cucumber	Pusa Sanyog	45	50	Delhi
Bitter gourd	Pusa Hybrid	22	40	Delhi

Source : Narendra Singh, 1997; Sirohi, P.S., 1999.

Table 11.6 : Vegetable Hybrids Identified/Released by Public Sector

Brinjal (Eggplant)	Arka Navneet, Pusa Hybrid-5, Pusa Hybrid-6, Pusa Hybrid-9, NDBH-1, ABH-1, ABH-2, ABG-2, Phule Hybrid-5
Tomato	Pusa Hybrid-1, Pusa Hybrid-2, Pusa Hybrid-4, FMH-1, Arka Vardhan Pusa Sambandh (KT-4), TH-802
Cauliflower	Pusa Hybrid-2
Cabbage	Pusa Synthetic
Muskmelon	Pusa Rasraj, Punjab Hybrid-1
Watermelon	Arka Jyoti
Bottle gourd	Pusa Manjari, Pusa Meghdoot, Pusa Hybrid-3
Pumpkin	Pusa Hybrid-1
Cucumber	Pusa Sanyog
Summer squash	Pusa Alankar
Capsicum	Pusa Deepti
Chilli	CH-1

Source : Narendra Singh and V.K. Verma, 1998.

Table 11.7 : Vegetable Hybrid Identified/Released for Cultivation Through AICVIP (1990-1997)

Brinjal	*Tomato*	*Capsicum*
1. Arka Navneet	1. ARTH-4	1. KT1
2. Pusa Hybrid-6	2. MTH-6	Cabbage
3. Pusa Hybrid-5	3. ARTH-3	1. Pusa Synthetic
4. ARBH-201	4. Arka Vardhan	2. Sri Ganesh Gol
5. NDBH-1	5. Pusa Hybrid-2	3. NATH-401
6. ABH-1	6. KT-4 (Pusa Sambandh)	4. BSS-32
7. MHB-10	7. NA-601	Cauliflower
8. MBH-39	8. FMH-1	1. Pusa Hybrid-2
9. NDBH-6	9. NA-501	Muskmelon
10. ABH-2	10. DTH-4	1. M-3 hybrid
		Watermelon
		1. Arka Jyoti
		Carrot
		1. Hybrid-1

Table 11.8 : List of Popular Hybrids of Private Sector

Tomato	Vaishali, Karnataka Hybrid, Lerica and NS-815
Brinjal	Suphal and HOE-404
Chilli	Agri, NS-1101 and HOE-808
Capsicum	Indira, Bharat, Lerio, Early Bonty, NS-33 and Hira
Cabbage	Cabbage No. 8, Questo, NS-22, Hari Rani Gol, Krishna, Vishesh
Cauliflower	Snow Crown, BSS-18, NS-60 and NS-90
Bottle gourd	Barad and Kavery
Watermelon	Madhur, Milan, Nath-101 and MHW-4
Muskmelon	Abhjeet, MCH-5 and MCH-6
Okra	Varsha, Vijay, Vishal

Source : Kalloo *et al.*, 1998 National Symposium ISVS, Souvenir, Silver Jubilee.

Table 11.9 : List of Promising Hybrids, an achievement of "Promotion of Hybrid Project"

Tomato	Avinash-2, Hemlata, TH-2312, Ratna, RHTH-13, DTH-6, ARTH-3
Brinjal (Eggplant)	NDBH-8, ARBH-201, PDBH-13, IIHR-500A, X Arka Keshav, and IIHR-104 X IIHR-491
Chilli	BSS-188, BSS-141, HOE-818, HOE-888, MHP-59, ARCH-236, Kiran
Cabbage	K-1, CBH-127, Kt CBH-95 and KT CBH-139, Golden Acre, Pride of India
Cucumber	CH-13, PCUCH-1, DH-9, 18 and 17 (developed from gynoeceous lines), KH-1
Onion	MS-65 X PBR-243 and MS-65 X PBR-245, Hybrid-63, Hybrid-35

Source : Kalloo *et al.*, 1998. National Symposium, ISVS, Souvenir, Silver Jubilee.

Table 11.10 : Hybrid Seed Marketed in Vegetable Crops (1995-96)

Crop	*Seed marketed (kg)*	*Source*
Tomato	21000	Country
Brinjal	8250	Country
Chilli	1700	Imported
Cabbage	18000	Imported
Cauliflower	4000	Country
Gourds	16300	-do-
Melons	8700	-do-

Source : Seed Association of India.

Production Technology for Rare/Minor Vegetable Crops

In our country more than 70 types of vegetables are grown but maximum emphasis has been given on important vegetables like tomato, brinjal, chilli, cauliflower, cabbage, pea and few important cucurbits. Besides, a number of minor vegetables are grown in different parts of the country. Though presently the area under these minor vegetables is very limited, it is expected that in near future there will be great demand of these vegetables. Even today, these vegetables are fetching very high price in multistar hotels and other tourist restaurants. In Himachal Pradesh, cultivation of asparagus and broccoli is increasing very fast. Among all the vegetables in cole family, broccoli is rated as more remunerative. Recently, two improved varieties of broccoli, namely Palam Samridhi (Green headed) and DOG PPB. 1(Purple head) have also been developed for cultivation. Demand for supply of seed of these vegetables is now coming from various states.

Like asparagus and broccoli there are a number of other minor vegetables such as Faba bean, Summer bean, Lima bean, Winged bean, Velvet bean, Chive, Leak, Welsh onion, Brussels' sprouts, Chinese cabbage, *Momordica cochinchinensis, Coccinia indica, C. cordifolia, Melorthia heterophylla*, Curry leaf, drumstick, agathi, waterleaf, Indian spinach, parsnip, celery, lettuce, globe artichoke, sweet corn, baby corn etc. Looking to the importance of these crops, it is desired that there should be well chalk out plan to cover these vegetables under various research projects to generate the information on various aspects so that the commercial cultivation of these minor vegetables can be popularized.

Chemical Weed Control in Vegetable Crops

Weeds cause substantial damage to crop plant and reduce the yield considerably. Grasses and broad leaved weeds frequently harbour insect-pest and diseases which may later attack the crop. Several herbicides have been tested to control the weeds in a number of vegetable crops. Among herbicides Stomp, Goal, Basalin, Sencor, Lasso and Tribunil have been found very effective in several vegetable crops. These herbicides are widely being used by the farmers to control the weeds in vegetables.

Table 11.11 : Selected Herbicides for Control of Weeds in Important Vegetable crops

Sr. No.	*Herbicides*	*Active ingredient (kg/ha)*	*Crops*	*State of application*	*Control of weeds*
1.	Pendimethalins	1.0	Brinjal	1-10 days after transplanting	Broad leaf weeds & Grasses
		0.5	Garden pea	Pre-emergence	-do-
2.	Oxybluorfen	0.25	Tomato	Pre-plant spray	Broad leaf weeds & Grasses
3.	Fluchlonalin	1.0	Tomato	Pre-plant spray	Broad leaf weeds
		2.0	Onion	Pre-plant spray	Broad leaf weeds
		2.5	Okra	4 days before sowing	Broad leaf weeds
4.	Metribuzin	0.3-1.1	Tomato & pepper	Pre-plant soil spray	Broad leaf weeds
5.	Alachlor	1.5	Okra	Pre-emergence	Grasses and broad leaf weeds
6.	Methabenzthiozuron	1.87	Garden pea	Pre-emergence spray	Broad leaf weeds
7.	Decthal	6.7-11.2	Brinjal	Pre-emergence after earthing	Annuals primarily Grasses
		6.7-11.2	Cauli-flower	Immediately after sowing and also as pre-plant spray	Annuals primarily Grasses
		6.7-11.2	Onion	Immediately after seed sowing or transplanting	Annuals primarily Grasses
		6.7-11.2	Radish	Immediately after seed sowing	Annuals primarily Grasses

Growth Regulators in Vegetable Crops

Plant Growth Regulators (PGR) are organic compounds, other than nutrients, which in small amounts promote, inhibit or otherwise modify any plant physiological processes. Now-a-days plant growth regulators are being used to increase the production of number of vegetable crops (Table 11.12). Application of GA_3 @ 325 ppm induces staminate flowers in gynoecious lines of muskmelon and cucumber, thus are used for maintaining such lines for hybrid seed production. Cycocel is effective to induce leaf curl virus tolerance in tomato. Ethephon sprayed on the plant at 2-4 true leaf stage increased female and hermaphrodite flowers in several cucurbits thus increased the yield. In tomato, chilli and pepper, spray of ethephon at ripening stage enhances ripening. Parachlorophenoxy acetic acid at 50 to 100 ppm sprayed at the stage of flowering increased fruit set at high and low temperature conditions in tomato (Panditor *et al.*, 1979).

Integrated Plant Nutrient System for Vegetable Production

In most of the Indian soils, nitrogen is deficient but phosphorus and potash are available in sufficient quantities. However, in areas deficient in phosphorus and potassium as indicated by soil testing, about 60-100 kg/ha P_2O_5 and 50-120 kg. nitrogen/ha are recommended for vegetable crops, depending on the requirement of individual crop. The use of micro-nutrients in vegetable production is gradually becoming important. Although a part of the requirement is met by application of manure, compost or poultry manure, deficiencies in certain area of the country are still common, and use of micro-nutrient fertilizers in such region has been found beneficial. Sprays of 2 per cent sulphate and borax solution have been found to increase the yield to tomato.

In simple terms Integrated Plant Nutrient System (IPNS) is a balance use of chemical fertilizer, organic manure, such as the form yard manure (FYM), crop residues, animal and human wastes, and bio-fertilizers. The IPNS aims at sustainable productivity with minimum deleterious effects of chemical fertilizers on soil health and environment.

In vegetable production, role of organic manure is much more as compared to other cereal crops. It has been proved experimentally that vegetables produced by the application of organic manure possesses good

Table 11.12 : List of Growth Regulators Along with Their Important Uses in Vegetable Crops

Sr. No.	*PGR*	*Concentration (mg/l)*	*Method of application*	*Crops*	*Attributes affected*
1.	Gibberellic acid (GA_3)	10-20	Foliar spray	Watermelon, Tomato	Sex expression Good yield
		40-100	Seed treatment or foliar spray	Okra, Tomato, Brinjal	Seed germination, fruit set and yield
		1000	Foliar spray	Cucumber	Maintaining Gynoecism
2.	Cycocel (CCC)	500	Seed soaking	Okra	Salt tolerance
		500	Root dipping and foliar spray	Tomato	Control leaf curl virus, fruiting and yield
		250	Root dipping of transplants	Tomato	Salt tolerance
		1%	-do-	Onion	-do-
3.	Ethephon	100-500	Foliar spray	Cucurbits, Tomato	Flowering, fruiting, sex expression and yield were improved
		1000	Pre-harvest	Tomato	Fruit ripening
		2000	Post-harvest	Tomato chillies	Fruit ripening
4.	Parachlor-phenoxy acetic acid (PCPA)	50-100	Foliar spray at full bloom	Tomato	Fruitset at low and high temperature conditions
5.	Planofix (NAA)	10	Foliar spray	Chilli	Reduces flower and fruit drop and improved fruit set and yield
6.	Malic hydrazide (MH)	50-150	Foliar spray at 2 and 4 true leaf stage	Bottle gourd Round melon	Fruit set and yield

firmness and have long storage life. Organic amendments in the form of oil cakes and neem, mahua, GNC and Castor suppress the population of nematodes and other harmful pathogens like *Fusarium and Rhizoctonia.* Beside, press mud and digested sludge are being used to raise other crops.

The micro-nutrients, namely boron manganese, iron, molybdenum and copper play an important role in vegetable production. Boron is effective in controlling the malady of fruit cracking in tomato and quality produce in terms of total soluble solids, ascorbic acid and flesh appearance.

Recently, application of bio-fertilizers in vegetable crops has been found very effective. Bio-fertilizers harper atmospheric nitrogen with the help of specialized soil micro-organisms. Such nitrogen fixing micro-organisms are either free living in soil and symbiotic with plants and directly or indirectly contribute towards the nitrogen nutrition of the plants. In onion, inoculation with *Azospirillium brasiliens* sp. Nov. and VAM at nursery stage and in the main field recorded an additional yield of 22.93 t/ha. and saved 25 per cent recommended doses of NPK fertilizers. Thus production of vegetables through organic farming has high demands in export and some farmers have started organic farming by trial and error methods (Pandey and Singh, 1998).

Water Management

Vegetables in general are heavy users of moisture and draw a large share of irrigation resources. The need for high yielding and short duration varieties for water use efficiency is much more than low yielding ones. Drip or trickle irrigation has proved useful in growing tomato and okra in Maharashtra, with a saving of 56 and 69 per cent, respectively. At the Tamil Nadu Agricultural University, the comparative effect of,furrow and drip irrigation were tested on tomato, okra, brinjal, beet root, radish, chillies and sweet potato. The germination and growth were greater in drip method than the furrow method. The weed infestation was less in the drip method compared to the furrow method. In drip method, water reaches only at the root zone to the required depth, thus, plants use nutrients.

Table 11.13 : Water Requirements and Yield of Vegetable Crops

Vegetable	*Water used (cm)*		*Water saving (%)*	*Yield increased (%)*
	Drip	*Control*		
Tomato	10.76	49.20	78.0	43.00
Okra	8.60	53.53	83.0	13.00
Beet root	17.73	85.76	79.0	4.00
Radish	10.81	46.41	76.0	3.00
Chilli	41.77	109.71	61.0	20.75
Brinjal	24.47	69.18	64.0	0.81
Sweet Potato	25.20	63.14	60.0	38.0

Source : "Production Technology of Vegetable Crops" by Shanmugavelu, K.G., 1989.

Increase in Production Period of Some Crops

On the basis of the temperature requirement for curd irritation and development, cauliflower varieties are available now-a-days which can supply curds in the market throughout the year in the northern plains of the country (Narendra Singh, 1998). Similarly radish is cultivated and used round the year. It is winter season crop, however, in north Indian plains it is grown as late Kharif and Rabi vegetable. Generally most of the tropical varieties start bolting without forming marketable roots in the later part of December or January, so, it is not practicable to grow one variety of any group (temperate, sub-tropical). Thus, varieties suited to various conditions/periods have been developed. Therefore, it is very important to select the right variety for sowing in a particular season. Now-a-days tomato can be grown almost throughout the year in the country. This is due to development of heat tolerant, cold tolerant and disease resistant varieties. In northern plains tomato is grown continuously from June to March covering most period of year. Low temperature setting varieties such as Ostenkinskiz, Cold Set and Pusa Sheetal can be grown in severe winter conditions. Similarly Hot Set, HS-102, Saladette can set fruit in summer. Spray of Parachlorophenoxy Acetic Acid at 50 and 100 ppm at flowering stage sets fruits during summer and winter conditions. During rainy season due to severe incidence of leaf curl tomatoes are not being grown in many parts of the country. However, the development of tomato leaf curl resistant varieties H-24 and H-36 have led to the production of tomato under such conditions.

Due to development of Kharif onion, two crops of onion are being taken in northern plains of India. Kharif onion is the growing of onion in Kharif season (off-season), i.e. from June to November. There is scarcity of onion from November to March and during such period Kharif onion proves to be a boon to the farmers. This not only increases the total onion production but also provides fresh onion to the consumers at reasonable rate and good return to the farmers. Apart from this, it avoids the storage losses of Rabi onion, because if there is no Kharif onion we have to store the Rabi onion from November to March. During this period most of the onion starts sprouting, shrinking and rotting. The varieties which are most suitable for cultivation in Kharif season are N-53, Agrifound Dark Red, Arka Kalyan and Baswant-780. These varieties require mild climate without extreme of low and high temperatures. The seeds are first treated with Thirum 2-3 g/kg. of seeds and sown in the nursery from the last week of May to first week of June. Nursery beds must be treated with Captaf @ 2g/l of water before sowing. Seedling are transplanted from first week of July to August or when they are 7-8 weeks old. Depending upon the rains, 8-10 irrigations are enough. Irrigation should be stopped 15-20 days before obtaining the maturity to improve the keeping quality of bulb.

Integrated Pest Management

Generally, vegetables are attracted by a number of insect pests. Due to plant canopy and succulency, vegetables suffer maximum from pest damage. In vegetables more than 40 per cent yield loss is caused due to pest attack. As a result, growers face heavy loss due to degradation of quality and marketability. Unlike cereals, the green pods, fruits and leaves are mostly used as vegetables, which are more prone to retain the pesticide residue. Even though vegetables cover only 2.5 per cent of total cropped area, 17.16 per cent of total insecticides are consumed in vegetable cultivation. The persistency of toxic chemicals in consumable parts limits the choice of pesticides and make vegetable pest management more sensitive and challenging. Residual toxicity is of particular consequence in produce for export. Shipment from the country are rejected because of residual toxicity above a maximum residue level (MRL). According to the chairman of the spices exports, chilli farming of Andhra Pradesh have to adopt IPM technology to reduce the use of pesticides to improve export, as consignment have been rejected due to pesticide residues. Under the IPM, we assess exhibiting pest situation and utilize all the available pest control methods in a compatible manner to keep the pest population below economic threshold level and above maintenance threshold level of natural enemies.

In recent past, throughout the world efforts have been made to control the vegetable pest by use of natural enemies, parasite predators besides host specific insect viruses and other entomo-pathogenic micro-organisms and to a considerable extent success has been achieved. In tomato, fruits borer can be successfully controlled by use of *Trichogramma* and Ha NPV (Nuclear Polyhedrosis Virus). Okra shoot and fruit borer can be checked by *Trichogramma brassliensis*. Diamondback moth of cabbage can be controlled successfully by *Bacillus thuringiensis*. No doubt IPM technology has emerged an effective and eco-friendly approach to combat the pest problem in vegetable crops. But farmer's ignorance about this approach and apprehension that natural enemies do not totally suppress the pest population and low populations of pest is enough to cause heavy loss. Further lack of availability of these bio-agents and their multiplication is another problem in adoption. To make the IPM technology more popular among the growers, an intensive effort on research and extension is needed.

Pollination Management in Vegetable Crops

An eco-friendly and relatively less known practice in developing countries of enhanced vegetable yield is pollination management. This method of bringing the pollinators to the crop in bloom has been widely used in many countries. A honeybee colony with around 20000 bees in one colony of *Apis indica* is capable of locating accurately and foraging on vast areas. Today in the west, bee keepers rent their hive to agriculturist in the flowering season. Use of bees in cross pollination is the cheapest, eco-friendly and self-sustainable method to boost the yield to meet the growing demand for the food. In Israel, bumble bee has been found more effective pollinator than honey bee. As like honey bee and bumble bee, carpenter bees visit only some plants but are excellent pollinators (Pandey and Singh, 1998).

Inter-generic Grafting in Vegetable Production

In vegetable production, there are several problems of soil borne diseases and pests and nematodes and it is strenuous to incorporate resistance to such stresses in the varieties. Therefore, intergeneric grafting has been proved very effective in a number of vegetable crops. Cucumber grafted on pumpkin gives resistance against *Fusarium* spp. and grafting on figleaf gourd provides low temperature resistance. Watermelons are generally grafted on bottle gourd and rarely on pumpkin. Melons are grafted on the same species but are very rarely on white gourd and pumpkin. Interspecific grafting are very common in brinjal plant also. Scarlet brinjal and *Solanum torvum* are popular root stocks for egg plant to give resistance mainly against *Fusarium* and bacterial wilt, respectively. In grafting technology, Japan has taken lead and it is growing 32 per cent tomato, 50 per cent brinjal, 93 per cent watermelon and 72 per cent cucumber as grafted plants (Paroda and Kalloo, 1995).

Pruning and Training of Vegetable Crops

Pruning away some branches within that tangled mass of vegetation inhibits the growth of certain diseases, producing micro-organisms and the combination of light and air circulation promotes more rapid drying. Removing crossing limb also prevents would created by rubbing. Proper pruning and training have been found to improve earliness and yield in several cucurbits. In muskmelon the female/hermaphrodite flowers are borne on the side branches arising from higher nodes. If the pruning of the side branches is done upto 7th node, the growth and vigour of the plant improves and flowering is early and ultimately yield is improved. It has been observed that fruits arising from 9-12th nodes are more sweet in taste. In watermelon the female flowers are borne on the main branches. Hence, female flowers and yield can be increased by nipping the main shoot from 5-6th node and allowing 3-4 well developed main branches to develop. By this technique number, yield and sweetness of fruits has been improved substantially. In round melon also pruning to four primary branches have resulted in larger number of fruits and higher yield because of the same reason.

Training is also very important practice to train the tomato, cucumber and other beans and cucurbits. Training of indeterminate tomato provides ideal conditions to express the full potential of growth and fruiting. Vegetable growers of Madhya Pradesh and Maharashtra are cultivating cucurbits mainly on bower system of training. This system of training does not only enhance the vegetative growth and yield but also give quality fruits. Bottle gourd grown on this system bears uniform size and colour of fruits which fetch high price in the market.

Vegetable based Cropping System

Vegetables are short or medium duration crops. They vacate fields early or in a short time. Small and marginal farmers can even cultivate vegetable crops year the round. Vegetables have cropping intensity of 400 per cent. In North India, two crops each of radish, turnip, beet root, cauliflower, knol-khol and potato are quite possible during rabi season. Long duration vegetable crops like brinjal, tomato, beans, pea, okra, cluster bean and cucurbits though begin yielding early and continue for longer period. Inter-cropping of vegetables in sugarcane, maize, gobhi, saron and sraya is possible. Inter-cropping of palak, onion and radish with tomato, cauliflower and cabbage is more profitable. Relay cropping of vegetables as filler crop in a normal cropping is best for the small and marginal farmers. Some of the vegetable crop rotations which have been found remunerative are:

1. Maize – Potato – Onion
2. Okra – Potato – Tomato
3. Early cauliflower – Potato (early) – Round melon
4. Tomato – Potato –Watermelon
5. Cowpea – Radish – Potato – Pumpkin
6. Kharif onion (green) – Potato – Chilli
7. Butter gourd – Potato – Bottle gourd
8. Luffa – Early Potato – Garden pea – Round melon

Use of Mulches in Vegetables Production

Mulches are covering material to the soil surface. They are mainly used to reduce or increase the temperature. High temperatures affect seed germination, vegetative growth, flowering, pollination, fruit set and yield. Mulch also improves the quality of vegetables by avoiding their direct contact with soil.

Organic mulches can reduce the soil temperature upto some extent. In potato, mulching hastened and improved the sprouting, plant growth and yield in early crop. It reduces the rotting of seed tuber at high temperature. In tomato during summer, mulching gives higher yield. Organic mulches have been used successfully in cucurbits, chilli, brinjal, and early cauliflower for obtaining comparatively high yields. Mulches protect the roots of the plants from heat, check evaporation, and conserve soil moisture, reduce weed infestation and modify the soil and air micro-climate.

In general plastics are used to increase the soil temperature specially during winter. Polyethylene sheets (clear and black) are used as mulches. Under the transparent film, the soil temperature rises by 2-10°C during day time but the retention of the heat energy is poor during night. However, black film shows better retention. Covering of nursery bed with the transparent plastic sheet of 300 or 400 gauge for 30 to 45 days during summer months has been found to effectively control the soil pathogens. Soil solarization prevents the seeds and seedling rot caused by *Verticillium, Rhizoctonia, Fusarium, Sclerotium* etc. and thereby improve seedling growth of brinjal, chilli, cauliflower, cabbage, onion, etc. Plastic sheets used immediately after seed sowing are helpful in early germination by increasing soil temperature and conserve the moisture.

River Bed Cultivation of Vegetable Crops

The river bed cultivation is very old practice of growing vegetables on the bank or basin of rivers. There are several advantages of river bed cultivation, viz. early yield, ease in irrigation, high net return per unit area and additional crop. Mostly cucurbits are grown in river beds. Besides, cucurbits, tomatoes are successfully cultivated due to its deep root system. Cucurbits are sown in the month of November to December in trenches/channels. The trenches are dug in North-West direction to manage the availability of higher temperature. The depth of channels is 45-90 cm. depending on height of water table. Generally 60 cm. to 90 cm. is the height of water table in river beds. Width of channels is kept about 45 cm. and length depends upon area and location. Sometimes circular pits of about 35 to 45 cm. in diameter are prepared having a depth of about 90 cm. The trenches are filled with compost/FYM, soil and N, P, K requirements of the crops. These trenches are left for few days and if possible pre-sowing irrigation is done to settle down the various layers of materials in the trenches. Distance between trench is kept 2-2.5 m. depending upon the variety and type of the crop to be raised. Seed sowing for early crop is done in 1st or 2nd week of November at a spacing of 45-60 cm. in the trench at a depth of 3 to 4 cm. Two seeds are generally sown at one place. If the temperature is very low, pre-sprouted seeds are sown for smooth germination. Mulching is done to enhance seed germination. In North-West India, the temperature in December to January goes down to 1-2°C, the protection is provided by thatch screen made at locally available material. This protection serves as wind break to save the crop from chilling winds and checks the sand drifting.

Biotechnology

In recent past, biotechnology has emerged as a powerful tool for alleviating hunger, disease, overcoming energy shortage and improving self-sufficiency of developing countries. It is useful in many areas like *in vitro* multiplication of elite planting material genome mapping and marker assisted selection and in development of transgenic plants. Genetic engineering of vegetable Brassicas for insect and fungal resistance is imperative to achieve an eco-friendly approach towards integrated pest management. Transgenic plants carrying Bt genes for insect resistance are about to be marketed in USA. No doubt this branch of science has immense potential and can play an important role in understanding the numerous and mysterious complex phenomenon in plants and animals which will prove boon to the welfare of the mankind. However, a point of caution is essential at each and every step. Good efforts in this direction are underway both by public and private sector.

Post-harvest Management of Vegetable Crops

Green vegetables due to high moisture content are inherently more liable to deteriorate especially under tropical conditions such as ours. Owing to lack of production, planning and climatic factors, gluts occur frequently leading to distress sale, poor prices to growers and wastage. The post-harvest losses estimated as about 20-40 percent of the total fruit and vegetable production go as waste, costing more than Rs.30,000 million annually. Thus income of the growers and per capita availability of produce come down.

Research in post-harvest has probed into screening of vegetable varieties and hybrids for prolonged shelf life and processing character, standardization of different storage systems including controlled atmosphere system for different vegetable crops, improvement of packaging and transportation system suited to Indian conditions; harnessing solar energy for drying as well as storage utilization of wastes for the development of economically viable products and initiating post-harvest research specific to improve export potential.

Export-Oriented Vegetable Farming

Vegetables are now being considered as one of the most potential commodities for export. The value of refresh, canned and dehydrated vegetable exports has been to the tune of Rs.363.44 crores during 1996-97.The Agricultural and Processed Food Product Export Development (APEDA) has identified traditional vegetables like onion, potato, bitter gourd and chilli and non-traditional vegetables like asparagus, celery, sweet pepper, paprika, sweet corn, baby corn, green peas, French bean, cherry-tomato and gherkin having good export potential. Onion accounts for 70 per cent of total foreign exchange earning among fresh vegetables. Among other vegetables, 60 per cent share goes to okra, 20 per cent to green chilli and 20 per cent bitter gourd, French bean, capsicum and other mixed vegetables. Among the traditional category of vegetables, onion, okra, bitter gourd, green chillies, etc. meet the requirement of

Indian expatriates in SE Asia and Gulf countries and to some extent in the U.K. The non-traditional items including vegetables like cabbage, cauliflower, lettuce, capscicum etc. go to E.C. countries, where growing condition are not ideal during November to March. India's varied agro-climatic conditions are major asset in terms of natural resources, which can be utilized in accelerating the vegetable production.

References

Agrawal, P.K. (1997), Hybrid Vegetable Seed Requirements—Supply and scope in India. In summer school on *Hybrid Seed Productions Technology of Vegetables*, April, 7-26, 1997.

Anonymous (1972-93), Annual Reports, All India Coordinated Vegetable Improvement Project (AICVIP), New Delhi, Varanasi.

Anonymous (1990-97), Annual Reports, All India Coordinated Vegetable Improvement Project (AICVIP), New Delhi, Varanasi.

Anonymous (1999), Vegetable Research at a Glance Souvenir of the Department of Vegetable Crops, Punjab Agricultural University, Ludhiana-141 004 (XVIII Group meeting of All India Coordinated Vegetable Improvement Project, October, 11-14, 1999).

Arora, S.K. (1999), Present Scenario of Vegetable Production in India. Published in *Recent Advances in Bio-sciences for Sustainable Food Security*, (Eds.) R.C. Sihag and other, AAREM, CCS Haryana Agricultural University, Hissar.

Bhatnagar, P.S. (1998), Notified Varieties of Horticultural Crops. *ICAR News* (Oct. – Dec. 1998), p. 15.

Bose, T.K., Som, M.G. and Kabir, J. (1993), *Vegetable Crops* Naya Prakash, Kalyani, West Bengal.

Chadha, K.L. (1998), "History of Vegetable Research in India". *Silver Jubilee National Symposum* of Indian Society of Vegetable Science held at Varanasi (U.P.), December 12-14, 1998.

Gopala Krishnan, T.R. (1996), Ujwala, a Bacterial Wilt Resistant Chilli Variety. *ICAR News* (Oct. – Dec., 1996). p. 23.

Kalloo, G. (1988), *Vegetable Breeding*, Vol. III C.R.C. Press, Fla, U.S.A.

Kalloo, G. (1995), Status of Vegetable Production in India with special reference to Vegetable Hybrid Technology, *Vegetable Research in India*, PDVR, Varanasi, pp. 125-52.

Kalloo, G., Banerjee, M.K. Sanjeet Kumar and Chander Prakash (1998), Hybrid Vegetable Technology in India: An Over View. *Silver Jubilee National Symposium of ISVS Souvenir*, December 12-14, 1998 at Varanasi (U.P.).

Kirti Singh (1998), "Challenges in Vegetable Production in Twenty-First Century." *National Symposium on Emerging Scenario* in Vegetable Research and Development, Dec. 12-14, 1998, pp. 1-11.

Narendra Singh (1997), IARI released vegetable hybrids for all over India. *ICAR News* (July-Sept., 1997), p. 14.

Narendra Singh (1998), Cauliflower for all seasons. *ICAR News* (April-June, 1998) p. 15.

Narendra Singh and Verma, V.K., (1998), "Recent Trends in Vegetable Production Technology". ISVS Souvenir: *Silver Jubilee National Symposium*, December 12-14, 1998, Varanasi (U.P.), India.

Pandey, A.K. and Singh, K.P. (1998), Vegetable Production Technology Towards Productivity Enhancement. ISVS Souvenir: *Silver Jubilee National Symposium*, December 12-14, 1998, Varanasi (U.P.), India.

Pandita, M.L., Arora, S.K. and Kirti Singh (1979), Effect of plant regulators on the fruit set, early and total yield of tomato var. HS-101 (*L. esculentum* Mill.) during summer season. *Haryana J. Hort. Sci.* 8: 112-16.

Pareek, O.P. and Samadia, D.K. (1999), Watermelon (Mateera) varieties developed by NRCAH. *ICAR News* (April-June, 1999).

Paroda, R.S. and Kalloo, G. (1995), Vegetable Research with special reference to hybrid technology in the Asia and Pacific Region.

Shanmugavelu, K.G. (1989), "Production Technology of Vegetable Crops", A Book Chapter.

Sirohi, P.S. (1999), Bitter gourd Pusa Hybrid-1, First Commercial F_1 Hybrid. *ICAR News* (April-June, 1999), p. 14.

Yadav, I.S. (1996), Horticultural varieties/Hybrids with biotic and abiotic stress resistance. *ICAR News* (Oct.-Dec., 1996), p. 21.

Yadav, I.S. (1998), Bacterial-wilt resistant tomato hybrids – A success story, *ICAR News* (July-Sept., 1998), p. 14.

12

REGIONAL DIMENSIONS OF AGRICULTURAL GROWTH POTENTIALS*

SURENDRA SINGH

Introduction

It is believed that increasing influence of agricultural technology creates hetrogeneties and inequalities by breaking down the community structures, norms, and beliefs of farmers' society (Newman, *et. al.* 1980). It also evolves diversified farming patterns with the concentration of agricultural production growth that led to widen its areal gaps particularly in Indian conditions (Bhat and Learmonth, 1968) and also alters the magnitude and intensity of agricultural growth potentials. Non-land capital intensification increases agricultural income, output, production efficiency and productivity (Solow, 1957, 1963). But these increments are due to the role of the capacity-utilisation of yield (i.e. production) potentials playing in the intensification of agricultural activities. In fact the conditions of agricultural growth potentials phenomena are internally co-associated and areally co-varied with the conditions of existing production processes. Therefore, the logical study of agricultural growth potential phenomena may be helpful in examining the consequences of induced technology in connection with finding out suitable areas of further enhancement of production efficiency. Indeed, without establishing input-output relationship of agricultural activities, the tendencies of production potential components cannot be specified

* This is the modified version of the paper 'Agricultural Growth Potentials and Regionalisation'.

and componental relationship between production potentials and input intensification cannot be stated. The agricultural production function approach is, therefore, adopted for specifying regional variations of agricultural growth potentials.

Thus, the attention is focused essentially on two important aspects of agricultural growth potentials: (a) to establish a normative frame of agricultural production function by which the tendencies of the magnitude and intensity of agricultural growth potentials can be studied, and (b) to identify the areas of high intensity of agricultural growth potentials for preparing regional-investment public policies particularly for developing economies where agricultural potentials are enough to use.

Identification of Components of Production Potentials

Various studies of assessing agricultural yield potentials have been carried out on the basis of description of attributes of natural resource endowments (Hayami and Ruttan 1971, Buringh, *et. al.* 1975). But the approaches of these studies are based on absolute measurements of yield potentials rather than relative ones. Production function approach may produce workable solution with evolving systematic tendencies and regional patterns of integrated nature of agricultural growth potential phenomena. Note that the concept of growth potentials is related with differentiation of existing yield conditions and its maximum expectations.

Untapped yield gap between *existing yield*, Y, and its *highest possible yield*, A, (that can be obtained on theoretical considerations or on experimental basis as on farmer's farm) determines the total *magnitude* of yield potentials per unit of land, P_p as $P_p = (A-Y)$, while its *intensity* I_p is its magnitude per unit of existing yield $I_p = [(A-Y)/Y]$. The term *production efficiency*, PE, is directly related with and proportional to the intensity of existing yield (Bhatia, 1967; Singh, 1974-75) as existing yield per unit of the highest possible yield, $PE = (Y/A)$.

It must be noticed here that all these components of agricultural growth potentials phenomena vary areally as well as temporally due to acceleration of production potential processes that are governed by input intensification forces of agricultural activities. Biotechnological researches in the field of agriculture and forestry particularly in plant genetics protect plant growth (Winzel, 1987) and their applications in agricultural intensification influence the growth and enhance crop-yields by increasing level of the highest possible yield over time. This process of *potential generation* must intensify the yield potential phenomena by enhancing 'potential multiplier' effects in agricultural activities. On the other hand, enhancement and application of bio-chemical (use of chemical fertilizers) and agro-engineering (use of machines in irrigation, tillage and crop-threshing) researches are helpful in intensifying the existing conditions of yield by utilising the intensity and magnitude of production potential phenomena. These forces act as 'potential absorber' and accelerate *potential utilisation* process in farming systems. These forces and processes govern agricultural growth potential system. But the systematic areal relationship of production potentials with input intensification cannot be established without taking into account the suitable agricultural production function.

Production Functions and Their Parameters

It is widely recognised by agricultural production economists that agricultural production follows the law of diminishing marginal product to intensity everywhere in the world (Spillman, 1923). Cobb-Douglas production function that has been/is being widely used for analysing areal as well as spatial (or locational) structures of agricultural production (Hanumantha Rao, 1968; Visser, 1980, 1982), is fundamentally based on 'lognormal law of constant production elasticity'. While the production processes in agricultural activities should always be operated on the law of 'concave elasticity of production' for which Spillman (1933) proposed 'exponential yield curve'. It holds semi-logrithamic linearity for production potentials.*

Leaving aside the critical aspects and reviewed discussions of concerned literature available on production function approaches* a slightly less complex form which follows 'reciprocity law of concave production elasticity' must produce the normative and real solution of the conditions of agricultural production processes and their growth potentials (Singh, 1980). It is mathematically symbolised as:

$$Y(X_m) = [A(1.00 + B_m X^{-1}_m)^{-1}] \qquad \ldots (1)$$

subject to

(i) X_m and Y are non-negative variables,

(ii) m is number of input factor,

* For further details of the mathematical forms and logical reasoning of agricultural production functions, see Spillman and Lang (1924), Heady and Dillon (1961) and Heady (1964).

(iii) A & $B_m > 0$ are the constants,

where A = the highest possible or maximum expected level of yield in the system because, in the above equation, $X_m \rightarrow \infty$, so that $B_m X_m^{-1} \rightarrow 0$, then $Y = A$; B_m = rate of yield potentials per unit of agricultural productivity because the simplified form of the above equation for B_m is

$$B_m = [(A - Y)/(Y/X_m)] = [(A - Y)/Y].X_m, \text{ and} \quad ...(2)$$

$$B_m X_m^{-1} = [(A - Y)/Y] = Ip\,(x_m) \quad ...(3)$$

Thus term $B_m X_m^{-1}$ denotes the intensity of yield potentials in the basic form of agricultural production function.

Componential Equilibria and Regional Structure

Simplification of the basic form of production function (Eqn. 1) for $PE\,(x_m)$ and $P_p\,(x_m)$ and its differentiation with respect to X_m as :

$$PE\,(x_m) = X\,(B_m + X_m)^{-1} \quad ...(4)$$

$$P_p\,(x_m) = B_m A\,(B_m + X_m)^{-1} \quad ...(5)$$

$$M_p\,(X_m)^* = \frac{B_m A}{(B_m + X_m)^2} = \frac{B_m}{A}\left(\frac{Y}{X_m}\right)^2 = \left(\frac{A-Y}{A}\right)\left(\frac{Y}{X_m}\right) \quad ...(6)$$

$$P_e\,(x_m)^* = \frac{B_m}{(B_m + X_m)^2} = \frac{B_m}{A}\left(\frac{Y}{X_m}\right) = \left(\frac{A-Y}{A}\right)^{**} \quad ...(7)$$

confirm the facts that (a) the componential tendencies of production potentials, even the tendencies of marginal product to intensity, production elasticity, diminish non-negatively at a decreasing rate, and (b) the production efficiency, $PE\,(X_m)$, increases with decreasing rate asymptotically. Therefore, the present function does not specify maxima condition of agricultural production. Intensity of land rent, R, may specify the regional dimensions of agricultural growth potentials. In fact, without stating rent equation in present production function, the rent-production potential relationship cannot be established properly.

Land rent is the basic criteria of analysing agricultural intensification and land-use problems (Dunn, 1954; Visser, 1980, 1982). Recardean thesis of transfer of earnings of land which advocates that rent is the residual flow of return accruing to land, and the Dunn's

---

* The term $P_e\,(X_m)$ denotes Production elasticity which is equal to Marginal productivity, $M_p\,(X_m) = (dY/dX_m)$, per unit of Average Productivity, $A_p\,(x_m) = (Y/X_m)$, where dY/dX_m is first-order differentiation of the production function.

** These last terms of equalities have been found out by substituting equation (2) in them.

(1954) definition as a quantity derived by gaining difference between the value of total products per unit of land sold and its production cost including transportation charges, are the basic premises about the rent. Prices of production and production-factors are assumed invariably in the present study. According to these premises, the simple form of rent is, $R(x_m) = (Y - X_m)$. This form can be solved by substituting basic form of production function as :

$$\begin{aligned} R(x_m) &= [X_m (A - B_m - X_m)/(B_m + X_m)]. \\ &= PE. [A - (B_m + X_m)], \text{ s.t. } A \geq (B_m + X_m) \quad \ldots(8) \end{aligned}$$

It confirms that land rent is the multiplier of two factors: (i) production efficiency that has increasing effects on the quantity of rent, and (ii) the difference of A and $(B_m + X_m)$, which has a decreasing effect. The multiplied effect of these factors decreases quantity of rent at increasing rate upto a certain limit of input intensification when $A = (B_m + X_m)$. Note that maximisation is not feasible in this rent equation. However, *zero-rent criteria*, which satisfies minimisation of rent as $MR(X_m) = dR/dX_m = 0$, must determine the level of maximum utilisation of production potentials, $\bar{P}p\ (x_m)$ at $\bar{X}_m$ level of input intensity. Putting first-order differential of equation (8) as zero.

$$MR(x_m) = [B_m (A - B_m - X_m)/(B_m + X_m)^2] = 0 \quad \ldots(9)$$

and solving it for X_m and P_p as

$$\bar{X}_m = (A - B_m) \text{ and } \bar{P}_p = B_m \quad \ldots(10)$$

one can confirm about the quantity of marginal rent that is equal to the quantity of the differences observed between marginal product to intensity and production elasticity because the simplified form of equation (9) may be written as

$$MR(X_m) = M_p(x_m) - P_e(x_m) = 0, \quad \ldots(11)$$

Thus, quantity of marginal rent becomes zero at the intersection point of $M_p(x_m)$ and $P_e(x_m)$ curves at $\bar{X}_m$ input levels.

This criterion must divide whole areal structure of growth potentials into two clear-cut segments. For further divisions, *potential-difference-determinant criterian* can be chosen. According to this criterian, a farmer must work on his farm in favourable farm conditions till he gets higher returns of rent than the quantity of yield potentials as: $MR(x_m) = P_p(x_m)$. The solution of this condition with the help of substituting equations (5) and (9) and its simplifications for X_m and P_p must determine the level of optimal utilisation of production potentials, $\hat{P}_p(X_m)$ at input level of $\hat{X}_m$, as:

$$\hat{X}_m = [(A - B_m - AB_m)/(A + 1)],$$

and $$\hat{P}_p(x_m) = B_m(A + 1) \qquad \ldots(12)$$

According to these equilibria, the entire areal structure of growth potentials can be divided into three segments or phases of agricultural growth potential availability* # (Fig. 12.1). The concerned areas of these phases may be nomenclatured as (a) the areas of *Immediate Growth Potentials* (IGPs) that include very high availability of yield potentials due to higher magnitudes and intensities of marginal products and production elasticity. Marginal product to intensity is far higher than production elasticity. Therefore, rate and intensity of land rent and marginal rent are higher. These areas of higher magnitudes of production potentials must immediately be utilised by increasing input intensification. (b) The areas of second phase of production potential availability which may be named as *Future Growth Potentials* (FGPs). These areas fall between the range of $\hat{x}_m$ and $\hat{X}_m$ levels of input intensities. The rent conditions are not much favourable although marginal product to intensity and production elasticity vary within their medium ranges. (c) The areas of the third phase of growth potential availability is called *Low Growth Potential* areas (LGPs). They have stagnation in the rate and intensities of the components of growth potentials with the very low forces of potential generation. Rent

---

* The following are the logical conditions of the growth potential components under various phases of potential utilisation as

(i) *IGPs* where $M_p(x_m) > P_e(x_m)$; $P_p(x_m) > \hat{P}_p(x_m)$; $0 < X_m < \hat{X}_m$.

(ii) *FGPs* where $M_p(X_m) > P_e(x_m)$; $\hat{P}_p(x_m) > \hat{P}_p(X_m) > \bar{P}_p(X_m)$; $\hat{X}_m < X_m < \bar{X}_m$

(iii) *LGPs* where $M_p(x_m) < P_e(x_m)$; $P_p(x_m) < \bar{P}_p(X_m < X_x$.

\# Note that the fourth phase of agricultural growth potential availability which can be named as the areas of Very Low Growth Potentials (VLGPs) can also be distingushed by considering the reverse condition of equation (11) as $P_e(x_m) - M_p(x_m) = P_p(x_m)$. But this phase has insignificant magnitudes of potential components and is not analysed here (see Fig. 1).

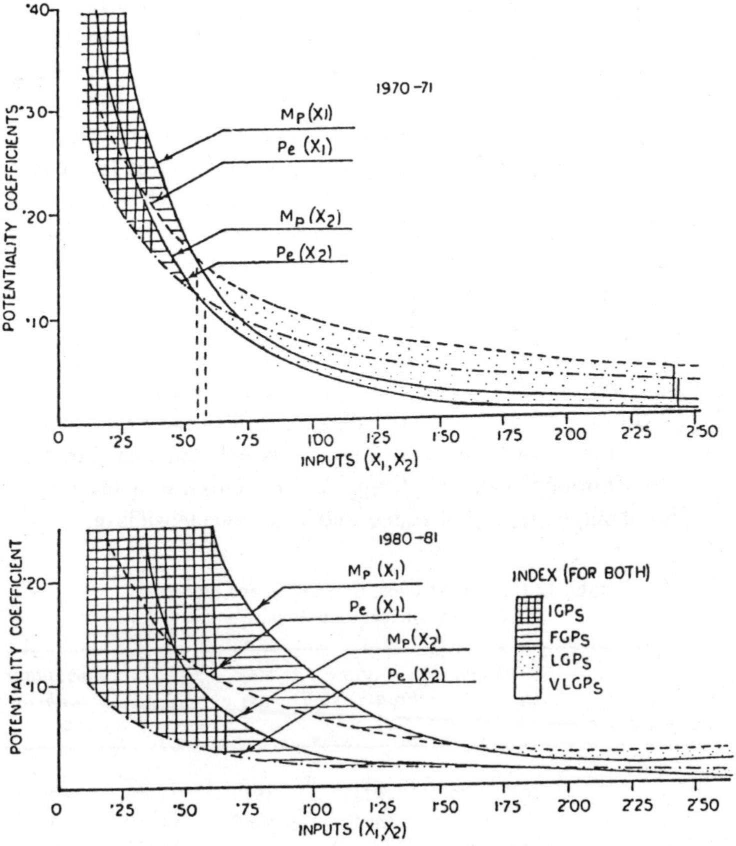

Fig. 12.1 : Phases of Agricultural Growth Potential

conditions are not applicable in these areas on account of their negative observations.

The Test Procedure

A micro-areal unit of about 1000 sq.km., Amroha tehsil of Moradabad district which lies in the middle part of fertile Ganga-Ramganga *doab,* has been chosen. Revenue *mauzas* (i.e., villages as the smallest areal units) that are 602 in number in the tehsil, have been considered for analysing regional dimensions of growth potentials.

For testing theoretical model, two important input variables: *Agricultural technology* (X_1) as an indicator of the availability of non-land capital per unit of land and *Labour input* (X_2), have been considered. Natural input is not included due to homogeneous conditions of physical phenomena of the study area. Input variable of agricultural technology incorporates intensities of irrigated area, use of chemical fertilizers, High Yield Varieties and number of tractors per unit of agricultural land, while labour input includes agricultural labour force (cultivators plus agricultural labourers per unit arable land) for each of areal unit. On the other hand, *yield index*— aggregate agricultural production per unit of agricultural land (Y)— has been calculated by summing up the yields of principal crops on the basis of their crop-equivalents (Singh and Chauhan, 1977) for 1970-71 and 1980-81.

Table 12.1 which depicts over all areal tendencies and decadal changes of agricultural phenomena highlights that increasing intensity of agricultural production from 0.523 to 1.389 (165.67%) evolves regional uniformity with the reduction of 4.94 per cent areal variations of its distributional patterns during 1970s. This rapid increase in agricultural output per unit of arable land in Amroha tehsil is on account

Table 12.1: Areal Variations, Correlations and Tendencies of Change in Input and Output Variables

	Mean	*Average Productivity* (Y/X_m)	*S.D.* (σ)	*C.V. (%)*	*Correlation with Y*
(A) 1970-71					
X_1	.6446	.8113	.4549	70.571	.7242
X_2	1.0636	.4917	.5335	50.169	.3624
Y	.5230	—	.1073	20.523	1.0000
(B) 1980-81					
X_1	.6720	2.0678	.2975	48.201	.6990
X_2	1.2967	1.0716	1.0179	78.499	.1535
Y	1.3896	—	.2166	15.584	1.000
(C) Decadal Change (in %)					
X_1	+ 4.251	+ 154.875	—	– 22.370	—
X_2	+ 21.916	+ 117.938	—	+ 28.330	—
Y	+ 165.698	—	—	– 4.939	—

Note: *C.V.* = Coefficient of areal Variability, i.e., relative index calculated as : C.V.(%) = [(σ/mean). = 100].

Source: Empirical raw data for input as well as output variables have been compiled from various sources such as Land Revenue Collection office of Tehsildar, Tehsil Amroha and labour data from the official of the Census Operation UP, Lucknow.

of (a) unification in crop-patterns; sugarcane, a commercial crop, has become dominated crop throughout the area during successive decade, and (b) changes in the attributes of agricultural technology from irrigation intensification to the wider application of High Yielding Varieties particularly of sugarcane and wheat crops and tractorisation (bio-engineering technology) during Green Revolution period (Singh, 1985). But there seems over all insignificant increase (4.25%) in intensification of non-land capital. Intensity of labour input and its areal variations are constantly increasing by 21.92 per cent and 28.33 per cent respectively during the decade. Its relationship with the index of production is weak in early 1970s and becomes insignificant during this decade.

Estimation of Results and Interpretation of Regional Variations

Employing best-fitted approach of regression method in 'two-factor model' of the basic form (Eqn.1), the potentiality parameters (A and B_m) and the component-values are computerised for 1970-71 and 1980-81. The real numerical values of these parameters are as :

For 1970-71 :

$$Y(x_{1,2}) = [.7245\,(1.0 + .1174X_1^{-1} + .0903X_2^{-1})^{-1}] \quad ...(13)$$

where $\overline{X}_1 = .6071$, $\widehat{X}_1 = .3027$, $\overline{X}_2 = .6342$, and $\widehat{X}_2 = .3298$,

For 1980-81 :

$$Y(x_{1,2}) = [1.6830\,(1.0 + .0772X_1^{-1} + .0250X_2^{-1})^{-1}] \quad ...(14)$$

where $\overline{X}_1 = 1.6058$, $\widehat{X}_1 = .5501$, $\overline{X}_2 = 1.6580$, and $\widehat{X}_2 = .6023$.

These numerical expressions generalise the systematic and regional behaviour of potential phenomena of the tehsil in the following manner.

Increasing intensification of labour input and changing attributes of the input index of agricultural technology during successive decade lead two simultaneous changes in the structure of agricultural growth potentials of Amroha area (a) A gradual decadal increase of 132.30 per cent (from .7245 to 1.6830) in the level of the highest possible yield A, which is the result of acceleration of potential generation processes, wider application of High Yielding Varieties particularly in sugarcane and wheat crops. (b) Weak absorption capacity of growth potentials which can really be observed by decreasing rate of yield-potentials per productivity unit, B_m, Absorption rate of non-land capital potentiality [i.e. production potentials to agricultural technology, $P_p(x_1)$] diminishes 34.24 per cent (from .1174 to .0772) with an insignificant increase (4.25%) in intensity of technology. While the absorption rate of labour-potentiality [production potentials to labour input, $P_p(x_2)$] decreases 72.31 per cent (.0903 to .0250). It counts fast decay rather than absorption rate of capital-potentiality. Note that the higher labour intensification in agriculture, although increasing its productivity, by 118.0 per cent (from .492 to 1.07), i.e. 37 per cent slower than the rate of capital productivity during 1970s (Table 12.1), may stagnate production conditions by creating disguised unemployment problems in future conditions of the area.

On account of strong potential generation forces working in the area and weak absorption rate of growth potentials, there is an over all increasing tendency of the magnitude and intensity of yield potentials. The input levels and maximum and optimal utilisation of production potentials, $\bar{X}_m$ and $\widehat{X}_m$, are also shifting outwards from origin with widening the componential gaps (Table 12.2, Fig. 12.1). Consequently, the classification limits of regional patterns expand too much on areal scale (i.e., the case of areal diversity) so that over all magnitudes of yield potentials must be diluted over area.* But, in present case, the percentage of total magnitude of production potentials particularly in the areas of IGPs w.r.t. agricultural technology is generated only 2.04 per cent, that is comparatively lower than the percentage of areal expansion, 5.80 per cent during the period of successive decade (Table 12.3). Therefore, ratio of change in growth potentials in these areas of IGPs is very low (.351), i.e., far below unit, and the emerging regional patterns of IGPs are shifting from the North-Central part of Amroha tehsil (1970-71) to the Ramganga low lands and the Ban-Karula *doab* (1980-81).

Similarly, the changing patterns of labour-potentiality depict that the negligible area of IPGs of early 1970s have been expanded up to 15.81 per cent particularly in the surrounding areas of main townships and larger villages where agricultural labour can be absorbed in non-

---

* Indeed, when production processes are accelerated by utilising the growth potentials, intensity of yield-potentials tends subsequently down towards saturation point. But, in present case, on account of rapidity of the rate of marginal rent and enhancement of the magnitude of the highest possible yield *A* during 1970s, there seems regional disequilibria with an increase in the areas of IGPs in Amroha tehsil.

Table 12.2 : Significant Growth Rates and Intensity Levels of Agricultural Potentiality in Amroha Tehsil

Rates of Growth Potentials	*Regional Inequalities and Partial Potentiality Levels*							
	$A_p(X_1)$	$M_p(X_1)$	$P_e(X_1)$	$P_p(X_1)$	$A_p(X_2)$	$M_p(X_2)$	$P_e(X_2)$	$P_p(X_2)$
1970-71								
1. High	1.72450	.48190	.27944	.20245	1.72450	.37066	.21494	.15572
2. Equilibrium	1.00000	.16204	.16204	.11740	1.00000	.12464	.12464	.09030
3. Low	.27550	.01230	.04464	.03234	.27550	.00946	.03434	.02488
1981-81								
1. High	2.6830	.33020	.123078	.20713	2.68300	.10693	.03985	.06708
2. Equilibrium	1.00000	.04587	.04587	.07720	1.00000	.01485	.01485	.02500
3. Low	—	.02139	—	—	—	.00693	—	—

Notes : 1. Four regional classes of Growth Potentials are as the areas of (i) IGPs (very high levels of growth rates); (ii) FGPs (optimum-high growth rates between high and equilibrium levels); (iii) LGPs (optimum-low growth rates between equilibrium and low levels); and (iv) VLGPs (below low levels of growth and intensity).

2. The growth levels : equilibrium, high and low, have been identified by following logical aspects of the model as described in text.

agricultural activities in near future. In such areas of IPGs, the rate of increase of magnitude of yield-potentials is higher (38.48%) than the rate of areal expansion (15.81%) during the decade and, therefore, ratio of change of the labour-potentials is far higher (2.43) than unity (Table 12.3). Further more, in the areas of FGPs to agricultural technology that are situated in the south-central parts of the tehsil (Fig. 12.2), the temporal increase in the magnitude of yield-potentials (14.89%) and its areal expansion (14.25%) proceed simultaneously at similar rate. Therefore, these areas of FGPs maintains constantly the intensity of Capital-potentiality during the successive decade where ratio of the temporal change is nearly unit (Table 12.3).

Conclusion

In this paper a normative agricultural production function by which the parameters of production potentials can easily be identified has been presented. This function, which is fundamentally based on reciprocity law of established agricultural input-output relationship that proves better solution than the others, can be utilised for preparing regional-investment-strategy for area development problems of agricultural conditions. It states logically that agricultural yield potentials, marginal product to intensity and production elasticity diminish to follow concavity, while agricultural production efficiency increases asymptotically with decreasing rate. During 1970s, increasing level of the highest possible yield index from .7245 (1970-71) to 1.6830 (1980-81) and shifting outwards the ranges of the input levels of maximum and optimal utilisation of production potentials ($\bar{X}_m$ and $\hat{X}_m$) — the maximum input level of capital-potentiality ($\bar{X}_1$) from .6071 to 1.6058, labour-potentiality ($\bar{X}_2$) from .6342 to 1.6580 and the optimum input level of capital-potentiality ($\hat{X}_1$) from .3027 to .5501, and labour–potentiality ($\hat{X}_2$) from .3298 and .6023 (for detail, see equations 13 to 14) $\hat{X}_2$ enhance intensity and magnitude of production potentials with creating regional disequilibria in its patterns particularly in the areas of IPGs of the low lands of main rivers in the Amroha area. These areas require immediate need of the application of agricultural technology for proper utilisation of local yield potentials with the best areal conditions of agricultural activities.

Table 12.3: Decadal Changes in Total Magnitude* of Production Potentials (P_p)

Areal Classes	*1970-71*			*1980-81*			*Changes (in %)***		
	Input Ranges	*Total Area (%)*	*P_p (in %)*	*Input Ranges*	*Total Area (%)*	*P_p (in %)*	*Area*	*P_p*	*Growth Potential Ratio of Changes ($\Delta P_p / \Delta$ Area)*
(A) Potentiality Magnitudes w.r.t. Agricultural Technology (X_1)									
1. IGPs	.050 – .303	35.47	44.81	.050 – .551	41.27	46.85	+5.80	+2.04	.3511
2. FGPs	.303 – .607	42.15	31.30	.551 – 1.606	57.01	45.55	+14.86	+14.25	.9590
3. LGPs	.607 – 2.514	14.14	23.14	1.606 – 3.000	1.72	7.60	– 12.42	– 15.54	– 1.2512
4. VLGPs	2.514 – 3.500	8.24	.75	–	–	–	–	–	–
(B) Potentiality Magnitudes w.r.t. Labour Input (X_2)									
1. IGPs	.050 – .330	.74	13.99	.050 – .602	16.55	52.39	+15.81	+38.40	2.4288
2. FGPs	.330 – .634	4.56	27.27	.602 – 1.658	51.10	30.18	+46.54	+2.91	.0625
3. LGPs	.634 – 2.539	25.47	37.55	1.658 – 3.000	32.35	17.43	+6.88	– 20.12	– 2.9244
4. VLGPs	2.539 – 3.500	69.23	21.18	–	–	–	–	–	–

Note: Percentages of decadal increase (+)/decrease (–) are simply differences occurred between the percentage figures of area as well as production potentials of 1970-71 and 1980-81.

* Real values of total magnitudes of $P_p(X_m)$ are calculated by integrating it as Total magnitude of

$$P_p(X_m) = \int_0^x m[AB_m (B_m + X_m)^{-1} \int d X_m = AB_m [\log(B_m + X_m)].$$

** It is calculated dividing changing % of growth potentials (ΔP_p) by changing areas percentages (Δ Area) of various input ranges.

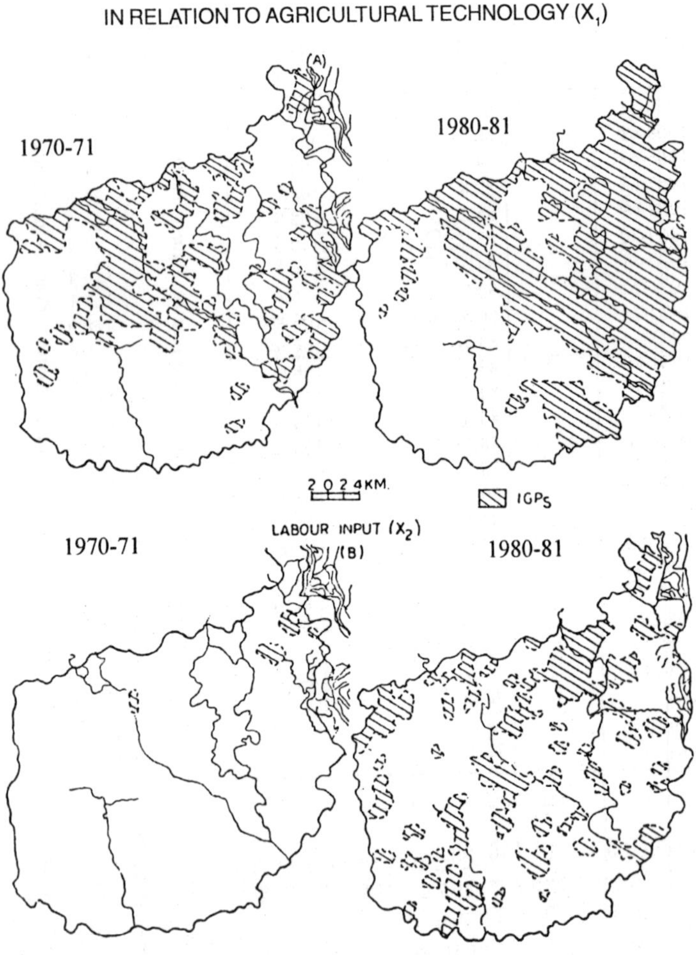

Fig. 12.2 : Areas of Very High Agricultural Growth Potentials

Indeed, growth potential phenomena also plays an important role in the spatial structure of agricultural intensification. It can be specified by employing the form of yield potentials (Eqn. 5) in the locational aspects of rent conditions by varying pricing policies of marketable production and/or its factors.

References

Bhat, L.S. and A.T.A. Learmonth (1968), 'Recent Contribution to the Economic Geography of India: Some Current pre-occupations', *Economic Geography*. Vol.44, No. 3, p. 196.

Bhatia, S.S. (1967), 'A New Measurement of Agricultural Efficiency in Uttar Pradesh, India', *Economic Geography*, Vol.43, No.3, pp. 244-60.

Buringh, P., Van Heemst, H.D.J. and Staring, G.J. (1975), *Computation of the Absolute Maximum Food Production of the World,* Department of Tropical Soil Science, Agricultural University, Wageningen, The Netherlands.

Dunn, Jr. E.S. (1954), *The Location of Agricultural Production*, University of Florida Press, Gainesvilla, p. 6.

Hanumantha Rao, C.H. (1968), 'Production Functions for Hyderabad Farms', in A.K. Khusro (ed.) *Reading in Agricultural Development*, Allied Publishers, India, pp. 160-72.

Hayami, Y. and Ruttan, V.W. (1971), *Agricultural Development: An International Perspective*, The Johns Hopkins University Press, Baltimore.

Heady, E.O. and Dillon, John L. (1961), *Agricultural Production Functions*, Kalyani Publishers, Ludhiana.

Heady, E.O. (1964), *Economics of Agricultural Production*, Prentice-Hall of India Pvt. Ltd., New Delhi.

Newman, M., Ouedraogo I, and Norman D. (1980), 'Farm-Level Studies in the Semi-Arid Tropics of West Africa, in *Proceedings of International Workshop on Socio-economic Constraints to Development of Semi-Arid Tropical Agriculture,* published by International Crops Research Institute for the Semi-Arid Tropics, Patancheru P.O., Andhra Pradesh, India, pp.241-63.

Singh, Jasbir (1974-75), *An Agricultural Atlas of India: A Geographical Analysis,* Vishal Publications, Kurukshetra, p. 251.

Singh, Surendra (1980), 'Reciprocity Model, Agricultural Development and Regional Planning', *Transactions,* Institute of Indian Geographers, Vol.2, No.2, pp.37-47.

Singh, Surendra (1985), *Integrated Area Planning and Development.* Technical Report of Research Project, submitted to University Grants Commission, New Delhi, pp.70-98.

Singh, Surendra and Chauhan V.S. (1977), 'Measurement of Agricultural Productivity—A Case Study of U.P., India', *Geographical Review of India*, Vol.39, No.3, pp. 222-31.

Spillman, W.J. (1923), 'Application of the Law of Diminishing Returns to Same Fertilizer and Feed Data', *Journal of Farm Economics*, Vol.5, pp.36-52.

Spillman, W.J. and Lang, E. (1924), *The Law of Diminishing Returns*, World Book Co., New York.

Spillman, W.J. (1933), 'Exponential Yield Curves in Fertilizer Experiments', U.S.D.A., *Technical Bulletin* 348, Washington.

Solow, R.M. (1957), Technical Change and the Aggregate Production Function', *Review of Economics and Statistics,* Vol. 39, No. 3, pp. 312-20.

Solow, R.M. (1963), *Capital Theory and the Rate of Return*, Amsterdom, North Holland.

Visser, S. (1980), 'Technological Change and the Spatial Structure of Agriculture', *Economic Geography*, Vol. 56, No. 4, pp. 311-319.

Visser, S. (1982), 'On Agricultural Location Theory', *Geographical Analysis*, Vol.14, No.2, pp. 167-176.

Wenzel, G. (1987), 'Can Biotechnology be of Help to Plant Protection in Tropical and Sub-tropical Countries', *Plant Research and Development* (Institute for Scientific Co-operation, Tubingen, F.R.G.), Vol. 26, pp. 79-86.

13

PULSES PRODUCTION IN U.P. SINCE INDEPENDENCE

Crisis, Constraints and Cure

YASIR SAYEED HANAFI

Introduction

Pulses are an important component of foodgrain crops. Because of their high nutritive value (protein content ranges between 17 to 27 per cent), they form an important segment of balanced diet. They have inbuilt mechanism to fix nitrogen in their root nodules, adaptability to a wide range of agro-ecological and cropping systems. India grow such a variety of pulse crops which none of the countries in the world grows. Over a dozen pulse crops are grown under different agro-ecological regions. However their average productivity is very low as compared to other countries. Pulses are of immense value not only for human nutrition but also for agriculture and dairy farming. Straws and hays of cereals used as cattle feed are deficient in lysine whereas legume hay is rich in amino acid and makes a valuable addition to cattle feed (Singh, R., 1998). The nitrogen depleted from the soil by cereal cultivation can be replanished by adjusting it with pulse cultivation can be grown even in tough agro-climatic conditions.

The Problem

Before Independence the landuse pattern was more balanced in terms of the area under foodgrains and commercial crops, i.e. 70 per cent in foodgrains and 30 per cent under commercial crops. Among foodgrain crops, pulses' share was also desirable in terms of area and production, therefore the availability of pulses was nearly sufficient enough at that time. On the basis of the standard requirement but after independence, it was noticed that major wheat growing area was transferred to Pakistan and on the whole 1/5 or 20 per cent of total population and 1/4 or 25 per cent of the total cultivated area of wheat went to Pakistan, hence the scarcity of foodgrains was realized in India. As a result, the emphasis was given more on wheat through means of irrigation and various other inputs. Irrigation started increasing all over India in most of the pulses belts. Because of increased irrigation instead of growing pulses, wheat became the top priority, even when it was considered as a commercial crop. As a result, the wheat productivity increased about three times to pulses productivity in irrigated regions, because the better performance of wheat it started encroaching the major areas of pulses and only the marginal areas left under pulses where productivity was very low.

It is evident from the scenario of India that the area and production of pulses almost stagnant during last four decades but the population increased with unprecedented growth rate which causes severe decline in availability from 70.95 grams/day to 36.98 grams/day in the year 1955 and 1995 respectively. The main reason for the decline in per capita availability of the pulses is attributed to the sluggishness in the growth of area, production and yield of these crops (Bhushan and Sobti, 1992). The share of the pulses in total foodgrain production which was 16.55 per cent during 1950-51 came down to 7.84 per cent in 1994-95 (S. Lal and B. Prakash, 1996). While analysing the other reasons of low productivity of pulses in various parts of the country, it is observed that non-availability of high yielding, disease resistant varieties (as in case of wheat and rice), cultivation on marginal and sub-marginal lands under moisture deficit and low fertility and poor pest management are the major constraints in realizing optimum yield potential.

Besides, there is no effective mechanism for facilitating the transfer of latest research findings and technologies developed by research bodies and institutes. Nigam (1993), stated subsidiary status, socially backward crop, poverty, traditional, social status, lack of experience and motivation also contributed to low production of pulses in the country. Satya Priya (1989), stated that the major constraints in the increasing pulse production appears to be the absence of any significant technological break through evolving high yielding and more responsive pulse breeds. Kanwar (1991), noted that the list of improved varieties and technologies goes on increasing but their adoption and diffusion rate is low.

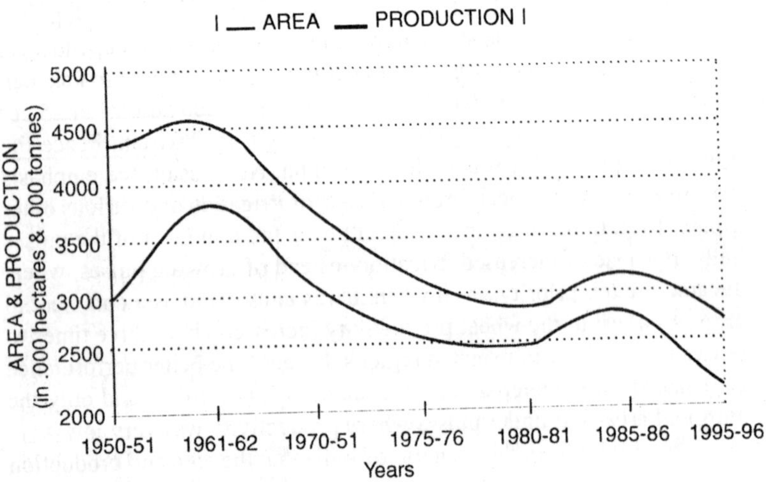

Fig. 13.1 : Trend of Area and Production of Pulses Since Independence

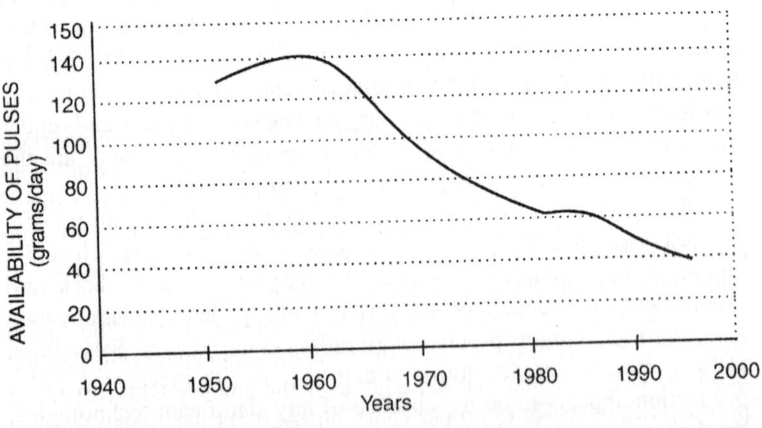

Fig. 13.2 : Declining Trend of Pulses' Availability Since Independence

OBJECTIVES

The main objectives of the study are:

- to analyse the pulses crisis of Uttar Pradesh at district level in terms of availability in grams/head/day during 1985-86 and 1995-96.
- to find out the decadal decline of availability of pulses in Uttar Pradesh as a whole.
- to analyse the regional variation in availability of pulses.
- to discuss the changing pattern of availability of pulses.
- to find out the factors of pulses crisis and remedial measures for its development.

Data Base and Methodology

The secondary sources of data are being used in this analysis, issued from the Agricultural Statistics and Crop Insurance, Krishi Bhawan, Lucknow, Ministry of Economics and Statistics Division, State Planning Institute, Lucknow and Ministry of Economics and Statistics, New Delhi.

The method used to find out the availability of pulses in grams/head/day is to divide the total production of pulses in grams by total population and 365 (number of days in a year) in each district. The population in the given study is calculated on the basis of the growth rate of population in each district during 1981 and 1991. The productivity and availability of all the districts divide into five categories and plotted on map to show the regional variations and to show the decadal decline of availability, curve is plotted on the X-axis and Y-axis.

Productivity Variation and Regional Distribution of Pulses Availability

It is evident from the earlier discussion that the area under pulses remain stagnant and the better pulses area was encroached by wheat. Therefore, the production either remain stagnant or decline. The percentage share of area under pulses in the state as a whole declined from 14.66 per cent in 1985-86 to 13.74 per cent in 1995-96, and production share came down to 5.58 per cent from 9.10 per cent in the same span of time.

It is estimated from the study of 1985-86 and 1995-96, that the over all productivity of pulses declined from 893 kg/hect. to 781 kg/hect.

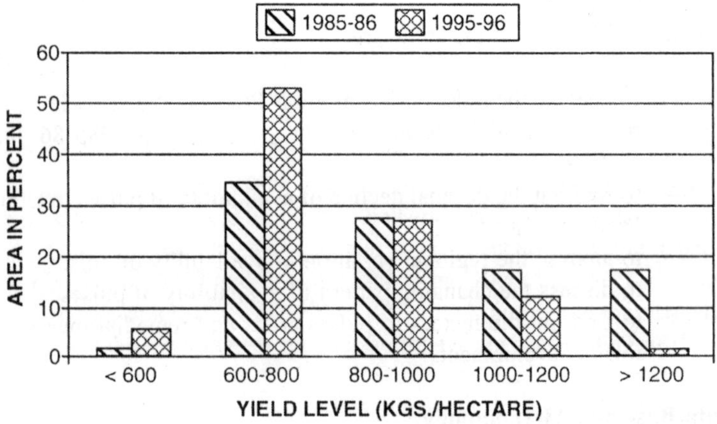

Fig. 13.3 : Changing Pattern of Area under Pulses

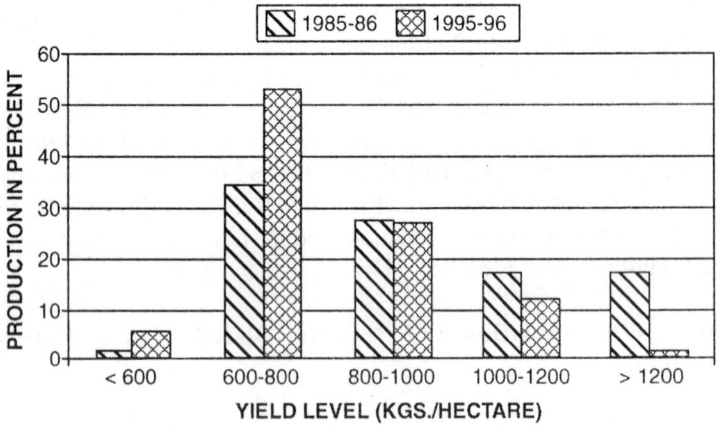

Fig. 13.4 : Changing Pattern of Production under Pulse

During 1985-86, it ranges between 511 kg/hect. to 1404 kg/hect. in the districts of Uttarkashi and Kanpur (R) respectively while in 1995-96, it varies from 466 kg./hect. to 1210 kg./hect. in the districts of Haridwar and Agra respectively. On the other hand, in case of cereals it touches upto 3000 kg/hect. in some of the districts.

Table 13.1 : Changing Pattern of Area and Production in Different Yield Levels

	1985-86				1995-96			
Yield Level kg/hectare	*Area (Hectares)*	*Area (%)*	*Prod. (Tonnes)*	*Prod. (%)*	*Area (Hectares)*	*Area (%)*	*Area (Tonnes)*	*Area (%)*
>1200	389162	12.27	505713	17.86	23883	0.86	28902	1.33
1000-1200	461288	14.55	504918	17.83	251874	9.08	274897	12.69
800-1000	875341	27.60	789362	27.88	705635	25.43	596734	27.55
600-800	1372408	43.28	989002	34.93	1592825	57.41	1153795	53.26
<600	72889	2.30	40633	1.44	200178	7.22	111991	5.17
Total	3171088	100.00	2831428	100.00	2774395	100.00	2166319	100.00

Yield level (>1200 kg/hect.) :

1985-86 Kanpur (R), Agra, Kanpur (U), Etawah, Ghaziabad and Allahabad.

1995-96 Agra

Yield level (1000-1200 kg/hect.):

1985-86 Ghazipur, Fatehpur, Budaun, Etah, Farrukhabad, Mainpuri, Bulandshahr, Jaunpur and Barelly.

1995-96 Firozabad, Etah, Mainpuri, Kanpur (R) and Allahabd.

Yield level (800-1000 kg/hect.):

1985-86 Meerut, Jalaun, Varanasi, Sultanpur, Mirzapur, Moradabad, Balia, Faizabad, Raibarelly, Unnao, Aligarh, Pratapgarh, Rampur, Azamgarh and Mathura.

1995-96 Farrukhabad, Mirzapur, Nainital, Etawah, Rampur, Aligarh, Kanpur (U), Muzaffarnagar, Mathura, Budaun, Siddhartnagar, Jalaun, Basti, Jhansi, Pilibhit and Bijnor.

Yield level (600-800 kg/hect.) :

1985-86 Deoria, Barabanki, Shahjahanpur, Nainital, Basti, Gonda, Bijnor, Hamirpur, Jhansi, Dehra Dun, Banda, Hardoi, Gorakhpur, Lucknow, Lalitpur, Muzaffarnagar, Sitapur, Tehri Garhwal, Saharanpur, Bahraich and Pithoragarh.

1995-96 Pratapgarh, Fatehpur, Barelly, Lalitpur, Ghaziabad, Meerut, Hamirpur, Gonda, Deoria, Banda, Faizabad, Mau, Moradabad, Varanasi, Gorakhpur, Saharanpur, Azamgarh, Sonbhadra, Jaunpur, Tehri Garhwal, Sultanpur, Barabanki, Unnao, Khiri, Pithoragarh, Raibarelly, Bahraich, Dehradun, Maharajganj, Almora, Hardoi and Shahjahanpur.

Yield level (<600 kg/hect.):

1985-86 Pilibhit, Chamoli, Garhwal, Almora, Khiri and Uttarkashi.

1995-96 Lucknow, Bulandshahr, Sitapur, Uttarkashi, Ghazipur, Chamoli, Garhwal, Balia and Haridwar.

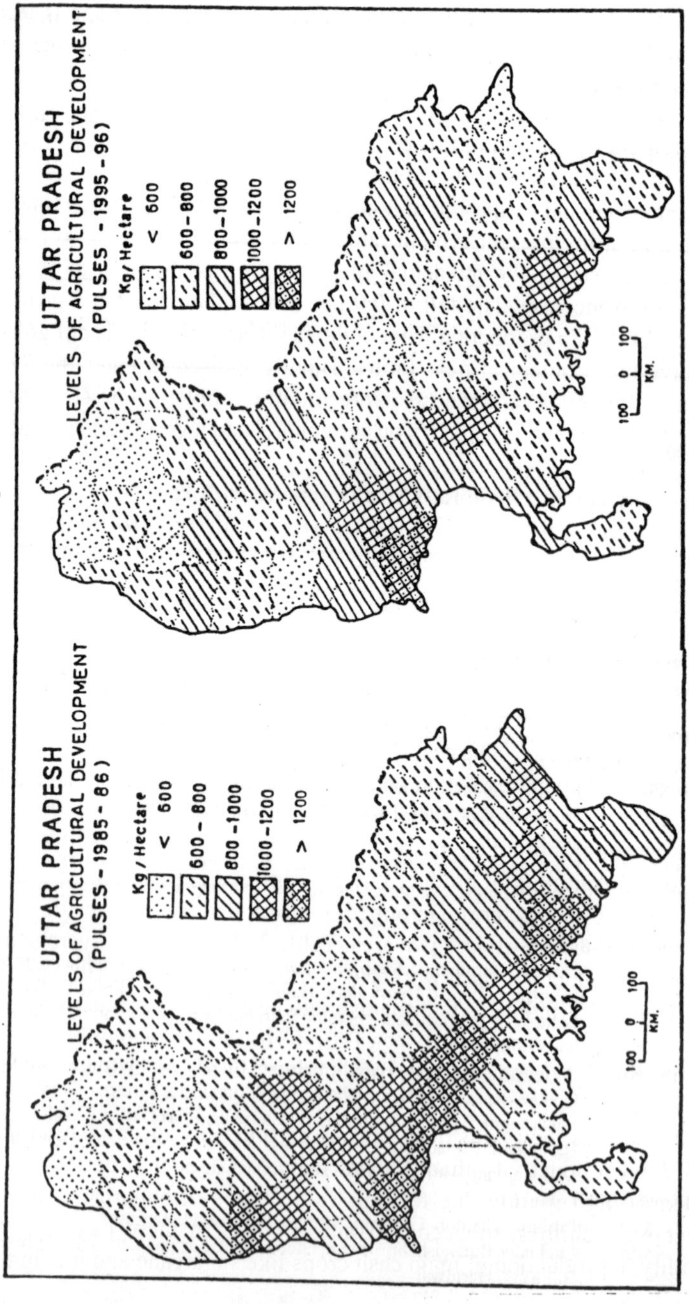

Fig. 13.5: Levels of Agricultural Development in Uttar Pradesh

It is revealed from Table 13.1, that the situation of productivity of pulses in the U.P. as a whole is not satisfactory. There were only 6 districts, namely Kanpur (R), Agra, Kanpur (U), Etawah, Ghaziabad and Allahabad, where the productivity was above 1200 kg/hect. in 1985-86 and 1995-96 only Agra remain in this category. The productivity ranges between 1000-1200 kg per hectare was noted in 9 districts, namely Ghazipur, Fatehpur, Budaun, Farrukhabad, Mainpuri, Bulandshahr, Jaunpur and Barelly in 1985-86 while in 1995-96 only 5 districts, namely Firozabad, Etah, Mainpuri, Kanpur (R) and Allahabad fall in this category. A large number of districts (36) came under the categories ranges between 600-1000 kg/hect. in 1985-86 and spread on most of U.P. in 1995-96 as 48 districts fall in this category. The earlier trend is continued in the lowest category, i.e. less than 600 kg/hect. and it is noted that there were only 6 districts, namely Pilibhit, Chamoli, Garhwal, Almora, Khiri and Uttarkashi fall in this category during 1985-86 while in 1995-96, Lucknow, Sitapur, Bulandshahr, Uttarkashi, Ghazipur, Chamoli, Garhwal, Balia and Haridwar fall in the productivity level below 600 kg/hectare.

It is estimated that 2.3 per cent area of total pulses was under very low category of yield and contributing only 1.44 per cent of total production during 1985-86, while in 1995-96, the total areal spread in this category increased to 7.22 per cent which contributed 5.17 per cent in total production. The next category of low productivity ranging between 600-800 kg/hectare, occupied the largest area, i.e. 43 per cent and contributing only 35 per cent in total production during 1985-86, and after a decade in 1995-96, this category occupied 57 per cent of the area and 53 per cent of the production of total pulses. If we analyse the situation of the above two categories of productivity, i.e. below 800 kg/hectare, in terms of area, it is revealed that there is a significant increase from 45 per cent to about 65 per cent during a time span of 1985-86 and 1995-96. The higher spread of lower productivity is a matter of great concern because it is negative indicator in the development of pulses. The medium productivity level between 800-1000 kg/ha. does't show any big change in areal spread and production as well, the area becomes about 25.5 per cent from 27.5 per cent production share remain fluctuating around 27.5 per cent in the same time span. In the high productivity level between 800-1000 kg/ha shows decline both in area and production from 14.55 per cent to 9 per cent and from 17.83 per cent to 12.69 per cent respectively. The very high productivity level or more than 1200 kg/ha. shows a severe decline both in area and production as well, area becomes only 0.86 per cent from 12.27 per cent while production declined from 17.92 per cent to only 1.33 per cent, in the same period. The lower spread of high productivity area is again a matter of great concern which is a negative indicator for agricultural development.

It is obvious that the situation of the area and production is not satisfactory at any productivity level and it is revealed that the area under lower productivity level is increasing while decreasing in higher productivity level and both are the negative factors for the development of any crop. So the problem needs special attention from planners and if such a trend continues in the coming decade, the situation would be very critical and must be undertaken for development on priority basis.

The Changing Pattern of Pulses' Availability

The situation of pulses' availability in U.P. as a whole, shows a declining trend from about 131 grams/head/day in 1950-51 to about 38 grams/head/day in 1995-96. It is evident from Table 13.2, the highest availability of pulses is noted in Jalaun (about 487 gms/day) and lowest availability in the district of Chamoli (1.69 gms/day) during 1985-86, while in 1995-96, the highest availability is noted in Hamirpur (about 387 gms/day) and lowest in Chamoli again (1.81 gms/day). If we analyse the percentage of population with the availability, it is found that during 1985-86, only 22.86 per cent of population in U.P. have got the pulses according to standard requirement, i.e. 80 gms/day (ICMR) and rest of the population was malnourished in terms of pulses. The districts in which the availability of pulses is more than the standard requirements were Jalaun, Hamirpur, Jhansi, Banda, Lalitpur, Fatehpur, Etawah, Kanpur (U), Kanpur (R), Etah, Budaun, Allahabad, Aligarh and Agra. But the situation becomes worst during 1995-96, as only 7.64 per cent population of U.P. could remain in the level of more than 80 gms/day of availability of pulses and more than 92 per cent of population becomes malnourished. The number of districts self-sufficient in pulses availability becomes only seven, namely Hamirpur, Jalaun, Lalitpur, Jhansi, Banda, Kanpur (R) and Fatehpur. The districts achieving required level of pulses are mostly the Bundelkhand region of U.P. where pulses' share is quite high in total foodgrains. The declining trend in availability is more serious in next category, ranges between 60-80 gms/day, that out of 9 districts only one district namely, Mirzapur remain in this category. On the basis of percentage share of population, it is noted that

16.51 per cent of population came under this category during 1985-86 and its share came down to only 1.23 per cent during 1995-96. The next category of availability ranges between 40-60 gms/day was recorded in ten districts mostly belongs to central U.P., namely Hardoi, Barabanki, Unnao, Pratapgarh, Farrukhabad, Mathura, Barelly, Sitapur, Faizabad

Table 13.2 : Changing Pattern of Per Cent Population in Different Availability

	1985-86		1995-96	
Availability (Grams/Head/Day)	*Population (Numbers)*	*Population (%)*	*Population (Numbers)*	*Population (%)*
>80	28047870	22.86	11769220	7.64
60-80	20257430	16.51	1894266	1.23
40-60	22910908	18.67	18671964	12.11
20-40	28442244	23.78	58448794	37.92
<20	23048280	18.78	63353561	41.10
Total	122707732	100.00	154137805	100.00

Availability (>80 gms/head/day) :

1985-86 Jalaun, Hamirpur, Jhansi, Banda, Lalitpur, Fatehpur, Etawah, Kanpur (U), Kanpur (R), Etah, Budaun, Allahanad, Aligarh and Agra.

1995-96 Hamirpur, Jalaun, Lalitpur, Jhansi, Banda, Kanpur (R) and Fatehpur.

Availability (60-80 gms/head/day) :

1985-86 Mirzapur, Sultanpur, Bahraich, Ghazipur, Goda, Shahjahanpur, Raebarelly, Balia and Mainpuri.

1995-96 Mirzapur.

Availability (40-60 gms/head/day) :

1985-86 Hardoi, Barabanki, Unnao, Pratapgarh, Farrukhabad, Mathura, Barelly, Sitapur, Faizabad and Jaunpur.

1995-96 Bahraich, Etawah, Etah, Gonda, Sonbhadra and Allahabad.

Availability (20-40 gms/head/day) :

1985-86 Varanasi, Basti, Bulandshahr, Azamgarh, Khiri, Pilibhit, Gorakhpur, Pithoragarh, Ghaziabad, Rampur and Lucknow.

1995-96 Siddhartnagar, Basti, Sitapur, Shahjahanpur, Raebarelly, Pratapgarh, Hardoi, Budaun, Mainpuri, Aligarh, Agra, Firozabad, Sultanpur, Varanasi, Unnao, Balia, Ghazipur, Khiri, Farrukhabad, Barabanki, Azamgarh and Pithoragarh.

Availability (<20 gms/head/day) :

1985-86 Deoria, Nainital, Bijnor, Moradabad, Meerut, Saharanpur, Tehri Garhwal, Almora, Muzaffarnagar, Garhwal, Uttarkashi, Dehradun and Chamoli.

1995-96 Maharajganj, Barelly, Faizabad, Gorukhpur, Jaunpur, Pilibhit, Bulandshahr, Mau, Deoria, Rampur, Nainital, Garhwal, Tehrigarhwal, Lucknow, Uttarkashi, Mathura, Kanpur(U), Almora, Moradabad, Bijnor, Saharanpur, Ghaziabad, Haridwar, Meerut, Dehradun, Muzaffarnagar and Chamoli.

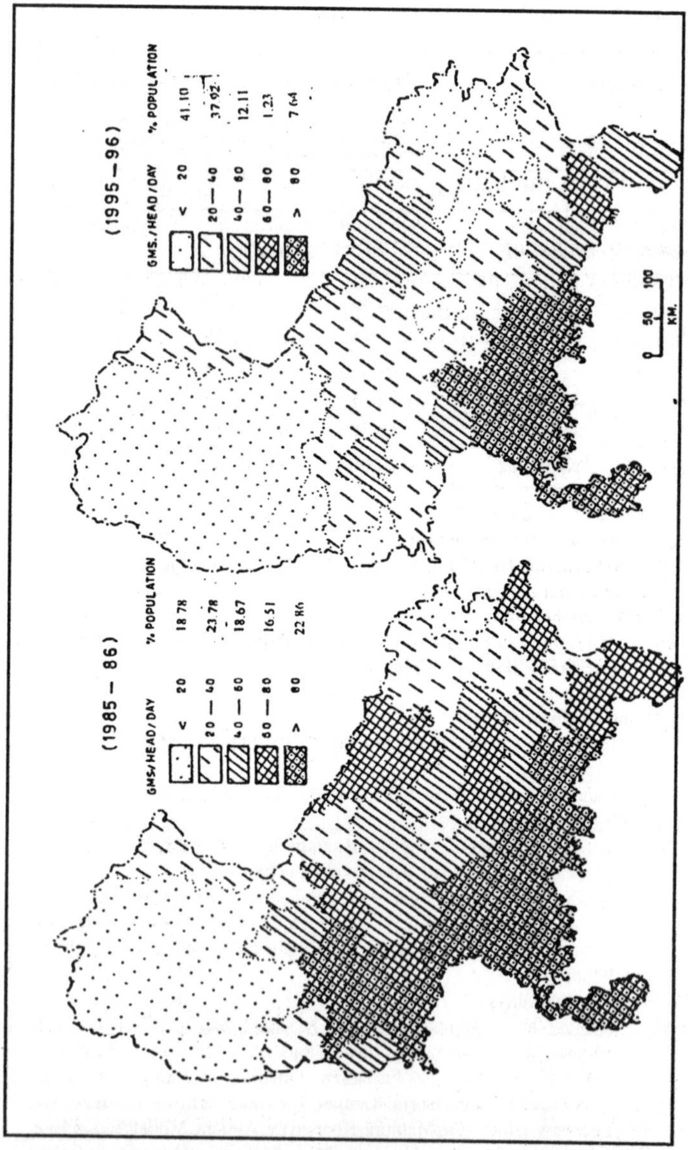

Fig. 13.6 : Changing Pattern in Availability of Pulses (1985-86 to 1995-96)

and Jaunpur while during 1995-96, Bahraich, Etawah, Etah, Gonda, Sonbhadra and Allahabad found in this category. The lowest two categories (20-40 gms/day and below 20 gms/day) of availability are the matter of great concern where the number of the districts are increasing from 24 in 1985-86 to 49 in 1995-96 which occupies almost whole of Uttar Pradesh except the districts of Bundelkhand region and a few pockets like Bahraich, Etah and Etawah. It is also revealed that about 79 per cent of the population of U.P. cannot even achieve 40 gms of pulses per day during 1995-96 while in 1985-86, the share of population in this category was only about 42 per cent.

Achievements in Pulses Development

Before Independence, pulses improvement work confined to collection and evaluation of land races in different regions. Farmers were growing local cultivars which lack genetic purity. But after Independence Indian government established various agencies like the Indian Institute of Pulses Research (IIPR), and All India Co-ordinated Pulses Improvement Project, which developed large number of high yielding varieties. Some of them are resistant or tolerance to major diseases.

Research on cropping systems enabled to identify efficient cropping systems. It helped in nitrogen economy upto 40 kg/ha. to the succeeding crop. Critical inputs for optimum production were identified. A modest application of 20 kg sulphur per hectare along with other nutrients increased the productivity of pulses (Ali, M., 1994).

Based on economic importance, major diseases of pulses in different agro-ecological zones are identified and their cost-effective cure and stable management taken up.

The major emphasis of research was laid to identify the key pests of different pulses and develop a long-term integrated pest management strategy based on low inputs.

Research programme in agriculture engineering are oriented towards post-harvest technology. Consequent to this, mini dal mill for splitting pulses seed was developed. The unit has an effective output of 100 kg of finished dal per hour.

Constraints

Rainfed situation — Still the pulses producers think that the pulses grown under rainfed situations, as a result they are grown on marginal and sub-marginal lands of rainfed areas. Importance of irrigation does not realised for pulses, as only 10 per cent area under pulses is irrigated in India as a whole. Uttar Pradesh ranked second with about 24 per cent area under irrigation next only to Haryana, where it is about 26.4 per cent. Since major area under pulses is rainfed, adoption of improved package of practices become risky and is usually avoided by farmers.

Low yield — Yield of pulses are generally low due to the existence of traditional varieties. Several high yielding, disease resistance and input responsive varieties of pulses have been developed but they could not be adopted due to lack of awareness of farmers and sometimes due to non-availability of seeds.

Low output — The studies conducted during 1990-91 in the cost of production of pulse crops and potatoes, cereals in the district of Kanpur (R), revealed that net income from the cultivation of rabi pulses was quite low in comparison to the income derived from cultivation of potatoes, mustard and wheat. Due to low net profitability in production of pulses, farmers do not show positive response for increasing pulses production and diverting their areas under cultivation of these crops.

Risk — Higher risk associated with cultivation of pulses is a major constraint in increasing the production of pulses. Yield of pulses do not remain stable and fluctuate due to high susceptibility of pulses to disease and pests and rainfed situations.

Technology — It has often been argued that no major break through in the development of technology of pulses production has been achieved, thereby resulting in stagnation in production of pulses. But it is not true, several high yielding, early maturing, stress, diseases and pests resistant varieties of pulses crop have been evolved. Surveys of farmer's field also revealed that farmers do not apply the fertilizers to the pulses. Even if they did, the level of application of fertilizers remains much below the recommended level. Similarly, it has been proved that pulses do respond to irrigation but farmers still cultivate them under rainfed conditions.

Complementarity — Pulses are generally grown under mixed cropping with cereals. As the irrigation facilities are being extended, the area under coarse cereals are being replaced with superior cereals as a result the total area under pulses either declined or stagnant.

Low marketable surplus — Most of the farmers grow pulses for their own domestic requirement on a limited area. This results in low marketable surplus with the farmers. Due to low marketable surplus, the farmers sell their produce at the village level only to the local traders who do not pay remunerative price to the farmers for pulses. Low receipts for their produce also discouraging them to grow pulses on a larger area.

Suggestions

Pulses represents a group of crops and each crop has its own requirement for input and environment. Each crop should therefore get individual consideration for crop enhancement. Crops like pea and lentil with high productivity should be expanded.

Reliance on improved production technology, high yielding and stress-resistance varieties, integrated pest and disease-management technology should be adopted to increase the productivity of the crops and to reduce the onfarm losses.

Sincere efforts should be made to create storage space in towns and villages near the major markets and adequate protection measures against the storage-pest should be provided. Development of industrial units for pulse-based food products such as soups, biscuits, noodles, etc. and their export should be provided.

The big gap between the farmer's price and retailers price should be reduced for attracting returns to the pulse growers. Greater involvement of non-government agencies and co-operatives are to be ensured, specially for utilisation of credit facilities.

Development of early-maturing cultivars for multiple cropping sequence to increase the overall productivity. Plant types suitable for inter-cropping with cereals and commercial crops should be the priority of research.

Technology developed for rainfed areas, farming systems, water management and biological nitrogen fixation should be made more effective, so as to develop the location-specific production technology for different pulse crops.

Development of crop management systems for efficient use of natural and applied inputs in production of different crops and supply of inputs such as seed, fertilizers, irrigation, plant-protection chemical and equipment should be available.

The weed management in pulses requires an integrated approach that utilises effective cultural, mechanical, biological, ecological and chemical methods in a mutually supported manner into the crop production system with due considerations of economic, environmental and sociological consequences.

Cultural practices such as method and time of sowing, crop density and geometry, crop species and varieties, method and time of fertilizer application, mulching, inter-cropping, method and time of irrigation have pronounced effect on crop-weed interferences so these practices should be apply according to requirement, i.e. narrow row spacings are known to suppress the weed growth, however, degree of suppression vary greatly (Sinha *et. at.,* 1988).

Rotation procedures recognise that certain weeds are often associated with specific crops. Rotation among crops having drastically dissimilar lifecycles or cultural conditions so as to break the cycles of weeds are among the most effective of all weed control methods.

Conclusion

It is concluded from the above analysis that a very sharp decline of pulses availability is recorded in U.P. and India as well. The low productivity of pulses in various parts of the State and country as well, are due to the non-availability of high yielding, disease resistant varieties, cultivation on marginal and sub-marginal lands under deficit moisture and fertility and poor pest management are the major constraints in realising optimum yield potential. In the absence of any other substitute to protein rich food, the situation becomes very critical and special care should be taken to maintain the balanced diet of the rural areas. A large number of laudable suggestions have been listed, however, they will be applicable in Indian context can be well understood if some integrated approach is adopted. It is evident that the state has become self-sufficient in foodgrain only in this decade, but the studies should be focus on following issues on priority basis for a balanced cropping pattern and proper direction of planning for pulses in the country.

(a) Genetic enhancement of yield and quality,
(b) Cropping system research,
(c) Integrated nutrient and water management,
(d) Integrated drought management,
(e) Integrated pest management,
(f) Development of crop models for high and sustained pulse production,
(g) Collection, evaluation and conservation of germplasm,
(h) Post harvest technology, and
(i) Onfarm research.

References

Ali, Masood (1994), *Agronomy,* (Eds.) 25 Years of Research on Pulses in India, Ali, M., Asthana, A.N. and Mehta, S.L., Indian Institute of Pulse Research, Kanpur, pp. 19-21.

Asthana, A.N. (1998), Pulse Crops Research in India, *The Indian Journal of Agricultural Sciences,* Vol. 68, No. 8, pp. 448-52.

Asthana, A.N. and Chaturvedi, S.K. (1999), *Pulses : A Little Impetus Needed,* The Hindu Survey of Indian Agriculture, Kasturi and Sons Ltd., Chennai, pp. 61-65.

Bhan, V.M. and Mishra, J.S. (1998), *Efficient Use and Management of Agro-Chemicals for Increasing Pulse Production,* Agriculture Situation in India, Vol. LV, No. 4, pp. 187-95.

Bhushan, B. and Sobti, R. (1992), Pulses : Present Status and Prospects, *Yojana,* 36(13).

Chopra, K (1975), *Pulses Production in India,* Regional Development (mimeo), Jawaharlal Nehru University, New Delhi.

Nigam, R.K. (1993), *Constraints and Challenges in Transfer of Technology in Pulse based Cropping Systems,* Summer Institute on Management of Pulses in Cropping Systems, pp. 213-20.

Pandey, R.K. and Sarup, S. (1996), Supply Prospects of Foodgrain Production in India, *Yojana,* March 1996.

Satya Priya, V.S. (1989), *Pulses in India,* Oxford & I.B.H. Publishing Co. Pvt. Ltd., New Delhi, pp. 121-30.

Singh, R. (1998), Socio-Economic Dimensions of Pulses Cultivation in Haryana, *Agricultural Situation in India,* Vol. LIV, pp. 755-57.

Singh, A.C. *et. at.* (1988), *Physiological Analysis of Yield Variation in Irrigated Pigeon Pea in Relation to Time of Sowing, Row Spacing and Weed Control Measures.* Indian Agriculture, 32(2) : 177-185.

Sud, S. (1996), Food Economy : Some Reflections. *Yojana,* October, 1996.

14

PULSES CRISIS IN INDIA
An Inter-State Analysis

MANSOOR ALI & AHMAD MUJTABA SIDDIQUI

Introduction

Pulses are considered as a rainfed crop because they are drought resistant plants and can be grown under very harsh environmental conditions. They form an integral part of Indian dietry system and very rich source of vegetable protein (Protein contents ranging from 17 to 27%) which is vital for body growth and development. Pulses provide two to three times more protein than many cereals. Besides this they are also a cheap source of protein. Owing to these factors it has considered as a boon for poor and a life saving commodity for them. Apart from this they enrich the soil fertility through nitrogen fixation with the help of bacteria present in their root. They also improve the soil structure through their typical tap root system which opens the soil into deep strata and the heavy leaf drop increases the content of organic matter in soil. Pulses are the most suitable for crop rotation and promote the multiple cropping which maintains the sustainability of vulnerable agriculture. They have an inherent capacity of adaptability to a wide range of agro-ecological cropping system and management variables. Due to the above factors pulses has become an important crop of Indian agricultural system and are great in demand.

Although they have very high remunerative value but area under pulses production remains virtually stagnant. There is hardly any improvement in production and productivity, since the last four decades in India, whereas every individual crop especially foodgrain crops have recorded a remarkable improvement. The availability of pulses per capita per day has declined from 64 gm in 1951-56 to 33.2 gm in 1998. The

FAO/WHO has made a recommendation of 80 gm of pulses/capita/day. The declining trend in productivity and availability seldom creates the scarcity, because the growth rate of population and demands are higher than the growth rate of production and availability. The major reasons of low productivity and availability of pulses in various parts of the country are of multiforked, these are the non-availability of high yielding, non-disease resistant varieties, cultivation on marginal and sub-marginal lands under deficit moisture and fertility, poor management, insufficient infrastructure, lack of incentives, faulty marketing system which discourages investment in purchased inputs etc. So there is a need to re-evaluate the strategies and there is necessity to chalk out a proper system through which all the above said variables should be properly managed to enhance the productivity as well as their availability.

Objective and Methodology

The basic objective of this study is to analyse the fluctuation in availability per capita/day. Further the study has been supported by fluctuation in area, production and productivity. An effort has been made to evaluate the factors of poor performance and finally critical assessment and suggestions have been formulated to improve the pulse production and productivity. The study about fluctuation in above mentioned variables has been done on State level from 1970-71 to 1994-95 at different interval of time. The availability of pulses per capita/day has taken into an account at decadal level of major pulse growing State. The eleven most important pulses growing States are Madhya Pradesh, Uttar Pradesh, Maharashtra, Rajasthan, Bihar, Orissa, Karnataka, Andhra Pradesh, Gujarat, Haryana and Tamil Nadu, contribute 96.6 per cent to the total production. Therefore, the pulse situations can be understood by examining the trend in these States. The time series data from 1970-71 to 1994-95 of total pulses were collected from Agricultural situation in India published by Directorate of Economics and Statistics, New Delhi. The calculations have been done by simple mathematical methods.

Declining Trend of Availability in Pulses – An Analysis

The slow growth in pulses has resulted in monotonic fall in per capita availability of pulses from 59.09 gm/day in 1970-71 to 45.66 gm/day in 1990-91. This fall in availability per capita is attributed to various socio-economic factors, such as decreasing area under pulses production, faulty public distribution system, and improper available facilities required for pulses, and lastly, the lack of suitable programmes and policies. Besides these new alternative sources of protein, greater demand which has resulted due to better standard of living has played a vital role. The availability is continuously decreasing since Independence. In 1970-71 total production of pulses was 11.818 million tonnes from the area of 22.534 million hectares which changed to 12.316 million tonnes in 1981-85 and finally in 1990-91 the production was 14.064 million tonnes. The area considered under pulses in 1990-91 was 24.397 million hectares. In case of availability in 1970-71 as per capita, it was 59.07 gm/day which decreased to 42.49 gm/day in 1980-81 but it slightly increased to 42.66 gm/day in 1990-91. In 1970-71, there were four States out of eleven major pulses growing States in India where per capita availability was more than the FAO recommendation, i.e. 80 gm./head/day. These States were Madhya Pradesh, Uttar Pradesh, Rajasthan and Haryana have a value of per capita availability as 131.02 gm/day, 95.18 gm/day, 188.95 gm/day and 221.92 gm/day respectively. The rest of States have very low availability. The acute deficient states in 1970-71 were Gujarat, Andhra Pradesh, Karnataka, Maharashtra and Bihar, where availability per capita of pulses per day in grams were 16.93, 28.34, 40.54, 42.17 and 47.98 respectively. During the period of 1980-81, the situation further deteriorated. In almost all the States availability decreased. The same four States maintained their position but availability declined. In 1990-91 the highest availability was recorded in Madhya Pradesh, i.e., 120.22 gm/head/day followed by Rajasthan, Orissa and Haryana with a value of 107.51, 92.33 and 90.00 gm/head/day. The spatial analysis shows that availability is decreasing continuously without any hindrance. There are only two States in India where situation has improved, i.e., Orissa and Gujarat.

If we take into account the total protein nutrition derived from other protein sources such as foodgrain, milk and its products, eggs, fish, meat, etc. then 55 gm/capita/day requirement of pulses may be the realistic target. The consideration of above minimum requirement has revealed that in 1970-71 there were five States which have sufficient availability of pulses in gms/capita/day. These States were Orissa, Uttar Pradesh, Madhya Pradesh, Rajasthan and Haryana. They have maintained their position in 1980-81 and 1990-91. In 1990-91 acute shortage in terms of availability was in the States of Andhra Pradesh, Bihar, Karnataka and Gujarat. The per capita per day availability in these States was 29.63 gm, 30.0 gm, 33.62 gm and 41.72 gm. The highest

Table 14.1 : Per Capita Availability of Pulses in grams/day

State	*1970-71*	*1980-81*	*1990-91*
Madhya Pradesh	131.02	105.59	120.22
Uttar Pradesh	95.18	62.37	54.45
Maharashtra	42.17	36.26	50.26
Rajasthan	188.95	93.56	107.51
Bihar	47.98	32.64	30.00
Orissa	58.30	92.05	92.33
Karnataka	40.54	34.16	33.62
Andhra Pradesh	28.34	21.23	29.63
Gujarat	16.93	21.64	41.72
Haryana	221.92	107.07	90.00
Other States	16.11	10.53	9.87

decrease in terms of availability has been registered in Haryana and Rajasthan.

Fluctuation in Area and Production of Pulses

The uncertainty in production of pulses is one of the major factors which discourage the farmers to restrict the area under this crop. In this study inter-state fluctuation in areas and production has been examined and the analysis showed that area under pulses production is almost stagnant with minor increase at certain point of time. In 1970-71, total production of pulses was 11.818 million tonnes from 22.534 million hectares. Madhya Pradesh contributed 16.8 per cent, Uttar Pradesh 26 per cent and Rajasthan 15 per cent to the total production. These States covered about half of the area to the total pulses cultivated area. In 1970-75 the highest area was covered by Madhya Pradesh, i.e., 20 per cent of the total area under pulses cultivation followed by Rajasthan, U.P. and Maharashtra i.e., 16.4 per cent, 14.9 per cent and 10.8 per cent respectively. But in terms of production Uttar Pradesh shared the largest contribution, i.e., 23.20 per cent of the total production followed by Madhya Pradesh, Rajasthan and Maharashtra with a contribution of 21.1 per cent, 12.3 per cent and 7.9 per cent respectively. During the period of 1976-80 and 1981-85 the situation is more or less remained the same. In 1976-80 the largest area was shared by Madhya Pradesh i.e., 20.5 per cent followed by Rajasthan and Uttar Pradesh but the maximum contribution in production was shared by Uttar Pradesh, i.e., 20.9 per cent followed by Madhya Pradesh, 17.7 per cent and Rajasthan 14.5 per cent. But in 1981-85 Gujarat, Karnataka and Orissa have

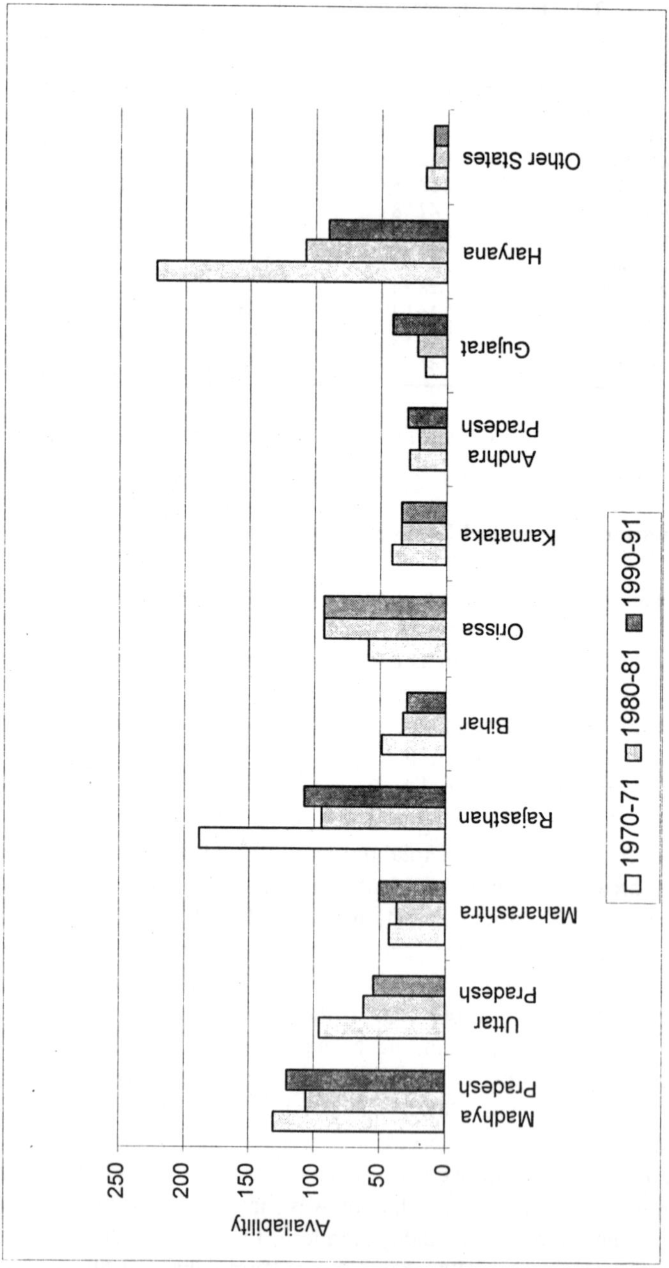

Fig. 14.1 : Per Capita Availability of Pulses in Gram per day

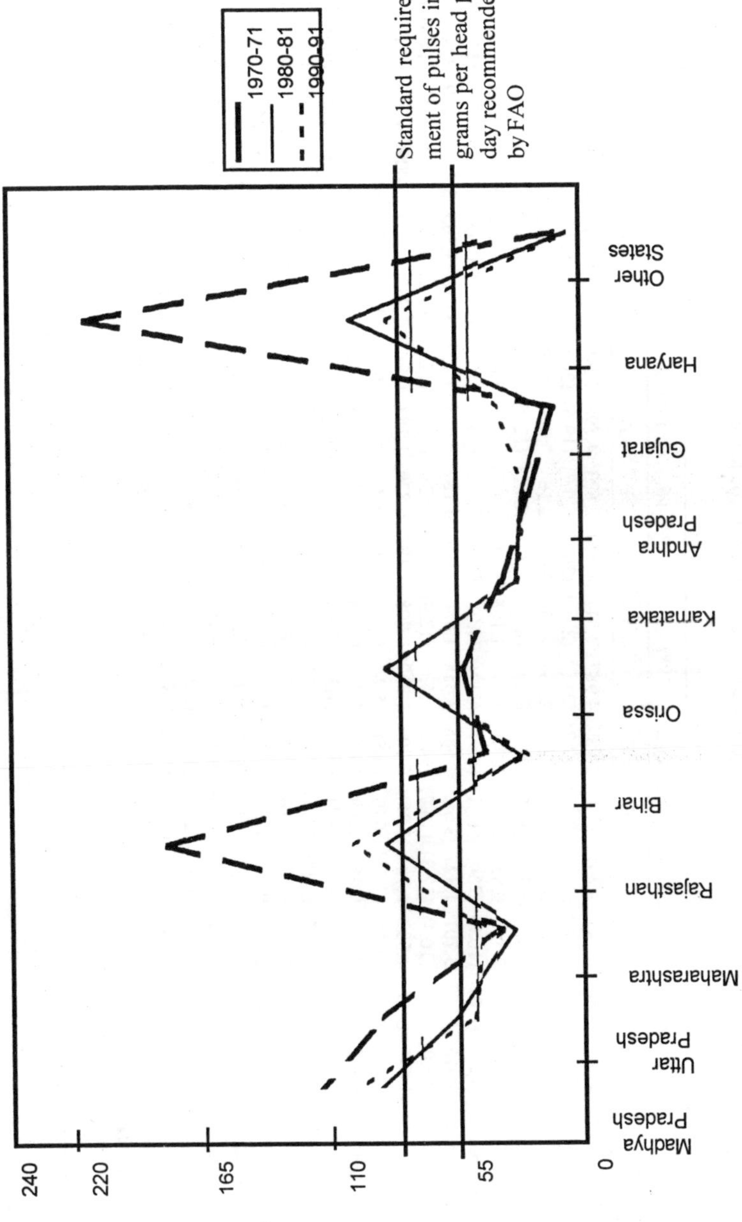

Fig. 14.2 : Surplus and Deficit in Per Capita Availability of Pulses (in gram per day)

Table 14.2 : Share in Area and Production

States	1970-71		1971-75		1976-80		1981-85		1986-90		1990-91		1992-93		1993-94		1994-95	
	A	P	A	P	A	P	A	P	A	P	A	P	A	P	A	P	A	P
1. M.P.	4.246	1.992	4.541	2.291	4.724	1.939	4.987	2.547	4.720	2.623	4.798	2.902	4.746	2.914	4.450	3.363	4.826	3.565
	(18.8)	(16.8)	(20.0)	(21.1)	(20.5)	(17.7)	(21.2)	(20.7)	(20.4)	(20.7)	(19.6)	(20.6)	(21.8)	(18.9)	(20.8)	(26.5)	(20.1)	(26.5)
2. U.P.	3.725	3.069	3.363	2.507	2.971	2.293	2.966	2.559	3.00	2.564	3.009	2.758	2.926	2.592	2.889	2.488	3.072	2.441
	(16.5)	(26.0)	(14.9)	(23.2)	(12.9)	(20.9)	(22.6)	(20.8)	(13.0)	(20.2)	(12.3)	(19.6)	(13.4)	(16.8)	(13.5)	(19.6)	(12.8)	(18.1)
3. Maha-	2.491	0.776	2.455	0.856	2.784	0.979	2.796	1.108	3.149	1.459	3.257	1.444	3.205	1.402	3.343	2.013	3.613	1.597
rashtra	(11.0)	(6.6)	(10.8)	(7.9)	(12.1)	(8.9)	(11.9)	(9.0)	(13.6)	(11.2)	(13.3)	(10.2)	(14.7)	(9.09)	(18.6)	(15.8)	(15.6)	(11.9)
4. Rajasthan	3.616	1.777	3.701	1.327	3.612	1.588	3.658	1.586	2.910	1.182	3.685	1.722	3.018	1.365	3.316	1.069	3.560	1.315
	(16.0)	(15.0)	(16.4)	(12.3)	(15.7)	(14.5)	(15.6)	(12.9)	(12.6)	(9.3)	(15.1)	(12.2)	(13.8)	(6.4)	(15.5)	(8.42)	(14.8)	(9.8)
5. Bihar	1.645	0.987	1.532	0.784	1.386	0.709	1.220	0.798	1.193	0.839	1.187	0.917	1.082	0.829	1.009	0.755	1.084	0.940
	(7.3)	(8.3)	(6.8)	(7.5)	(6.0)	(6.5)	(5.2)	(6.5)	(5.1)	(6.6)	(4.8)	(6.5)	(4.9)	(5.38)	(4.7)	(5.9)	(4.5)	(7.00)
6. Orissa	0.845	0.467	0.980	0.462	1.456	0.667	1.719	0.973	1.997	1.066	2.033	1.062	2.076	1.113	0.902	0.387	2.166	0.855
	(3.7)	(3.9)	(4.3)	(4.3)	(6.3)	(6.0)	(7.3)	(7.9)	(8.6)	(8.4)	(8.3)	(7.5)	(9.52)	(7.2)	(4.2)	(3.05)	(9.0)	(6.37)
7. Karnataka	1.131	0.404	1.307	0.490	1.384	0.534	1.591	0.566	1.636	0.575	1.483	0.550	1.649	0.581	1.460	0.599	1.611	0.638
	(5.0)	(3.4)	(5.8)	(4.5)	(3.0)	(4.9)	(6.8)	(4.6)	(7.0)	(4.5)	(6.1)	(3.9)	(7.5)	(3.7)	(6.6)	(4.7)	(6.7)	(4.7)
8. Andhra	1.451	0.450	1.395	0.383	1.367	0.367	1.416	0.550	1.527	0.699	1.636	0.716	1.646	0.757	1.573	0.609	1.500	0.590
Pradesh	(6.4)	(3.8)	(6.2)	(3.5)	(5.9)	(5.3)	(6.0)	(4.5)	(6.6)	(5.5)	(6.7)	(5.1)	(7.5)	(4.9)	(7.3)	(4.8)	(6.2)	(4.3)
9. Gujarat	0.423	0.165	0.391	0.142	0.508	0.206	0.755	0.455	0.759	0.412	0.932	0.627	0.915	0.556	0.898	0.538	0.946	0.541
	(1.9)	(1.4)	(1.7)	(1.3)	(2.2)	(1.9)	(3.2)	(3.7)	(3.3)	(3.2)	(3.8)	(4.4)	(4.1)	(3.6)	(4.2)	(4.2)	(3.9)	(4.03)
10 Haryana	1.141	0.813	1.66	0.617	0.972	0.761	0.817	0.411	0.602	0.446	0.732	0.536	0.529	0.380	0.477	0.470	0.518	0.485
.	(5.0)	(6.9)	(4.7)	(5.7)	(4.2)	(6.9)	(3.5)	(3.3)	(2.6)	(3.5)	(3.0)	(3.8)	(2.42)	(2.46)	(2.2)	(3.7)	(2.16)	(3.6)
11 Tamil Nadu													2.575	1.092	0.981	0.397	1.085	0.446
.													(11.8)	(7.0)	(4.6)	(3.1)	(4.5)	(3.3)

recorded an increase in area under pulses. Gujarat recorded 48.6 per cent increase in area whereas Karnataka and Orissa recorded 14.9 per cent and 18.06 per cent increase in Area. In 1986-90 Maharashtra has recorded 12.62 per cent increases in area. Andhra Pradesh, Karnataka and Orissa have also recorded increase in area but in Rajasthan area under pulses cultivation decreased by 20.4 per cent. In 1990-91, the highest area under pulses cultivation was in Madhya Pradesh, i.e., 19.6 per cent equal to 4.798 million hectare followed by Rajasthan, Maharashtra and Uttar Pradesh, i.e., 15.1 per cent, 13.3 per cent and 12.3 per cent equals to 3.685, 3.287 and 3.009 million hectares respectively.

In terms of production, the maximum contribution came from Madhya Pradesh, i.e., 2.902 followed by Uttar Pradesh and Rajasthan, i.e. 2.758 and 1.722 million tonnes. In 1992-93 again Madhya Pradesh has shared largest area in, i.e. 4.746 million hectares followed by Maharashtra, Rajasthan and Uttar Pradesh, whereas in terms of production, Madhya Pradesh has maintained its position at first with a value of 2.914 million tonnes. In Uttar Pradesh total pulses production was about 2.592 million tonnes, and in Maharashtra it was 1.402 million tonnes. In case of 1993-94 and 1994-95 the situation of area under pulses cultivation and production remain as it was previously almost in all the States of India. It except in Orissa where it has improved remarkably while in Haryana it has declined.

In an analysis fluctuation in area and production taken into account, it depicts that from 1970-71 till 1994-95 area has continuously decreased in all pulse growing States. In 1971-75 the highest decrease was recorded in area in Uttar Pradesh whereas 15.9 per cent of increase was recorded in Orissa over 1970-71. In 1976-80 the highest decrease in area under pulses cultivation was recorded in Uttar Pradesh while an increase about 48.5 per cent in area was noticed in Orissa. But in 1981-85 and 1986-90 maximum increase was noticed in Haryana and Karnataka. From 1990-91 to 1991-92 every State has decreased their area under pulses production except Orissa, Karnataka and Andhra Pradesh. In 1993-94, the situation improved marginally and it again got improved in 1994-95. In 1994-95 every State has recorded a positive fluctuation leaving behind Madhya Pradesh and Andhra Pradesh. But the fluctuating trend in production of pulses in India revealed that in every State it decreased. Rajasthan and Bihar have noticed 25.3 per cent and 20.5 per cent decrease while only Karnataka and Maharashtra have registered an increase in production by 21.2 per cent and 10.3 per cent whereas in

Table 14.3 : Fluctuation in Area

	States	*1971-75*	*1976-80*	*1981-85*	*1986-90*	*1990-91*	*1992-93*	*1993-94*	*1994-95*
1.	Madhya Pradesh	6.94	4.02	5.56	–5.35	1.65	–1.08	–4.2	–2.5
2.	Uttar Pradesh	–9.71	–18.2	–0.16	0.13	0.3	–2.75	–1.2	6.3
3.	Maharashtra	–1.44	13.4	0.43	12.6	3.42	–1.59	4.3	8.0
4.	Rajasthan	2.35	–2.40	1.23	–20.4	26.6	–0.18	9.9	7.3
5.	Bihar	–6.86	–9.53	–11.9	–2.2	–0.5	–10.5	6.7	7.5
6.	Orissa	15.9	48.5	18.06	16.1	1.8	2.1	–56.5	140.13
7.	Karnataka	15.5	5.89	14.9	2.82	–9.35	11.1	11.5	10.3
8.	Andhra Pradesh	–3.85	–2.00	14.9	2.82	–7.13	0.61	–4.5	–4.6
9.	Gujarat	–7.5	29.9	48.6	15.2	22.7	–1.8	–1.8	5.3
10.	Haryana	–6.5	–8.8	–15.9	–26.3	21.5	27.7	–9.8	8.6
11.	Tamil Nadu							–61.9	10.6

Table 14.4 : Fluctuation in Production

	States	*1971-75*	*1976-80*	*1981-85*	*1986-90*	*1990-91*	*1992-93*	*1993-94*	*1994-95*
1.	Madhya Pradesh	15	–15.36	31.35	2.98	10.6	0.41	1.5	6.0
2.	Uttar Pradesh	–18.3	–8.53	11.6	0.19	7.5	–6.0	–3.9	–1.9
3.	Maharashtra	10.3	14.36	13.17	31.6	–1.0	2.9	43.6	–20.68
4.	Rajasthan	–25.3	19.6	–0.12	–25.4	45.6	–21.6	–21.6	23.04
5.	Bihar	–20.5	–9.56	12.5	5.13	9.29	–9.65	–8.9	24.5
6.	Orissa	–1.07	44.3	45.8	9.5	–0.37	4.8	–65.2	120.7
7.	Karnataka	21.2	8.9	5.9	1.5	–4.3	5.6	3.1	6.4
8.	Andhra Pradesh	–14.8	–4.17	49.8	27.0	2.43	5.72	19.5	0.57
9.	Gujarat	–13.9	45.0	120.8	9.45	52.2	11.3	–3.2	0.57
10.	Haryana	–24.1	23.3	–45.9	8.5	20.2	29.1	23.6	–3.2
11.	Tamil Nadu							–63.6	12.3

1976-80 Gujarat, Orissa, Haryana, Rajasthan and Maharashtra have increased their production by 45.0 per cent, 44.3 per cent, 23.3 per cent, 19.6 per cent and 14.36 per cent respectively. In 1981-85 the production increased in almost all the states except in Haryana and Rajasthan, i.e. 45.9 per cent and 0.12 per cent. The same situationwas in 1986-90 except Rajasthan where production decreased by 25.4 per cent. In 90-91 highest increase in production was noticed in Gujarat and next to it was Rajasthan followed by Haryana with a value of 52.2 per cent, 45.6 per cent and 20.2 per cent respectively. While in 1992-93 a decrease in production was registered in Rajasthan, Bihar and Uttar Pradesh i.e., 21.6 per cent, 9.65 per cent and 6.0 per cent orderly, considering the 1990-91 as above. But in 1993-94 the situation of pulses production was not uniform, as in some States it decreased while in some States it increased. Maharashtra, Haryana and Andhra Pradesh got highest increment in production by 43.6 per cent and 23.6 per cent and 19.5 per cent where as in Orissa Tamil Nadu and Rajasthan it fall heavily i.e. 65.2 per cent and 61.6 per cent and 21.6 per cent respectively, and lastly in 1994-95 Orissa has increased her production by 120.7 per cent, Bihar 24.5 per cent, Rajasthan 23.4 per cent. The maximum fall in production was recorded in Maharashtra, i.e. 20.68 per cent.

The trend of productivity shows that it is also decreasing continuously. In 1990-91 Uttar Pradesh have maximum yield i.e. 916 kg/hect followed by Bihar, Haryana with the value of 772 kg/hectare and 732 kg/hec. The lowest yield was in Karnataka equals to 370 kg/ hect. While in 1994-95, maximum yield was in Haryana, i.e., 936 kg/ hect next to it was Bihar, i.e., 795 kg/hect. followed by Madhya Pradesh and Gujarat, i.e., 739 kg/hect., 572 kg/hect. respectively and the lowest yield was in Rajasthan, i.e., 369 kg/hect.

Conclusion

From the above analysis the fact has been established that per capita availability of pulses in gm/day is continuously decreasing, due to the decrease in production and an encroachment in area under pulses cultivation by other cereal crops. So, there is an urgent need to minimize the gap between production and per capita availability through a proper planning, which should be on priority basis. The planning and policies should be multifaceted. Farmers should be encouraged to cultivate the pulse crops on the main land rather than marginal land and for this they should be granted some incentive and financial help. Besides this

Table 14.5 : Productivity of Pulses (kg/ha)

	States	*1970-71*	*1971-75*	*1976-80*	*1981-85*	*1986-90*	*1990-91*	*1992-93*	*1993-94*	*1994-95*
1.	Madhya Pradesh	469	504	410	510	555	604	614	679	739
2.	Uttar Pradesh	824	745	771	862	854	916	886	861	795
3.	Maharashtra	311	349	351	396	463	443	437	602	442
4.	Rajasthan	491	358	439	433	406	467	457	322	369
5.	Bihar	60	511	511	654	703	772	766	748	867
6.	Orissa	553	471	458	566	538	522	536	429	395
7.	Karnataka	357	374	385	355	351	370	352	411	396
8.	Andhra Pradesh	310	274	268	706	457	437	460	388	393
9.	Gujarat	390	363	405	602	542	672	608	599	572
10.	Haryana	712	578	782	502	740	732	718	985	936
11.	Tamil Nadu							424	405	411

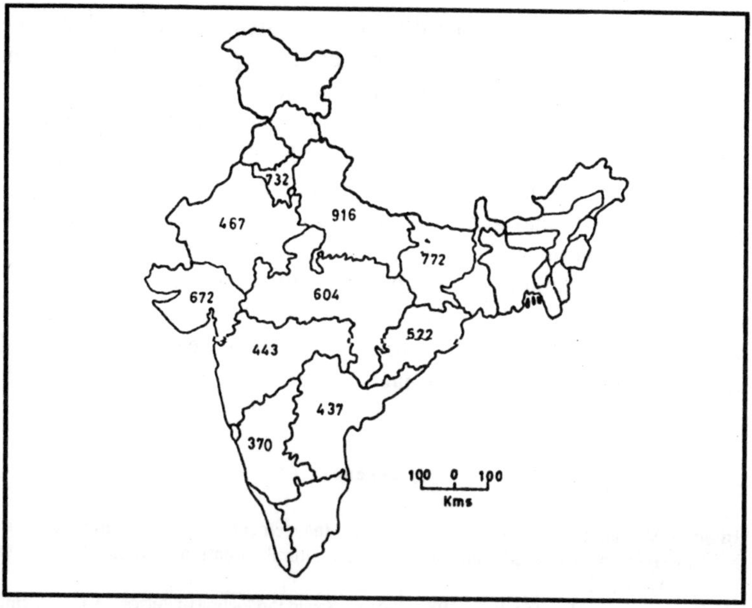

Fig. 14.3: Productivity of Palses (kg/ha) (1990-91)

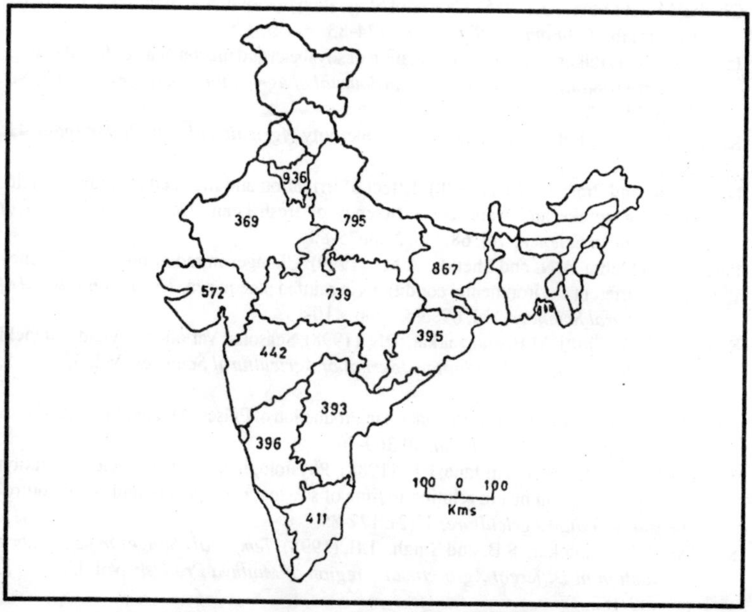

Fig. 14.4: Productivity of Pulses (kg/ha) (1994-95)

marketing system and public distribution system for pulses should be improved considerably to maintain the effect support price. Government should extend the proper training, methods of farming and plant protection technology measures to small farmers. Pulses are considered as a rainfed crops, so there is a need to develop the new varieties of pulses which should be drought resistant and high yielding. New biotechnological and genetic innovations should be incorporated to develop the hybrid varieties of pulses of short maturity periods. The environmental component for pulses cultivation must be improved through better management practices, including timely sowing, moisture conservation, better plant stand establishment, seed treatment and rhizobium inoculation weed management and plant protection measures.

References

Bhan, V.M. and Singh, A.N., (1991), "Seed Management – A tool for increasing in production of oilseeds and pulses." Agricultural Situation in India, September 1991, pp. 213-217.

Gangawar, A.C. and Pandey, R.C. (1982), "Stagnation in Production of Pulses – An Economic Analysis", *Agricultural Situation in India*, 27: 283-87.

Ghatha, I.S. and Singh, J. (1985), Causes of Stagnation in Production of Pulses and Oilseeds in Punjab, *Economic Affairs*, 28: 774-83.

Jagpat, J.G. and Holkar, S., (1998), Evaluation of soyabean and pigeon pea lies for advantage in inter-cropping systems. *The Indian Journal of Agricultural Sciences*, Vol. 68, No. 2, pp. 241-43.

Kumar, A. (1986), Imbalances in Pulses Productivity, *Agricultural Situation in India*, 41: 23-27.

Nandan, R. and Prasad, U.K. (1998), Effect of irrigation and nitrogen on growth, yield, nitrogen uptake and water-use efficiency of fresh bean. *The Indian Journal of Agricultural Science*, Vol. 68, No. 2 pp. 75-80.

Patel, N.R., Mehta, A.N. and Sheikh, A.M. (1999). Changes in radiationwise efficiency under different environmental conditions in rainfed pigeon pea, *The Indian Journal of Agricultural Sciences*, Vol. 69, No. 6, pp. 410-15.

Ramteke, S.D., Chitti, M.B. and Takkar, P.N. (1998), Seasonal Variation in yield and yield components in gram, *The Indian Journal of Agricultural Sciences*, Vol. 65, No. 5, pp. 251-54.

Rao, I.V.R. and Ray, A.K. (1985). Stagnation in Production of Pulses: A Quantitative Analysis. *Agricultural Situation in India*. 40:369-76.

Sinha, A.C., Mandal, B.B. and Jana, P.K. (1988), Physiological Analysis of yield variation in irrigated pigeon pea in relation to time of sowing, row spacing and weed control measures. *Indian Agriculture*, 32(2): 177-85.

Sisodiya, A.S., Nahatkar, S.B. and Singh, T.B. (1998), *Temporal changes in pegeon pea production in Different Agro-climatic region of Madhya Pradesh*. Vol. LV, No. 3, pp. 149-152.

15

CORRELATION OF WHEAT PRODUCTIVITY WITH FERTILIZER CONSUMPTION AND IRRIGATION
A Case Study of Uttar Pradesh

MANSOOR ALI & YASIR SAYEED HANAFI

Introduction

The prosperity and development of a country is the composite reflection of many attributes. It cannot depend simply on its scientific and technological possession or on its mere territorial sovereignty. It has also rests upon one of the most vulnerable front, i.e. food self-sufficiency and food security, means upto what extent a country is self-sufficient in foodgrain production and its assured availability. In recent times if a country wants its all-round development a desire to have some influence in world politics, then it should be and must firmly be footed on its agricultural sector for its food self-sufficiency and food security. Keeping in view the world political scenario, one is not very much sure about a nuclear war in this millennium but it is quite obvious that there must be a war of grains. Today foodgrain is not merely an item or a stuff to feed one's growing population but it has become an item of politics, and in coming centuries it will be used as a weapon for both the peaceful and aggressive purposes. This dimensional shift in the usage of foodgrain itself speaks about its importance.

Since independence Indian agriculture has passed through several experimental and developmental phases and the most remarkable phase was the period of Green Revolution. A sharp increase in agricultural production was registered by using high yielding variety seeds, chemical fertilizers, plant protection measures, increasing rate of irrigation and improved farm machinery. Taking India as a whole we are self-sufficient in foodgrain production as well as its assured availability, but at regional level, district level or even lower to it, i.e. village level, we are not self-sufficient in foodgrain production and availability. In case of U.P., which is one of the most balancing and representing State of India in terms of foodgrain production, in some of its parts, food shortages still persist. This is because of higher population growth than the foodgrain growth and secondly, it is due to the non-availability and non-accessibility to the new agricultural technology. This latter reason is also adding the regional disparities in the level of production (Ali Mohammad, 1992). The imbalance is not only in production and productivity but it also persists in terms of availability because of uneven growth of population. It may also be due to several other factors such as regional differences in size of land holding, tenureal system, technological factors, farm management and plant protection measures, social factors, taboos and existence of infrastructure like transportation, marketing and electricity. At this time there are only two options before us to tackle this problem, either through areal expansion of foodgrain crops under cultivation or simply by increasing the productivity per hectare of foodgrains. India has increased its production by four fold since 1950, in which the contribution of productivity increase is about 80 per cent while the area expansion contributing only about 20 per cent. The adoption of various modern inputs, farming techniques and mechanized system in agriculture helped to increase the yield per hectare which consequently help the nation to achieve self-sufficiency in foodgrain production but still all parts of U.P. have not attained the required level of self-sufficiency in foodgrain availability due to spatial variations in production and population pressure. Therefore, to overcome the problems social injustice and inequality, the imbalances in levels of agricultural productivity should be minimized to attain an overall self-sufficiency not only at national level but also at regional level.

Objectives

The basic objective of this study is to examine and analyze the spatial variation in productivity of wheat, fertilizer consumption and irrigation in Uttar Pradesh during the period 1985-86 to 1995-96. For this purpose only wheat has been taken into consideration because it is the most important cereal crop in terms of area, production and yield. It also contributed about 35 per cent of the total foodgrain production of India and covered about 20 per cent of net sown area in 1996. The other selected variable is fertilizer consumption, which is one of the important factors of Green Revolution, and is a vital supporting element for HYV seeds along with irrigation. The irrigation is the life breath of the modern agricultural system. Apart from this, growths of the above said factor have also been analyzed with reference to growth in yield. For this analysis data of two point of time has been taken at an interval of ten years, i.e. 1985-86 and 1995-96. Firstly, because a single year cannot give a clear picture about spatial and temporal variations and secondly, in these years especially after 1980, the agricultural production increased phenomenally which erase the begging bowl image of the country and now India is in a position to chalk out a balance sheet for the strategies of the future.

Data Base and Methodology

The source of data which is extensively used in this study is of secondary nature published by the Directorate of Economics and Statistics, Ministry of Agriculture and Food, Government of U.P., Agricultural Situation of India published by Directorate of Economic and Statistics, New Delhi, Economic Survey and Agricultural Statistics, Government of India and Hand Book of Fertilizer.

The present study consists of three sections:

- The first section deals with the analysis and variations in fertilizer consumption and irrigation throughout the State at district level.
- The second section deals with the analysis and variations in fertilizer consumption and irrigation throughout the State at district level.
- The third section deals with the assessment about the variation and a correlation between the yield *vs.* fertilizer consumption, yield *vs.* irrigation and fertilizer consumption *vs.* irrigation. The correlation is estimated by the Spearman method at different agro-climatic regions in U.P.

Spatial Variation in Productivity of Wheat

Wheat is one of the most significant foodgrain crops of Indian dietary system. It occupies about 33 per cent of the total cropped area and contributes about 35 per cent in total foodgrain production of the country. Its production has increased from 6 million tonnes in 1950 to 68 million tonnes in 1996-97. In Uttar Pradesh it occupied about 39.5 per cent of the gross cropped area in 1985-86 while in 1996-97, this figure increased to 44.5 per cent. The increase in area is mainly confined wherever the irrigation is available. The production of wheat increased from 53.7 per cent in 1985-86 to 57.16 per cent in 1995-96.

Table 13.1, shows the variation in productivity and trend of growth in yield level in U.P. It is evident from the table, that during 1985-86 more than 50 per cent of the districts have recorded the yield level below the State average, i.e. 1980 kg/ha. While the districts of western U.P., namely Bulandshahr, Ghaziabad, Meerut and Muzaffarnagar recorded a very high yield level even higher than the national average, i.e. 2700 kg/ha. The low level of yield was registered in almost all the hilly tract of U.P. (except Nainital); Almora has recorded the lowest yield of about 997 kg/ha. and in the districts of Bundelkhand region, e.g. Jhansi, Lalitpur and Mirzapur were also very poor in per hectare productivity. But during 1995-96, almost all the districts of U.P. have shown improvement in yield level, because of the improved infrasturctural conditions and adoption of modern farming techniques, HYV seeds and increased rate of assured irrigation. As a result there are 25 districts, where the yield level recorded around the State average, i.e. 2453 kg/ha. and there are 16 districts where yield level surpasses the national average of about 2700 kg/ha. These districts are mostly confined to the western U.P. and Ganga-Yamuna *doab* region, namely Agra, Bulandshahr, Ghaziabad, Mathura, Meerut, Muzaffarnagar and Rampur.

On the basis of yield/hectare, the whole U.P. has been grouped into five categories of agricultural development plotted on Figs. 15.1 and 15.2 for 1985-86 and 1995-96 respectively to compare the pattern of regional variation of yield. The category of very low yield level (below 1400 kg/ha.) occupied by 11 districts in 1985-86, and this number comes down to 4 districts during 1995-96. In terms of percentage the area under this category decreased from 10.48 per cent to only about 2.11 per cent and production decreased from 6.1 per cent to only about 1.05 per cent, in the same time span. The second category of yield level (1400-1800 kg/ha.) covered an area of about 28.63 per cent during 1985-86 and decreased to about 4.82 per cent of the total area under wheat in 1995-96, while the production share declined to about 3.04 per cent from 24.24 per cent in the same period of time. The third category of medium yield level ranges between 1800-2200 kg/ha. occupied an area of about 30.76 per cent and

Table 15.1 : Changing Pattern of Productivity of Wheat (kg/ha.), Fertilizer Consumption (kg/ha.) and Irrigation (per cent) in Uttar Pradesh (1985-86 to 1995-96)

	Productivity of Wheat		*Fertilizer Consumption*		*Irrigation*		*Growth*		
	1985-86	*1995-96*	*1985-86*	*1995-96*	*1985-86*	*1995-96*	*Productivity*	*Fetilizer Consumption*	*Irrigation*
(1)	(2)	(3)	(4)	(5)	(6)	(7)	(8)	(9)	(10)
Agra	2520.49	3191.94	65.77	122.88	53.42	63.2	26.64	86.83	18.31
Aligarh	2682.71	2960.7	63.85	60.11	76.49	84.99	10.36	–5.86	11.11
Allahabad	1657.69	2159.43	85.13	137.53	44.13	63.62	30.27	61.55	44.16
Almora	996.76	1160.64	5.93	4.2	12.48	12.67	16.44	–29.17	1.52
Azamgarh	1829.76	2196.37	74.36	39.92	52.73	39.15	20.04	–46.32	–25.75
Bahraich	1528.22	1962.25	47.98	41.95	15.05	20.18	28.40	–12.57	30.19
Balia	1669.2	2251.11	91.29	104.45	45.02	59.64	34.86	14.42	31.95
Banda	1024.94	1499.42	18.42	19.75	25.56	32.57	46.29	7.22	27.43
Barabanki	1763.2	2180.92	80	105.91	51.73	77.23	23.69	32.39	49.29
Barely	2038.24	2393.79	98.61	141.08	55.94	84.4	17.44	43.07	50.88
Basti	1765.89	2303.98	64.68	113.58	44.89	53.2	30.47	75.60	18.51
Bijnor	1973.99	2461	115.69	146.92	57.4	77.76	24.67	26.99	35.47
Budaun	2248.39	2537.97	82.34	105.19	44.96	67.37	12.88	27.75	49.84
Bulandshahar	3124.72	3432.3	92.47	103.2	89.42	98.96	9.84	11.60	10.67
Chamoli	1042.47	1396.28	7.83	4.77	6.65	7.19	33.94	–39.08	8.12
Dehradun	1571.16	1773.38	32.14	46.63	42.51	42.49	12.87	45.08	–0.05
Deoria	1901.41	2261.29	111.16	120.06	50.4	53.74	18.93	8.01	6.63
Etah	2280.62	2477.31	62.2	84.13	61.8	78.62	8.62	35.26	27.22
Etawah	2312.57	2743.74	78.34	75.37	60.88	72.78	18.64	–3.79	19.55
Faizabad	2103.02	2500.17	92.16	68.41	54.54	82.73	18.88	–25.77	51.69
Farrukhabad	2489.34	2975	117.92	138.03	53.39	70.26	19.51	17.05	31.60
Fatehpur	1822.98	2330.19	63.93	80.74	44.44	60.09	27.82	26.29	35.22
Firozabad		2884		94.87		64.1			

(Contd.)

Table 15.1 (*contd.*)

	Productivity of Wheat		*Fertilizer Consumption*		*Irrigation*		*Growth*		
	1985-86	*1995-96*	*1985-86*	*1995-96*	*1985-86*	*1995-96*	*Productivity*	*Fetilizer. Consumption*	*Irrigation*
(1)	(2)	(3)	(4)	(5)	(6)	(7)	(8)	(9)	(10)
Garhwal	1043.48	1273.35	4.41	2.45	10.52	11.66	22.03	–44.44	10.84
Ghaziabad	3006.74	3519.09	111.78	165.48	59.27	98.94	17.04	48.04	66.93
Ghazipur	1964.65	2210.24	105.06	145.17	55.66	59.58	12.50	38.18	7.04
Gonda	1668.1	2357.38	36.35	61.37	27.06	36.05	41.32	68.83	33.22
Gorakhpur	1777.2	2315.1	100.73	139.84	43.81	54.06	30.27	38.83	23.40
Hamirpur	1247.63	1607.22	11.25	30.41	18	31.84	28.82	170.31	76.89
Hardoi	1857.99	2536.83	58.98	45.15	45.98	66.64	36.54	–23.45	44.93
Haridwar		2450.04		187.7		76.21			
Jalaun	1695.78	2383.16	31.05	19.69	22.62	41.5	40.53	–36.59	83.47
Jaunpur	1930.39	2484.94	115.08	90.5	53.25	75.39	28.73	–21.36	41.58
Jhansi	1391.47	2090.46	18.71	43.13	26.12	46.37	50.23	130.52	77.53
Kanpur (Rural)	2590.56	2885.46	68.46	94.45	49.38	60.84	11.38	37.96	23.21
Kanpur (Urban)	2423.01	2532.77	139.27	180.22	74.59	70.42	4.53	29.40	–5.59
Khiri	1831.94	2296.97	63.31	76.81	36.86	46.63	25.38	21.32	26.51
Lalitpur	1337.42	2002.64	23.56	69.99	44.97	53.32	49.74	197.07	18.57
Lucknow	1818.2	2223.66	110.18	103.44	60.02	79.92	22.30	–6.12	33.16
Maharajganj		2406.25		94.68		46.55			
Mainpuri	2351.79	2912	85.61	159.52	65.6	90.2	23.82	86.33	37.50
Mathura	2486.45	3148.96	74.31	132.08	69.95	79.89	26.64	77.74	14.21
Mau		2215.96		96.25		68.22			
Meerut	3306.88	3430.74	114.79	146.72	93.06	99.39	3.75	27.82	6.80
Mirzapur	1103.61	2129.77	43.41	89.38	33.69	61.65	92.98	105.90	82.99
Moradabad	2165.19	2708	88.26	209.44	67.23	94.58	25.07	137.30	40.68
Muzaffarnagar	2829.61	3038.21	108.74	164.73	82.19	95.23	7.37	51.49	15.87

(*Contd.*)

Table 15.1 (*contd.*)

	Productivity of Wheat		*Fertilizer Consumption*		*Irrigation*		*Growth*		
	1985-86	*1995-96*	*1985-86*	*1995-96*	*1985-86*	*1995-96*	*Productivity*	*Fetilizer Consumption*	*Irrigation*
(1)	(2)	(3)	(4)	(5)	(6)	(7)	(8)	(9)	(10)
Nainital	2355.51	2638.86	178.24	231.62	67.42	79.42	12.03	29.95	17.80
Pilibhit	2063.22	2711.73	130.46	173.63	71.14	91.52	31.43	33.09	28.65
Pithoragarh	1279.89	1547.31	6.99	5.07	7.2	8.13	20.89	–27.47	12.92
Pratapgarh	1779.43	2179.99	93.3	100.41	47.8	75.16	22.51	7.62	57.24
Raibarelly	1718.74	2018.46	70.47	81.2	67.38	81.8	17.44	15.23	21.40
Rampur	2586.79	3314	121.14	121.07	67.71	90.65	28.11	–0.06	33.88
Saharanpur	2416.2	2711.12	106.86	137.96	67.65	81.98	12.21	29.10	21.18
Shahjahanpur	2199.74	2950.83	107.58	138.67	64.89	87.29	34.14	28.90	34.52
Siddhartnagar		2057.81		128		37.91			
Sitapur	1563.27	2160.33	56.3	92.52	32.91	53.89	38.19	64.33	63.75
Sonbhadra		1180.13		43.42		25.17			
Sultanpur	1964.73	2140	66.23	82.71	39.46	63.16	8.92	24.88	60.06
Tehri Garhwal	1263.74	1433.07	5.97	3.89	17.56	17.11	13.40	–34.84	–2.56
Unnao	1696.45	2238.58	71	75.06	57.79	73.6	31.96	5.72	27.36
Uttarkashi	1197.34	1819.45	13.74	10.91	19.21	19.85	51.96	–20.60	3.33
Varanasi	1711.33	2353.12	137.92	133.77	62.58	77.48	37.50	–3.01	23.81
Total	1980.11	2452.69	78.02	100.9	51.09	64.47	23.87	29.33	26.19

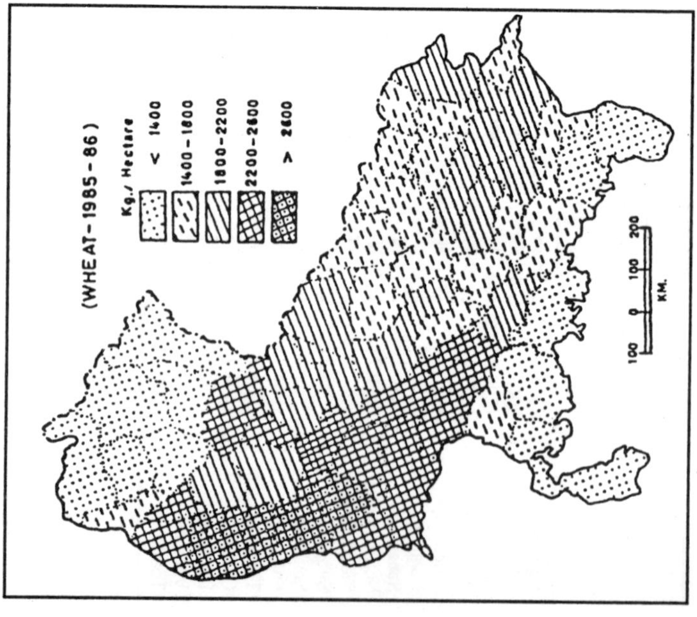

Fig. 15.1: Uttar Pradesh—Levels of Agricultural Development

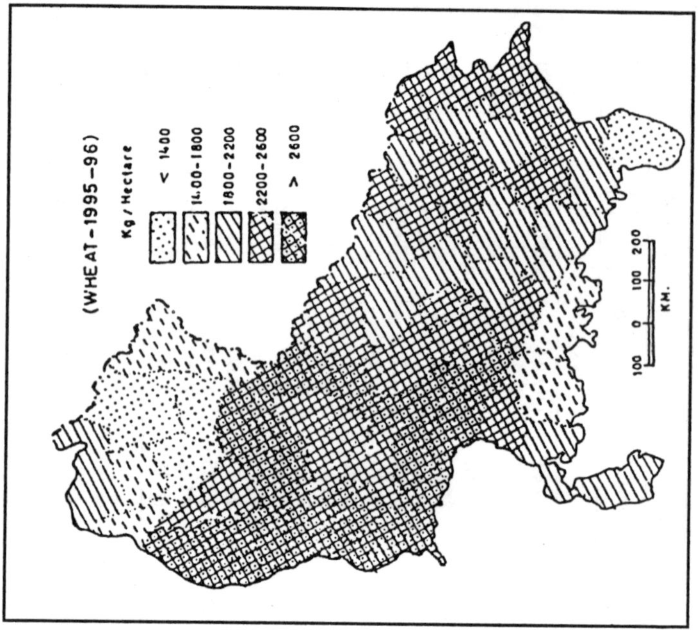

Fig. 15.2: Uttar Pradesh—Levels of Agricultural Development

about 18.25 per cent during 1985-86 and 1995-96 respectively and produced about 30.32 per cent and 18.25 per cent of the total wheat production of U.P. at the same point of time. The category of high yield level (2200-2600 kg/ha.) occupied an area of about 19.86 per cent during 1985-86 and it increased to a high level of 40.76 per cent during 1995-96 of the total area under wheat cultivation and shared about 23.96 per cent in 1985-86 and about 39.68 per cent in 1995-96 of total wheat production. The fifth category of very high yield level (more than 2600 kg/ha.) covered an area of about 10.27 per cent during 1985-86, about 31.10 per cent in 1995-96, which contributed in total production about 15.33 per cent and 39.98 per cent in 1985-86 and 1995-96 respectively. It is concluded that the first three categories of yield level shows a declining trend both in area and production while the higher yield level registered a positive growth both in area and production. In 1985-86, almost whole of the State was under very low, low and medium level of wheat productivity except Ganga-Yamuna *doab* which was under the high and very high level of wheat productivity. But during 1995-96, except a few districts of hilly tract of Kumaon and Garhwal and Bundelkhand region, almost all the districts of U.P. recorded under medium, high and very high level of wheat productivity (Figs. 15.1 & 15.2).

Spatial Variation of Fertilizer Consumption and Irrigation

Figures 15.3 and 15.4, show the pattern of fertilizer consumption in U.P. it is clearly revealed that there were 29 districts in U.P. during 1985-86, where the fertilizer consumption was above the State average, i.e. 78.02 kg/ha while remaining districts were below it, and there were only 17 districts during 1985-86 in which the fertilizer consumption was about 100 kg/ha., namely Nainital, Kanpur (U), Varanasi, Pilibhit, Rampur, Farrukhabad, Bijnor, Jaunpur, Deoria, Ghaziabad, Lucknow, Muzaffarnagar, Saharanpur, Ghazipur and Shahjahanpur. The very low fertilizer consumption was observed in all the hilly districts and trans-Yamuna districts of Hamirpur, Banda, Mirzapur and Lalitpur. During 1995-96, almost half of the districts of U.P. shows fertilizer consumption above the State average, i.e. 100.90 kg/ha. The high level of fertilizer consumption (more than 140 kg/ha.) is recorded in 13 districts, namely Bareilly, Faizabad, Ghaziabad, Ghazipur, Gorakhpur, Haridwar, Kanpur (U), Mainpuri, Meerut, Moradabad, Muzaffarnagar, Nainital and Pilibhit. The low level of fertilizer consumption was again recorded in all the hilly districts (except Nainital) and trans-Yamuna districts of

Lalitpur, Jhansi, Jalaun, Hamirpur and Banda. Some of the districts show declining trend in fertilizer consumption in 1995-96 as against to 1985-86, these districts are Almora, Tehri Garhwal, Pithoragarh, Chamoli, Uttarkashi, Jalaun, Bahraich, Hardoi, Aligarh, Azamgarh, Etawah, Lucknow, Jaunpur and Farrukhabad. This decrease in fertilizer consumption is due to the non-availability of HYV seeds and insufficient irrigation etc. For spatial analysis, fertilizer consumption has been grouped into five categories. It is evident from Figures 15.3 and 15.4, that during 1985-86, the high to very high level of fertilizer consumption was recorded in Ganga-Yamuna *doab* and a few districts in eastern U.P. such as Deoria, Jaunpur and Varanasi while rest of the regions come under medium, low to very low level of fertilizer consumption. The overall situation of fertilizer consumption has been improved during 1995-96 with more or less the same pattern of regional variation.

Irrigation is the lifeline of the modern agricultural system. For the proper agricultural development assured irrigation is essential. In this study, spatial variation of irrigation with respect to productivity of wheat has been taken into consideration in U.P. During 1985-86, gross irrigated area was about 51.05 per cent of the gross sown area under all crops and 28 districts were lying below this level of State average, mostly belongs to the hilly region, Bundelkhand region and eastern U.P. On the other hand there were only 19 districts where the irrigated area was more than 60 per cent, namely Meerut, Bulandshahr, Ghaziabad, Muzaffarnagar, Kanpur (U), Aligarh, Pilibhit, Mathura, Mainpuri, Moradabad, Etah, Etawah, Nainital, Rai Bareilly, Rampur, Saharanpur, Shahjahanpur, Varanasi and Lucknow. In 1995-96, the situation of irrigation improved considerably as the irrigation occupied the 64.47 per cent of the total cropped area, and almost all the districts of U.P. lie under high to very high level of irrigation except the hilly tract and Bundelkhand region the irrigation recorded low. There are some districts during this point of time where the irrigation occupied almost cent per cent of the gross cropped area such as Bulandshahr, Ghaziabad, Muzaffarnagar, Moradabad, Pilibhit, Rampur and Mainpuri. It becomes possible only because of the availability of modern inputs and infrastructure facilities. The spatial variation of irrigation throughout all the districts of U.P. is very clear from Figs. 15.5 and 15.6.

Changing Pattern of Wheat Productivity, Fertilizer Consumption and Irrigation

It is evident from Tabel 15.1, that all the districts of hilly tract and Bundelkhand region have low wheat productivity, low fertilizer

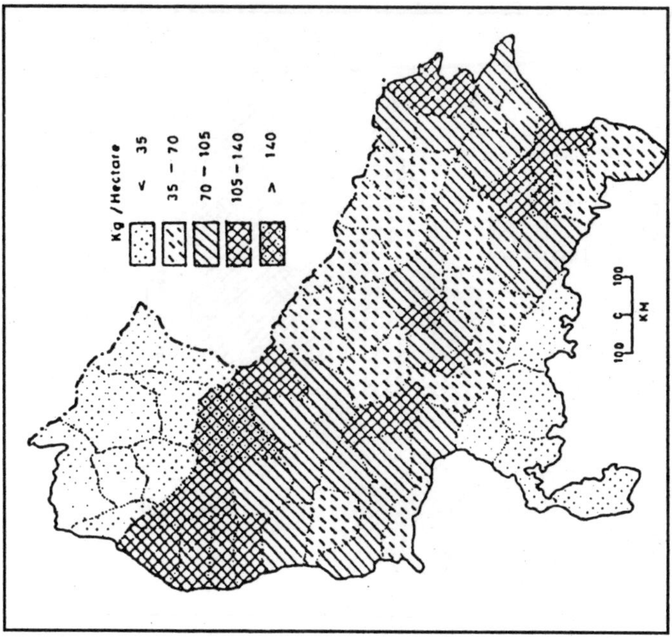

Fig. 15.3 : Uttar Pradesh—Fertilizer Consumption (1985-86)

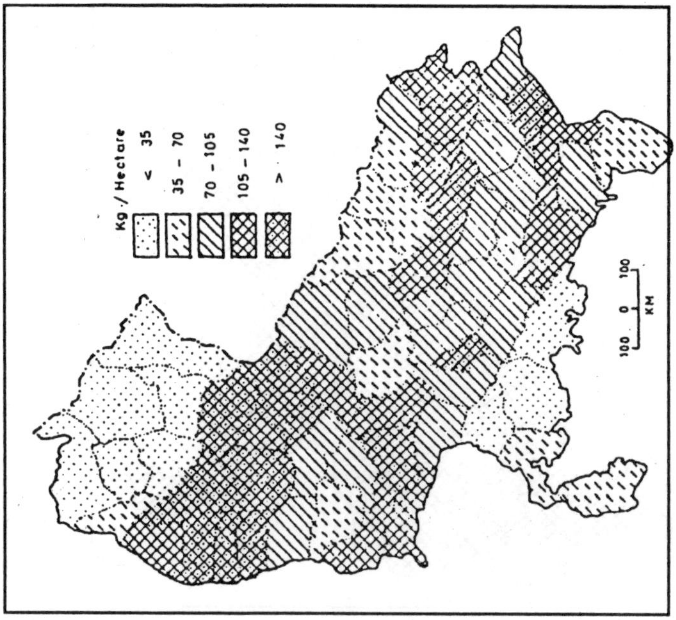

Fig. 15.4 : Uttar Pradesh—Fertilizer Consumption (1995-96)

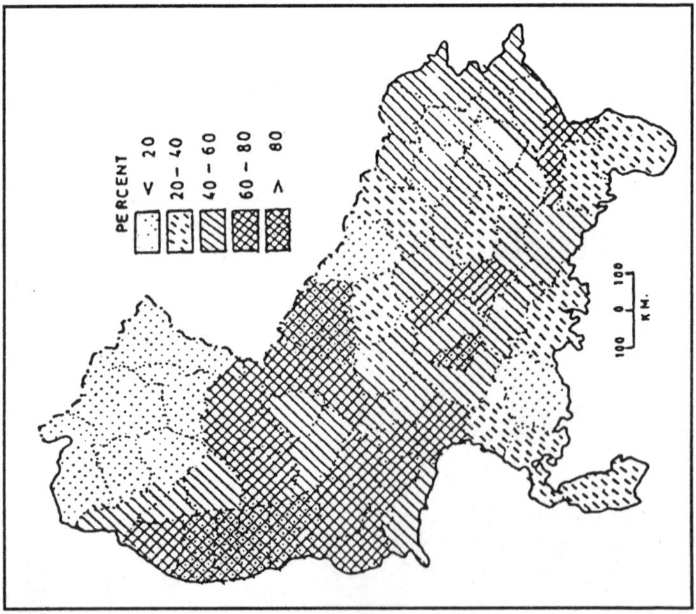

Fig. 15.5: Uttar Pradesh—Levels of Irrigation (1985-86)

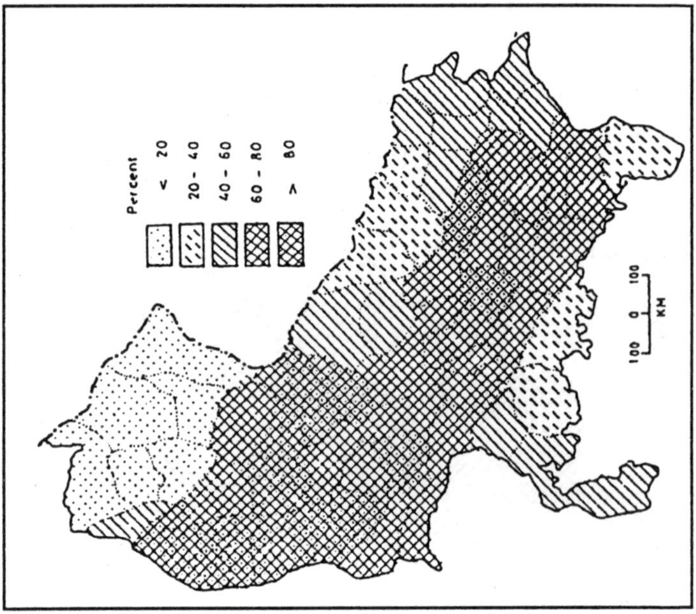

Fig. 15.6: Uttar Pradesh—Levels of Irrigation (1995-96)

consumption and low irrigation such as Almora, Chamoli, Garhwal, Pithoragarh, Tehri Garhwal and Uttarkashi. For example in Almora, the productivity was very low at both points of time, i.e. 996.70 kg/ha. in 1985-86 and 1160.64 kg/ha. in 1995-96, as compared to the State averages, and same is the case with Fertilizer Consumption, i.e. 5.93 kg/ha. and 4.20 kg/ha. while irrigation occupied only 12.48 per cent and 12.67 per cent of the cropped area during 1985-86 and 1995-96 respectively. The growth of these variables also recorded very low, i.e. growth in productivity registered 20.04 per cent, while fertilizer consumption and irrigation shows declining trends with the magnitude of –46.32 per cent and –25.75 per cent respectively. The same condition of declining trend of fertilizer consumption and irrigation with slight increase in productivity also persists in rest of the hilly districts. The districts of Bundelkhand region follows the same trend of low productivity, low fertilizer consumption and low irrigation but the trend of growth shows a considerable improvement in all these variables which is due to the improvement in the agriculture system, adoption of modern tools and other inputs like assured irrigation and promotional policies of government for agricultural development. The regions of semi-desert, arid and sub-humid (or tarai region), shows high productivity, high fertilizer consumption and high irrigation in most of the districts which shows high growth rate in all the said variables. For example, Agra of semi-desert region had productivity of wheat about 2520 kg/ha. in 1985-86, increased to 3194.94 kg/ha. in 1995-96, and very high increase in fertilizer consumption, i.e. from 65.77 kg/ha. to 122.86 kg/ha. and the irrigated area becomes 63.20 per cent from 53.42 per cent in the same span of time, so the growth in fertilizer consumption is very high, i.e. 86.83 per cent, while the growth in productivity of wheat and irrigation are 26.64 per cent and 18.31 per cent respectively. In case of Farrukhabad district of arid region, the productivity increased to 2975 kg/ha. from 2489.34 kg/ha., fertilizer consumption is increased to 138.03 kg/ha. from 117.92 kg./ha. whereas irrigation increased to 70.26 per cent from 53.39 per cent in the time span of 1985-86 and 1995-96. In case of Pilibhit district of sub-humid or Tarai region the productivity of wheat becomes 2711.12 kg/ha. from a low of 2063.22 kg/ha. along with fertilizer consumption which becomes 173.63 kg/ha. from 130.46 kg/ha. and irrigated area becomes 91.52 per cent from a low of 71.14 per cent in the same span of time, their values of growth estimated to be 31.43 per cent, 33.09 per cent and 28.65 per cent in case of productivity, fertilizer consumption and irrigation respectively. In 1995-96, the condition of all these valuables, improved considerably in almost all the districts of the State except the districts of hilly tract and Bundelkhand region but the magnitude of growth in irrigation is better than the fertilizer consumption.

Correlations in Wheat Productivity, Fertilizer Consumption and Irrigation

The analysis of correlation is done in different agro-climatic regions of U.P. on the basis of Spearman's correlation method. It is evident from the estimates that there is a strong correlation among these variables in different agro-climatic unit or it can be said that where the productivity of wheat is higher, the fertilizer consumption and irrigation is also higher, and where the productivity of wheat is lower, the fertilizer consumption and irrigation is also recorded lower. But there are some exceptions to this connotation.

The correlation estimated by the Spearman's method between productivity of wheat and fertilizer consumption, productivity of wheat and irrigated area, and between fertilizer consumption and irrigated land, in different agro-climatic region depicts a very clear picture of correlation. The productivity of wheat and fertilizer consumption has positive correlation in all the agro-climatic unit at both the intervals of time with few exceptions such as in the semi-arid region, a very weak correlation between productivity of wheat and fertilizer consumption during 1985-86 with the value of –0.0302, but in 1995-96, the correlation becomes positive with the value of 0.394795. In Tarai districts the correlation of wheat productivity and fertilizer consumption crepts towards weak from positive correlation with the values of 0.238466 in 1985-86 and –0.36318 in 1996-96. Bundelkhand region shows improvement in the values of correlation between wheat productivity and fertilizer consumption, i.e. 0.050129 and 0.237573 in 1985-86 and 1995-96, respectively. The semi-desert districts of the State have strong correlation between wheat productivity and fertilizer consumption in 1985-86, i.e. 0.638112 which become weaker, i.e. 0.548417 in 1995-96. In case of productivity of wheat and irrigation all the agro-climatic regions of U.P. have strong to very strong positive correlation except in Bundelkhand region where in1985-86 it was –0.25357 but after a decade in 1995-96, a very strong positive correlation exists with the value of 0.7604. In case of fertilizer consumption and irrigation, the trend of correlation becomes weak positive from strong positive in semi-desert,

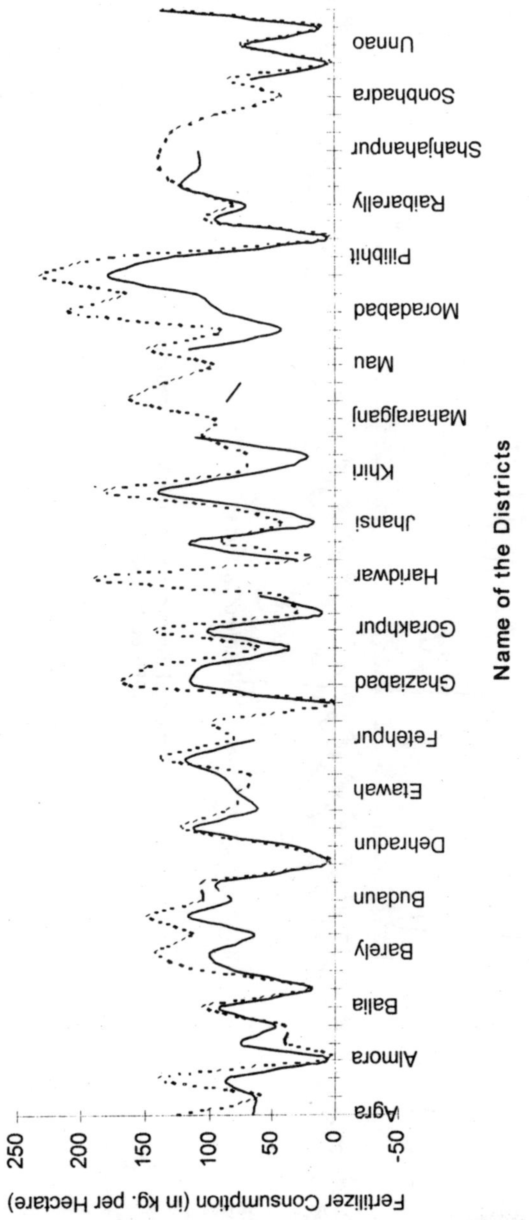

Fig. 15.7: Changing Pattern of Fertilizer Consumption in Uttar Pradesh 1985-86 to 1995-96

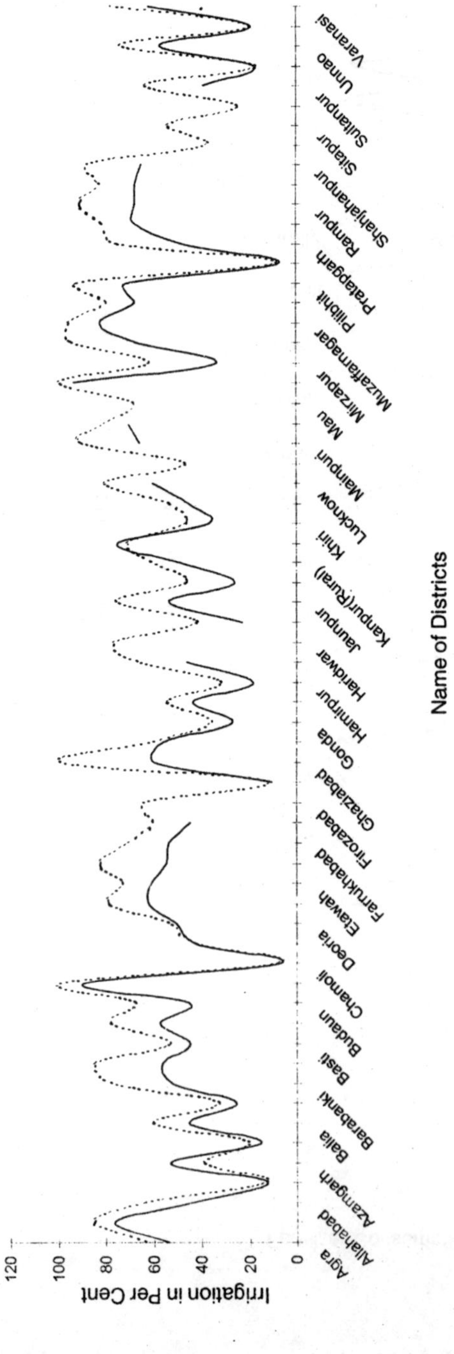

Fig. 15.8: Changing Pattern of Irrigation in Uttar Pradesh 1985-86 to 1995-96

arid and semi-arid. The Tarai districts show a very adverse situation where the value of Spearman's correlation decreased to –0.41134 from 0.467696, which indicates a faulty system of irrigation and inadequate fertilizer distribution and consumption. Among all the regions, Bundelkhand districts shows a good positive correlation, i.e. as the productivity increases, the fertilizer consumption and irrigation also increases as well. In the hilly districts the correlation between fertilizer consumption and irrigation shows nearly perfect positive, i.e. 0.935085 in 1985-86 and 0.949688 in 1995-96 (Table 15.2).

Table 15.2 : Spearman's Correlation Between Productivity of Wheat & Fertilizer Consumption, Productivity of Wheat & Irrigation, and Fertilizer Consumption & Irrigation

Agro-climatic Regions	*Prod. vs. F.C.* 1985-86	*Prod. vs. F.C.* 1995-96	*Prod. vs. Irii.* 1985-86	*Prod. vs. Irii.* 1995-96	*F.C vs. Irii.* 1985-86	*F.C. vs. Irii..* 1995-96
Semi-Desert	0.638112	0.548417	0.886660	0.505401	0.716480	0.376598
Arid	0.593635	0.483042	0.754941	0.472314	0.668336	0.412852
Semi-Arid	-0.03020	0.394795	0.324210	0.758854	0.777930	0.547538
Tarai or Sub-Humid	0.238466	-0.363180	0.560944	0.664304	0.467696	-0.41134
Hilly or Humid	0.832891	0.635011	0.827965	0.626885	0.935085	0.9949688
Bundelkhand	0.050129	0.237573	-0.253570	0.760400	0.604187	0.773115

Semi-Desert Region	:	Agra, Aligarh, Bulandshahr, Etah, Etawah, Ghaziabad, Mainpuri, Mathura and Faizabad.
Arid Region	:	Allahabad, Barabanki, Farrukhabad, Fetehpur, Hardoi, Kanpur (U), Kanpur (R), Lucknow, Meerut, Muzaffarnagar, Pratapgarh, Raibarelly, Sitapur and Unnao.
Semi-Arid Region	:	Azamgarh, Bahraich, Balia, Basti, Budaun, Deoria, Faizabad, Ghazipur, Gonda, Gorakhpur, Jaunpur, Khiri, Moradabad, Shahjahanpur, Sultanpur, Varasani, Mau, Maharajganj and Siddhartnagar.
Tarai or Sub-Humid Region	:	Bareilly, Bijnor, Nainital, Pilibhit, Rampur, Saharanpur and Haridwar.
Hilly or Humid Region	:	Almora, Chamoli, Dehradun, Garhwal, Pithoragarh, Tehri Garhwal and Uttarkashi.
Budelkhand Region	:	Sonbhadra, Mirzapur, Lalitpur, Jhansi, Hamirpur, Jalaun and Banda.

Prod. = **Productivity** of Wheat, F.C. = Fertilizer Consumption and Irri. = Irrigation.

The correlation between the magnitudes of growths of productivity of wheat, fertilizer consumption and irrigation shows that it is very weak and unpredictable (Table 15.3). It is seen that the correlation between the growths of wheat productivity and fertilizer consumption is negative in four agro-climatic regions, namely arid, semi-arid, tarai and hilly region. But semi-desert region shows a very strong positive correlation, i.e. 0.776557 while in Bundelkhand region it is weak positive, i.e. 0.041666. The correlation between the growths of wheat productivity and irrigation shows positive in all the six agro-climatic region but very strong positive correlation is observed in arid region which is very close to perfect positive correlation, i.e. 0.819839. On the other hand correlation between the growths of fertilizer consumption and irrigation varies from strongly negative to weak positive in different agro-climatic units of U.P. It means that optimum output in agricultural sectors has been achieved in the existing conditions only by applying the modern agricultural inputs. It does not mean that, there is no scope for further enhancement in productivity, but it can achieved by the proper planning. So there is a need to evaluate and change the existing cropping pattern, land use pattern and agricultural system to earn the optimum output using the limited resources because every resource has its limitation and restrictions.

Table 15.3 : Spearman's Correlation

Agro-climatic Regions	*Growth in Prod. vs. F.C.*	*Growth in Prod. vs. Irri.*	*Growth in F.C vs. Irri.*
Semi-desert	0.776557	0.081973	0.282087
Arid	– 0.15001	0.819839	0.023088
Semi-arid	– 0.03626	0.146934	0.117773
Sub-humid (Tarai)	– 0.38650	0.298991	0.196399
Humid (Hilly)	– 0.24473	0.226471	-0.41954
Bundelkhand	0.041666	0.164078	-0.16871

Prod. = Wheat productivity, F.C. = Fertilizer consumption and Irri. = Irrigation.

Conclusion

The correlation of wheat productivity with fertilizer consumption and irrigation is not uniform throughout the State, though the technological factors are more or less uniformly available. The gap in production and fertilizer consumption and irrigation is due to environmental variations at micro-level. The correlation of fertilizer consumption and irrigation with wheat production is positive in different agro-climatic regions but varies from one homogeneous region to another. A large number of districts of the State have low to very low percent growth in productivity of wheat fertilizer consumption and irrigation. The injudicious and indiscriminate use of fertilizer consumption and haphazard expansion of irrigation may create a serious problem for agricultural development. Thus for sustainable and remunerative agricultural development, the diffusion of irrigation and fertilizer consumption should be in right perspective. As in some districts, increase in fertilizer consumption has a diminishing return in terms of productivity of wheat. So there is a need to evaluate it, and replaced it with biofertilizer and green manure to enhance the productivity. The organic farming should be adopted in which the maintenance of soil fertility and the control of pests will be achieved through the enhancement of biological processes and ecological interaction. Certainly it will have long lasting effect on both physical and human world and will be helpful in retaining the sustainable growth and development.

References

Agarwal, A.N. (1980), *Indian Agriculture*, Vikas Publishing House, New Delhi.

Bhalla, G.S. and Alagh Y.K. (1979), *Performance of Indian Agriculture*, Sterling Publishing House, New Delhi.

Burns, W. (1944), *Technological Possibilities of Agricultural Development in India.* Superintendent, Government of Punjab, Lahore.

Ghosh, T.K. and Kashyap, S.P. (1996), District Level Planning in India: *An Overview of Agro-climatic Regional Planning Approach,* edited by G.S. Guha and S.P. Kashyap, *Agro- Climatic Planning in India,* Concept Publishing Company, New Delhi. Vol. 1, pp. 214-51.

Hussain, M. (1980), *Agricultural Geography of India*, Concept Publishing Company, New Delhi.

Jha, D.N. (1989), *Agriculture and Regional Planning*, Mittal Publication, New Delhi.

Joshi, S.N. (1995), Yield Gap Analysis in Agro-Climatic Sub-Regions, Edited by D.N. Basu and S.P. Kashyap, *Agro-Climatic Regional Planning in India*, New Delhi, Vol.2, Concept Publishing Company.

Mohammad, A. (1989), *Food Production and Food Problems in India*, Concept Publishing Company, New Delhi.

Mohammad, A. (1992), Regional Imbalances in Levels of Agricultural Productivity, Edited by Noor Mohammad, *New Dimensions in Agricultural Geography,* Vol.1, Concept Publishing Company, New Delhi.

Mohammad, A., Ali, M. and Hanafi, Y.S. (1998), "Response of Fertilizer in Wheat Productivity: A case study of Uttar Pradesh", *The Geographer*, The Aligarh Muslim University Geographical Society, Department of Geography, A.M.U. Aligarh, Vol.45. No.2, pp. 1-21.

Mohammad, N. (1991), Technological Change and Spatial Diffusion of Agricultural Innovations in Trans-Ghagra Plain, Edited by Noor Mohammad, *Perspective in Agricultural Geography*, Vol. 5, Concept Publishing Company, New Delhi.

Nagarajan, S. (1997), *Wheat: Promise of Value-added Products*, The Hindu Survey of Indian Agriculture, Kasturi & Sons Ltd., Chennai.

Nagarajan, S. and Singh, G. (1998), Sustaining Wheat Revolution: Retrospect and prospects, *Indian Journal of Agricultural Sciences*, Vol. 68, No.8, pp. 396-404.

Raychaudhuri, S.P. *et al.* (1963), *Soils of India*, Indian Council of Agricultural Research, New Delhi.

Shafi, M. (1984), *Agricultural Productivity and Regional Imbalances: A case study of Uttar Pradesh*, Concept Publishing Company, New Delhi.

Sharma, B.L. and Bhardwaj, P. (1998), Sustainable Agricultural Development, Edited by H.S. Sharma and S. Chattopadhayay, *Sustainable Development*, Concept Publishing Company, New Delhi, pp. 183-94.

Singh, R.L. (1971), *Regional Geography of India*, National Geographical Society, Varanasi.

Tapeshwar Singh (1998), Fertilizer Use, Food Security and Sustainable Agricultural Development: An India Experience, *The Geographer*, The Aligarh Musilm University Geographical Society, Department of Geography, A.M.U Aligarh, Vol. 45, No. 2, pp. 78-92.

16

LAND-USE CHANGES AND STATUS OF AGRICULTURAL PRODUCTION IN INTER-STATE CHANDIGARH REGION, NW INDIA

YADVINDER SINGH & DHIAN KAUR

Introduction

Ever since the dawn of civilization land-use changes have been taking place from time-to-time. Along with, there have been extension of farmlands for increasing food production to meet the demand of growing population. Urbanization is the major factor in influencing use of land. With the development of new urban areas or with the expansion of existing ones, there have often been encroachments on the fertile agricultural lands. Same is the story of the development of the Capital City of Chandigarh lying in NW India.

The landscape of Chandigarh and its satellite towns of SAS Nagar (Mohali) in Punjab and Panchkula in Haryana, is amongst the most well planned and well developed urban systems in India. Parts of agriculturally fertile and well developed Punjab-Haryana Rolling Plains lie in the S, SW and NW of this urban system and cultivated rolling piedmont plains encircle it on the N, NE and SE. In order to regulate the land-use and urban growth in the peripheral region of Chandigarh, the Inter-State Chandigarh Region (ISCR) with Chandigarh City as its core was demarcated in 1976 by Government of India, Co-ordination Committee on Regional Planning to cover an area of 2,513 sq. km.

At the time of attaining Independence in 1947 India experienced the World's one of the largest population migrations in human history and this brought in its wake a great setback to agricultural operations in

NW India for several years. As an aftermath, foodgrain shortages were faced till mid-sixties and the government had to rely on heavy imports of food. In order to attain food self-sufficiency an era of Green Revolution was begun in India around 1965 with the introduction and cultivation of Mexican wheats mainly in Punjab, Haryana, Western Uttar Pradesh and Ganganagar district of Rajasthan. Performance of Green Revolution in India has been debated and evaluated amongst others by Frankel (1971), Chakravarti (1973), Randhawa (1974), Singh (1974), Chadha (1979), Bidwi (1983) and Shiva (1989). Recently, agricultural development in South Asia has been monitored by Singh (1997) as based on district by district data and field truthing which has resulted in broad delimitation of agro-ecological regions. However, there is very little assessment at regional or local levels regarding land-use and agricultural production in the context of development and urbanization in Punjab and the adjoining Haryana region. For ISCR in fact no such information is available. Therefore, from 1989-1994 the writer was involved in evaluating impact and implications of development on various ecosystems in ISCR for the 25 years period of 1967-68 to 1990-91. As a result of this evaluation, the present analysis of data on land-use changes and agricultural production in DAE of ISCR is presented.

Circumvention of the Analysed Region

In order to embrace the physical features in workable outlay by taking *tehsil* as a unit for database, ISCR circumvention was extended by the writer to cover 5,391.50 sq. km. area lying between 30°17′-31°11′ north Latitude and 76°16′-77°29′ East Longitude. Thus the evaluated ISCR region includes (i) Union Territory of Chandigarh forming the core area, (ii) Punjab area: Kharar and Ropar tehsils of Ropar district, Rajpura tehsil of Patiala district and Fatehgarh Sahib tehsil of the same district, (iii) Haryana area: Kalka and Narayangarh tehsils of Ambala district (now Kalka as a separate district), and (iv) Himachal area: Parts of Nalagarh tehsil of Solan district circumventing Siwaliks ISCR. Four ecosystems as Natural Hilly Ecosystem (NHE), Heterotrophic Urban-Industrial Ecosystem (HUIE), Semi-Natural Drainage Ecosystem (SNDE), and Domesticated Agro-Ecosystems (DAE) and their areas were clearly demarcated but the main analysis centres around DAE which is the dominant ecosystem covering 4,415 sq. km area, i.e. 81.88 per cent of total area of ISCR but only 64 per cent of the total area of ISCR region is under cultivation.

Data Base

Secondary data relating to spatial spread of different ecosystems and various indicators of agriculture were compiled from Revenue Records (RR) and District Statistical Abstracts (DSA).

Land-Use Classification*

The DAE primarily comprises of (a) agricultural fertile highly developed upland and flood plain lying to the S, SW and NW of the HUIE, (b) cultivated piedmont plain located N, NE and SE of the HUIE, and (c) cultivated *choe* (seasonal stream) terraces and *choe* valley low lands in the DAE. Over the last three decades or so since the beginning of Green Revolution in India there has been noticeable changes in agricultural land-use. Therefore, in order to show the changes in agricultural land utilization pattern in DAE the information given in RR and DSA is classified as follows:

Forest

These constitute the most vital class of agricultural land-use. Area under forests in the present ecosystem has not changed much. During the period under review, from 1967-68 to 1972-73, it increased by 9.35 per cent. Then during the next 5 years period it fell by 13.61 per cent. The area showed 7.11 per cent increase as it became 47,040 ha. in 1982-83. But again a slight decline of 1.98 per cent by 1987-88 was seen. It increased to 49,499 ha. in 1990-91 which showed a marginal increase of 6.25 per cent over 1967-68 figure. This is primarily due to introduction of agro-forestry and social forestry in the region. Otherwise the natural forests with dominant native species, *Butea monosperma* (*dhak*) forests which existed in the forties and fifties along side Attawa and Kanthala *choes* have completely been destroyed and all the land on *choe* margins and some even on the bed has been put under agriculture. Under agro-social forestry programmes primarily *Eucalyptus* has been cultivated.

Agro-forestry refers to adoption of the method of growing woody perennials along with agricultural crops on the same unit of land.

* Although land-use and land-cover are closely related and inter-changeable terms yet strictly speaking according to NRSA (1989) land-use refers to "man's activities and various uses which are carried on land" and land-cover refers to "natural vegetation, water bodies, rock/soil, artificial cover and others resulting due to land transformation."

Cultivation of *Eucalyptus* and *Populus* trees in rows within the fields and along boundaries as a regular practice, has been adopted nearly three decades ago in the ISCR. This practice of growing trees on farm lands for generating additional income and employment quickly gained momentum. But there had been indiscriminate cultivation of *Eucalyptus* all around because of its fast growth, lesser soil coverage, least post plantation care and more economic gains apart from enthusiastic approach of the foresters and industrialists. However, after mid-eighties the popularity of the tree amongst agriculturists has suffered a drastic change because of the enlightenment brought about through scientific research.

Land not Available for Cultivation

Land not available for cultivation showed almost a gradual increase of 17.88 per cent over the period, from 61,161 ha. in 1967-68 to 72,100 ha. in 1990-91. There has been a tremendous increase (164.10%) in the land used for non-agricultural purposes which has primarily been due to the up-coming of satellite towns of SAS Nagar and Panchkula as well as construction of Satluj-Yamuna Link (SYL) Canal. Area under this category had more than doubled from 25,104 ha. In 1967-68 to 54,480 ha. in 1972-73. Barren and non-cultivable land showed a marked decrease from 36,507 ha. in 1967-68 to only 5,800 ha. in 1990-91 indicating a decline of 529.43 per cent.

Fallow Land

The area under this category markedly dropped from 18,989 ha. in 1967-68 to 8,500 ha. in 1982-83 (44.76% of total i.e. – 55.24%) but during 1982-83 to 1990-91 the area of fallow land increased by 63.17 per cent.

Culturable Waste

Culturable waste recorded a gradual reduction in area from 24,988 ha. in 1967-68 to 9,240 ha. in 1990-91. However, the culturable waste as very less in 1987-88, i.e. only 6,963 ha. The fluctuations are due to the fact that urban earmarked land remains under utilized or lies vacant with growth of wild plants.

Through the use of fertilizers and water, barren lands, culturable waste as well as fallow land have been brought under cultivation of mainly rice and wheat.

Net Sown Area and Total Cropped Area

The net sown area in the ecosystem increased marginally by 2.4 per cent from 1967-68 to 1990-91, largely through the extension of the plough to new lands. The total cropped area increased from 451,464 ha. in 1967-68 to 538,400 ha. in 1990-91. There has been a gradual increase over the years in the area sown more than once. It shows an overall 58.20 per cent increase. This depicts a welcome trend towards intensive cultivation.

Change in Cropping Patterns

Due to extensive and intensive agriculture during 1967-68 to 1990-91 period and through use of High Yielding Varieties (HYVs), agro-chemicals (fertilizers, weedicides, etc.), frequent irrigations and farm mechanization, large tracts of barren-fallow-culturable waste lands have been brought under cultivation particularly for wheat and rice crops. At the same time there was continuous diversion of fertile agricultural lands for non-agricultural purposes. Therefore, the net sown area of DAE increased only by 2.4 per cent being mainly through the extension of agriculture to new lands. There has been extensive use of ground waters (tubewell irrigation) for crop production with the result that the tubewell irrigated area increased from 65,752 ha. (1967-68) to 2,07,500 ha. (1990-91). Also fertilizer consumption relevant to per hectare of net sown area showed an increase of 113.95 per cent during the period under review.

This, the impact of Green Revolution on crop production has been immense. There has been emphasis on multiple cropping and use of HYVs. A big change from long duration to short duration crops was distinctly noticeable. There has been overwhelming dominance of wheat-rice rotation year after year over the same lands. During summer fallow lands were hardly ever left for restoring soil fertility. Instead, by adopting multi-cropping pattern farmer stated more and more use of HYVs, fertilizers, repeated irrigations, agro-chemicals and mechanical farming. Long duration crops as cotton and sugarcane cultivation was not favoured and so also the cultivation of barley, sorghum, pearl millet, gram, rapeseed and mustard was discarded. Many of these crops are now grown on rain-fed soils or on poor soils. In addition to wheat and rice crop combination, potato and sugarcane crops are favoured. With availability of ground water irrigation facility, ground nut, pulses and oilseed crops are replaced. Rather area under these crops has been diverted to other crops as wheat, rice, potato, etc.

Agricultural Production

In ISCR during 1967-68 to 1990-91 the Green Revolution resulted in 272.48 per cent increase in grain production although the area under foodgrains had increased by only 73.38 per cent. During the 25 years' period wheat and rice production showed remarkable increase of 250.35 per cent and 850.09 per cent respectively. This extremely high boost in production is explained by adoption of modern technology, intensive cultivation and reclamation of new lands for wheat and rice cultivation. The area under the two crops has increased by 80.8 per cent and 209.55 per cent respectively but at the cost of many other crops.

As far as pulses and oilseeds are concerned the total production is not proportionate to area increase. Per hectare yield of wheat increased from 1,342-1,839 kg in 1967-68 to 2,190-3,565 kg in 1990-91. Rice also showed sharp increase in the lowest and highest per hectare yield. Lower yields correspond to *barani* (non-irrigated) or poorly irrigated areas that like in Kalka and Narayangarh tehsils in Haryana. For wheat the year 1990-91 showed 93.85 per cent increase in highest yield and 63.18 per cent increase in case of lowest yield of 1967-68 base year. Rice yield maintained a steady increase amounting to 164.35 per cent in lowest yield and 211.20 per cent in highest yield. Broadly speaking during 1967-68 to 1990-91, the per hectare yield of wheat is just nearly double but in case of rice the increase in yield is more than three times. This is really a very remarkable achievement.

The yield of maize has been fluctuating but during 1987-88 the highest per hectare yield increased to 2,051 kg (46.08% increase) but it dropped to 1,970 kg/ha. in 1990-91 (40.31%) increase as compared to 1967-68 yield. Barley yield/ha. showed a steady increase over the period with the lowest yield showing 55.17 per cent and the highest yield showing 116.79 per cent increase. For pearl millet the yield shows high degree of disparity. It is interesting to note that maize, barley, sorghum and pearl millet reflect very modest per hectare yield when compared with wheat and rice.

By and large, yield of sugarcane and potato has shown a steady increase. Sugarcane reflected nearly 66.67 per cent increase over 1967-68 figure. While potato indicated 77.21 per cent increase in the lowest and 55.13 per cent increase in the highest/ha yield. Gram production was very variable over the years since high rains during winter lower the per hectare yield. Groundnut yield showed a gradual fall and also there has been no major improvement for cotton with the lowest and highest per hectare yield indicating an increase of only 33.09 per cent and 13.11 per cent when 1967-68 and 1990-91 figures are compared. Rapeseed and mustard yield is highly variable over the years with highest yield increasing by 66.57 per cent in 1990-91 over 1967-68 figure. The fluctuating per hectare yields of these crops were dependent on the weather conditions during growing and harvesting seasons.

In DAE of ISCR wheat, rice, sugarcane and potato have experienced appreciable increase in yield while groundnut grown on non-irrigated soils has experienced a decline in area as well as yield. Cotton cultivation is not of very high commercial order in DAE of ISCR. Barley, sorghum, pearl millet, gram, rapeseed and mustard are largely grown on *barani* or poorly irrigated soils. The main thrust in the agricultural production has been for yield increase in the case of wheat, rice, maize, sugarcane and potato.

Discussion

It was recently found that *Eucalyptus* cultivation causes heavy damage to the adjoining crops by lowering down of water table, depletion of soil of nutrients due to lesser leaf production in proportion to bole size and delayed leaf composition (Kohli 1992). Also, it has earlier been found by Kohli *et al.* (1990) that plantation of *Eucalyptus* as a monoculture or as a shelter belt in agricultural lands exercises negative influence on winter crops in terms of plant density, root and shoot growth, biomass and economic yield. Field *bund* monoculture plantation of *Eucalyptus* has been shown by Singh and Kohli (1992) to have drastic effect on adjacent crops through release certain chemicals into the field environment (atmosphere and rhizosphere). This means practice of agro-forestry with adoptation of *Eucalyptus* plantations have to be followed with caution and restraints. Agro-forestry as a sustainable land-use system and for resource conservation has been recommended by Yadav (1990) and Singh and Singh (1990). This would naturally help in meeting short falls in the supply of fuel wood, fodder, timber, etc. and for proper water shed management. Of course, selection of woody species meant for cultivation under agro-forestry programme needs to be done carefully under expert advice of agronomists and botanists.

There is absolutely no doubt that the Green Revolution introduced in India in mid-sixties proved to be a boon for the farmers since it resulted in marked increase in agricultural production. The main strength of this agricultural revolution laid on three surmises as (i) genetic manipulation of seed to improve yield, i.e. creating HYVs, (ii) cultivation of short duration HYVs, application of fertilizers, application of frequent irrigations, eradication of weeds and diseases from crops through applications of weedicides and insecticides, and (iii) mechanization of farm operations and taking proper care to boost production in the agro-ecosystem. Unfortunately intensive agriculture centred around wheat-rice rotational cultivation, resulted in non or less cultivation of traditional crops. This led to the erosion or even destruction of genetic diversity base of agriculture in north India. Instead of cultivation of diverse native varieties suited to different soil and water conditions, monocultures of single or few varieties from exotic genetic sources or their manipulations have been cultivated. Intensive agriculture resulted in longer retentions of pests and fungal or microbial inoculum in soils because the age-old practice of leaving ploughed lands fallow had been abandoned.

There have been several other after-effects of Green Revolution in ISCR such as (i) deterioration in quality of surface and ground waters, (ii) depletion of ground waters, (iii) waterlogging and salinization/ alkalinization, (iv) soil pollution and degradation, etc. These form subject matter of another communication.

Summing up, it may be stated that in DAE of ISCR in spite of marked changes in land-use due to urbanisation resulting in diversion of fertile agricultural lands to non-agricultural purposes as well as several after-effects of Green Revolution as noted earlier, there has been a great development in agriculture sector as reflected through high increase in farm productivity during 1967-68 to 1990-91 period.

Acknowledgements

The writers wish to express their gratitude to Professor G.S. Gossal, Prof. (Mrs.) Swaranjit Mehta and Prof. M.S. Gill for inspiration and encouragement.

References

Bidwai, P. (1983), Indian Agriculture in Trouble : Consequences of Green Revolution. New Delhi: *Times of India*. February 22, 1983, p. 6.

Chadha, G.K. (1979), Production Grains of New Agricultural Technology. Panjab Univ. Publ.

Chakravarty, A.K. (1973), Green Revolution in India. *Ann. Assoc. Amer. Geogr. 63*: 319-330.

Frankel, F. (1971). *India's Green Revolution: Economic Gains and Political Costs.* Princeton: Univ. Press.

Kolhi, R.K. (1992), Allelopathic implications of *Eucalyptus* in agro-ecosystems. Nat. Symp. on "*Allelopathy in Agri-ecosystems*", HAU, Hissar Feb. 12-14, 1992. Special Lecture Abstract, pp. 1-5.

Kohli, R.K., Singh, D. & Verma, R.C. (1990), Influence of *Eucalyptus* shelter belt on winter season agro-ecosystem. *Agri. Ecosystems & Environment* 33: 23.31.

NRSA (1989), Manual of Nationwide Land-use/Land Cover using satellite Imagery Part I. National Remote Sensing Agency, Department of Space, Government of India, Balanagar, Hyderabad. pp. I-vi, 1-58.

Randhawa, M.S. (1974), *Green Revolution: A case study of Punjab*, New Delhi, Vikas Publishing House.

Shiva, V. (1989), The violence of the Green Revolution: Ecological Degradation and Political Conflict in Punjab. Dehra Dun: Research Foundation for Science & Ecology Publ.

Singh, D. & Kohli, R.K. (1992), Reasons of poor under floor vegetation of *Eucalyptus*. In: Tauro, P. & Narural, S.S. (Eds.) *Allelopathy in Agro-ecosystem*. HAU, Hissar Publ. pp. 114-17.

Singh, G.B. & Singh, H.K. (1990), Agro-forestry for resource conservation. *Proc. Internatn. Symposium on Water, Erosion, Sedimentation and Resource Conservation*, CSWCRTI, Dehra Dun. pp. 376-89.

Singh, J. (1974), *An Agricultural Atlas of India: A Geographical Analysis*. Kurukshetra: Vishal Publication.

Singh, J. (1997), *Agricultural Development in South Asia: A Comparative Study in the Green Revolution Experiences*. New Delhi: National Book Organization.

Yadav, J.S.P. (1990), Agro-forestry as a sustainable land-use system. Proc. International Symposium on Water, Erosion, Sedimentation and Resource Conservation, CSWCRTI, Dehra Dun. pp. 364-75.

17

PLANNING FOR THE GROWTH OF AGRICULTURAL PRODUCTIVITY AND ECONOMIC DEVELOPMENT

A Study of Dadri Tehsil (Haryana)

A.K. CHHAUKAR & Y.K. MITTAL

Study Area

The study area 'Dadri Tehsil of Bhiwani District of Haryana lies between 28°22′55′′ to 28°33′49′′ north latitudes and 75°48′57′′ to 76°28′10′′ east longitudes which is in the South-Western part of Haryana (Fig. 17.1). The total area of the study region is 1378.85 sq. km. ranging between arid to semi-arid climate, having nearly 300 mm. of average annual rainfall. The topographical patterns of the study area and its existence to geomorphic process have closer relationship with climatic aridity of the recent and past geological periods. The topography of the region is a mixture of sandy undulating plain, dunal plain and a pocket of old alluvial plain with some Aravalli outcrops.

Planning the Development

The study of agricultural growth and its impact on the economy constitutes a significant aspect to provide a good basis for regional planning and economic development. Therefore, it is essential to examine and understand the regional diversity in natural conditions, inequalities in the distribution of various aspects of agricultural modernization and to explain imbalances in the levels of land use, crop land use occupancy etc. The regional imbalances in the distribution of resources and

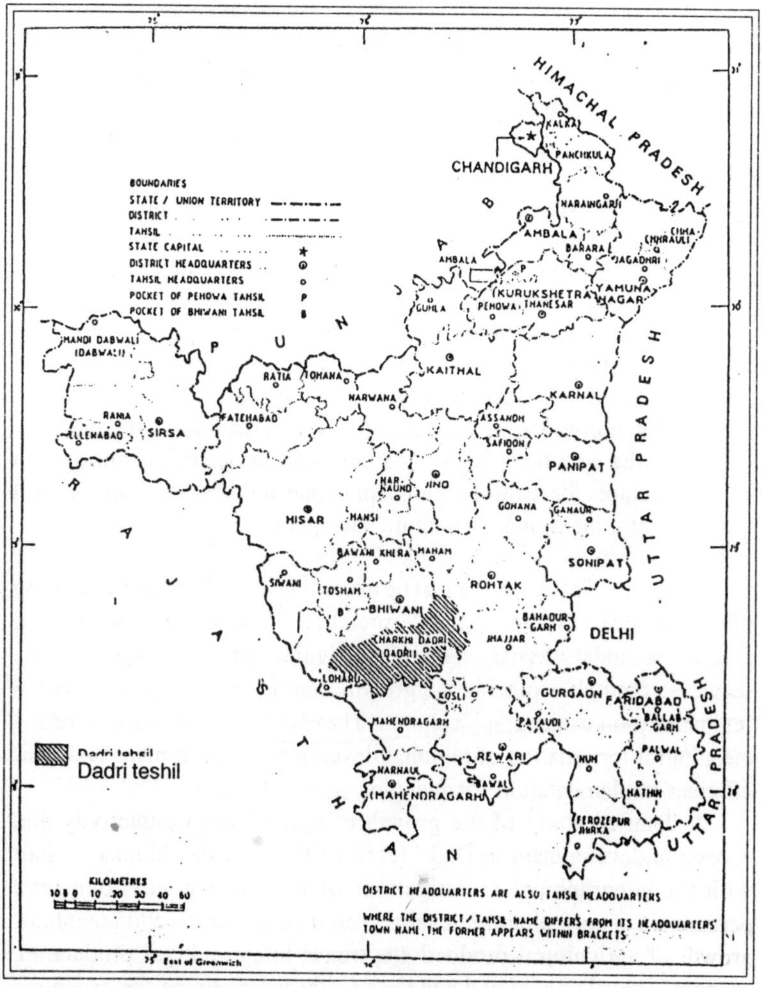

Fig. 17.1: Haryana Administrative Divisions, 1991

inequalities in the levels of resources development strike and act as irritants so provoke geographers to redress them. Therefore, a geographic analysis of the terrainal characteristics are responsible to modify the use of geographical area and influence the land use, cultivation of various crops and agricultural productivity.

Dadri Tehsil of Bhiwani district of Haryana is still suffering from economic backwardness and neglected vital socio-economic services. These are because of negative discrimination planning concept based on political oriented and expenditure oriented regional planning. Further, the inability to successful implementation of regional development plans is due to –

— the lack of information regarding regional diversities in natural conditions and imbalances in human circumstances which are responsible for regional inequalities in development of economic activities;

— the inadequate information at spatio-temporal scale concerning crop land occupancy, rural industrial development, agro service centres and vital socio-economic services; and

— the non-availability of division of an area into viable planning units with their major/medium rural service centres or growth centres for fruitful regional planning at grossroot level for rural betterment and agricultural development.

The above deficiencies must be overcome by attempting monitoring of biophysical environment, interpretation of geographic patterns of primary/secondary/tertiary economic activities and vital socio-economic services, equitable placing of growth centres and purpose-oriented regionalisation of geographical area. These are the prerequisites for the meaningful formulation of regional development action-plans and their efficient implementation for planning perspectives.

A detailed study of the growth of agricultural productivity and economic development in Dadri tehsil of Haryana should make a start with the geographical investigations of the physical environmental parameters of agricultural relevance, resource utilisation and potentials, growth of agricultural productivity, trends in agricultural production, economic development and suggestions for the planning for economic development to an application of a model for delimitation of viable planning units and placing of service centres. Such an analysis ought to highlight certain situations at spatial and temporal scale, and these are:

— Regional diversities in natural conditions and imbalance in resource utilisation and potentials interface responsible for inequalities in spatial patterning of socio-economic manifestations.

— Areas of dynamism and stagnation in terms of economic development and areas of prosperity and backwardness in levels of socio-economic development; particularly agricultural development in the developing regions.

So far the situational analysis was carried out and the functional gaps were identified, and now, the need arises for making specific recommendations for planning. As such, the ensuing profiles strive at achieving this goal whereby the state government, a primary locational decision maker in regional planning could mould regional policies and economy. It would successfully accomplish resources and opportunities for the regional development so as to redress the existing regional inequalities in resources development.

In order to achieve these objectives, the essentials are the area-based action-programmes based on positive-discrimination planning concept for effecting improvements in agricultural productivity, rural small scale/household industry and vital socio-economic services. The action programmes are the prerequisites for planning for the Agricultural productivity.

Planning for Socio-economic and Technological Infrastructure

Of the much needed inputs to increase foodgrain output in the study area, land reforms deemed to play a pivotal role. The emphasis here has to be on economically viable size of operational holding rather than on merely implementing land reforms. The viable size is the basic requirement for optimal use of agricultural land, including water and human resources. Moreover, it will encourage the farmers to modernise their farm operations with the use of new farm technology.

The size of farms and capability of land in terms of land suitability for irrigation restrict the degree of agricultural capitalization at the unviable size of holdings (under 3 hectares), which dominate the area under reference in particular. Therefore, for future planning and accomplishing better field productivity results through maintaining the viable size of operational holdings, the five pronged drive may be implemented, namely,

— Enact a legislation to fix a minimum size of family holding below which the sub-division of farms be not allowed.

— Imposition of ceiling on agricultural holdings and physical distribution of surplus land to small land farmers.
— Preparation and maintenance of up-dated land records reflecting genuine tenurial system.
— Redefinition of self-cultivation (*khud-kasht*) be that those land owners who stay in close proximity to the holding and cultivate the land by personal and family labour.
— Surplus family labour force be provided alternate employment in occupations other than agriculture in rural areas through the decentralisation process of small scale industry and diversification in rural economy with emphasis on mixed farming, i.e. mini-dairy farming/piggery/poultry farming-cum-crop farming/bee keeping.

The operational holdings under 3 hectares are economically unviable size for the implementation of package programmes. To overcome this problem and the other operational problems faced by small-sized operational holdings, the community approach should be adopted for operational purposes by small farmers. The farmers should overcome many of the handicaps of small size of land holdings if the suggested processes in farming are adopted. Promulgation and acceptance of these approaches in the study area will ensure to improve farm production efficiency.

Since the vagaries of rainfall and long dry spells are common features in this part of the State, the strengthening of secondary and tertiary system of irrigation is essential for agricultural development which otherwise is inherited by favourable terrain having slope under 3°, average temperture conditions above the threshold and fine/coarse loamy soils. A comprehensive primary system of irrigation is needed to increase crop production and labour demand per hectare. Irrigation should not be treated as an end in itself, rather it should be considered as a mean to increase productivity from the soils. Therefore, the new outlook has to be production-oriented and more attention should be paid towards

— Maximizing production from the available irrigation resources.
— Strengthening existing secondary and tertiary systems so as to make them primary irrigation system and to improve intensity of irrigation, particularly in the dunal and sandy undulating plain.

- — Improving the efficiency of irrigation, i.e. to provide water to field crops during both cropping seasons.
- — Introducing sprinkler irrigation systems for making the efficient use of scarce water resources.
- — Husbanding rainwater with efficient dry farming technology and soil mulch farming techniques etc.
- — Tailoring cropping pattern and crop sequencing to the existing natural conditions, particularly, soil texture/structure/moisture conditions.
- — Extending irrigation facilities to the dunal plain and sandy undulating plain.

The most important immediate measure should be to develop suitable mechanized implements for different farm operations and the same should be made available to small sized and medium sized farmers at subsidised rates. The use of modern farm implements should be promoted through the established agro-service centres. Such a process of selective mechanisation and agro-based household industries should be established. In spite of progress made in the use of bio-chemical inputs in recent years, the full potential of agriculture is far from being realised. Essentially, a reflection of the environmental fact that, by and large, the cropping system in the study area is still dominated, the coarse foodgrains and yields are still relatively low.

Policy makers and development planners must devise and implement measures to upgrade the yield level of coarse grain crops which occupy about 20 per cent of the total cropped area. As such, it is unfortunate that while the farmers are increasingly resorting to high-yielding varieties, they are not providing them requisite nutrition. Therefore, it is not surprising that the feasible yield level of coarse grains is not being fully exploited. Further it is suggested that an emphasis on bio-technological revolution be given by subsidising green manure ziad crops, particularly cluster bean and green gram. The liberal introduction of these crops in arid areas will maintain soil health without any financial strain on the small and medium size-class farmers. A stress be laid on the need for promoting fertilizer-use efficiency and economy through the use of bio-fertilizers, organic manures and agronomic practices.

Planning for Land-use and Agricultural Land Utilisation

It is evident that the land resources have not utilised optimally in accordance with their potentiality and this has directly influenced the socio-economic life of the people. As such, it necessitates the planning for land use and agricultural land utilization. Thus, the contours of the Eight-tier Integrated Action Plan for agricultural transformation be finalised and the same be implemented as under

- Social forestry,
- Forestry protective measures,
- Improving land-use efficiency,
- Cover-crop cultivation and mulch farming techniques,
- Restructuring cropping pattern and dryland farming,
- Mixed crop system in rotation with intensive green manure fallowing and organic fertilization,
- Size-class oriented agricultural development projects, and
- Incentive-oriented farm products pricing policy and marketing facilities.

Any appreciable improvement in ecological balance and rural economy can be made in the sandy undulating environment provided the villagers are made to participate in Green the Area Programmes for instance. The greening drive in arid land stretches should be followed and the villages be convinced that this process will set a new record in afforestation. Soil conservation in the erosion prone areas has to be done on war footing with massive afforestation on barren and unculturable land where social forestry has to be undertaken to check water erosion in the dunal plain.

Social forestry has a pivotal role to play in the drought-prone arid and semi-arid areas of Dadri tehsil which have a negligible share of the geographical area under forest, i.e. about 0.75 per cent *vis-à-vis* the critical value of 20 per cent for forest-environment in plain area as envisaged in the National Forest Policy. Moreover, the biological balance will be achieved in these areas by social forestry and social conservation. At the same time, these social forestry projects can generate rural employment opportunities and these will improve the physio-social-economic climate of the area.

There is no scope for horizontal expansion of area under cultivation of crops but there is still sufficient scope for increasing cropping intensity. It should be possible to further increase land-use efficiency to at least 200 per cent level. Land-use efficiency patterns and dynamics for the reported time period reveal that cropping intensity have not been particularly promising for most of the study area. Furthermore, with the population increasing at a natural rate of about 2 per cent per annum and the declining man-land ratio, it will become difficult in near future to balance the annual food requirements with the yearly production unless land-use efficiency is improved within the accessible irrigation and dry-farming technological facilities. Introduction of efficient cropping systems and crop-sequences by adopting scientific soil and management techniques would open a new era in the efficient land utilisation, i.e. vertical expansion of cultivation in the area under study.

Soil erosion is a serious problem in drought-prone areas during the hot dry season due to the high detachability of the coarse soils in the dunal and sandy undulating plains. The suitable measure is to reduce soil erosion with water conservation by following cover crop cultivation and mulch-farming techniques. Suitable cover crops are leguminous pulses which have long been used in soil conservation and in soil fertility maintenance as green manures. Mulch-farming technique means the application of crop residue mulches on a soil surface. The best mean of obtaining mulch on a soil surface is a proper built-in rotational sequence in the cropping pattern ensuring an adequate quantity of crop residue as left over. Moreover, it will maintain an adequate level of organic matter while giving better yields than conventional farming.

Diversify cropping should be the slogan for the farmers in the area. Industrialisation of agriculture is the broad process wherein the total agricultural production adopts the characteristics of the modern industrial economy. More emphasis should be given to the status of crops like oilseeds, pulses, fodders and legumes in the cropping pattern. A concerted effort should be made to maximise oilseeds production in the study area where crop ecology is favourable for mustard, in particular.

The future of Indian agriculture lies in dryland farming because rainfed farming fields constituted about 70 per cent of the arable land in the country and it was from these fields that higher production could be expected in the near future. The agricultural performance level was very low in the dryland farming areas and it was definitely possible to raise this level by 100 per cent through the dry farming technologies available today at the Jodhpur-based Central Arid Zone Research Institute (CAZRI) one of the units of the Indian Council for Agricultural Research (ICAR).

There are wide yield gaps in the major foodgrain crops between the potential yield level a result of improved green revolution technology *vis-à-vis* the average-yield level, even in the agriculturally healthy areas.

It has been observed that bigger gaps exist in the study area should be scanned in the viable planning units.

Therefore, measures have to be devised to increase the number of breeding animals so that extensive development requirements of the proposed dairy industry can be met at large-scale farms.

Comfortably, all agricultural trading practices should safeguard the interests of cultivators who constitute a considerably high percentage of the main workforce in rural areas.

Therefore farm prices policy should be incentive-oriented and ideally be woven into the overall economic matrix, in such a way, as to ensure a smooth growth of both agricultural and non-agricultural sectors. Only co-operatives could narrow the gap between the consumer's price and the producer's price as they have lower profit margins.

Agricultural economy cannot sustain without an increase in industrial activity. The main problems of the rural areas are mass unemployment and inequality in social well-being. These problems can be mitigated with balanced rural industrialisation which can bring about a balanced and integrated rural development under Rural Industries Scheme. A preferential treatment should be given to village-based industries depending on village resources and banks should become an equal partner in this process. Moreover, the tiny industry and household industries need to be encourages and strengthen so as to increase the female beneficiaries percentage which presently is very low.

Industries which are not energy-intensive should be identified for proliferation in rural areas where power supply is presently a constraint. Special marketing organisations should be created to assist rural artisans, besides providing concessional credit, freight-subsidies, training facilities, free consultancy to small scale industrial units etc. Agro-based industry should receive high priority in credit allocation from the financial institutions and growers should be encouraged to set-up agro-processing units within the framework of co-operative societies. Moreover, attempts should be made to reorient industrial growth to serve the objective of employment generation, dispersal of small-scale industry in the rural areas and to increase the contribution of small scale industrial units to industrial production, particularly in the dunal and sandy undulating plains. Rural Industrial Supervision Boards be established to monitor the development rural small scale industry, particularly, the cottage industry.

Planning for Equitable Distribution of Vital Socio-Economic Services and Rural Service Centres

Provision of adequate vital socio-economic services in the area is prerequisitic for accelerating the pace of economic development and to ensure the spread effect of such economic development.

In addition, service population and distance of accessibility recommended norms respectively, 30,000 people and 6 to 8 kilometres as yard-sticks, be used for planning the basic socio-economic services in qualitative as well as quantitative terms in the viable planning units.

Under planned economic development, education, medical, banking, telephone, veterinary, electricity, metalled road, and potable water facilities are essential in rural areas to stimulate the regional development process and make rural life more comfortable. The equitable distribution of these services is crucial not only for promoting economic growth but also in creating social equity and in improving the quality of rural socio-economic environment. That is why provision of basic socio-economic services for the rural masses has been accepted as a constitutional goal.

No plan to bring about a balanced regional development of this backward region of Haryana will succeed without examining the existing geographic distribution of these facilities and identifying functional gaps for locating additional growth centres. It should be based on the concepts of

- Minimising physical accessibility of villages to social service places;
- Reduction of village population pressure for service places;
- Adoption of national minimum programme or of distance/ population norms as recommended by the Planning Commission; and
- Active participation of rural masses in upgrading socio-economic environment.

Education is one of the most important factors in achieving rapid economic development. Programme of formal education needs to be stressed as an instrument of socio-economic change in rural areas. The spatial distribution of high/higher secondary schools is uneven, especially, very wide functional gaps are prominent. Planned efforts have to be made for making provision of adequate formal educational facilities within a convenient distance of 5 kilometres. In addition, a major rural service centre should be provided with a high/higher secondary school, women craft centres and industrial training units within easy accessibility.

Public health care is fundamental to regional progress and it is a measure of energy and productive capacity of rural masses. Loss of health influences productivity as well as efficiency in the regional production, both in the sphere of industry as well as agriculture. Medical resources in the form of primary health centres of dispensary should be made available within a distance of 5 kilometres and mobile medical facilities may also be made available in rural areas.

Banking facilities and telecommunication services are grossly lacking in many parts of the study area. Moreover, the distribution patterns are highly skewed. It is recommended that banking services are to be provided at every major rural service centre, particularly, Agricultural bank for rural development providing subsidy on large-scale for basic inputs in farming, dairy farming, poultry-piggery, bee-keeping and agro-based household industry.

Equitable regional planning and development could be achieved by altering the accessibility pattern of villages to the growth by altering the accessibility pattern of villages to the growth centres which may be termed as spatial engineering.

The boundary of a viable planning unit was kept close to the hexagon's peripheries coinciding with the village boundaries. These can be adopted as ideal units for socio-economic planning at grassroot level.

The ideal hexagonal at grassroot level viable planning units may be where inter-centre distance is kept 16 kilometres or the distance between hexagons enter and its peripheries is 8 kilometres. In this study these norms were maintained because 8 kilometres' distance was considered a convenient walkable distance per hour on level to nearly-level slopes. The spatial planners may use the recommended service-population (3,000 people) and convenient walkable distance (8 kilometres) norms as the starting points for determining the location of service centres which should provide vital socio-economic service to ruralites. Presently, these are not adequately provided to rural masses because of the uneven distribution pattern of major rural service centres in Dadri tehsil of Bhiwani district of Haryana.

References

Bhatia, S.S. (1967), A New Measure of Agricultural Efficiency in Uttar Pradesh, India, *Economy Geography*, Volume 43.

Chauhan, T.S. (1987), *Agricultural Geography: A Study of Rajasthan State,* Jaipur, Academic Publishers.

Gupta, A. Das (1978), *Economic and Commercial Geography*, Calcutta, A. Mukerjee and Co. Pvt. Ltd.

Husain, M. (1979), *Agricultural Geography*, Delhi, Interalia India Publications.

Husain, M. (1998), *Agricultural Geography,* Jaipur, Rawat Publications.

Khusro, A.M. (1964), Returns to scale in Indian Agriculture, *Indian Journal of Agricultural Economics*, Vol. 19.

Mohammad N. (Ed.) (1980), *Perspectives in Agricultural Geography*, New Delhi, Concept Publishing Company.

Randhawa, N.S. (1974), *Green Revolution : A Case Study of Punjab*, Delhi, Vikas Publishing House.

18

IMPACT OF INSTITUTIONS ON AGRICULTURAL DEVELOPMENT IN BURDWAN, WEST BENGAL

N.K. DE & MISS. ANANYA TARAPHDER

Introduction

People unite and organise themselves with an exact aim, which is known as an institution. The dictionary meaning of institution, however, is an organisation for promotion of some public object. The institutions have their own spatial existence. From time immemorial institutions exist but change its form with space and time. Now institutions have become a part and parcel of modern society. According to the services rendered by the institutions, these can be categorised as direct or indirect servicing centres. Active service centres include Banks, Co-operatives, etc. whereas the Government Policy implementing organisations act as a passive/ indirect one. The institutions can also be classified as government or non-government organisation.

With the passage of time, institutions change their forms, character and services they render in accordance with the changing aim and motive of the society. The motive force is generated from necessity. Conscious people started agriculture with distinct plans and programmes. Vertical and horizontal use of land was necessitated by population pressure. Institutions with their various functions change the agricultural scenario of a particular region.

Through an institution one can avail the benefits of large scale production system. So the number of institutions as well as people having connections with them are increasing day by day. Now-a-days the influence of institutions is felt in every sphere of life including the modern cultural activities and agriculture.

On a global scale, the importance of institutions are well established. But in a developing country like India, due to poverty, lack of education and consciousness, as well as faulty property rights (cause of fragmented small holdings) all farmers cannot avail of the facilities extended by the institutions equally. Keeping all these aspects in mind a modest attempt has been made in the present paper to highlight the institutional influence on the agricultural scenario of Burdwan district, West Bengal. In this paper stress has been given to examine how a tradition bound subsistence agriculture has been transformed into a modern, commercial and mechanised agricultural base, within a span of thirty years because of institutions.

Study Area

The name Burdwan is the British expression of the term "Barddhaman" meaning "an expanding one". Cultural landscape of this area is a dynamic one. Economic superiority of agricultural community is dominant especially in the Eastern part of the district. It is a very peaceful district which has developed both in agriculture and in industry. The latitudinal extent of the district is from 22°56′N to 23°53′N and longitudinal one is from 86°48′E to 88°25′E which covers an area of 7028 sq. kms. having a total population of 6034706 (1991).

Methodology

The methodology followed in the present paper can be divided in three phases. Pre-field phase – it consists of collection of secondary data and information from journals, government reports and available literatures (both published and unpublished); Field phase – it includes collection of primary data from selected areas; Post-field phase – it includes arranging, re-arranging, tabulating and analysing the data and present them in pictorial forms (maps and diagrams). As the present paper is a preliminary one, it is primarily based on secondary information. Primary data is related to the people's perception towards agricultural institutions mainly.

Pictorial representation is of three types – Bargraphs/Composite bars, Regression/trend lines, temporal trends with reference to yearwise use of N.P.K., pesticides and diffusion of HYV seeds (Aus, Aman, Wheat,

Jute, etc.). The parametric data (collected on infrastructural facility) is analysed in terms of (a) area *vis-a-vis* road length and (b) population *vis-a-vis* road length.

$$\left.\begin{aligned} \text{by} = Y-\bar{y} &= r\frac{dx}{dy}(X-\bar{x}) \\ X-\bar{x} &= r\frac{dy}{dx}(Y-\bar{y}) \end{aligned}\right] \text{ where } r \text{ (correlation coefficient)} = \frac{\Sigma xy}{N\,dx\,dy}$$

Institutions in Burdwan

The institutions that are directly and indirectly related to the development of agriculture in Burdwan include: Principal Agricultural Office; Agricultural Irrigation Department; Minor Irrigation Department; Damodar Valley Command Area Development Agency; Indian Farmers' Fertilizer Co-opertive; District Planning Committee, Burdwan; Block Development Office; Panchayat Samiti; Zilla Parishad; Fishery Department; Different Nationalised Banks and Burdwan Central Co-operative Bank; Public Works Department; Agricultural Marketing Department, etc.

These institutions can be classified as :

I. Active Institutions.
II. Passive Institutions.

I. Active/Implementing Institutions are –

(i) Agricultural Irrigation Department.
(ii) Minor Irrigation Department.
(iii) Indian Farmers' Fertilizer Co-opertive (IFFCO).
(iv) Panchayat Samiti.
(v) Block Development Office (B.D.O.).
(vi) Zilla Parishad.
(vii) Fishery Department.
(viii) Financing Institutions – Co-operatives Society and Banks.
(ix) Public Works Department.
(x) Agricultural Marketing Department.

II. Passive/Advisory Institutions are –

(i) Principal Agricultural Office (P.A.O.).
(ii) District Planning Committee (D.P.C.).
(iii) Damodar Valley Command Area Develoment Agency (D.V.C.A.D.A.).

(iv) Agricultural Marketing Department.
(v) Primary Agricultural Credit Society (P.A.C.S.).

There are some institutions which have dual role to play as an active institution as well as a passive one [here I (x) and II. (iv)]

Role of Institutions

In Burdwan the institutions are all active from the time immemorial. The concept of community storage through "Dharmagolas" (village community godowns to store cereals) were present even in remote villages which were under the supervision of village leaders. The co-operative movement was initiated in Burdwan in 1917. In 1918, Sridharpur Co-operative Bank started giving loans for fertilizer, pesticide, oil cake manufacturing etc. though in reality the co-operative farming came into being in the district in the fifties, only.

The role of the institutions includes –

(A) Direct/Active Role
(B) Indirect/Passive Role.

(A) *Direct/Active Role :* To help farmers in storage and marketing and to avail of credit facility.

(B) *Indirect/Passive Role:*

(i) To impart advice to the farmers,
(ii) To give demonstration to attract farmers in package programmes,
(iii) The application of package practices, and
(iv) To choose specific areas for special work programmes.

(A) Direct Role of the Institutions on Agriculture

In the credit and marketing sector the banks determine the scales of finances to be given as loans to the persons concerned as per government directives. Agricultural marketing department controls the prices of agricultural products in the regulated markets mainly. The primary agricultural credit societies (PACS) help the farmers at the grassroot level by sanctioning loans as well as maintaining close contact with the day-to-day problems faced by the farmers in the field etc.

Table 18.1 : Sub-Divisionwise Distribution of Selected Institutions, 1995

Sub-Division	*No. of Bank Branches*	*No. of PACS Branches*	*No. of Cold Storage*	*No. of Seed Farms*	*No. of Markets*		
					R	*W*	*P*
Burdwan	134	249	44	10	1	15	35
Kalna	47	114	17	04	0	10	20
Katwa	68	157	05	04	0	12	26
Asansol	142	41	08	02	2	23	53
Total	391	561	74	20	3	60	134

PACS — Primary Agricultural Credit Society
R — Regulated
W — Wholesale
P — Primary
Source : Agricultural Marketing Department.

It may be mentioned in this connection that the total number of branches of different nationalised banks in Burdwan was 225 only in 1985 which increased to 391 in 1995. The number of PACS in Burdwan were nominal in 1985 which increased to 562 in 1995 (Table 18.1, Fig 18.1).

(B) Indirect Role of the Institutions on Agriculture

The organisazing power of the people of Burdwan being strong, acceptance of the intensive agricultural district programme, commonly known as Package Programme was very easy to be introduced in 1962. As such, Burdwan was the first and foremost district in the State of West Bengal to initiate this Programme. The cultivators' adoption of these packages to increase agricultural production also involves a package of advisory services by competent technical staff.

To make the package programme a grand success training was imparted by the government personnel to the educated and affluent class of cultivators mainly. The role of institutions are concentrated in the following aspects (Tables 18.2 and 18.3, Fig. 18.2).

(a) Preparation of farm plans.
(b) Demonstration of the use of optimum doses of fertilizers and irrigation water.
(c) Seed and soil testing.
(d) Jute retting and stepping.

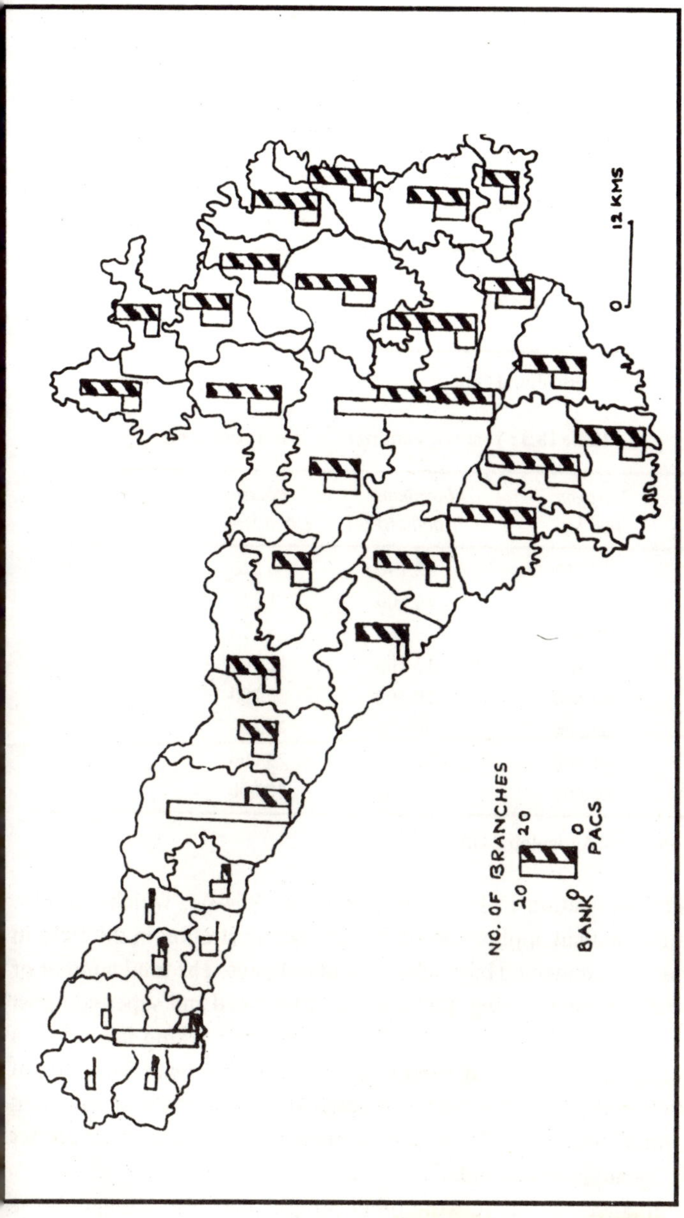

Fig. 18.1 : Burdwan District: Impact of Financing Institutions on Agriculture (1995)

(e) Use of plant protection measures.
(f) Demonstration on the use of improved agricultural implements etc.

Table 18.2 : Yearwise Plant Protection Measures, 1995

Year	*Pesticides ('000 t)*	*Weedicides ('000 t)*	*Fungicides ('000 t)*
1968-69	256	10	—
1983-84	848	46	0
1993-94	1421	64	31

Source : Principal Agricultural Office.

Table 18.3 : Yearwise Fertilizer Use in Burdwan, 1995

Year	*Nitrogen ('000 Mt)*	*Phosphate ('000 Mt)*	*Potash ('000 Mt)*	*Total ('000 Mt)*
1961-62	7.720	2.130	0.220	10.070
1964-65	18.360	10.900	1.230	30.490
1980-81	28.760	9.260	4.120	42.140
1985-86	46.200	15.100	12.200	73.500
1990-91	63.500	29.500	29.200	122.200
1991-92	63.500	30.400	29.800	123.700
1993-94	61.000	25.000	23.000	109.000
1994-95	63.000	30.000	30.000	123.000

Source: Principal Agricultural Office.

Field application in Burdwan started in 1964-65, which includes the actual practical application of the oral demonstration in the field in the areas well connected by roadways and railways. The total number of demostrations (line sowing, preparation of seed bed and super compost etc.) given in 1964-65 were 10,522. Soil and seed testing laboratories were set up in 1964-65 and 1966 respectively in Burdwan Sadar. Plant protection measures were taken up under the supervision of Principal Agricultural Office (P.A.O.), Burdwan. Field demonstrations were further assisted by audio-visual aids.

Simultaneously, there were other programmes also alongwith the field applications, which include specific local programmes.

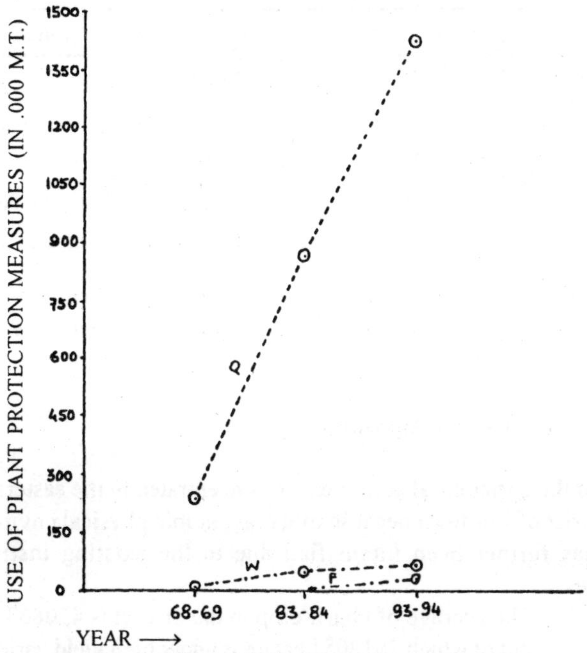

Fig. 18.2A : Temporal Trend of Plant Protection Measures

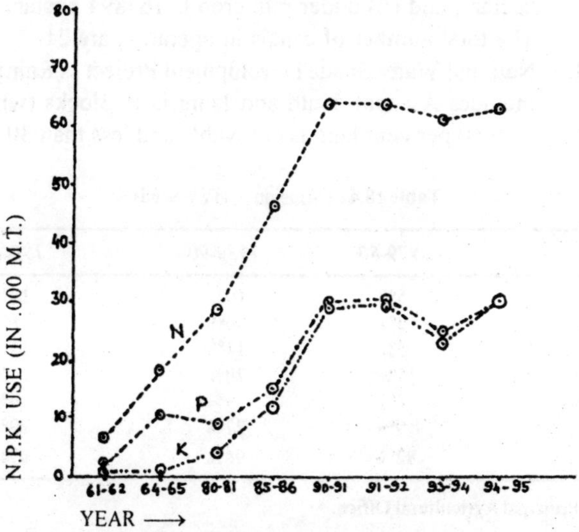

Fig. 18.2B : Temporal Trend of N.P.K. Use

Programmes	*Blocks Involved*
Soil conservation, Water Shade Development	Kanksa
Land reclamation	Kanksa and other lateritic tracts
Irrigation and drainage works	Bhatar
Construction of approach roads	Memari
Distribution of quality seeds	Burdwan, Galsi, Memari, Purbasthali, Kalna, Katwa, Bhatar

Further horticulture, jute, pulse, wheat development programmes were also organised in those areas which are not suitable for rice cultivation.

Institutions *vis-a-vis* Agriculture

Most of the agricultural activities are concentrated in the eastern half of the district of Burdwan because of its favourable physical environment. This has further been intensified due to the existing institutional facilities.

I. The acerage of kharif crop in the district is 450863 hectare, out of which 261205 hectare is under high yield variety seeds (HYV) – (Table 18.4, Fig. 18.3).

II. The area coverage of irrigation (i) under kharif crop is 39020 hectare, and (ii) under rabi crop is 167894 hectare. The total number of canals in operation are 21.

III. National Water Shade Development Project in Rainfed Area includes Asansol, Kulti and Jamuria II Blocks (where less than 50 per cent land is cultivable and less than 30 per cent

Table 18.4 : Diffusion of HYV Seeds

Crops	*1979-80*	*1989-90*	*1990-91*
Aus	5%	10%	10%
Aman	3%	6%	8%
Boro	5%	14%	15%
Wheat	15%	20%	25%
Mustard	2%	9%	9%
Potato	9%	27%	29%
Jute	82%	96%	97%

Source : Principal Agricultural Office.

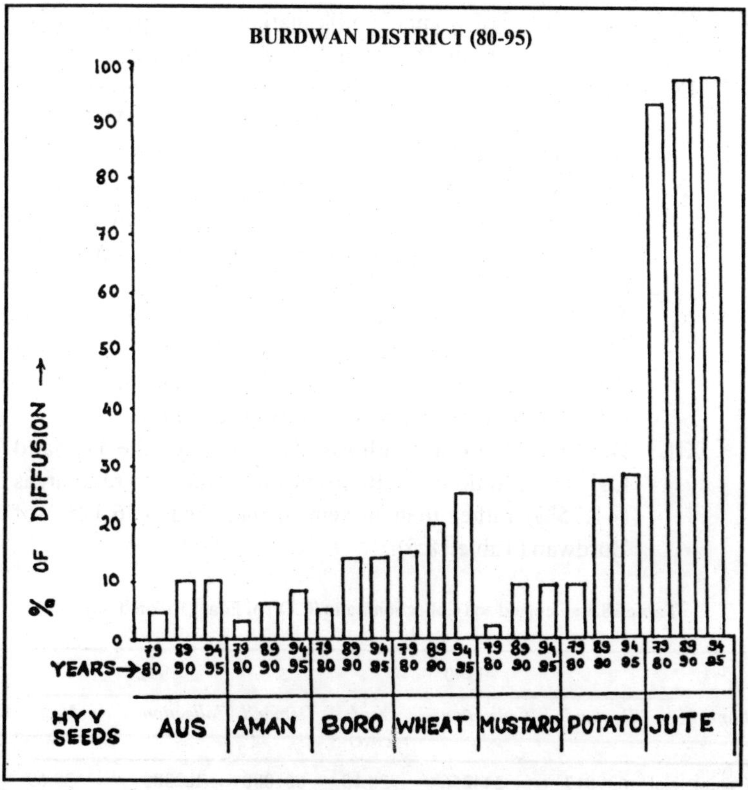

Fig. 18.3 : Diffusion of HYV Seeds

land is under irrigation). The agricultural production has increased considerably here as an after effect.

IV. The cultivable waste lands once lying fallow have been used for cultivation in Durgapur, Ausgram-I & II blocks because of the waste land development programme.

V. Special Area Development Programmes in Ausgram I & II and in Kanksa show a new horizon to the landless labourers.

VI. The dry land farming has been extended to 1400-1500 acres of land in the western part of the district.

VII. Mechanization is more extensively used in those areas where connectivity is high (Memari, Burdwan Sadar Block etc.) (Fig. 18.4). The correlation co-efficient between area and road length is positive and moderate ($r = +0.45$).

VIII. The number of women's milk marketing co-operatives are increasing rapidly (Kalna and Burdwan Block).

IX. Veterinary and other associated services have been extended even to the remote villages (e.g. Balgona and Malkita in Burdwan Sadar).

X. Burdwan District Rural Development Agency (DRDA) through Tribal Rural Youth's Self-Employment Projects (TRYSEM) has a direct and positive impact on mechanization of agriculture.

XI. The fisheries department has taken up programmes of pisciculture in water logged abundoned colliery area. Zilla Parishad has already constructed a tourist Bungalow on the side of a big lake which is used for pisciculture.

XII. Because of the agricultural development the Demand Collection Ratio (C.D. Ratio) has been more in rural areas (41.75%) rather than in semi-urban areas (26.12%) of Burdwan (Table 18.5).

Table 18.5 : Demand and Collection Ratio (C.D.) of Loan (Rs. on '000)

Bank	1990			1992		
	Demand	*Collection*	*% of recovei*	*Demand*	*Collection*	*% of recovery*
Commercial Bank	639817	244256	38.18	661080	262389	39.69
RRB	63375	19147	30.21	122700	22400	18.26
Co-op.	329203	241491	73.36	326905	281351	86.06
Total	1032395	504894	48.90	1110685	566140	50.97

Source : District Planning Committee.

Table 18.6 : Small Savings

Year	*Total*		*Eastern Zone*		*Western Zone*	
	Target	*Achievemem*	*Target*	*Achieveme...*	*Target*	*Achievement*
1988-89	62.00	62.18	22.00	31.16	40.00	31.02
1989-90	80.00	94.79	36.00	42.21	44.00	52.58
1990-91	108.00	100.54	48.00	48.57	60.00	51.97

Source : District Planning Committee.

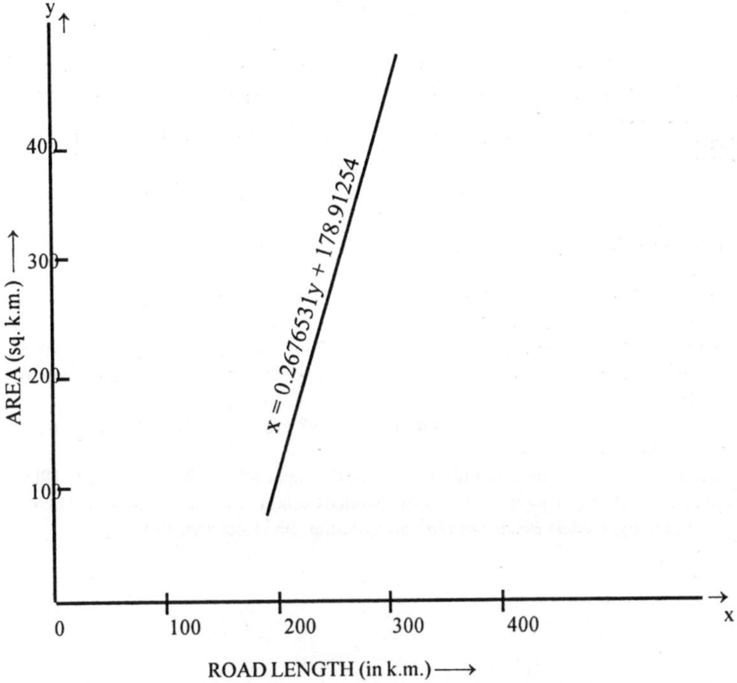

Fig. 18.4: Regression Line Showing Relation between Area and Road Length

Conclusion

From the above analysis it is evident that the institutions in Burdwan have not only increased agricultural production but also has a direct and positive impact on the district's economy. As a result agro-based industries – Rice Bran Oil Mill, Rice Mill, Flattened rice mills etc. have flourished rapidly. Availability of assured prices and storage facility has further enhanced the agricultural development.

This rising trend of positive impact of institutions were very much prevalent almost in every field of agriculture till 1980s. Since then an awareness is slowly developing among the farmers about the negative impact of advanced agricultural technology.

It is of utmost importance to protect the local (native) variety seeds from extinction, to control pests through bio-technology and to check the overuse of chemical fertilizer (resulting in land, water and soil pollution) through institutions, working at the grassroot level.

References

Barman, S. and M.R. Choudhury, (1980), Technological Innovation in Galsi and Memari Blocks in Burdwan District. In *Indian Journal of Landscape Systems,* Vol. 3, Nos. 1 & 2. September 1980.

Burdwan District Rural Development Agency, (1992) Annual Action Plan.

Burdwan Central Co-operative Bank, (1992), Memoirs, Platinum Jubilee 1917-1992.

Chadha, G.K. (1979), *Production Gains of New Agricultural Technology*, Publication Bureau, Punjab University, Chandigarh.

Datt, R. and Sundharam, K.P.M., (1995), *Indian Economy*, S. Chand and Company Ltd., New Delhi.

District Planning Committee, (1994-95), Planning Reports from Blocks.

Government of West Bengal (1951), *Burdwan District Gazetteer*.

Government of West Bengal, (1966), Nirmal Mitra (Supervisor). A short note on Agricultural Development in West Bengal 1965-66. Department of Agriculture and Community Development.

Lead Bank Office (United Commercial Bank), (1985 & 1995). District Credit Plan for Burdwan District.

Principal Agricultural Office, Burdwan, (1982-1992), Annual Agricultural Reports and Plans.

Sengupta, B. (1995), "Tourist Centres in Abundoned Colliery Area" In: Anandamela (Bengali Version), *Ananda Bazar Patrika Ltd.*, Calcutta, 6th December, 1995.

19

AGRICULTURAL RESEARCH INSTITUTIONS AND DEVELOPMENT OF INDIAN AGRICULTURE

A Geographical Analysis

JABIR HASAN KHAN & MOHAMMAD YUSUF

Agriculture contributes about one-third of national income and nearly 75 per cent of the rural population earns its living from agriculture and agro-based industries. Growth of agriculture depends upon a number of natural, technological, institutional and cultural factors. In the last decades, a number of efforts have been made to develop the Indian agriculture by chiefly providing better facilities of seeds, chemcial fertilizers and establishment of research institutions. This has enabled the country to be, by and large, self-sufficient to feed the increasing population. Rapid improvement in productivity and production of selected agricultural crops, since adoption of the Green Revolution Technology from the mid-sixties, has been conspicuous only in small pockets of well endowed irrigated areas. It brought imbalances in regional development of Indian agriculture. It will be of crucial significance, not only on account of the need to reduce regional disparities, but also essentially to raise production levels, the far greater attention is required to bring an accelerated growth in areas which have relatively lower growth. The generation of location-specific, new technology through research and its adoption by farmers are key factors for overall development of Indian agriculture and to bring equilibrium in its regional development.

Keeping in view these observations, in the present paper an attempt has been made to highlight the regional variations in distribution of research institutions engaged in promotion and development of agriculture in India.

Methodology

The data regarding State/Union Territories (State/UTs)-wise distribution of Agricultural Research Institutions (ARIs) in India, have been collected both from primary and secondary sources of information. Central Research Institutes (CRIs), National Research Centres (NRCs), National Bureau (NB), State Agricultural Universities (SAUs) and Zonal Research Stations (ZRSs) which are permanent in nature and fully engaged in the agriculture research, have been included to find out variations in the geographical distribution of ARIs in India. The State/UT has been taken as the smallest unit of study. Two parameters (area and population) have been selected for identification of variations in the spatial distribution of ARIs in India. There is direct relation of areas to the agriculture in terms of growing crops, rearing animals or even setting up the institutions. The population has also relation with the agriculture because whatever is produced in the field, is supposed to feed population directly or indirectly. In fact, both area and population affect the growth of agriculture. Therefore, total number of ARIs in a State/UT per thousand square kilometres of its area, and per lakh of its population have been found out.

Analysis of Agricultural Research Institutions

Indian Council of Agricultural Research (ICAR) is the apex organization responsible for sponsoring, promoting, conducting, co-ordinating research, education and extension in the agriculture and its allied sectors in the country. Under ICAR, there are 42 Central Research Institutes, 22 National Research Centres, 4 National Burea, 70 All India Coordinated Research Projects, 9 Project Directorates on Vegetables (New Delhi), Oilseeds, Rice Research and Poultry (Hyderabad), Cropping Systems, Cattle (Meerut), Pulses (Kanpur), Water management (Rahuri-Ahmadnagar) and Wheat (Karnal), 109 Krishi Viggyan Kendras and 414 *Adhoc* Schemes/Projects.[1] Moreover, ICAR also assists 27 State Agricultural Universities, and 124 Zonal Research Stations, that have been established in the Agro-Climate Zones (ACZs), in the country.[2] State/Union Territorieswise distribtuion of ARIs, i.e. CRIs, NRCs, NB, SAUs and ZRSs has been given in the Appendix.

Research in the field of agriculture is conducted at three levels, namely, national, state and regional/zonal.

The important institutions fully engaged in the agriculture research at the national level are CRIs, NRCs, and NB. Some general Universities such as Agra, Allahabad, Annamalai, Gorakhpur, Kanpur, Guru Nanak Dev, Manipuri, Banaras Hindu University, Vishwa Bharti, North-Eastern Hill University, Meerut and Rajasthan are also imparting education and conducting research in agricultural sciences. Moreover, some voluntary organisations and related Government organisations, i.e., Department of Scientific and Industrial Research, Non-conventional Energy Sources, Environment, Electronics, Ocean Development, Indian Council of Medical Research and Ministries of Labour, Education, Irrigation and Power etc., are partially engaged in the field of agricultural research.

There are 27 SAUs which are imparting education and conducting research on various aspects of agricultural sciences in their respective states. In the country, 124 ZRSs based on Agro-climatic Zones have been established to fill up the gap between technology generated by the institutions and practised by farmers. The purpose of ZRS is to strengthen need-based regional research in agriculture in the country under the National Agricultural Research Projects launched in 1979.

State/UTs-wise distribution of ARIs in India as given in Table 19.1 and State/ UTs ranked under five categories of very high, high, medium, low and nil on the basis of the raito of ARIs in a State/UT in relation to its area and population depicted in Table 19.2 indicate that there are great variations in spatial distribution of ARIs in India.

There is no even single research institution in the state of Mizoram and Sikkim and UTs, i.e. Chandigarh, Dadra and Nagar Haveli, Daman and Diu, Lakshadweep and Pondicherry, while, Uttar Pradesh has 27 institutions, which is the highest figure among the States/UTs.

There is highly uneven distribution of ARIs in terms of area. Delhi, Haryana, Kerala and Goa have very high concentration of ARIs in terms of area while two States and five UTs have not any research institution.

Andaman and Nicobar Islands and Arunachal Pradesh are in the highest rank in respect of ARIs in relation to population.

Table 19.2 also reveals the fact that the States/UTs having very high rank in respect of number of ARIs in relation to their area, are generally in low to medium rank in terms of proportion of ARIs in the context of their population and *vice versa*. It may be due to uneven distribution of population and differences in the area of various States/ UTs of India.

Table 19.1 : Distribution of Agricultural Research Institutions in India

States/UTs	*Area in thousand sq. kms.*	*Population in lakhs*	*Types of ARIs*			*Total*	*ARIs/1000 sq. kms.*	*ARIs/Lakh Population*
			CRIs/N RC/NB	SAUs	ZRSs			
(1)	(2)	(3)	(4)	(5)	(6)	(7)	(8)	(9)
Andhra Pradesh	275.04	665.08	4	1	7	12	0.04	0.02
Arunachal Pradesh	83.74	8.65	1	—	1	2	0.02	0.23
Assam	78.52	224.14	—	1	6	7	0.09	0.03
Bihar	173.88	863.74	1	2	6	9	0.05	0.01
Goa	3.70	11.70	1	—	—	1	0.27	0.09
Gujarat	196.02	413.10	1	1	9	11	0.06	0.03
Haryana	44.21	164.64	9	1	3	13	0.29	0.08
Himachal Pradesh	55.67	51.71	2	2	4	8	0.14	0.16
Jammu & Kashmir	222.24	77.19	—	1	—	1	0.13	0.01
Karnataka	191.80	449.77	2	2	11	15	0.08	0.03
Kerala	38.68	290.90	5	1	5	11	0.28	0.04
Madhya Pradesh	443.45	661.81	4	2	12	18	0.04	0.03
Maharashtra	307.71	789.37	5	4	9	18	0.06	0.05
Manipur	22.33	18.37	—	—	1	1	0.04	0.05
Meghalaya	22.43	17.75	2	—	1	3	0.13	0.17
Mizoram	21.08	6.90	—	—	—	—	—	—
Nagaland	16.58	12.10	—	—	1	1	0.06	0.08
Orissa	155.71	316.60	4	1	10	15	0.10	0.05
Punjab	50.36	202.82	1	1	5	7	0.14	0.03
Rajasthan	342.24	444.06	3	1	9	13	0.04	0.03
Sikkim	27.10	4.06	—	—	—	—	—	—

Table 19.1 (Contd.)

States/UTs	*Area in thousand sq. kms.*	*Population in lakhs*	*Types of ARIs*			*Total*	*ARIs/1000 sq. kms.*	*ARIs/Lakh Population*
			CRIs/NRC/NB	SAUs	ZRSs			
(1)	(2)	(3)	(4)	(5)	(6)	(7)	(8)	(9)
Tamil Nadu	130.06	558.59	2	2	7	11	0.08	0.02
Tripura	10.49	27.57	—	—	1	1	0.10	0.04
Uttar Pradesh	294.41	1391.12	13	3	11	27	0.09	0.02
West Bengal	88.75	680.78	3	1	6	10	0.11	0.01
Andaman & Nicobar Islands	8.25	2.81	1	—	—	1	0.12	0.36
Chandigarh	0.11	6.42	—	—	—	—	—	—
Dadra & Nagar Heveli	0.49	1.38	—	—	—	—	—	—
Daman & Diu	0.11	1.02	—	—	—	—	—	—
Delhi	1.48	94.21	5	—	—	5	3.38	0.05
Lakshaweep	0.03	0.52	—	—	—	—	—	—
Pondicherry	0.49	8.08	—	—	—	—	—	—
Total	3287.26[3]	8463.03[4]	68	27	124	219	0.07	0.03

Table 19.2 : Rank of States/UTs based on ARIs in relation to Area and Population

Rank	*Area*	*Population*
Very High 0.20 and above	Delhi, Haryana, Kerala and Goa	Andaman and Nicobar Islands and Arunachal Pradesh
High 0.10-0.19	Himachal Pradesh, Punjab, Meghalaya, Andaman and Nicobar Islands, West Bengal, Orissa and Tripura	Meghalaya and Himachal Pradesh
Medium 0.05-0.09	Assam, Uttar Pradesh, Karnataka, Tamil Nadu, Maharashtra, Nagaland and Bihar	Goa, Haryana, Nagaland, Maharashtra, Manipur, Orissa, and Delhi
Low 0.04 and Below	Andhra Pradesh, Madhya Pradesh, Manipur, Rajasthan, Arunachal Pradesh and Jammu and Kashmir	Kerala, Tripura, Assam, Gujarat, Karnataka, Madhya Pradesh, Punjab, Rajasthan, Andhra Pradesh, Tamil Nadu, Uttar Pradesh, Bihar, Jammu and Kashmir and West Bengal
Nil	Mizoram, Sikkim, Chandigarh, Dadra and Nagar Haveli, Daman and Diu, Lakshadweep and Pondicherry	Mizoram, Sikkim, Chandigarh, Dadra and Nagar Haveli, Daman and Diu, Lakshadweep and Pondicherry

An examination of States/UTs-wise list of ARIs in India (Appendix) brings the fact that there are also great variations in the distribution of ARIs within the states. For example, in Uttar Pradesh majority of ARIs are located in few cities, i.e. Izzatnagar, Meerut, Kanpur, Mathura, Jhansi, etc. that are situated in the western part of the State. It has been also observed that there is clustering of ARIs in the cities which are either the capital of the states or having metropolitan character. For instance, there are five ARIs in Andhra Pradesh out of which four are located in Hyderabad. In some of the States ZRSs have not been still established in all the ACZs. For example, in Jammu and Kashmir six ACZs have been identified but no ZRS has been established so far in the said zones.

Conclusion and Suggestions

India is a vast country, endowed with great variety of natural, cultural and human resources that provide great scope for development and diversification of agriculture. It needs to direct efforts towards location-specific and need-based research. Therefore, an equilibrium may be brought in the distribution of ARIs for maintaining the balance in the growth and development of Indian agriculture.

The following suggestions are highlighted which may bring equilibrium in the distribution of ARIs for overall growth and development of Indian agriculture:

(i) To establish at least one research institution in the State/ UTs where there is not still any reserch institution.

(ii) To establish at least one Agricultural University in each State[5].

(iii) To shift existing ARIs from capital/metropolitan cities to remote/rural /semi-urban areas as per need.

(iv) To distribute ARIs in all regions of a State/UT rather than to concentrate them in few cities of a particular region.

(v) To pay attention to diversify agriculture according to the needs and environmental conditions of an area or region in the field of crops sciences, animal husbandry, fisheries, forestry, horticulture, sericulture, pisciculture, silviculture and agriculture engineering and management.

(vi) To bring equilibrium in the distribution of ARIs in India in respect of their ratio both in relation to area and population of State/UTs.

(vii) To re-demarcate ACZs in all States/UTs after considering their physical, cultural and socio-economic set up at micro-level.

(viii) To establish co-ordination among the ARIs.

(ix) To implement recommendations of Commissions and committees, e.g. National Commission on Agriculture 1976[6], and Review Committee on Agricultural Universites 1978[7].

APPENDIX

STATES/UTS-WISE LIST OF ARIS IN INDIA

Andhra Pradesh

1. Central Tobacco Research Institute, Rajahmundri.
2. Central Research Institute for Dryland Agriculture, Santoshnagar, Hyderabad.
3. National Academy of Agricultural Research and Management, Rajendranagar, Hyderabad.
4. National Research Centre for Sorghum, Rajendranagar, Hyderabad.
5. Andhra Pradesh Agricultural University, Rajendranagar, Hyderabad.
6. ACZs 6, ZRSs 7 : Lam (Guntur), Ankapalle, Tirupati, Jagtiyal, Nandyal, Rastakuntba and Chintalpalli.

Arunachal Pradesh

1. National Research Centre for Yak, Dirang.
2. ACZs, 2. ZRS 1: Shergaon (Sangti).

Assam

1. Assam Agricultural University, Jorhat.
2. ACZs 6, ZRSs 6 : North Lakhimpur, Jorhat, Shillong, Karimganj and Diphu.

Bihar

1. Indian Lac Research Institute, Namkum, Ranchi.
2. Rajendra Agricultural University, Pusa, Samastipur.
3. Birsa Agricultural University, Kanke, Rachi.
4. ACZs 6, ZRSs 6 : Pusa, Purnea, Sabour, Dumka, Chinaki and Ghatshila.

Goa

1. ICAR, Research Complex for Goa.

Gujarat

1. National Research Centre for Groundnut, Junagarh.
2. Gujarat Agricultural University, Sadar, Krishinagar, Dantiwada.
3. ACZ 8, ZRSs 9 : Navsari, Bharuch, Surat, Anand, Dantiwada, Bhachau, Targhdia, Junagarh and Arnej.

Haryana

1. Central Soil Salinity Research Institute, Karnal.
2. Central Institute for Research on Buffaloes, Hisar.
3. National Dairy Research Institute, Karnal.
4. National Institute of Animal Genetics, Karnal.
5. National Bureau of Animal Genetic Resources, Karnal.
6. National Research Centre for Integrated Pest Management, Faridabad.
7. National Research Centre for Equines, Hisar.
8. National Biotechnology Centre on Animal Production, Karnal.
9. National Research Centre for Arid Horticulture, Hisar.
10. Haryana Agricultural University, Hisar.
11. ACZs 2, ZRSs 3 : Karnal, Bawal and Hisar.

Himachal Pradesh

1. Central Potato Research Institute, Shimla.
2. National Research Centre for Mushroom, Chambaghat, Solan.
3. Himachal Pradesh Krishi Vishwa Vidyalaya, Palampur.
4. Dr. Yashwant Singh Parmar University of Horticulture and Forestry, Solan.
5. ACZs 4, ZRSs 4 : Dhaulakuan, Bajaura, Mashobra and Kukumseri.

Jammu & Kashmir

1. Sher-e-Kashmir University of Agricultural Sciences and Technology, Srinagar.
2. ACZs 5, ZRS – Nil.

Karnataka

1. Indian Institute of Horticulture Research, Sadasivanagar, Bangalore.
2. National Research Centre for Cashew, Gojukendra, Puttur.
3. University of Agricultural Sciences, Hebbal, Bangalore.
4. University of Agricultural Sciences, Dharwad.
5. ACZs 10, ZRSs 11 : Bidar, Raichur, Bijapur, Sirsa, Hebbal Bangalore, Nogamangla, Navile, Shimogo, Dhariwar, Mudgere and Brahmvar.

Kerala

1. Central Tuber Crops, Research Institute, Sreekariyam, Trivandrum.
2. Central Plantation Crops Research Institute, Kasaragod.
3. Central Marine Fisheries Research Institute, Cochin.
4. Central Institute of Fisheries Technology, Willington Island, Cochin.
5. National Research Centre for Species, Mari Kunu, Calicut.
6. Kerala Agricultural University, Trichur.
7. ACZs 5, ZRSs 5 : Pillicode, Vellayani, Pattambi, Ambalvayal and Kumarakom.

Madhya Pradesh

1. Indian Institute of Soil Science, Maharana Pratap Nagar, Bhopal.
2. Central Institute of Agricultural Engineering, Bhopal.
3. National Research Centre on Soyabean, Indore.
4. National Research Centre on Weed Sciences, Jabalpur.
5. Jawahar Lal Nehru Krishi Vishwa Vidyala, Jabalpur.
6. Indira Gandhi Krishi Vishwa Vidyla, Raipur.
7. ACZs 12, ZRSs 12 : Raipur, Jagdalpur, Ambikapur, Jabalpur, Sehore, Pawarkhera, Morena, Tikamgarh, Chindwara, Indore, Khargone and Jhabua.

Maharahstra

1. Central Institute of Cotton Research, Nagpur.

2. Central Institute of Fisheries Education, Jai Prakash Road, Bombay (Mumbai).
3. Central Institute for Research on Cotton Technology, Matunga, Bombay (Mumbai).
4. National Bureau of Soil Survey and Land Use Planning, Nagpur.
5. National Research Centre for Citrus, Nagpur.
6. Konkan Krishi Vidyalaya, Dapoli, Ratnagiri.
7. Mahatma Phule Krishi Vidyapeeth, Rahuri.
8. Marathwada Agricultural University, Parbhani.
9. Punjabrao Krishi Vidyapeeth, Krishi Nagar, Akola.
10. ACZs 9, ZRSs 9 : Vengurla, Karjat, Igatpuri, Kolhapur, Pune, Sholapur, Aurngabad, Yavatmal and Sindhewahi.

Manipur

1. ACZ 1, ZRS 1 : Sangnaipet (Imphal) (Shillong).

Meghalaya

1. ICAR, Research Complex for North-Eastern Hills Region, Barapani (Shillong).
2. National Research Centre for Mithun Bishnupur, Shillong.
3. ACZ 1, ZRS 1 : Barapani (Shillong).

Nagaland

1. ACZ 1, ZRS 1 : Medziphema.

Orissa

1. Central Rice Research Institute, Cuttack.
2. Central Institute of Fresh-Water Aquaculture, Kausalyaganga, Bhubaneshwar.
3. Water Technology Centre for Eastern Region, Bhubaneshwar.
4. Orissa University of Agriculture and Technology, Bhubaneshwar.
5. ACZs 10, ZRSs 9 : Kunjhar, Ranital, Bhubaneshwar, Udayagiri, Semiliguda, Jeypore, Bhawanipatna, Chiplima and Mahispat.

Punjab

1. Central Institute for Post-Harvest Engineering and Technology, Ludhiana.
2. Punjab Agricultural University, Ludhiana.
3. ACZs 5, ZRSs 5 : Kandi, Gurdaspur, Ludhiana, Faridkot, Bhatinda.

Rajasthan

1. Central Arid Zone Research Institute, Jodhpur.
2. Central Sheep and Wool Research Institute, Avikanagar, Malpura.
3. National Research Centre for Camel, Jorbeer, Bikaner.
4. Rajasthan Agricultural University, Bikaner.
5. ACZs 9, ZRSs 9 : Jodhpur, Sriganganagar, Fatehpur (Sikar), Sumerpur (Pali), Durgapur (Jaipur), Navagoan (Alwar), Udaipur, Banswara and Kota.

Tamil Nadu

1. Sugarcane Breeding Institute, Coimbatore.
2. Central Institute of Brackishwater Aquaculture, Madras (Chennai).
3. Tamil Nadu Agricultural University, Coimbatore.
4. Tamil Nadu Veterinary and Animal Science University, Madras (Chennai).
5. ACZs 7, ZRSs 7 : Varidhachalam, Paiyra, Coimbatore, Aduthurai, Aruppukottai, Kanyakumari and Thadiankudisai.

Tripura

1. ACZ 1, ZRS 1 : Lembucherra (Agartala).

Uttar Pradesh

1. Indian Grassland and Fodder Research Institute, Jhansi.
2. Indian Institute of Sugarcane Research, Lucknow.
3. Vivekananda Parvatiya Krishi Anusandhan Shala, Almora.
4. Central Institute of Horiculture for Northern Plains, Lucknow.

5. Central Soil and Water Conservation Research and Training Institute, Dehra Dun.
6. Indian Veterinary Research Institute, Izzatnagar, Bareilly.
7. Central Institute for Research on Goats, Farah, Makhdoom, Mathura.
8. Central Avian Research Institute, Izzatnagar, Bareilly.
9. National Bureau of Fish Genetic Research Allapur, Allahabad.
10. National Biotechnology Centre on Animal Health, Izzatnagar, Bareilly.
11. National Research Centre for Meat and Meat Products Technology, Izzatnagar, Bareilly.
12. National Research Centre for Coldwater Fisheries, Haldwani.
13. National Research Centre for Agro-Forestry, Jhansi.
14. Chandra Shekhar Azad University of Agriculture and Technology, Kanpur.
15. Govind Ballabh Pant University of Agriculture and Technology, Pantnagar, Nainital.
16. Narendra Deva University of Agriculture and Technology, Faizabad.
17. ACZs 10, ZRSs 11 : Ranichauri, Pantnagar, Daurala, Nagina, Shahjahanpur, Madhurikund, Kanpur, Bharati, Sardarnagar, Kumarganj and Mirzapur.

West Bengal

1. Central Research Institute for Jute and Allied Fibres, Barrackpore.
2. Central Inland Capture Fisheries Research Institute, Barrackpore.
3. Jute Technology Research Laboratories, Calcutta.
4. Bidhan Chandra Krishi Vishwa Vidyalaya, Mohanpur.
5. ACZs 6, ZRSs : Pedong, Pundibari, Raundia, Mohanpur, Jhargam and Mathurapur.

Andaman And Nicobar Islands

1. Central Agricultural Research Institute for Andaman and Nicobar Group of Islands, Port Blair.

Delhi

1. Indian Agricultural Research Institute, Pusa, New Delhi.
2. Indian Agricultural Statistics Research Institute, Pusa, New Delhi.
3. National Bureau of Plant Genetic Research, Pusa, New Delhi.
4. National Biotechnological Centre for Crop Science, New Delhi.
5. National Centre for Agricultural Economics and Policy Research, Krishi Bhawan, New Delhi.

References

1. Indian Council of Agricultural Research. *Annual Report 1991-92*. ICAR, New Delhi, pp.170-280.
2. Randhawa, N.S., Agricultural Research in India: An overview of its Organization, Management and Operations, 1987, *FAO Research & Technology Paper 3*, Rome, Annex 7.
3. India: Ministry of Information & Broadcasting. India 1992: *A Reference Annual 1992*, INB, New Delhi, pp. 371-416.
4. Census of India 1991, *Final Population Totals 1991,* Ministry of Home Affairs, New Delhi, pp. 9-19.
5. India: Education Commission. *Report of Education Committee on Agriculture (1964-66)* 1966, Ministry of Education, New Delhi, p. 349.
6. India: Ministry of Agriculture & Irrigation, National Commission on Agriculture 1976, *Part XI: Research, Education and Extension. Report 1976,* ISI, New Delhi.
7. Randhawa, N.S., Report of Review Committee on Agricultural Universities, 1978, ICAR, New Delhi.

20

METHODOLOGICAL ISSUES IN THE FARM SIZE
Productivity Studies in India

NISAR AHMAD KHAN

Introduction

The issue of the relationship between farm size and productivity has been of general interest to both social scientists and policy makers. Russian Scholars (Lenin, Chayanov and Lewsin) carried out substantive research on the topic during the earlier part of twentieth century and more recently, the issue has been kept alive through numerous studies in a number of countries particularly in India. The inverse relationship between farm size and productivity has been observed in many underdevloped economics with widely different climatic conditions, structure of land holdings and cropping patterns [See Berry and Cline (1979) and Griffin (1974)] for studies pertaining to Latin America and Asia respectively.

The inverse relation acquired significance as it led to believe that small farms make more efficient use of resources than large farms and thus, providing ground to argue that the small farmers are superior to large ones on purely economic grounds. The well known policy implication of this is that an agricultural development strategy based on the promotion of small rather large farms can serve both growth and income distribution objectives.

In India the debate about the farm size and productivity relationship started with the publication of Farm Management Studies (of India, 1954-57). The debate was initiated by A.K. Sen in a paper entitled 'An aspect of Indian agriculture' published in *Economic Weekly* in 1962. Sen in his paper stated a proposition based on Farm Management Surveys (FMS) that, by and large, productivity per acre decreased with the size of holding. Thus, maintained Sen, productivity was more on small farms as compared to large farms. Although Sen himself expressed some caution regarding the statistical basis of the proposition concerning this inverse relation (especially in his subsequent paper of 1964), the phenomenon was taken more or less as well established by most economists who proceeded to provide a number of alternative explanations for the observed tendency.

Ashok Rudra and others questioned the statistical validity of the inverse relationship between farm size and productivity. They argued that while the inverse relationship may hold in certain areas, it is not a universal phenomenon and cannot be said to operate in all parts of the country. The issue was hotly debated between the follwers of A.K. Sen (Deepak Mazumdar, 1965; C.H.H. Rao, 1966; G.R. Saini, 1971; Khusro, 1973; Pranab Bardhan, 1973; K. Bhardwaj, 1974; A.K. Ghose, 1978; Bhattacharya and Saini, 1972) and Ashok Rudra (A.P. Rao, 1967; Usha Rani, 1971; Chattopadhyay, 1976). The methodological objections about the inverse relationship between farm size and productivity formed the basis of the said debate.

Methodological Objections

Various objections have been made to the inverse size productivity relationship, both with respect to its statistical validity and to its economic limitation.

Rudra and Chattopadhyay (1976) expressed their doubts about the statistical validity of the results obtained by many studies pertaining to size-productivity relationship. They argue that the results in many studies are based on the test of significance for the coefficients of simple linear regression fits in two variables. Thus A.P. Rao, Saini, Usha Rani Hanumantha Rao and Bhattacharya all assume the following form:

$$\text{Log}\, Y = \text{Log}\, A + B\, \text{Log}\, X$$

Where Y is value of output and X is farm size, whereas Krishna Bharadwaj uses the same form but interpret Y as value of output per acre. Khusro alone dispense with logarithms and uses the simple form:

$$Y/X = A + BX$$

Where *Y* and *X* are as before. None of these researchers, however, gave any justification whatsoever for the forms assumed by them. They seem to be unconcerned with the fact that the conclusions drawn by them on the basis of the *t*-tests carried out by them for the significant difference of the regression coefficient from zero is dependent on the assumption that the regression relations assumed by them are valid (Chattopadhyay, M. and Rudra, A., 1976).

A glaring case of driving misleading conclusions on the basis of statistical test is that of Bhalla, S. S. (1970) who concluded on the basis of his study that "the inverse relationship between farm size and productivity is confirmed and indeed, appears to be quite pronounced, as shown by the high degree of the relationship (high *t*-statistics)". Commenting on the above conclusion of Bhalla (1984), Paul Barbier writes "as we know K. Popper, Bhalla is not habititated to confirm any theory, he may only say that the theory is not rejected".

Rudra (1982) further argues that a significant inverse relationship between size and productivity does not necessarily mean that the relationship holds in all ranges of size variable. Thus, if *Y* decreases with *X* in a certain range of values of *X*, but does not depend on *X* in any systematic fashion for other values of *X*, then it is all the same quite likely that in fitting a curve one would get a downward slope or in carrying out rank correlation test one would get a negative rank correlation. In either case, if one gets negative values — but not significantly different from zero when tested individually — one would be justified in suspecting precisely this: that the inverse relationship holds in certain ranges of *X* but not in others.

Paul Barbier (1984) says that most of the statistical tests which have been carried out to verify the empirical existence of the size-productivity inverse relationship appear to have a low degree of reliability. With a view to asses the possible impact of the methods used on the results obtained, Barbier examined the FMS data for the year 1971-72 relating to the Hoogly district in the State of West Bengal and concluded by saying "The results obtained from this exercise have actually confirmed the above doubts about the validity of the statistical procedures used to this data. For one thing, we did not find any kind of monotonous inverse relationship, and, for another thing, we are not even sure that functional relationship exists at all between the size of the farm and the productivity of land."

Paul Barbier (1984) has further pointed out that many of the major studies of inverse relationship publish their findings without any indication of the standard deviation of yields around the mean levels in each size class. These standard deviations could be large for all size classes, implying that yields in reality vary randomly over the entire rane of farm sizes.

Some researchers have pointed out that the inverse relationship may be due to the use of aggregate data. Aggregation results into smoothening of data and may lead to the spurious findings of a continuous inverse correlation where none exists in the underlying data. Most of the studies pertaining to size-productivity relationship have used the data available from Farm Management Surveys which presents informations as aggregated into size groups of holdings. Such aggregation is bound to affect some results more than others. Classifying and presenting information on the basis of size-groups of holdings implicitly assumes that the characteristics of farms under study depend predominantly upon their belonging to a certain size group. To the extent that they do not, by pooling together the information about the individual holdings falling within a single size-group, the variations in their traits will be lost, as what one gets is an average figure for the group as a whole. Thus, even an exceptional attribute of a single farm would be shown as if it were an average trait of the group (Bharadwaj, K., 1974).

Rudra (1982) argues that pooling or aggregation can falsify the nature of dependence of productivity on farm size in both directions. Thus, if within a village, productivity of land is invariable with respect to farm size but if the productivity of land is different in different villages and if the villages with higher productivity of land have small average farm sizes, then putting together the data from different village would reveal a spurious inverse relationship. If on the other hand, average productivity of land is the same in every village and if within each village the inverse relationship holds, then if different villages have got different average ranges of farm sizes, the intra-village inverse relationship would get obliterated in the process of pooling of inter-village data. Thus, use of such data may be expected to give highly misjudging results.

The first exercise with disaggregated data in India was carried out by A.P. Rao (1967) who fitted a logarithmic linear function to farm level data all belonging to the same village. His conclusion was: "contrary to the findings of the Farm Management Studies, according to the present study productivity remained constant over all holding sizes in all the villages, which indicate that holding size has no effect on productivity."

Rao was supported by Rudra (1968a) who in his analysis of individual holdings in 20 villages noted that 18 out of 20 villages failed to reveal any dependence of yield per acre on farm size, while in the case of one there was, in fact, a positive association between yield and size, and the remaining one revealed no systematic pattern commenting on Rudra's (1968a) results, C.H.H. Rao (1968) pointed out that the results obtained by Rudra were perhaps due to the use of yield per gross cultivated area. Gross cultivated area is reckoned on the basis of actual land-use and counts in repetitive cropping on the same piece of land. (It is equivalent to net cultivated area or the size of farm multiplied by intensity of cultivation.) To the extent therefore that intensity of cropping varied systematically with size (particularly if inversely), Rao argued, Radra's formulation would be biased towards eliminating the inverse relation between size and yield per acre. Rudra (1968b), in his reply, questioned the concept of size of farm (net cultivated area) as a proper measure of land input and also pointed out that the relation between size of farm and intensity of cultivation was not invariably inverse as Rao supposed.

Saini (1971), using disaggregated farm management data and relating yield per acre (net) to size of holding (net area), reported that inverse relation held systematically on the basis of a log linear functional fit in most cases (22 out of 25).

Usha Rani (1971), who also used disaggregated data, found, "the regression coefficient in 14 out of the 15 cases is negative but if the '*t*' test is applied at the 5 per cent level of significance then the regression coefficient is found significant only in 7 out of 15 cases and hence no generalization regarding the relationship can be made. Further, if the test at one per cent level of significance is applied, the regression coefficient is found significant only in one out of 15 cases. Hence one can even conclude that yield per acre remains constant over different size groups of farmers."

The above results led Rani to conclude "This controversy of relationship between the size of farm and yield per acre was based on the aggregated data of FMS and on disaggregated data from some other sources, but the results were not put to statistical tests. After taking care of these factors, the conclusion which emerges from the present exercise is that the whole controversy and all the explanations offered to prove the different observations had a very weak statistical basis."

The most voluminous work that has been undertaken on this problem is that by Bhattacharya and Saini (1972). They used disaggregated FMS data for individual forms. Separately for each sample village, and applied statistical tests for examining the relationship between farm size and gross value of output per acre. They considered two districts, namely, Muzaffarnagar in U.P. and Ferozepur in Punjab. The results obtained by them in their own words is a under:

"The negative correlation between farm size and productivity is, therefore, clear for this region (Muzaffarnagar) in the sense that such correlection is observed within most of the sample villages and could not have arisen due to aggregation over villages." "But on the whole, the size productivity correlation is not at all clear for this region (Ferozepur)."

The different results obtained by them for two regions, led them to suggest, "Even if one does not carry out completely separate villagewise analysis (as done here) it may often be necessary to introduce dummy variables representing changes in the intercept from village to village. If this is not done, the analysis will frequently be invalid and the true relationship distorted by the aggregation over villages."

Chottopadhyay and Rudra (1976) estimated coefficients of correlation between farm size and two indicators of farm productivity and conclude, "It is seen that one cannot discover any tendency of yield per hectare decreasing with farm size on the basis of these data. The rank correlation coefficients are mostly non-significant and they are also not predominantly of any sign. For most of the crops there are about as many negative signs as positive. In any case there is no scope for propounding a general law."

S.S. Bhalla (1979) observed that the inverse relationship between farm size and productivity is a reflection of substantive differences between small farms and large farms, rather than a product of sample selection bias or village factors correlation with farm size.

M.R. Carter (1984) using a pooled farm level data obtained from Farm Management Surveys taken in Haryana during the agricultural year 1969-70 to 1971-72, found that the inverse relationship is not a reflection of bias resulting from sample selection based on farmer literacy nor is it a misidentification of village effects.

Recently Chattopadhyay and Sengupta (1997) carried a study, using farm level disaggregated data for 1989-90 for West Bengal. The analysis has been carried out an exactly the same line as those carried out by Bhattacharya and Saini (1972). They divided the entire State into six agro-climatic zones. Sixty Blocks were selected from these six zones. From these 60 Blocks, 60 villages were selected. As to the selection of household as an ultimate unit of enquiry, all the households as well as total operated area in each household for each selected village under each block were recorded.[1] The recorded household against each selected village were categorised into five size classes of operational holdings. From each size-class two samples were taken by random procedure.[2] In this way all 600 farmers were selected. The size-productivity relationship was examined for all varieties of paddy cultivated by the farmers of 600 selected households. Both linear and log-linear relationship were examined showing value of output per hectare of paddy. (V/A) against net cultivated area (A) separately for the holdings within each sample village.

They supplemented regression analysis by computing Kendall's rank correlation coefficient (tau) between (V/A) and A separately for each sample village. They also undertook the overall Chi-square tests applied for combining the villagewise test for different zones. A similar procedure was applied for combining the test based on tau.

In order to investigate the effects of aggregation over villages. Chattopadhyay and Sengupta applied standard analysis of homogeneity of the villagewise regression lines for each region. This means they examined whether or not the size productivity relationship for the different villages could be specified by a simple linear or log-linear relation. Standard analysis of covariance procedure was applied to test the suitability of the model.[3]

Chattopadhyay and Sengupta have summarised the findings of their study by saying, "Thus, our results suggest that relationship between size and productivity is more or less uniform across the villages, village-specific factors such as soil fertility, irrigation, facilities etc., tend to alter the magnitude of this effect. If one uses aggregated data to study such relationship, he has to consider an intercept dummy as a shift parameter to capture such inter-village differences. Otherwise the conclusion drawn from such data well be ambiguous. Most of the earlier studies based on aggregated Farm Management data and used regression analysis suffer from such limitation."

So the studies conducted by Bhattacharya and Saini, S.S. Bhalla, M.R. Carter and Chattopadhyay and Sengupta have shown that inverse size-productivity relationship is not because of the use of aggregate data and there is no need to doubt the statistical validity of the relationship.

Another important problem with the studies pertaining to size-productivity relationship, is the appropriate definition of "Size". The central role played by size of farm in research endeavours means that size must be defined in an analytically useful way. However, size is a relative concept, and studies that do not recognise this fact are of limited usefulness. The problem of size has recently been addressed by H.E. Doran (1985) in a methodological vein. He notes that a common method is to divide the sample arbitrarily into two groups on the basis of some measure of farm size, and then to estimate a separate production function for each group. On the basis of these different production functions, inferences are drawn about efficiencies, which then form the basis of policy pronouncements.

Doran offers a procedure for drawing a distinction between large and small farms based on statistical techniques from switching regression. Gold-fled and Quandt propose that the dividing line be determined by the data, with large and small being determined by sizes more than (and less than) the aggregate mean plus (and minus) one standard deviation. Both methods seem to represent refinement to what heretofore, has been a quite arbitrary division.

The problems with farm size as an explanatory variable have been emphasized by Krishna (1964). He found that the same farm management survey data on which most of the empirical work was based would support the finding that holdings between 13 and 16 acres yield both the maximum and minimum gross output per acre and that holdings of 1-3 acres yield both the maximum and minimum output per unit of input cost.

There is also the serious problem of land fragmentation. The studies generally aggregate fragmented holdings and treat the total as one unified piece of land. Sau (1973) reports that in Madhya Pradesh, where fragmentation is least serious, a farm of 40-50 acres will usually encompass five separate plots averaging 8.2 acres in size. Sau further reports that a sample survey of 11 villages in the dry region of Poona district shows a farm of 150 acres consisting of 11 parcels each averaging approximately 14 acres in size. The unit of cultivation in the largest size group (100-150 acres) is 11 times the average size of a fragment in that group. The inconvenience, limitations, and organising difficulties of a big farmer with land in 7-10 scattered fragments can easily be imagined. Compounding this, we have different soil and microclimatic conditions across parcels.

It has also been argued that partial productivity measures, like yield or labour product, result in ambiguity about the relative efficiency of farms of different sizes. Land productivity may be low when labour productivity is high and *vice versa*. Farm efficiency comparison should be based on the productivity of area alone. This is notoriously difficult to measure because resources can only be aggregated in value terms, and many problems attend on the prices used and on the measurement of fixed capital between farms. One approach is to value resources at prices which are thought to reflect social, rather than private, scarcity values. Berry and Cline (1979) contains examples of total factor productivity analysis, and the results seem to confirm the inverse relationship for overall farm efficiency.

An equally important empirical problem arise because of the particular functional form assumed. The majority of the studies have employed a Cobb-Douglas production function apparently because of its computational simplicity rather than its technical superiority or relevance to actual production conditions.

In addition to the above conceptual and empirical problems, the research on farm size and productivity seems virtually to have ignored important aspects of production relations and organisational matters. In appraising this literature Ghose A.K. (1979) writes,

> "The surprising feature of the research on the subject is that whereas theorists have forced not directly on size but typologies based on production relations, empirical research has been confined almost wholly to testing the size-productivity relationship. No attempt has been made, for example, to determine whether the inverse relation is observed when farms are considered in terms of single type of production relations. The major explanation for this deficiency in empirical research lies on the conventional assumption that most peasant farms employ hired labour. In reality a great deal of variation in size may exist among farms of each type and the correlation between farm size and mode or organisation of production is not always large."

To investigate the relationship between the type of farm organisation and the size of area actually farmed, Ghose analysed data for the Hoogly district in West Bengal and the Ferozepur district in the Punjab. His findings illustrate the risk of using farm size as an explanatory variable. He notes,

> "In Hoogly, the various types of farms (Peasant, peasant-tenant, etc.) do not seem to different significantly with regard to farm size; all types of farms are found in each size group. An employer farm

is not necessarily a large farm, nor is a peasant farm necessarily small. It is of course true that as average farm size increases, the proportion of farm that are wage-labour based increases as well, but it is clear that even in very small size-classes a significant proportion of farms is found to be wage-labour based. In Forozepur, on the other hand, wage-labour based farms are generally larger in size than peasant farms. But even here, there are quite a few very large peasant farms so that farm size by itself does not tell us very much about the organisational basis of production."

In spite of the said limitations, the critiques of the inverse relationship have not rejected the validity of the inverse relationship in all circumstances. They are basically against such sweeping generalisation as, "..... Thus, by and large, the inverse relationship between farm size and productivity is a confirmed phenomenon in Indian agriculture and its statistical validity is adequately established by an analysis of disaggregated data" (Saini, 1971), "...... over the years, the inverse relationship has almost achieved the status of a stylised fact of peasant agriculture," (G.S. Bhalla, 1979) and "..... The previous chapters of this have considered the relative productivity of small and large farms from both theoretical and empirical standpoints and reached the general conclusion that the former normally generate higher land productivity". (Berry and Cline, 1979). Their view is that such a relationship could not be regarded as a universally valid law operating in Indian agriculture.

Conclusions

The issue of inverse relation between yield per acre and the size of holding is highly complex. There has been considerable debate over the methodology and the exact nature of the relationship. However, in spite of several methodological objections to the inverse size-productivity relationship, the critiques of the inverse relationship have not rejected the validity of the inverse relationship in toto. We conclude by saying that the various studies pertaining to the relationship between farm size and productivity indicates that the negative relationships, although widespread, are not always strong. The weak nature of the relationship becomes more evident if pooling and grouping of data are avoided, and even where the relationship is significantly negative over the whole range of farm size, it need not hold for particular segments. There cannot, therefore, be much confidence in claims which portray the inverse relationship as laws but the frequency of their occurrence does provide meaningful information in suggesting that they represent certain widespread tendencies in Indian agriculture.

Notes

1. If the number of households in the selected village is less than 200, then a second village adjacent to the nucleus village within a radius of five kilometres from the nucleus village was taken and total number of households in each village or cluster of villages was noted.
2. Following five-size classes were formed on the basis of the total operated area (in hectare) under each cultivator : (i) Less than 1.00 hect., (ii) 1.00-2.00, (iii) 2.00-4.00, (iv) 4.00-6.00, and (v) 6.00 hect and above.
3. Scatter diagram showing *V/A* against *A* on arithmetic and also on double log scale for the 60 sample villages indicate that *a*'s are different for different villages but the *b*'s are constant. Hence the model $y=a+bx$ where y and x donote *V/A* and *A*, respectively, used in this exercise, seems to be realistic.

References

Barbier, P. (1984), Inverse relationship between farm size and productivity : A product of Science or imagination, *Economic and Political Weekly,* Vol. XIX, No. 52-53.

Berry, R.A. and Cline, R.W. (1979), *Agrarian structure and productivity in developing countries*, Baltimore, John Hopkins University Press.

Bharadwaj, K. (1974), *Production Conditions in Indian Agriculture : A study based on Farm Management Surveys*, Occasional Paper 33, Department of Applied Economics Cambridge University Press, Cambridge.

Bharadwaj, K. (1994), *Accumulation, exchange and development*, Sage Pubications, New Delhi.

Bhattacharya, N. and Saini, G.R. (1972), Farm size and productivity : A fresh look, *Economic and Political Weekly*, 7, 24 June.

Carter, M.R. (1984), The identification of the inverse relationship between farm size and productivity : An empirical study of peasant agricultural production, *Oxford Economic Papers,* Vol. 36, No. 1.

Chattopadhyay, M. and Rudra, A. (1976), Size productivity revisited, *Economic and Political Weekly*, Vol. XI, No. 39.

Chattopadhyay, M. and Sengupta, A. (1997), Farm size and productivity : A new look at the old debate, *Economic and Political Weekly,* Vol. XXXII, No. 52.

Doran, H.E. (1985), Small or large farm : Some methodology consideration, *American Journal of Agricultural Economics*, 67.

Ghose A.K. (1979), Farm size and land productivity in Indian agriculture : A reappraisal, *Journal of Development Studies,* Vol. 16, No. 1.

Griffin, K. (1974), *The Political Economy of Agrarian Change*, Macmillan London.

Krishna, R. (1964), Some Production functions for the Punjab, *Indian Journal of Agricultural Economics,* 19.

Rao, A.P. (1967), Size of holding and productivity, *Economic and Political Weekly*, 11 Nov.

Rani, U. (1971), Size of farm and productivity, *Economic and Political Weekly*, 26 June.

Rao, C.H.H. (1968), Farm size and yield per acre : A comment, *Economic and Political Weekly*, 14 Sept.

Rudra, A. (1968a), Farm size and yield per acre, *Economic and Political Weekly*, Special number, July.

Rudra, A. (1986b), More on returns to scale in Indian agriculture, *Economic and Political Weekly*, 3(43), Review of Agriculture.

Rudra, A. (1982), *Indian Agricultural Economics : Myths and Realities*, Allied Publishers, New Delhi.

Saini, G.R. (1971), Holding size, productivity and some related aspects of Indian agriculture, *Economic and Political Weekly*, 26 June.

Sau, R.K. (1973), *Indian Economic Growth : Constraints and Prospects*, Orient Longman, New Delhi.

Sen, A.K. (1962), An aspect of Indian agriculture, *Economic Weekly*, Vol. XIV, Annual number, Feb.

Sen, A.K. (1964), Size of holding and productivity, *Economic Weekly*, 2 May.

21

AGRICULTURAL DEVELOPMENT IN BIHAR

Critical Appraisal of Its Trend

ANIL KUMAR

Bihar with only 5.3 per cent of the land mass of the country, is the second most populous State of India, constituting nearly 10.29 per cent of national population. It is also expected that by the end of present century the state would further record an additional increase, at least by 1.6 crore, of population over 1991. The State is also the most ruralised as almost 90 per cent of the State population lives in rural areas and likewise about 81 per cent of the total working force of the state are engaged in agricultural activities. Agriculture alone contributes about 42 per cent to the state domestic product. This state has also the lowest per capita income in the country in spite of fertile alluvial soil stretching on the both sides of the river Ganga, favourable agro-climatic condition and rich mineral resources in the southern plateau region. This sounds a bit paradoxical, yet various factors have contributed to the large portion of its population, about 40.8 per cent, to remain below the poverty line.

Agriculture which happens to be the backbone of the state's economy is also the single most important sector for sustaining the livelihood of the majority of working force by providing employment and has to bear the burden of state's growing population at a reasonable caloric level through foodgrain production. At the same time agriculture has to make itself an economically viable sector as the per capita income of average farmer and employment generation in this sector has gone down in the State. Despite agriculture's overriding importance the constraints facing this sector have either increased or continued as before.

There is no doubt that the progress of agriculture in the State has been tardy and slow during the decades of development planning. The State has achieved 2.5 per cent of annual compound growth in food-grain production during eighties but during early nineties the growth rate has declined to 1.6 per cent. An effort has been made here to examine the agricultural development in the State of Bihar since launching the fourth five year plan which incidentally coincided with adaptation of scientific agricultural policy, a period known as Green Revolution, and level of sustainability since attained.

Trend of Agricultural Growth : Cropped Area

The strategies adopted during the earlier five year plans with emphasis on land reforms which aimed at increasing production proved satisfactory at earlier phases as the growth rate of agriculture achieved target of 4.4 per cent against the target of 4 per cent. But in the State where three-fourth of the population was engaged in agriculture, the backwardness persisted. In sixties and during the period known as Green Revolution emphasis was more given to extension of irrigation, farmer's access to modern input like HYV seeds, fertilizers and supported by effective planned efforts and government policies with positive result.

During fourth plan period net cultivated area constituted nearly 48 per cent of the geographical area of the State. It registered negligible change, yet at the initial phase of Green Revolution there was an increase of 11 to 14 per cent which started to decrease from 1979-80 and remained at 2 to 2.5 per cent since then. Only 44.57 per cent of the total area of the State was under cultivation during 1989-90 and in the eighth five year plan the figure further declined to remain at 42 per cent. Gross cropped area, marginally improved from 110.63 lakh hectares in fourth five year plan to 111.48 lakh hectares in sixth five year plan but declined to 105.12 lakh hectares in seventh five year plan and continued to slide to 94.50 lakh hectares in eighth five year plan. A gain of 22 per cent upto late seventies marks the peak from where total cropped area in the State sharply declined by the end of eighties. Intensity of cropping which has been 124.2 per cent during 1966-67, despite a substantial decline in gross cropped area during Green Revolution period, observed an increasing trend upto sixth five year plan periods (Table 21.1). During fourth plan period cropping intensity improved to 132 per cent and continued to maintain an increasing trend to about 138 per cent upto sixth five year plan. It declined to 136 per cent in seventh five year plan

Table 21.1 : Pattern of Land Utilization and Cropping Intensity

Year	*Net Area Sown (in lakh hect.)*	*Total Corpped Area (in per cent)*	*Copping Intensity (in per cent)*
1950-51	89.5	109.2	122.0
1960-61	80.3	111.0	138.7
1966-67	74.2	92.2	124.2
1967-68	82.8	108.9	131.5
1968-69	85.2	108.9	130.9
1969-70	83.9	110.6	131.8
1970-71	84.5	110.2	130.4
1971-72	82.7	106.8	129.1
1972-73	80.5	103.8	128.9
1973-74	83.7	107.6	128.6
1974-75	83.4	108.6	130.2
1975-76	84.7	112.8	133.2
1976-77	83.5	113.2	135.6
1977-78	88.4	115.6	136.9
1978-79	85.3	113.8	133.4
1979-80	79.0	104.1	131.9
1980-81	83.1	111.4	134.1
1981-82	78.6	106.2	135.2
1982-83	82.7	96.4	116.5
1983-84	75.8	102.5	135.3
1984-85	76.2	103.1	135.2
1985-86	76.9	105.1	136.5
1986-87	76.1	104.3	137.0
1987-88	74.8	103.2	138.0
1988-89	76.0	105.1	138.2
1989-90	77.2	104.0	134.6

Source : Bihar Statistical Handbooks, Bihar at a glance.

and reached a low of 130 per cent during eighth five year plan. In spite of the declining trend intensity of cropping reveals an increase of almost 10 per cent since 1966-67 in spite of fall both in net sown area and total cropped area. The declining trend of intensity even during early nineties is probably due to poor maintenance of public irrigation system and a significant increase in waste land in the State.

Foodgrains and non-foodgrains together constitute more than 95 per cent of gross cropped area. The cropping pattern shown in Table 21.2 further reveals that foodgrains occupy most of the cultivable land and there has been almost no change in this scenario since 1950-51.

It may be seen from Table 21.2 that area under foodgrains, which was 90.3 lakh hectares in 1950-51 achieved a peak during 1960-61 with 99.2 lakh hect., declined to 94.3 lakh hect. showing a decrease of

Table 21.2 : Area Under Major Crops

(Area in Lakh Hectares)

Crops	*1950-51*	*1960-61*	*1970-71*	*1989-90*	*Change in %*
Paddy	58.0	52.4	52.7	52.8	–8.6
Wheat	5.9	6.5	13.1	19.8	235.6
Maize	6.1	8.0	9.9	7.0	18.0
Total Cereal	70.1	75.9	82.6	82.2	17.3
Pulses	20.2	23.3	16.3	12.1	–40.1
Total foodgrains	90.3	99.2	98.9	94.3	4.4
Total Oilseeds	3.4	3.0	2.5	2.0	–41.2
Sugarcane	1.6	1.8	1.6	1.2	–25.0
Jute & Mesta	1.3	1.8	1.8	1.4	7.7

Source : *Bihar Statistical Handbooks and Bihar at a Glance.*

4.4. per cent in 1989-90. During the early parts of Green Revolution area under foodgrains increased but presented a declining trend through sixth five year plan to eighth five year plan. Actually there has been increase in area under foodgrains since 1950-51, indicating also the complete dependence of agriculture on foodgrains. Actually this increase in area under foodgrains is obvious in case of cereal crops which increased from 70.10 lakh hect. (1950-51) to 82.2 lakh hect. in 1989-90 showing a net increase in 17.3 per cent hectareage. Even this increase in hectareage in cereals was due to increase in wheat coverage because area under paddy had declined since 1951.

In the State paddy is the chief cereal crop occupying nearly half of the gross cropped area. Bihar accounts for 14.1 per cent of the aggregated area of paddy in the country during fourth five year plan but during eighth five year plan the figure declined to 11.7 per cent. Between these periods average area under wheat increased from 12.80 lakh hect. to 20.30 lakh hect. accounting for an increase of 59 per cent between fourth to eighth plan period. Bihar, a major maize producing State, experienced a decline in area from 9.12 lakh hect. in fourth plan period to 7.58 lakh hect. in eighth five year plan. The decline in area has been mainly in kharif maize. Area under pulses similarly declined from 15.65 lakh hect. to 9.37 lakh hectare between fourth to eighth five year plan, mainly due to shift of pulse area to wheat as wheat production is less risky and more important in context of food security on smaller size of holdings.

Among non-foodgrains, area under rapeseed and mustard increased from 0.85 lakh hect. to 1.10 lakh hect. during fourth to eighth five year plan. Similar gain in area have been observed in the case of potato, onion, sugarcane, banana whereas jute, a major cash crop in northeast part of the State and chillies, a cash crop in Begusarai, Samastipur, and Saharsa region lost area due to inefficient marketing system. It is further noted that area under jute and sugarcane remained constant even after Green Revolution (Table 21.3).

Table 21.3 : Cropping Pattern (in per cent)

Year	*Rice*	*Wheat*	*Maize*	*Pulses*	*Oilseeds*	*Other food crops*	*Sugar-cane*	*Jute*	*Total non-food crops*
1966-67	49.9	9.2	9.7	14.5	2.3	5.7	1.7	1.8	5.2
1967-68	49.7	10.2	9.5	16.3	2.3	4.7	1.1	1.5	4.7
1968-69	50.9	10.4	8.9	15.3	2.3	6.1	1.4	0.9	3.8
1969-70	50.1	10.6	8.9	15.6	2.3	5.6	1.5	1.3	4.3
1970-71	48.6	12.1	9.1	15.2	2.4	5.3	1.5	1.3	4.5
1971-72	51.2	13.5	6.8	14.5	2.4	4.7	1.3	1.3	4.3
1972-73	46.7	16.3	7.9	14.9	2.5	4.9	1.3	1.2	4.4
1973-74	48.9	12.6	8.8	14.7	2.6	4.8	1.3	1.4	4.9
1974-75	49.1	13.9	8.3	14.6	2.7	4.8	1.3	0.9	4.4
1975-76	47.8	16.5	7.7	13.9	2.9	4.4	1.2	0.9	4.5
1976-77	47.9	17.5	8.4	12.8	2.5	4.3	1.2	1.1	4.3
1977-78	49.0	16.5	7.8	12.9	2.7	4.1	1.2	1.4	4.7
1978-79	49.7	16.2	7.9	11.6	2.5	4.2	1.3	1.4	5.2
1979-80	49.1	16.4	7.9	12.0	2.3	4.1	1.3	1.4	5.5
1980-81	49.0	16.3	7.9	12.5	2.5	4.0	0.9	1.2	5.7
1981-82	49.8	15.2	7.9	11.8	2.2	4.1	1.1	1.3	6.6
1982-83	46.8	17.2	8.1	12.4	2.2	4.1	1.3	1.2	6.7
1983-84	51.3	12.3	8.5	12.4	2.5	4.0	1.3	1.3	6.4
1984-85	48.9	18.1	5.5	11.2	2.3	3.3	1.0	1.3	7.4
1985-86	49.1	17.4	6.1	11.1	2.3	3.1	1.1	1.9	7.9
1987-88	49.3	20.4	6.3	11.4	2.1	3.9	1.1	1.2	4.7
1988-89	50.4	20.0	6.5	10.8	2.0	3.7	1.2	1.3	4.1
1989-90	52.0	19.5	6.9	11.9	2.0	2.4	1.2	1.2	5.2

Source : *Bihar Statistical Handbooks and Bihar at a Glance,* D.O.S.E. Bihar.

Trend of Growth : Input Ingredients

The impact of the new agricultural policy and the period thereafter referred as Green Revolution in fact is predominantly dependent on infrastructural facilities created in the State under successive five year plans. Secured irrigation, use of HYV seeds and fertilizers together played a vital role in increasing agricultural production. The data presented in Table 21.4 indicates that the average irrigation intensity which was 21.60 per cent in 1966-67 increased to 30.70 per cent during 1989-90. But breakthrough in irrigation came after 1971-72. The net irrigated area has increased from 22.79 lakh hect. in 1969-70 to 36.80 lakh hect. in 1995-96, which worked out to be 27.10 per cent and 47.70 per cent of net sown area respectively. Tubewells emerged as a major source of irrigation in Bihar since fourth five year plan. Irrigated area under tubewell increased from 2.60 lakh hectares in 1969-70 to 17.28 lakh hect. in 1995-96, which accounts for nearly 50 per cent of the total irrigated area in Bihar. Throughout the period of Green Revolution canal irrigation remained almost stagnant at 10 lakh hect. Moreover area under canal irrigation declined in Bihar plain from 10.48 lakh hect. in 1980-81 to 10.34 lakh hect. in 1995-96. It is worth pointing out that irrigated area under the canal system and tubewells have not been getting sufficient water at right time due to poor maintenance of these irrigation structures. About 90 per cent of Government tubewells in the State have been abandoned either due to obsolete machineries or unavailability of electric supply. There is no doubt that almost one-third of gross cropped area is being presently provided irrigation but irrigation is mainly used as a guard for kharif crops.

Similarly consumption of fertilizer per hect. of gross cropped area which was only 6.14 kg. in 1968-69 increased to 74.32 kg. in 1988-89 and 77 kg. in 1995-96. However the level of fertilizer use had been much lower upto sixth plan period with 20 kg. per hect. which was one-third of per hectare use at country level. Even after sixth plan period due to unbalanced use of major nutrient (NPK) in the ratio of 17.3:5:1 against 4.2:2:1, uncertainties in fertilizer availability, untimely use and higher premium in case of urea and DAP in remote areas, farmers are not in position to get benefits of increased fertilizer use.

Area under HYV of seeds like consumption of fertilizer in the State, shown in Table 21.3, was less in the beginning of 1966-67 but situation gradually improved over the years. The percentage of area under HYV seeds to gross cropped area increased from 1.07 per cent to 1966-67 to 32.49 per cent in 1988-89. With uncertain irrigational level, and present level of fertilizer use have their obvious effect on HYV productivity which is below the expected level in the State.

Trend of Growth : Productivity

The comparative review of irrigation fertilizer and HYV points out that despite their positive effect on agricultural growth, there has not been a

Table 21.4 : Utility of Inputs and Productivity

Year	*Rain Fall (mm)*	*Net irrigated area (in per cent)*	*Area under HYV seeds (lakh hect.)*	*Inorganic fertilizer (in Yield per hectare in kg.) lakh tonnes*			
					Rice	*Wheat*	*Maize*
1966-67	874	21.60	0.99	0.00	334	437	1107
1967-68	1051	24.30	5.11	0.00	753	865	1003
1968-69	1262	26.10	6.20	0.67	776	865	887
1969-70	1256	27.10	8.36	1.10	674	835	929
1970-71	1249	25.60	3.27	0.99	852	1035	1124
1971-72	1295	28.80	18.10	1.08	974	1785	1161
1972-73	1180	28.80	21.93	1.19	947	1250	936
1973-74	1210	27.70	21.10	0.96	802	1236	1059
1974-75	1154	30.20	20.59	1.17	808	1353	650
1975-76	1139	31.70	23.54	1.35	923	1265	1004
1976-77	1193	34.50	27.29	1.56	895	1270	1063
1977-78	1294	34.00	30.68	1.73	987	1261	1036
1978-79	998	34.70	31.65	1.95	984	1385	1101
1979-80	1235	35.10	28.30	1.84	706	1107	947
1980-81	1270	35.50	36.50	2.05	1028	1355	1088
1981-82	1280	38.20	37.00	2.05	825	1342	904
1982-83	927	28.00	38.75	2.03	681	1400	1174
1983-84	1095	33.20	45.00	2.93	1016	1554	1165
1984-85	1429	00.00	50.00	3.81	1035	1616	1250
1985-86	1361	36.30	47.18	3.51	1128	1650	1220
1986-87	1288	36.70	54.78	3.60	1126	1660	1640
1987-88	1557	30.92	33.11	7.55	916	1539	1142
1988-89	1261	30.37	34.17	7.55	1140	1684	1526
1989-90	1233	30.70	00.00	0.00	1182	1645	1716

Source : *Bihar Statistical Handbooks*, Bihar at a glance.

satisfactory increase in agricultural production in Bihar. The proportion of productivity has not increased in the same ratio since 1966-67 as in the case of fertilizer and HYV. Agricultural productivity has a direct relationship to the availability of irrigation in general and in this state this factor is still far from being satisfactory. More favourable rainfall conditions are still deciding factor in yearly productivity.

Productivity of all the principal crops increased since the fourth five year plan but always less than the corresponding increase at national level. In 1969-70 Bihar had an edge over the country with respect of productivity of wheat (3.80 per cent), pulses (0.38 per cent), rapeseed and mustard (6.49 per cent) and potato (12.31 per cent) but during successive years State lagged behind in increasing production of principal crops. Despite a decline in area, average production of paddy increased from 44.00 lakh tonnes to 57.40 lakh tonnes between fourth to eighth plan periods. Inspite of this increase share of paddy in total foodgrains output declined from 53 to 47 per cent during the period. Production of wheat increased by two-fold and its share in foodgrains also increased from 23 per cent to 34 per cent during the period. Between 1969-96 productivity of maize increased by more than twice in Bihar inspite of 17 per cent decline in area during the period. It was possible due to increase in area under winter maize which recorded an average productivity of 30.07 quintal/hect. moreover winter maize productivity of 60 quintal/hect. is common in North Bihar. Productivity of pulses increased by 17 per cent between 1969-96. Bihar is still ahead to several states with respect to pulses productivity. But in the case of paddy and sugarcane the yield gap has increased to 25.95 and 46.35 per cent respectively since 1969-70.

In the State the growth rate in production of the main cereal crop like paddy has been 1.30 per cent annually. In the case of wheat the per annum growth rate is 5.20 per cent, while maize reveals less than 0.50 per cent growth rate per annum in production. The annual growth rate of hectareage under these three main cereal crops, it has been 2.70 per cent in wheat, but in paddy and maize there has been a negative growth rate of –0.1 and –1.6 per cent respectively. The growth rate of productivity of wheat has been significant compared to other cereal crops.

Table 21.5 : Growth Rate per Annum (1967-90)

Cereal	*Area*	*Production*	*Productivity*
Paddy	–0.1	1.3	1.4
Wheat	2.7	5.2	2.5
Maize	–1.6	0.4	1.2

Trend of Growth : Foodgrain Production

The area under different food crops fluctuated in response to rainfall and input ingredients but the total area devoted to foodgrains more or less remained almost unchanged since 1974-75. In foodgrain production there has been slight improvement from 7.51 million tonnes in 1964-65 to 7.88 million tonnes in 1970-71. Since then production gradually improved to 9.26 million tonnes in 1980-81. The positive trend continued during eighties and by the end of the decade production reached to 13.04

million tonnes. About 2.5 per cent of annual compound growth in foodgrain production was recorded during eighties which declined to 1.6 per cent during early nineties. In fact the improvement of about 75 per cent over 1964-65 registered in the foodgrain production has failed to produce real impact on the prevailing food situation in the State.

The per capita output of foodgrains in the State was 153.9 kg./ha. of gross cropped area in 1964-65. This figure declined to 126.85 and 120.15 kg. showing negative change of 17.6 and 5.3 per cent between the period 1970-71 and 1980-81 respectively in spite of 23.3 per cent increase in 1980-81 over the total output of foodgrains of 1964-65. Between 1981-91 foodgrain production registered 40.8 per cent improvement and likewise positive change of 4.5 per cent took place in per capita output during the decade.

Table 21.6 : Foodgrain Output

Year	*Output of total food-grain (in million tonnes)*	*Per capita output (in kg.)*	*Change in per capita output (in per cent)*
1964-65	7.51	153.90	(–) 3.00
1970-71	7.88	126.85	(–) 17.60
1980-81	9.26	120.15	(–) 5.30
1990-91	13.04	125.51	4.50

Sources : 1. Chand, M. *et.al.*, "Regional Planning in India," p. 298, Table 5 for 1964-65 and 1970-71.
2. *Bihar Statistical Handbook* (1982), Bihar at a Glance 1989, 1990-91, 92.

It is obvious that there exists a serious gap between the productivity of foodgrain and intensity of cultivation and input ingredients since the adoptation of new agricultural policy introduced in the State during sixties. Substantial growth in area sown more than once in the State has not increased to match the benefits of productivity to achieve the desired output target. In the perspective plan of 1978-79 of the State Government the investment in agricultural infrastructure was envisaged considering the future requirement of foodgrain and it proposed a target of 234 lakh tonnes of foodgrain production by 1988-89, but the State was able to produce only 127.9 lakh tonnes. Production since then improved to 195.73 lakh mt. tonnes in the year 1993-94.

Trend of Growth : Foodgrain Requirement

Let us examine the production of foodgrains in the State at the level of demand. Howmuch of foodgrain is required and made available by the agriculture sector in the State to feed the population?

Foodgrain production is supposed to sustain the population primarily by satisfying its food requirement at a reasonable caloric level. The National Commission has calculated the demand for foodgrain to meet nutrition requirement at the rate of 370 gm. of cereals and 70 gm. of pulses/day/person, which is not on the higher side even for a State like Bihar. Even at this rate the food requirement for human consumption by 2000 AD for the entire country, on a rough estimate, will be 153 million tonnes of foodgrain. Since the population of Bihar is about 13 per cent of the whole country, the food requirement of the State will likely to be 150 lakh tonnes. If an allowances of 10 per cent of gross production is made for loss at various stages, the total requirement will be something like 160 lakh tonnes in Bihar.

Based on the supply of 440 gm. of foodgrain upto 1980-81 and 500 gm. (considering 2600 calories/day/person) thereafter, the foodgrain requirement including requirement for seed (@5%), animal feed (@10%) and allowances for wastage (@12% upto 1981 and 9% thereafter) have been calculated in Table 21.7.

Table 21.7 : Foodgrain requirement

(in lakh tonnes)

Year	*Population (in lakh)*	*Requirement for Human Consumption*	*Seed*	*Animal Feed*	*Wastage*	*Gross Require-ment*	*Contin-gency*	*Produ-ction Target*
1978-79	645 (est.)	103.59	5.18	10.36	12.42	131.55	13.21	145.00
1980-81	699	112.25	5.61	11.22	13.46	142.54	12.75	155.30
1988-89	830 (est.)	151.47	7.57	15.14	13.62	187.80	12.00	199.80
1990-91	863	157.49	7.90	15.74	14.22	195.35	12.00	207.35
2000-01	927 (est.)	169.17	8.45	16.91	15.21	209.74	12.00	222.00

During the year 1980-81 against the requirement for consumption and gross requirement of 112.25 and 142.54 lakh tonnes of foodgrain, Bihar was actually able to produce 99 lakh tonnes. Again in the year 1988-89 the total foodgrain production in the State was about 128 lakh tonnes. It means that at reasonable level the requirement of foodgrain at the rate of 500 gm./day/head, which comes to about 151.47 lakh tonnes, is eighteen per cent more than the State has actually produced in the same year. Hence the deficit of about 23.5 lakh tonnes means that either deficit was met by import of foodgrain or a greater portion of population is getting less than required amount. This shortage is also reflected in per capita foodgrain availability as well. In 1990-91 the per capita availability of foodgrain, considering the production of 1989-90, was 375.42 gm./day/head in the State. For estimate of foodgrain requirement by the end of this century, an upward adjustment has been made to make it comparative at the 1991 population demand. The total foodgrain demand by the end of 2000 AD will cross the 200 lakh tonnes limit, and at the present growth rate of foodgrain production, the gap between desired intake and actual intake for the vast majority of people is bound to increase. The fall of 0.9 per cent in the compound growth rate of foodgrain production from eighties to early nineties is not going to solve the problem in near future. Bihar is poised to enter the 21st century along with its various socio-economic problems unrest in rural areas, higher labour dependency on agriculture, and level of rural poverty.

Trend of Growth : Productivity of Farm Workforce

In Bihar agricultural sector has to satisfy not only the food demand of its growing population but has to gainfully employ about 81 per cent of working force engaged in this sector and side-by-side make itself economically viable sector. Beside low value foodgrains and non-food crops high value cash crops are grown in the State and their combined value determines the profitability of agriculture. The brief review of the progress achieved since sixties in agriculture indicates increased productivity of all the principal crops during Green Revolution period but the increase has been less than the corresponding increase achieved at national level.

Agricultural productivity per farm worker also highlights the level of growth. Agricultural productivity per farm worker can be defined as productivity per hectare of cropped area divided by number of farm workers per hectare of net sown area. Table 21.8 depicts the average net domestic product per farm worker of agricultural sector at 1982 price.

Table 21.8 indicates that the average agricultural productivity per farm worker for the period between 1967-68 to 1969-70 was only Rs.755. During the last decade workers productivity in agricultural sector has increased to Rs.1239 in response to the growth rate achieved during eighties. Since the plains of Bihar has high density of population and high land productivity than plateau Bihar, its labour productivity is similarly high mainly due to high value crops of sugarcane, fruits, vegetables, chillies, tobacco and jute. Even then there has been no stability in production of main cash crops like sugarcane and jute in the

State. As a result there has been only minimal addition to productivity capacity and human development in the State during eighties and early nineties. At all India level and compared to some states the level of farm labour productivity achieved is on far lower side.

Table 21.8 : Level of Agricultural Productivity

Year	*Per Agriculture Worker (av. net domestic ag. product at 1982 price in Rs.)*
1967-68 to 1969-70	755
1980-81	785
1990-91	1239

Note : In this calculation only major crops have been considered.

In fact net productivity per farm population is slightly higher than the amount cited above. Based on market price of each crop produced in the villages and paid out cost involve, the average productivity of the canal irrigated Daudnagar block of Aurangabad district has been determined by Sharma (1990) between Rs.2000-4000 per hectare and net productivity per annum per unit of farm workforce as Rs.3700. Actually wages of agricultural labour have been included in paid out cost, hence the actual income of farmer is higher than the average, depending on size of operational holdings. The result of a micro study based on sample survey of cultivators of the Sahar village in Munger district reveals that small farmers contributing family labour to grow high value crops have higher per capita return than semi to medium operational holdings. Agricultural income, if family labour cost is deducted, increases in proportion to size of operational holding in spite of decreasing per capita production. Even in this micro study though the net productivity per hectare was Rs.3961, the productivity per cultivator remained as low as Rs.800 per annum. The net productivity consists of 58 per cent of the gross agricultural production. The productivity figure may vary from one region to another, yet in this State where 47 per cent of operational holding size is below 2 hectares, the low per capita return has put majority of the farmers at a distinct disadvantage. The case of agricultural labourers, constituting 37.2 per cent of State's working force is not better than marginal and small farmers. They are basically sustained by workdays created in agricultural sector. Sharma (1990) has observed that at present level of agricultural intensity no substantial improvement in total workdays has been achieved in this sector. Hence it is not possible to provide gainful employment to the total labour force in the State throughout the year. During crop seasons, over population of labour force and limited work days available per worker per year has actually lowered the length of work day to 4 to 6 hours and likewise tend to increase the average per capita paidout cost of agriculture in the State. The situation, thus, created is driving agricultural workforce to seek employment in other States. The shortage of labour force in various regions of Gangetic plain, having less than 0.4 man-animal form of horse power per hectare, during peak season has adverse impact on agricultural performance.

The growing apprehension among land owners about allowing share-cropping, thus leaving fields fallow, poor law and order condition and lack of proper dignity to the farmer in the society along with decreasing political and administrative support to them are few constraints beside poor irrigational and other infrastructural support. The paradox is that the chief ingredients of scientific agriculture has increased since 1967-68 but failed to provide the needed impact. Cultivation of certain cereal crops like paddy and wheat have become non-remunerative. The productivity at each level of measurement and production of crops both failed to sustain the population dependent on the performance of this sector. Since the level of poverty in the State critically depends on raising the productivity of agriculture, agriculture in Bihar has been responsible for State's highest record of 55 per cent people below poverty line. Thus efforts are needed to introduce radical land reforms to break the stagnation setting in the State after a short period of growth. Only a real agrarian transformation can make agricultural sustainable in Bihar.

References

Sharma, B.N. (1990), *Land use of Daudnagar Anchal, Aurangabad*, unpublished Ph.D. Thesis, T.M. Bhagalpur University.

Sipul, N. (1993), *Sahar : A Geographical Survey*, Department of Geography, T.M. Bhagalpur University.

Sah, Narottam (1974), *A Regional Profile of Indian Agriculture*, Vora & Com. Pub. Ltd., Bombay.

Chand, M. & Puri, V.K. (1983), *Regional Planning in India*, Allied Pub. New Delhi.

Chand, M. & Puri, V.K. *A Draft Perspective Plan, Bihar (1978-89)*, Bihar State Planning Board, Patna.

Chand, M. & Puri, V.K. *Bihar Statistical Handbook—1981*, Directorate of Statistics & Evaluation, Bihar Government Press, Patna.

Chand, M. & Puri, V.K. *Bihar at a Glance—1989-1992*, Directorate of Statistics and Evluation, Patna.

22

SUGARCANE MARKETING AND TRANSPORTATION IN INDIA
An Appraisal

R.C. TYAGI & S.S.A. JAFRI

India is the home of sugarcane, to which one can find references in the ancient and pre-historic literature such as the Vedas. It is evidently true that from India sugarcane (sucrose), which is universally used as an essential consumption item, spread to other countries. In India, mostly sugarcane is used as raw material for the production of sugar in the sugar mills. The demand for white sugar went up, particularly after the World War I, the import bill started proving a big drain on the Indian economy. The Government was, therefore, forced to encourage the modern sugar mills – Vacuum Pan Sulphilation (VPS) by passing the Sugar Industry Protection Act in 1932, under which an import duty on sugar was imposed. As a result of the protection to the sugar industry a phenomenal rise took place in the growth of factories as well as in the area under sugarcane cultivation. Gradually, sugar became the item of mass consumption and sugarcane became the most valuable cash crop for the cultivators. The most important thing for this crop is its perishable nature as it rapidly deteriorates with the passage of time converting sucrose into invert sugars which are non-crystallisable. The reason is not far to seek. The sugarcane is a juicy plant and when exposed to sun after its cutting, its juice dries up quickly and the recovery falls down. Not only that, even when the sugar plants remain standing in the field for a long time during summer season, the recovery declines.

The perishable nature of sugarcane crop also limits the options for the cultivators. They have to sell their sugarcane within a very short period, otherwise it will go dry and they would be put into a great loss. The farmers cannot store it. Sugarcane has to be cut from fields and it has to be transported immediately to some nearby sugar factory or sugar processing centre and there it must be crushed and juice converted into sugar without loss of time. Hence the organization of cane marketing and the role of different means of transport and good roads in factory areas are of considerable importance, calling for more urgent attention.

The area under sugarcane, its production and yield per hectare had shown an upward trend during the period 1975-78 to 1993-96 in the country. However, there had been variations in both area under cane and production from year to year due to whether condition and demand. The yield per hectare declined, both in U.P. and in India as a whole during 1975-78 to 1978-81 due to unfavourable weather conditions. During 1975-78 to 1993-96, in India the areas under sugar cultivation, production and yield increased by 29.7, 66.6 and 28.8 per cent respectively while in U.P. during the same period the area under sugar cultivation production and yield increased by 23.0, 66.7 and 35.8 per cent respectively (Table 22.1).

Table 22.1 : Average Acreage, Production and Yield/Hectare of Sugarcane

	All India			*Uttar Pradesh*		
Three Years (Average)	*Area (000 hect.)*	*Production (000 tonnes)*	*Yield pe. hectare (in tonnes)*	*Area (000 hect.)*	*Production (000 tonnes)*	*Yield per hectare (in tonnes)*
1975-78	2930	156859	53.5	1511	66798	44.1
1978-81	2788	144912	52.1	1463	59252	40.9
1981-84	3220	183310	56.9	1710	78690	46.0
1984-87	2964	171777	58.0	1570	76227	48.6
1987-90	3366	208973	62.1	1782	9338	53.1
1990-93	3701	241024	65.1	1882	105863	56.2
1993-96	3799	261288	68.9	1858	111384	59.9

Source : Based on Indian Sugar Year Book 1984-85 to 1996-97.

Sugarcane production is increasing in a fluctuating manner since 1975-78 to 1993-96 in the country. The sugarcane growing areas in the country have been broadly divided into two belts – Sub-tropical belt and Tropical belt. The sub-tropical belt consists of the States of the Uttar

Pradesh, Bihar, Punjab, Haryana, Rajasthan, Madhya Pradesh, Orissa, West Bengal and Assam. In this belt, generally sugarcane is planted in the month of February and March and is harvested from the month of November to April. The important characteristic feature of the sub-tropical belt is that it constitutes 74 per cent sugarcane area of the total area under sugarcane in India. Uttar Pradesh and Bihar share major part of the cane acreage in the country. This belt has been endowed by nature with rich and fertile alluvial soil of the Gangetic plain. On the other side, the tropical belt is mainly comprised of the States of Maharashtra, Karnataka, Andhra Pradesh, Tamil Nadu, Gujarat and Kerala. The climatic conditions of this belt are very much favourable to the sugarcane cultivation and the yield of sugar. The cane crop are generally sown in January-May and harvested in November-April. Apart from the factors such as irrigation and fertilizer use, climatic and soil differences between sub-tropical and tropical belts have their effect on the average yield of sugarcane per acre as also on its quality.

Although, the sugarcane production, area and yield is increasing in the country but also the problems of sugarcane marketing and transportation increasing up to a great extent and badly affecting cane growers. As already been mentioned, that perishable nature of this crop, weaken the farmers as they have to sell their crop to the sugar mills, Khandsari Units or gur manufacturers as soon as possible, just after its harvesting. This crop is one of the major cash crops of the country but unfortunately it is turning into a credit crop, because the farmers are not paid for cane crops for months and sometimes for the years by the sugar mills. This is also a critical situation for the cane growers, which is going on climbing up. All this is more true for U.P., where the State accounts 54 per cent of area of the total area under sugarcane in the country and about 47 per cent sugarcane produce of the total sugarcane produce in the country. Sugarcane crop has a major role as a cash crop in the Indian agricultural economy.

A noticeable features of the sugar industry is that majority of the factories obtain a considerable quantity of sugarcane from long distances. Only a few factories manage to get all the sugarcane they require from their gate area, that is, an area roughly within a radius of 15 kilometres or so. In North India, arrangements for purchasing cane from distant areas are made by opening outstation purchasing centres where cane growers deliver their sugarcane and from there the factories transport it by rail or road to their gates. In South India, except for a few factories delivery is taken from the factory gate even though the sugarcane might be coming from 80-100 kilometres from the factory.

For transport of sugarcane over long distances the factories offer transport facilities to cane growers by engaging their own vehicles or hired vehicles at their disposal. The cost of transport is recovered from the cane growers by adjustment in the cane prices or otherwise. In the States of Uttar Pradesh, Bihar, Haryana and Punjab, however, cane growers societies or unions have been organized for supplying cane to the sugar factories. In Uttar Pradesh, the entire supply of cane to factories is met by the cane growers unions.

The latest enactment in force in Uttar Pradesh and Bihar respectively are the Uttar Pradesh Sugarcane (Regulation of Supply and Purchase) Act, 1953 and the Bihar Sugarcane (Regulation of Supply and Purchase) Act, 1971. The Acts and Rules of various states as well as the Sugarcane Control Order, 1966, provide for reservation of areas or zones. In a reserved area, a factory has the right to purchase cane to the exclusion of any other factory and it has to purchase all the cane offered for sale to it. In an 'assigned area' more than one factory can purchase specified quantity of cane. Thus a 'reserved area' belongs to the factory concerned whereas an 'assigned area' does not. In several cases villages 'reserved' or 'allotted' to different factories are interspersed. Though there is a provision in all the States, Acts and the Rules and Orders framed thereunder, the reservation of areas or assigned areas for a season or seasons annually. In view of the different commissions instituted for sugar industry, it is essential to clarify, define and reserve the factory Zone on a long-term or a permanent basis depending upon the capacities of the factories. Thereby the sugarcane growers are expected to align their interests with these of the factory, and the factory in turn should see to it that the interests of the growers do not suffer.

In the opinion of the Sugar Industry Enquiry Commission, 1974 the annual consideration and issue of reservation order has been stated to be a very disturbing factor on several grounds. Firstly, it stands in the way of long-term planning for cane production as also for the development of the sugar factory areas. In addition to it pre-sowing agreement between the factories and the cane growers cannot be made. Reservation of areas for a period of at least five years with certain stipulation to meet the special situation was recommended by the Bhargava Commission. The Uttar Pradesh High Power Sugar Industry Advisory Committee (1963) was also in favour of reserved areas on a long-term basis.

The Cane Co-operative Societies have important role to play as a great agency supplying cane to the sugar factories. The factories are under obligation to pay the co-operative societies commission on their cane purchased directly from the farmers also. Although, in the States, there are two agencies for marketing of cane, viz., (i) Cooperative Development and Cane Marketing Union and (ii) direct purchase from the growers by the sugar mills. The sugar mills are supplied canes either through the individual cane growers or the Co-operative Development and Cane Marketing Unions to which the primary sugarcane societies are affiliated. The agencies for marketing of cane in the reserved areas of sugar mills are the primary sugarcane societies. Every Union is managed and organized by a Managing Committee which consists of members elected from amongst the primary societies. The primary societies in addition to the function of a cane marketing make advance of loans to the sugarcane farmers. The loans are realized from the farmers from the price of their cane supplied to the factory.

The share of the Co-operative in respect of supply of cane is on the decline in Bihar while the corresponding share has been on the increase in Uttar Pradesh. The decline trend in Bihar is owing to the fact that only a limited number of cane growers are the members of the Cane Marketing and Development Unions. Secondly, the unions in Bihar have been losing their interests and consequently their importance too in cane supply to the factories either due to non-payment of Union Commission or its lying in area for years.

The presence of two marketing agencies is said to be not desirable for the administrative set-up for cane marketing in Bihar in particular. It is suggested that a single efficient marketing agency for sugarcane as in Uttar Pradesh under the Cane Commissioner will prove more successful.

Price of cane fixed by the Government or paid by the factories has a direct bearing on cane production and its supply to the factories. Timely payment of the price to cane growers has its special importance. Although, the related statutory provision makes it obligatory on the part of sugar factories to pay the price within 14 days of its delivery, in actual practice, arrears of cane price have accumulated for years. Without doubt cane price area is one of the major factors that affect the fluctuation in sugarcane, sugar production as also sugarcane acreage. However, the arrears of sugarcane price in U.P. had a declining trend since 1992 to 1995 but the arrears of cane price has increased from the year 1996 and 1997 (Table 22.2).

There are a large number of factors that have some bearing on

Table 22.2 : Cane Price Arrears in U.P.

(Lakh Rs.)

Upto April 15th	*Private Sector*	*State Owned Sector*	*Cooperative Sector*	*Total State*
1991	6609.65 (11.42)	4835.77 (22.28)	4521.33 (17.56)	15966.75 (17.09)
1992	19170.31 (29.28)	8844.41 (35.87)	8728.74 (25.31)	36743.46 (30.15)
1993	14495.77 (20.68)	8531.33 (36.32)	6816.44 (21.55)	29843.54 (26.18)
1994	6695.02 (7.20)	4394.66 (15.94)	2105.30 (5.81)	13194.98 (9.65)
1995	11603.00 (7.91)	6993.00 (16.87)	2189.00 (3.70)	20785.00 (9.49)
1996	47687.00 (27.93)	16329.00 (33.46)	16973.00 (25.23)	80989.00 (28.87)
1997	59765.24 (38.90)	18687.16 (43.78)	18812.52 (30.90)	97264.92 (37.86)

Note : Figures in bracket are the percentage of the total.
Source : Based on Sugar & Cane Commissioner's Office, Lucknow.

sugarcane price in general. The most important and relevant factors that influence the price of sugarcane are: (i) Seasonal factors, (ii) Price of Gur and Khandsari, (iii) Price of alternative agricultural produce, and (iv) Fixation of price by the Government. These points need elaborate to clarify the method of fixation of cane price.

It is the mercy of monsoon that is decisive in agricultural life of the country. There is a good crop of sugarcane provided seasonal conditions such as timely and sufficient rainfall, required amount of moisture and absence of pest and disease prove conducive to the cane crop. Other things remaining as they are, the increased supply of cane due to higher yield leads to lower cane price. The sugar factories will be compelled to offer higher price to cane growers in case of lower cane production as a result of bad weather conditions.

On an average 30 to 35 per cent of the sugarcane produced in the country was utilized in the manufacture of sugar while about 54 to 58 per cent was used for the manufacture of Gur and Khandsari and the balance of 12 per cent goes to feeding, chewing, seeding and other uses. Although, the use of sugarcane increases in sugar factories since 1990 to 1996 but even than a major portion of sugarcane is used for the purposes other than manufacture of sugar. Table 22.3 shows the quantity of cane used for different purposes from 1976-77 to 1995-96. Recently suggestions have been made from certain quarters that Gur and Khandsari manufacture within the radius of 15 kms. of sugar factories may be banned so that the entire sugarcane produce in the area may be available to the factories.

Table 22.3 : Average Utilisation of Sugarcane for Different Purposes in India

	Percentage Utilisation of Sugarcane		
Three Years (average)	*Production of White Sugar*	*Utilised for Seed, Feed & Chewing etc.*	*Gur & Khandsari*
1978-81	34.4	11.8	53.8
1981-84	41.5	11.9	46.6
1984-87	40.4	12.0	47.6
1987-90	46.5	11.9	41.6
1990-93	49.6	11.4	39.0
1993-96	52.7	11.9	35.4

Source : Based on Sugar Year Book (1996-97).

It is well known fact that sugarcane occupies land for a longer period than any other agricultural crops. Its complete growth period extends from 10 months to 18 months. In U.P., Bihar and Punjab States the complete growth period of sugarcane takes a period full one year in the normal course. During this period two or more other crops including both food crops and cash crops can be grown, which can give the farmers a quicker return for their input invested in place of sugarcane. Paddy, maize, wheat, oilseeds, chilly and different types of pulse crops are the alternative produces. Sugarcane also needs larger investment in the inputs when compared to the wheat and paddy crops in which technological breakthrough has already been achieved. The price of these produces affect the price of cane payable by the sugar mills. Higher price of cereals and other money crops give impetus to the diversion of sugarcane area to their produce. The situation obtaining in this way compels the sugar mills to pay higher prices for the created scarcity of sugarcane supply. The adverse situation leads to the diversion of food crop and other cash crop acreage to growing of cane crop. Consequently the factories may enjoy the advantageous position in getting cane at the statutory minimum price fixed by the Government. Thus the price of alternative agricultural produce has a bearing on the cane supply position and cane price (Tables 22.4 and 22.5).

Table 22.4 : Stautory Minimum Cane Price

(Rs. per quintal)

Zone	*Years*				
	1991-92	*1992-93*	*1993-94*	*1994-95*	*1995-96*
South Bihar	26.00	31.00	34.00	39.10	42.50
North Bihar	29.35	35.04	38.98	42.80	47.88
Eastern U.P.	29.02	35.26	39.20	43.93	58.62
Central U.P.	28.83	35.37	39.82	43.86	48.58
Western U.P.	29.26	36.22	40.45	44.33	49.29
Punjab	27.88	34.44	39.16	43.57	46.29
Haryana	29.43	36.43	36.52	41.26	44.29
Rajasthan	27.01	32.76	39.63	40.22	46.09
Madhya Pradesh	31.15	37.50	39.84	42.61	48.25
Gujarat	35.26	42.95	47.17	55.05	61.49
Maharashtra	34.00	41.91	46.87	53.68	58.85
Karnataka	32.45	39.55	44.42	50.95	56.14
Andhra Pradesh	31.01	38.13	41.24	47.13	50.53
Tamil Nadu & Pondicherry	29.17	35.71	40.94	42.98	40.48
Kerala & Goa	26.48	35.88	38.16	41.14	47.01
Others comprising Orissa, W.Bengal, Assam and Nagaland	27.11	32.87	36.65	40.38	44.40

The Agriculture Price Commission (APC) was set up in 1965 to advise to the Government on the price policy for agricultural commodities including sugarcane. The Commission in its earlier reports on policy for sugarcane had observed that the fixation of Statutory Minimum Price (SMP) at a level lower than that recommended by the Commission not only adversely affected the supply of sugarcane but also resulted in escalating demand for sugar. Central Government fixes the sugarcane price for a sugar season on advice of CACP. There is difference between the sugarcane price recommended by Agricultural Price Commission and the price fixed by the Government during 1976-77 to 1996-97. The sugarcane price fixation based on the following four main articles, (i) a minimum cane price, (ii) a basic level of sugar recovery, (iii) a premium for every 0.1 per cent increase in sugar recovery over the basic level, and (iv) the average sugar recovery of the factory during a fixed period (optimum period).

The Central Government fixes each year the first three constituents of the formula after consultation with such authorities, bodies and association as are considered necessary by it to be consulted, notifies

Table 22.5 : Actual Cane Price Paid by Sugar Factories

(Rs. per quintal)

Zone	Years				
	1991-92	*1992-93*	*1993-94*	*1994-95*	*1995-96*
North Bihar	42.25/46.25	46.00/49.00	53.50/56.50	66.00/70.00	71.00/75.00
South Bihar	43.25/46.25	46.00/49.00	53.50/56.50	66.00/70.00	71.00/75.00
East U.P.	45.00/48.00	46.00/49.00	58.00/61.00	66.00/70.00	70.00/74.00
Central U.P.	45.00/48.00	46.00/49.00	58.00/61.00	66.00/70.00	70.00/74.00
West U.P.	45.00/48.00	46.00/49.00	58.00/61.00	66.00/70.00	70.00/74.00
Punjab	45.00/49.00	46.00/50.00	58.00/62.00	68.00/72.00	73.00/77.00
Haryana	45.00/49.00	46.00/50.00	56.00/60.00	66.00/70.00	70.00/75.00
Rajasthan	40.50/42.50	40.00/50.00	50.00/54.00	57.00/66.00	64.00/67.00
Madhya Pradesh	41.00/43.00	41.00/43.00	53.00/56.00	69.00/72.00	N.A.
Gujarat	22.50/28.00	26.00/32.50	31.00/50.00	50.00/73.00	43.50
Maharashtra*	29.00/46.68	27.77/48.95	36.00/61.00	46.00	46.00
Karnataka	30.89/45.00	29.36/50.00	45.00/65.00	56.50/60.40	58.00/64.00
Andhra Pradesh@	29.50	36.50	40.00	50.00	48.66/60.00
T.N. & Pondicherry@	29.06/35.00	31.00/44.40	36.35/55.11	52.50	56.00

Note : In Maharashtra, Gujarat and Parts of Karnataka the prices are generally ex-field.

@ Limited to 8.5% Recovery.

* 1st Advance.

Source : Based on Indian Sugar Mills Association, New Delhi (1996-97), p. 20.

the minimum price of sugarcane payable by each factory at the beginning of each year. It is also pointed out that the minimum statutory price fixed is the only minimum support price and the actual price received by the cane growers depend upon demand for and supply of cane. The minimum cane price protects the interest of growers in the year of shortage of cane production as the cane growers often receive higher cane prices from the factories. The Agricultural Price Commission in its report for the season 1968-69 also had recommended that the basic recovery to which the minimum cane price should be related, should be progressively lowered by 0.2 per cent every year until it reached 8.4 per cent by 1972-73. The Bhargava Commission (1974) recommended that the basic level of recovery should be fixed at 8.5 per cent in view of the fact that even in those regions where the average recovery had been the lowest in the country, recoveries of 8.5 per cent and above had been reached in several years in the past.

In the present method of averaging, the cane cost per quintal included in levy prices of sugar for a zone is the average of cane cost of all factories in the zone. This procedure results in the loss to factories of which the individual cane cost per quintal of sugar is higher than the Zonal average cane cost per quintal. It enables the factories with lower cane cost per quintal of sugar to derive more gain than the zonal average factory.

Optimum period though undefined specifically would mean the period during which the cane is at its best or near to best in quality and the average recovery of this period would represent the best performance of sugarcane in regard to sugar recovery. The minimum price payable by a factory during the season is calculated on the basis of the average recovery of the optimum period of the working of a factory in the preceding season. Government of India has fixed the optimum period for factories in different states and regions. In larger interest of the cane growers, the Sugar Industry Commission 1974 also recommended that the Central Government should announce the statutory minimum price for sugarcane for a crushing season ahead of the sowing of the cane that would be crushed in that season latest by early September each year.

Maharashtra is the highest recovery region and Tamil Nadu is the longest duration region. But the factory-wise disparity in duration and recovery within Maharashtra itself or within Tamil Nadu itself is considerably large, sometimes greater than in any other region of the country. So even if all the factories in India were concentrated in either Maharashtra or Tamil Nadu still at least 50 per cent of all the sugar factories would be below average in duration and recovery. Consequently, they would involve higher costs of production leading to sickness and affecting about 70 per cent of the sugar industry.

The aforesaid factors and facts imply that in respect of fixation of minimum sugarcane price during the last 50 years, the Government policy has not proved to be on a sound footing. Fixation of sugarcane price by the Government has been matched to suit the conditions arising from year to year or during one and the same season. Thus the unrealistic and unsuitable pricing policy of sugarcane adopted by the Government has also greatly contributed to the hectic fluctuations year to year of the cane marketing, cane acreage and cane production in the country. It is argued that the cost of production of cane by itself cannot be an adequate basis for fixation of cane price. Further it would be necessary to fix the price on a long-term basis, say at least for three years with the provision of suitable escalation to provide for the changing pattern of realization. On this line, it would be possible to ensure and stabilize a steady cane marketing and cane acreage in the country. It is also suggested that flexibility to an extent in price policy is necessary to provide to the sugar mills to be able to strike a balance between the actual price of cane and the required quantity of cane in keeping with the different situations obtaining. It is also essential for the Government to announce a minimum support price for Gur and Khandsari along with the announcement of a minimum statutory price of cane. On the other hand State Governments have been fixing very higher cane prices which alone constitute about 65 to 70 per cent of the total cost. The margin of the gross profit seems to be lowest and so a review of cane price beside reducing is required. The cost of other factors constituting the cost of sugar should be taken into consideration a fresh in view of the claim raised by the Sugar Industrial Complex and Indian Sugar Association during the sugar season 1985-86.

The Government announced the statutory minimum prices at Rs. 34.50, Rs. 39.10, Rs. 42.50 and Rs. 45.90 per quintal linked to a basic recovery of 8.5 per cent for the years 1993-94, 1994-95, 1995-96 and 1996-97 respectively. With the announcement of Statutory Minimum Price (SMP) State Governments simultaneously announced high State Advised Prices (SAP), despite being urged repeatedly to refrain from announcing such cane prices as only the Central Government had the authority to fix the sugarcane price under the Sugar Control Order, 1966. The U.P. Sugar Mills Association accordingly represented this matter to the State Government that it would not be possible to pay such a high state advised prices of the cane any more and subsequently filed a writ petition in the Allahabad High Court challenging the fixation of state advised cane prices. The Allahabad High Court by a landmark judgment dated 11 December, 1996, decided that the State Government had no power to fix the state advised prices for the cane under any status and quashed the order dated 15 November, 1996, issued by the U.P. State Government fixing the State advised cane price at Rs.72 per quintal for the season 1996-97. Further, the Court directed the Central Government to constitute a High Powered Committee to study the various aspects of the sugar industry and make recommendations to thoroughly revise the laws prevailing in India relating to sugar, sugarcane and sugarcane marketing.

Conclusion

About 60 per cent of the sugarcane is borne or carried to the sugar factories by bullock carts and rubber tyre carts on an average through pitiably bad roads. It is a known fact that bullock-carts are slow-moving means of carriage in comparison to motor trucks and trains and as such they take longer time in transporting the cane to the factories located at a distance of 5 to 20 kms. resulting in evaporation of sugar contents. In addition, the inadequacy of roads and feeder roads linking the village cane areas further add to losses in sugar recovery.

A conference of all Chief Engineers were held in 1934 at Nagpur for preparation of road development plan on National scale which is popularly known as Nagpur Plan. This plan aimed at bringing every village within 8 km. of main highway in a well developed area. However, it is held that progress of road development in the country has been hampered for want of funds. Despite considerably development of roads in India, the road and feeder roads are in pitiable condition specially in sugar factory areas causing great inconvenience and hardship to the cane growers of northern India for the purpose of cane marketing and transporting to the sugar mills.

The Bhargava Commission had suggested that as far as possible no cane grower should be allowed to transport his cane by bullock-cart over a distance of more than 8 kilometres. In Uttar Pradesh and Bihar most of the cane-growers carry their cane to the gates of the factories by bullock-carts within a radius of 10 to 16 kilometres. On economic consideration and checking cruelty to animals besides the huge loss of cane sucrose on account of driage due to delay in transport, the suggestion of Commission seems to be worthy of implementation.

The average distance of carriage of rail-cane was estimated by Tariff Board at about 60 kilometres, though in some cases the range of distance varied between 16 kilometres to 210 kilometres in the country. Before 1965, Bihar factories crushed about 33 per cent of their total cane crushed, carried by Rail. Now this percentage has fallen down and it is at about 25 per cent in Bihar. In spite of increased importance of road transport in the present context of sugarcane carriage, the importance of Rail cannot be underestimated.

The problem of sugarcane marketing and the problem of its transportation from field to crushing centres effect not only to the cane growers but also to the sugar mills due to loss of sugar contents. It is quite essential to make prompt and convenient payment of cane price as also the cane price arrears to the growers in order to ensure the required quantity of sugarcane to sugar factories. Further, it would be necessary to fix the price by Central Government on a long-term basis, say at least for three years with provision of suitable escalation to provide for the changing pattern of realization. These prices would be fixed by the Central Government as per Sugar Control Order, 1966 to avoid the clash between mills association and co-operative growers association. On this line it would be possible to ensure and stabilize a steady cane marketing and cane acreage in the country. A great inadequacy of Indian roads system is felt in view of the need of better marketing of agricultural produce particularly sugarcane. The roads and feeder roads are in pitiable condition, which required immediate attention, so to promote cane marketing and its transporting to the sugar mills. In such condition where sugarcane is a perishable item, it is necessary to transport it by quicker mode of conveyance like trucks or train instead of using bullock-carts.

References

Bhasin, P.C., 'Road Development in India', *Indian Roads Congress*.

Economic Trends, Vol. V, No. 19, 1st October 1976, Sickness in Sugar Industry.

Indian Sugar Year Book (1995-96-97), Vol. I, pp. 15-16, New Delhi.

Pillai M.P., 'A Realistic Cane Price Policy – The Need of the Hour', *Indian Sugar, Annual Number*, July, 1972.

Report of the Sugar Industry Enquiry Commission, 1974, Vols. I & II, Chapter XI, p. 1031.

S.I.E. Commission Report, Vol.II, Chapter II, p. 857.

The Bhargava Commission Report 1974, Vol. I, Part II, Chapter II, pp. 640-50.

23

DEVELOPMENT OF FLORICULTURE IN INDIA

YASIR SAYEED HANAFI

Introduction

After achieving the self-sufficiency on the food front the focus of Indian Agriculture has shifted to other fields of diversification and commercialisation. One of the options emerged, is in the field of floriculture. It is a field of Ornamental horticulture which consists of floriculture and landscape horticulture. Each is concerned with growing and marketing of plants and with the associated activities of flower arrangement and landscape designs respectively. According to Encyclopedia Britannica, "floriculture deals the production of flowers and ornamental plants, generally cut flowers, pot plants and greenery". The floriculture industry of India is consists of florist trade, nursery plants, potted plants, seeds and bulb production, micro propagation and extraction of essential oil from the flowers.

Floriculture has become a potential money spinner for the developing countries. It is a multi-million dollars trade abroad and a multi-crore industry in India as well. India is endowed with diverse ecological regions, varied climatic conditions and rich native flora which facilitated the availability and production of a wide range of floriculture products throughout the year. Besides, it has fertile soils, abundant sunshine, sufficient water, cheap and skilled labour is also easily available. At the same time, India is like a mine for the varieties of tropical ornamental plants such as Rhododendrons (43), Orchid (1600), Primula (43), Lonicera (23), Aster (14), Begonia (64), Impatiens (241), Iris (13),

Hydechium (24), Pandanas (7), Ixora (37), Gradenia (14), Lilium (11), Barleria (26), Ipomea (37), Thumbergia (10).

Objectives

The main objectives of the study are:

- To make aware about the importance, potential and opportunities of floriculture in India.
- To unveil the quite high return from this sector of agriculture.
- To analyze the growth of floriculture industry in India and predict its prospects in future.
- To make aware about the government's liberal policies and subsidies given to floriculture industry in India.
- To point out the constraints which restrict the growth of floriculture industry in India.
- To assess the potential markets and consumers for floriculture in India and abroad.
- To suggest the measures and methods by which floriculture industry will boost and to overcome the problems which create hindrance in its growth at domestic market and abroad as well.

Database and Methodology

The precise data of floriculture is not available, though we have been using and growing flowers for centuries. Earlier it has been used for religious and social offerings but its commercial value recognized later. The data given in the present study is of secondary nature which is collected from various statistical year books of Agriculture and Processed Food Export Development Authority (APEDA) and National Horticulture Board (NHB), Agriculture Survey of India published by HINDU. The collected data is simply plotted on X-axis and Y-axis to show the pattern of growth in acreage, production and earnings.

Global Trade and Opportunities for India

The worldwide consumption of floriculture products is estimated about 40 billion dollars. Cut flowers contributes nearly 60 per cent. The U.S., Japan and Western Europe are the major markets for floriculture products. The global floriculture industry is growing at an annual growth rate of 10 to 15 per cent. There has been an increase in the per capita consumption of floriculture products in the developed and developing countries. Western Europe consumes 50 per cent of the cut flowers produced worldwide. The Netherlands, the largest trader of floriculture products has shown a significant increase in export of floricultural products in early nineties. It exported 3.4 billion dollars worth of floricultural produce, about 65 per cent of the total cut flower export and 48 per cent of the potted plant exports. Recent estimates indicate a large expansion in floriculture product's consumption particularly in Eastern Europe, Japan, China, South Korea, Thailand, Indonesia and circum-pacific countries.

Export from the Netherlands to distant markets such as Japan and U.S. has been reduced. The East European markets is the target of the Netherland, and this would create a vacuum in the marketing of cut flowers and floricultural products in the United States, Japan and South Asian countries. Hence the prospects are good for new entrants. Floriculture is a sector in which India has unlimited opportunities because of its liberal policies towards horticulture and particularly floriculture trade.

Among the developing countries, Thailand's share is 2.7 per cent and Kenya's 1.3 per cent while India's share in the Global market of floriculture export is less than one per cent. India is centrally located in comparison with major important flower consumption centres in European and South Asian countries. Major markets for Indian floricultural products are Europe (Holland, Germany, the Netherlands, Switzerland, France and U.K.), the United States, the Gulf countries (Kuwait, Saudi Arabia and Oman) and Japan. Cut flowers export to Japan has significantly increased in the last two years. During 1996-97, India was the largest supplier of roses to Japan in terms of volume. Quality flowers can be sold in Japan and Europe particularly in winter while in Singapore, Hong Kong, South Korea and West Asia they can be exported throughout the year. The flower seed exports have tremendous possibilities especially to United States. Similarly tissue cultured plants and protected cultivable plants have good scope in Europe. Cut flower export to Australia is also begun recently.

Changing Scenario of Floriculture in India

The research work on floriculture, which started in late fifties and early sixties picked later and as a result now there are separate departments for this discipline in major agricultural research institutions and universities. In the initial year the emphasis was on gardening related aspects, the thrust shifted to commercial floriculture in later years.

Traditionally, flowers have been growing in India in the open fields, where they have been exposed to both biotic and abiotic stresses. In past, Indian floriculture has restricted itself to the growing of traditional crops like marigold, jasmine, China aster, Chrysanthemum and rose which have been used as loose flowers or garlands. Modern day floriculture focuses more on the production of high-value cut flower crops such as rose, gladiolus, carnation, orchids, tuberose, anthurium, lilium, and gerbera. The floriculture practiced mostly in the farm houses of affluent farmers, gives quite high return from unit areas. The glamour of export oriented floriculture, with its impressive projections of returns, particularly the potential for earning valuable foreign exchange, has tilted the balance in its favour.

The major problem affecting the growth of the domestic sector of floriculture is the non-availability of an organized marketing set-up. In view of the unorganised set-up, it is not possible to assess the market size of the flowers. Correctly considering the significant growth of this industry with an effect of changing life styles and under the increased urban affluence, the flower shops mushroom all over the country and increased purchase of floricultural products as gift items, and ornaments for interior decoration. Export oriented floriculture has picked up recently. The earning has increased from Rs.14.40 crores in 1991-92 to Rs.57.80 crores in 1995-96. It is evident from Table 23.1, that Tamil Nadu ranks first with 8384 hectares of land under floriculture followed by Karnataka, West Bengal, Andhra Pradesh, Rajasthan and Maharashtra with 7870, 3150, 3055, 2500 and 2045 hectares of land under floriculture respectively. Wide variations are also found in returns from the unit area for these crops in different regions. For instance, studies reported by different workers have indicated returns on jasmine cultivation to vary from Rs.10,000 per hectares in Andhra Pradesh to Rs.30,000 in major growing areas of Tamil Nadu to Rs.68,000 in Karnataka and more than Rs.80,000 per hectares in Maharashtra (Raghava, 1997).

The precise database of acreage and production of ornamentals in India is not available but it is evident from the report of Agricultural and Processed Food Export Development Authority (APEDA) and National Horticulture Board (NHB), that the total area under flower crops was estimated around 34,000 hectares during 1988-89, which

Table 23.1 : Area Under Flower Production

State	*Area (Hectares)*	*% Share of each State*
Andhra Pradesh	3055	10.60
Assam	31	0.11
Delhi	85	0.30
Gujarat	405	1.41
Haryana	425	1.47
Himachal Pradesh	25	0.09
Jammu & Kashmir	40	0.14
Karnataka	7870	27.32
Maharashtra	2045	7.10
Manipur	36	0.12
Punjab	158	0.55
Rajasthan	2500	8.68
Tamil Nadu	8384	29.10
Uttar Pradesh	600	2.08
West Bengal	3150	10.93
Total	28809	100.00

Source : Agriculture and Processed Food Export Development Authority (APEDA-1989).

includes 24,000 hectares under traditional flowers such as Marigold, Jasmine, China-Aster, Rose, Chrysanthemum, Tuberose and Crossandra and 10,000 hectares under modern flowers like Rose, Chrysanthemum, Carnation, Orchids, Lilies, Gladiolus, Garbera, Anthurium and Solidago. The area under flower crops increased to 38,000 hectares in 1992-93, and further to 53,000 hectares in 1994-95 and 64,000 hectares in 1995-96. In other words we can say that the acreage of floriculture

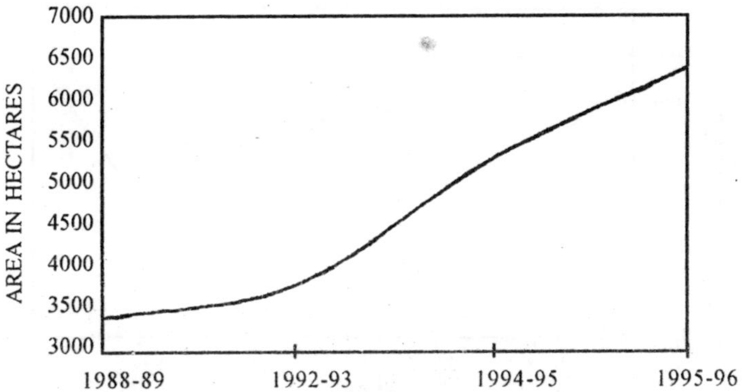

Fig. 23.1 : Growth in Area under Floriculture

becomes double in 1995-96 as compared to 1988-89 or showed a growth of hundred per cent increase during a time span of just 7 years (Fig. 23.1).

It is revealed from Fig. 23.2 and Table 23.2, that the floriculture export is increasing at an unprecedented rate from 1985-86 to 1995-96, particularly in the last three years from 1993-94, the export curve turned to be almost vertical, which shows bright prospect of floriculture industry in coming years.

Table 23.2 : Earnings from Floriculture Export

Years	*Earnings (in lakh rupees)*	*% Share (of total earning)*
1985-86	56	0.42
1986-87	*	*
1987-88	*	*
1988-89	467	3.53
1989-90	557	4.20
1990-91	*	*
1991-92	1445	10.91
1992-93	*	*
1993-94	1884	14.22
1994-95	3060	23.10
1995-96	5780	43.62
Total	13249	100.00

Source : Agriculture and Processed Food Export Development Authority (APEDA-1997).
Note—*Data not available.

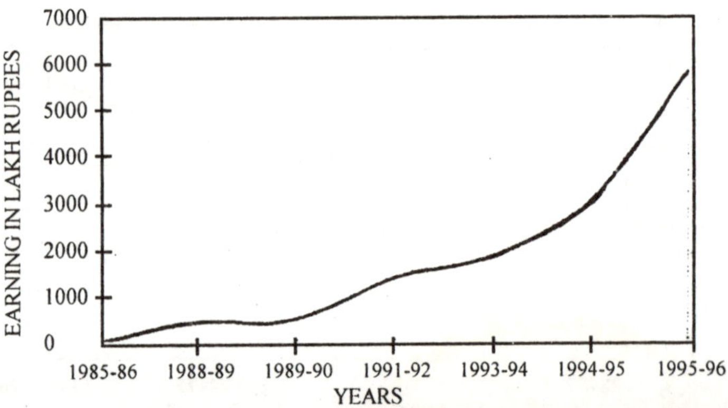

Fig. 23.2 : Growth in Earning of Floriculture Export

On the basis of data, it is estimated that the total export earning of 7 years (ignoring 4 unrecorded years) was Rs.13.249 millions from 1985-96 to 1995-96, and the share of individual year becomes more and more, and if we see the collective share of last 3 years in the total export, it is more than 80 per cent.

Flowers such as Rose, Jasmine, Crossandra, Champak, Chrysanthemum, Tuberose, Marigold and Aster are grown over large areas in Tamil Nadu, Karnataka, Andhra Pradesh, Bihar, West Bengal, Rajasthan, Delhi and Uttar Pradesh. Fragrant rose for oil and perfume grown in Aligarh, Hathras, Kanpur, Ghazipur and Kannuj in U.P., Madurai in Tamil Nadu, Belgam in Karnataka, Haldighati in Rajasthan and Amritsar in Punjab, Marigold is grown in U.P., Punjab, Haryana, Rajasthan, Bihar, Gujarat, Delhi and Karnataka.

The floriculture industry is growing rapidly in all of its spheres of acreage, production and foreign exchange earnings. All these become possible by government policies but still there are some drawbacks which creates hindrance in its growth at domestic level and abroad as well. Let us see the incentives given by government to this sector and what are the constraints in its growth?

Incentives

India has a good potential to enter in global trade as certain flowers and plants are grown in climates peculiar to India. In cut flowers it has started making an impact on the world market. India's share in the export of floriculture products in the world market is less than one per cent. The floriculture industry of India consists of florist trade, nursery plants, bulb production and extraction of essential oil from flowers.

Hence, the government has prioritised floriculture. Several industries either on their own or in collaboration with multinational companies have shown a keen interest in this capital intensive high tech production. To boost floriculture government gives following incentives on priority basis:

- The government allows subsidy on air freight for export of cut flowers and tissue cultured plants, subject to maximum of 25 per cent of IATA freight rates or Rs. 10 per kilogram for export to Europe and U.S. and Rs.6 per kilogram for export to West Asia and Southeast Asia whichever is less.

- Import duty has been reduced on several goods from 55 per cent which include live plants, bulbs, roots, cut flowers and ornamental foliage while the seeds, bulbs, tubers and cuttings or saplings for sowing or planting and tissue cultured material of any plant origin, are duty free.
- Import duty on seed development machinery, soil preparation equipment and specified goods for green houses has been brought down to 25 per cent.
- Government has announced a major change in policy as duty free import to Export Oriented Units (EOU) even if they export 50 per cent of their production.
- Setting up of appropriate infrastructure and suitable technology and equipment for pre-cooling and cold storage facilities has been provided at the international airports for storage of export consignment.
- The government has authorized different heads to issue certificates of origin in respect of horticultural export including floriculture products.
- Assistance is given for the purchase of refrigerated or insulated vans to 25 per cent of the cost of vehicles to a maximum of Rs.1.5 lakh per unit of APEDA.
- The cost for preparing product literature and publicity material can be reimbursed up to 40 per cent by APEDA.
- National Horticulture Board gives soft loans @ 4-5 per cent up to a maximum limit of Rs. one crore for establishment of infrastructure facilities like cold storage, pre-cooling units, packing and grading sheds and refrigerated transport.
- Subsidy is given up to 50 per cent of the cost for low-cost poly-houses, 40 per cent of the cost for medium cost units and 10 per cent or Rs. one lakh for high cost units.
- A steering committee has been formed for the promotion of export of floricultural products under the Ministry of Commerce.
- Karnataka agro-industry has started a small auction house at Bangalore for cut flowers on the pattern of the Aalsmeer Centre in the Netherlands.
- Model markets for flori-products are about to be established in Delhi, Mumbai, Chennai, Calcutta, Hyderabad, Pune and Bangalore by APEDA in collaboration with Central and State

Governments agencies and equipped with required infrastructural facilities.

- Assistance is available from National Bank for Agriculture and Rural Development (NABARD) to a number of hi-tech units at reasonable interest rates.

Constraints

In spite of an abundant and varied production base, India's floricultural industry is not growing accordingly. The low performance is attributable to the following constraints:

- High import duty on planting material and equipments.
- High freight charges and insufficient cargo-space in the air lines.
- Non-availability of cold storage facilities at international airports.
- Undeveloped greenhouse technology and improper facilities of tissue culture laboratories.
- Lack of detailed knowledge on post-harvest technology.
- Lack of training programmes on the pattern of Indian Training Institute for training the manpower for floriculture.
- Non-availability of highly qualified staff in Agricultural and Research Institutions for trade oriented practical courses.
- Non-availability of market surveys and pricing informations.
- Lack of appropriate planting materials, production technology, basic inputs and quality packing materials.
- Inadequate infrastructure for the production of floral crops leads to inadequate surpluses which may otherwise be exported.
- The export oriented unit projects area highly capital intensive which require the entrepreneurs to borrow money at high rate of interest. In most cases, a viable size of about 3 hectares requires a borrowed capital of about Rs. 3 crores, with an average interest rate of 18 per cent as a result the annual interest burden itself amount to Rs. 50 lakhs.

  Marketing of flowers is still disorganised. The flowers brought to wholesale markets in major cities but not packed scientifically during transportation.
- Wholesale flower markets and even retail shops in cities exists in open year. All these effect the life of the product.

- Non-availability of convenient flight connections to the major markets abroad.

Conclusion and Suggestions

It is concluded from the above discussion that India has immense potential of floriculture to exploit it commercially in the domestic market as well as for export. Estimates and surveys by various agencies shows tremendous growth in area, production and foreign exchange earning from this sector but its share in the global market is very meagre, i.e. less than one per cent. India's low share in global trade and unlimited potential reveals that still prospects of floriculture industry in India are very bright. To compete the global market, its products should be of high quality which need technical skill and modern technology. Because flowers and pot plants area largely produced in plant growing structures in temperate climates, floriculture is largely thought as a greenhouse, industry, there are, however, considerable outdoor culture of many flowers. The industry is usually very specialized with respect to its crops, the grower must provide precise environmental control. Exact scheduling is imperative since most floral products are seasonal in demands. Since the products are perishable, the transportation to market must function smoothly to avoid losses. The floriculture industry involves the grower, who mass-produces flowers for the wholesale markets and the retail florists who sales to public. The development of air freight has emphasized inter-regional and international competitions.

For further and smooth growth of floriculture industry, we should have to take the following steps on priority basis:

- There is a strong need for the development of required infrastructure, in major production zones.
- Still there is a need to setting up of appropriate infrastructure, suitable technology and equipments for pre-cooling and cold storage facilities at international airports for storage of export consignments.
- Government should take considerable steps to set up appropriate marketing infrastructure in the major production zones.
- Low cost technologies required on small holdings should be developed.
- Export oriented floriculture being highly capital intensive and

delayed in approval of loan request discourage the producers which should be checked.

- Convenient flight connections to major markets and sufficient cargo-space should be given to floriculture.
- Air freight should be reduced to reasonable levels like other commodities.
- Co-operative florist organizations should be established at regional levels.
- Detailed studies on post-harvest technologies of cut flowers should be carried out at research institutions.
- Training centres or diploma courses on floriculture should be set-up to train the personnel for growing and packing etc.
- Importance should be given to product promotion activities and advertising.
- Foreign collaboration will be very profitable for high quality floriculture products.

References

Chada, K.L. (1994), *Horticulture: Delayed Recognition of Potential*, The Hindu Survey of Indian Agriculture, Kasturi and Sons Ltd., Chennai, pp. 111-17.

Chada, T.R. *et al.* (1988), *Horticulture and Forestry Hand Book for Himachal Pradesh*, U.H.F. Solan.

Coats, A.M. (1968), *Flowers and Their Histories*, Adams and Charles Black, London.

Christopher, E.P. (1958), *Introductory Horticulture*, McGraw-Hill Book Company, New York.

Ghosh, S.P. (1999), *Horticulture : Eying the Export Market*, the Hindu Survey of Indian Agriculture, Kasturi and Sons Ltd., Chennai, pp. 141-45.

Raghava, S.P.S. and Dadlani, N.K. (1997), *Floriculture : Untapped Commercial Potential*, The Hindu Survey of Indian Agriculture, Kasturi and Sons Ltd., Chennai, pp. 139-43.

Raghava, S.P.S. and Dadlani, N.K. (1999), *Floriculture : Strategy Needs Review*, The Hindu Survey of Indian Agriculture, Kasturi and Sons Ltd., Chennai, pp. 147-49.

Randhawa, M.S. (1965), *Flowering Trees*, National Book Trust of India.

Singh, H. *et al.* (1997), *Horticulture Guide for Uttarakhand*, Trees for Life, New Delhi.

Singh, H. and Chada, T.R. (1971), *Horticulture Research and Development in Himachal Pradesh*, Department of Agriculture, Shimla.

Singh, J.P. (1994), *Floriculture : Growing Export Opportunities*, The Hindu Survey of Indian Agriculture, Kasturi and Sons Ltd., Chennai, pp. 129-35.

Thakur, A.R. (1960), *Horticulture in Hill Regions of North India*, Ministry of Food and Agriculture, New Delhi.

The New Encyclopaedia Britannica, (1993), 19:680:2b, 686:1b, Encyclopaedia Britannica Inc. Chicago.

Yadav, I.S. (1999), *Horticulture : Technology for the Farmers*, The Hindu Survey of Indian Agriculture, Kasturi and Sons Ltd., Chennai, pp. 151-53.

24

GROWTH AND DEVELOPMENT OF HORTICULTURE IN JAMMU AND KASHMIR (1947–1997)

MOHAMMAD SIDDIQUE

After Brazil and China, India has emerged as one of the major producer of fruits and vegetables in the world for it has produced over 320 lakh tonnes of fruits and 665 lakh tonnes of vegetables. Jammu & Kashmir, too, has increased its production from 7.60 lakh tonnes of fruits in 1989-90 to 9.10 lakh tonnes in 1995-96 and its export was 7.10 lakh tonnes in 1995-96. Highlighting the significance of horticulture as a major source of economy in our country, the President of India in his address to the Parliament has stressed the need to develop horticulture and remarked that besides other measures to increase the food production, the agricultural policy of the Government also aims at maximizing the production in horticulture, floriculture, medicinal plants and afforestation to increase our export in these areas (*The Hindu*, Feb. 22, 1999).

Of late, the greater demand for ensuring regular and undisrupted supply of vegetables and fruits has undoubtedly posed a serious problem severely affected by the inadequate supply of onions and potatoes and with unaffordable high price rise of these essential commodities in general and commoners in particular. Thus the horticultural products have assumed greater significance in our modern times because of the changing life style of the people, growing socio-economic transformation of the society and the demand in the international markets for it gives a good return.

Horticulture in Jammu & Kashmir is assuming much significance in the economy of the State which engaged 4.85 lakh families directly or indirectly in this sector. For the development of horticulture physical and climatic factors (undulating topography, water logging in low lying areas, marshy lands, untimely frost and snowfall, flood, famine, soil erosion, rapid run-off of rain water as a result of which loss of good fertile soil, siltation etc.) play havoc in some parts of the State. The small holdings and the paucity of agricultural lands have made limited scope for further extension. In such a physico-climatic framework, there is a growing need to maximize the production and productivity through providing inputs and modern technology to existing plantation.

Physico-Climatic Conditions and the Horticulture

As the State comprises three regions (i) The Jammu region, (ii) the valley of Kashmir, and (iii) The Ladakh region which may be characterized as the distinct regions in many respects: geographically, socio-culturally, economically and even politically. Demographically, the State differs greatly in the size of population, growth and distribution, density and occupational structure by age and sex. Most of the areas are uninhibited and barren. Fertility of the soil, productivity are obviously higher as compared to other states of the Great Plain. The valley of Kashmir is predominantly suitable for horticulture in which the Jhelum valley floor has been well known as the fruit bowl of India since the times immemorial. Despite the fact of some negative role of physico-climatic factors in some areas of the State, they do play positive role to growing various kinds of temperate and sub-tropical fruits. The important fruits grown in the valley of Kashmir are apples, pears, peaches, apricots, cherries, walnuts and almonds while mango, *ber, lichi*, guava, papaya, in the Jammu region. In Ladakh region, the agro-climatic condition is arid with great fluctuation in the temperature during day and night in different seasons of the year. The texture is such that it has low content of nitrogen and low to moderate content of phosphorus while potash ranges from moderate to high which altogether characterize alkaline in reaction and require regular irrigation. As the fertilizers being one of the main ingredients for higher production were not used initially due to lack of knowledge but when the farmers realized the benefits of the usage of fertilizers, they are now using and the results are encouraging. To improve the quality and quantity of horticulture (fruits and vegetables), higher yielding variety of plants and seeds which are available from Saspol Nursery were distributed as much as 1377 fruit plants during 1979-80 followed by improved variety of 2749 plants of apricots which were budded to replace the old apricots during 1979-80. A special attraction for tourists now is the sale of fresh fruits and vegetables lined all along the main Leh bazaar. It got boost the horticulture when the vegetable growers co-operative marketing society was established in 1962 which helped the farmers to strengthen their economic position by supplying with their horticultural produce at a reasonable price to the defence personnels (Army Camps) at different places in Ladakh region. The society has so far supplied 8667 tonnes of vegetables and fruits worth rupees 77.06 lakh.

The Jammu region which comprises of Jammu and R.S. Pura, Bhaderwah and Kishtwar, Poonch and Rajauri, Udhampur and Kathua, Ramban and Banihal and Kud and Batote have also much more specialities of vegetables followed by some sub-tropical fruits.

Growth in Area and Production of Horticulture

Jammu and Kashmir has recorded an impressive growth in area as well as in fruit marketed (lakh tonnes) over the years. Baramula, Jammu, Anantnag, Pulwama, Badgam and Srinagar districts are the major producers of fruits. Table 24.1 is self-explanatory and reveals that Fruit Growers Co-operative Marketing Society have played a marvellous job to help the growers in the growth and development of the horticulture in the State. In the initial stage, the area under horticulture was devoted to only 18 thousand hectares but arose to 63.01 thousand hectares in 1995-96. This substantial increase may be attributed by the following factors: (i) opening of Banihal tunnel (Jawahar Tunnel) in 1965 with a metallic road from Jammu to Srinagar and to Leh and Uri (now a National Highway 1A), (ii) growth of tourism in Kashmir, Ladakh and Jammu (Vaishno Devi), (iii) institutional role [banks, co-operatives, communication (T.V. and Radio)], (iv) agricultural educational research centres etc., (v) growth of urbanization, (vi) changing life style of the people, defence personnels and so on.

The production of fresh fruits especially in apples and dry fruits (almond and walnuts) followed by green vegetables (*Karham* and *haak*) have increased over the years due to local demands. The floating gardens in the Dal Lake supply the vegetables to Srinagar urban agglomeration. Table 24.2 gives a detailed statistical data and shows a high degree of fluctuation in the marketing of horticultural produce. The reasons could be attributed by the fact that insurgency in the valley of Kashmir and its effect in the neighbouring areas have made the economy in a shabby conditions.

Table 24.1 : Total Area Sown Under Different Crops (Jammu and Kashmir)

		Area Under Fruit and Vegetables (' 000 hac)	*% Area under Horticulture*	*Total Food Crops*
1955-56		18.00	2.61	689.00
1960-61		21.00	2.77	759.00
1965-66		22.00	2.99	747.00
1968-69		25.00	3.08	813.00
1973-74		34.00	4.06	837.00
1974-75		34.00	4.08	833.00
1977-78		47.00	5.34	880.00
1980-81		51.11	5.74	890.55
1984-85		54.91	5.91	929.99
1985-86		53.63	5.84	918.81
1986-87		52.57	5.64	931.90
1987-88		54.98	5.84	941.05
1988-89		59.57	6.47	921.32
1989-90		58.98	6.23	946.73
1990-91		60.04	6.28	955.53
1991-92		65.91	6.89	956.93
1992-93		61.47	6.44	955.11
1993-94		64.84	6.77	957.87
1994-95		62.96	6.66	945.28
1995-96		63.01	6.59	955.94
	1985-86	*1995-96*	*1985-86*	*1995-96*
Anantnag	7.89	9.07	12.11	74.94
Pulwama	11.86	13.90	23.98	57.96
Srinagar	5.57	5.29	22.27	23.75
Budgam	5.67	7.67	14.70	52.17
Baramulla	14.35	18.90	21.68	87.16
Kupwara	4.80	4.73	10.49	45.07
Leh	0.25	0.33	3.90	8.44
Kargil	0.19	0.20	3.06	6.53
Jammu	1.79	1.42	0.75	189.71
Udhampur	0.24	0.47	0.45	103.84
Doda	0.54	0.67	0.91	73.53
Kathua	0.29	0.27	0.25	105.49
Rajouri	0.10	0.06	0.07	88.81
Poonch	0.09	0.03	0.08	38.54
Total	53.63	63.01	6.59	955.90

Source :Digest of Statistics, J&K Government, 1995-96.

Despite the fact of limited agricultural land, the State recorded 8.17 lakh hectares of cultivated area during 1984-85, i.e. about 33.84 per cent of the total reporting area. The net sown area was recorded at 7.35

lakh hectares, i.e. 30.43 per cent of the reporting area. The irrigated net area was recorded by 3.09 lakh hectares, i.e. 42.07 per cent of the net sown area. Horticulture occupied by 54.91 thousand hectares of which 37 thousand hectares devoted to fruits and 17 thousand hectares were to put to vegetables. In such an agricultural situation, horticulture assumes a significant proportion in the State economy.

Table 24.2 : Fruit Grower Co-operative Marketing Society (Jammu & Kashmir)

	Fruit Marketed (lakh tonnes)	
1974-75	0.03	
1977-78	0.10	
1980-81	0.14	
1984-85	0.06	
1985-86	0.07	
1986-87	0.07	
1987-88	0.03	
1988-89	0.05	
1989-90	0.05	
1990-91	0.01	
1991-92	0.04	
1992-93	0.03	
1993-94	0.07	
1995-96	0.089	
	1985-86	*1995-96*
Anantnag	0.020	0.028
Pulwama	0.001	0.011
Srinagar	0.021	0.005
Budgam	0.010	0.007
Baramulla	0.011	0.060
Kupwara, Leh, Kargil	0.004 (Leh, Kargil)	(No data)
Jammu	0.001	0.029
Udhampur	—	0.001
Doda, Kathua, Rajouri	(Kathua 0.005)	(Negligible)
Poonch	—	0.002
Total	0.073	0.89

Source : Digest of Statistics, J&K Government, Department of Horticulture, 1995-96.

Import and Export in Horticulture

India has increased its horticulture exports significantly which have proved to be one of the most important area of overall growth and development. The traditional exports such as cashew, spices, coir and walnuts, fruits, vegetables, flowers, tissues culture and other ornamental plants have the country unmatched potential. Recognizing the benefits gained from exports, India is providing necessary infrastructure to encourage the further export and Rs.600 crores have been sanctioned for achieving the desired goal to increase the production and productivity through providing inputs and high technology to existing plantation. The other thrust is to provide assistance on post-harvest infrastructure and market information under the auspices of the National Horticulture Board.

The State of Jammu and Kashmir has recorded a rapid growth of population. In order to feed the teeming population, obviously import of the tropical fruits (banana, mango, watermelon etc.) are necessary items while the export of apples, dry fruits (almond, walnuts) are done on a large scale. Table 24.3 reveals the import and export of horticultural crops from 1973-74 to 1995-96 which shows an increase of both the in and out flow of horticulture commodities. The transport network of the State is highly developed which help in the transaction of local produce of horticulture in national market for gaining a good return.

As a matter of fact it may be noted from the statistical data (DOS) that 16 thousand buses and trucks were reported at Banihal terminal in 1950-51 to enter the valley of Kashmir which arose to 1.39 lakh followed by other vehicles of 19 thousand in 1985-86. This number further grew in size to 2.30 lakh in 1995-96 which reveals that the import-export of essential commodities including horticulture produce are on a higher side.

It may be worthwhile to note that the State exported fresh fruits 5424.75 thousand quintals of which apple (5324.66), pear (36.80), cherries (3.98) and others (59.31). The dry fruits accounted for 92.22 thousand quintals of which almond (16.89), walnuts (41.27), walnut kernals (23.63), jam and jellies (0.06) and others (10.06) during the normal year of peace (1984-85). The vegetables were exported during the harvesting season to a tune of 0.27 thousand quintal despite the local demand. The insurgency 1989 onward has slowed down the vehicle of economic growth in the valley of Kashmir.

Factors Associated with the Growth and Development of Horticulture

Impact of urbanization has been assessed in the Sixth Rehovot Conference (1971) in which the opinion expressed by the experts was

Table 24.3 : Trade and Commerce
(Jammu and Kashmir)

	Imported ('000 quintals)		*Exported ('000 quintals)*		
	Fruits	*Vegetables*	*Fresh Fruits*	*Dry Fruits*	*Vegetables*
1973-74	136.90	206.20	1598.61	90.80	13.00
1977-78	257.00	313.60	2515.10	81.80	3.50
1980-81	323.44	468.39	3821.70	94.95	0.41
1984-85	237.58	518.28	4553.63	98.61	0.27
1985-86	274.35	589.35	5424.75	92.22	—
1986-87	312.30	718.76	4883.44	110.11	—
1987-88	328.38	662.89	3316.76	82.92	—
1988-89	422.59	881.80	4780.04	70.21	0.27
1989-90	580.79	999.17	5011.27	168.64	—
1990-91	539.89	1013.47	3742.53	213.30	1.20
1991-92	701.03	1193.28	4830.64	209.30	9.52
1992-93	681.99	1217.96	6196.86	282.64	5.05
1993-94	802.74	1284.38	7385.90	247.24	2.45
1994-95	971.32	1426.90	5649.50	332.20	1.21
1995-96	1001.16	1387.07	6870.00	280.00	1.27

Source : Digest of Statistics, J&K Government, Department of Horticulture, 1995-96.

that the urban growth is the basis to the agricultural development (horticulture development) and the modernization of this sector of economy in economically less developed countries/regions is highly dependent on an urban infrastructure. Keeping in view of this fact, the State of Jammu and Kashmir has altogether 57 urban centres (1981) of all size classes which constitute 21.05 per cent of the local population. The growth and distributional patterns of urban centres are not uniform for it has varied topography, attitudinal variations and environmental and different geographical characteristics. In Jhelum valley floor, for instance, there are 18 urban centres out of 24 urban centres of the valley of Kashmir. The urban agglomerations of Srinagar and Jammu together account for 8.3 lakh population out of the total urban population of 12.6 lakh (i.e. 67.7 per cent). The remaining 55 small and medium size towns function mostly as the mandis or marketing centres of the horticultural products (fruits and vegetables). In this way, all the urban centres of the State in one way or the other are the focal points of innovations, progress and social and economic transformation within themselves but also exert the impact on the neighbouring villages for they characterize in having all the urbanizing factors in them such as small scale industries, cottage and household industries, processing, trade and commerce, transport and communication facilities, institutional establishments (banks and co-operatives), educational institutions and other social amenities and facilities, electricity, hospitals. However the impact of urbanization in the development of horticulture may be seen from the following indicators :

(i) use of fertilizers (animal dung, compost green manure and chemical fertilizers).
(ii) use of improved varieties of seed, plants.
(iii) use of improved elements (tractor, pump-sets, thrashers, sprayers duster).
(iv) adoption of plant protection measures (soil treatment, seed treatment, use of pesticides at the time of sowing, rat control).

It may be seen that nearer the villages to the urban centres are more highly exerted by the impact of urbanization in the horticultural growth and development than the farther located villages.

Problems and Prospects of Horticultural Growth and Development in the State

There are a number of problems arising out of the topographical characteristics, environmental conditions, isolation, political, social and economic factors which altogether are responsible for the growth and development of horticulture in the State. Himachal Pradesh as is situated on the same physico-climatic conditions has surpassed the former in many respects because of the human efforts, proximity of the State to the major market centres of India, the political stability of the State, and moreover the transport linkage even during the snowfall period. We shall now discuss the problems in case of Jammu and Kashmir first and shall examine the further prospects of horticulture sector in the State :

1. The first and foremost problem is the damage caused by the pests and diseases to the fruit plants. Majority of the orchards are located either near the settlements or along the roads which produce air pollution because of the heavy vehicular traffic.
2. Marketing of horticultural produce is a major problem. Only 30 per cent of the profit are received to the growers and 70 per cent are taken away by the middle men. As a result of which

the small growers are loosing their interest because of the less profit.

3. When the market price is high and growers expect high returns, their products get delayed because of the road blockage during the snowfall period or the landslides during the rainy season.
4. The problem of packaging always come in the way because of the long distance and high transport costs and the perishability factors of the fruits.
5. At the time of need, growers face difficulty in procuring the assistance given by the Department of Horticulture (Government) because of procedural delay.
6. Growing menace of communalism/regionalism is also a factor which shatters the basic philosophy of import and export of commodities at inter-regional level. Fair dealing always strengthen the trade and commerce to the satisfaction of both the parties.
7. In the age of competition, human effort is necessary to come forward with a view to safeguard their deteriorating economic condition.
8. The failure of snowfall, rainfall, i.e. environmental crisis often leads the growers in a difficult situation.

There are many more major and minor problems which come in the way of the growth and development of horticulture but these problems could be solved in the age of science and technology. However the future prospects of this sector of economy is bright because the State has been a temperate fruit bowl of India.

The State Government in collaboration with the Centre has launched various measures through its successive five year plans. A separate Department of Horticulture has been functioning and has adopted suitable policy to develop the horticulture in the State:

(i) Creation of suitable organizations to supply various input services and technical know-how. The Shere-Kashmir Agricultural University at Shalimar in Srinagar is an example besides other organizations to provide support to the horticulture industry by strengthening research and development and to adopt advanced technology.

(ii) Improvement in the quality of fruits and vegetables and regulation of marketing activities.

(iii) Schemes to ensure higher prices and incentives for small and marginal farmers/growers in the horticulture plantation programmes.

(iv) Adoption of improved methods of horticultural productions.

Besides the above plans and prospects of the State Government, National Horticulture Board has launched various schemes, e.g. post-harvest infrastructure and market information services, pre-cooling facilities to the growers and the cold storage facilities at the airport, drip irrigation system, trading and packing centres (40), pre-cooling units (15), plastic containers (5 lakhs), nutritional gardens in rural areas (50), juice vending machine (140), transfer of technology by training the farmers (2000), soft loans, development of marketing, various programmes of training through media [Newspapers, All India Radio (Srinagar, Jammu), Door Darshan (Srinagar)].

References

Raanam, Weitz (ed.), (1973), *Urbanization in the Developing Countries*, Report on the Sixth Rehovot Conference 1971, Praeger Publishers, New York.

Azad, K.C., Swaroop, R. and Sikka, B.K. (1987), *Horticultural Development in Hill Areas*, Mittal Publication, Delhi.

Digest of Statistics (1995-96), Government of Jammu & Kashmir.

Siddique, M. (1985), Urbanization in Jammu & Kashmir in *A Regional Analysis in Geography of Jammu and Kashmir*, (ed.) Majid Husain, Department of Geography and Regional Development, University of Kashmir, Srinagar, Ariana Publishing House, New Delhi, pp. 215-38.

Techno-Economic Survey of Jammu & Kashmir, 1969, NCAER, New Delhi.

Sharma, T.R. (1998), Horticulture Development in Himachal Pradesh, A Study of Apple Cultivation, *Kurukshetra*, Vol. 46, No. 12, September, pp. 50-52.

Raza, M., Ahmad, A. and Mohamad, A. (1978), *The Valley of Kashmir*, Vikas Publishing House, New Delhi.

Mahmoodur Rehman (1984-85), Government of Jammu & Kashmir, *Indicators of Economic Development*.

25

CROP-COMBINATION REGIONS IN SOUTH BIHAR PLAIN

RAMESHWAR THAKUR

Introduction

The study of crop-combination constitutes an important aspect of agricultural geography as it provides a good basis for agricultural regionalisation. Crops are generally grown in combination and a complete domination by a single crop in a given area at any time is rare. For comprehensive and better understanding of the agricultural mosaic of an agro-climatic region, the study of crop-combination is of great significance. The present work is an attempt to study the crop association for determining the crop- combination regions in the South Bihar Plain. The main objectives of the present work are: (i) To delineate crop regions to know the areas of dominance of the important cereal and non-cereal crops; (ii) To demarcate crop-combinations and to know the geographical conditions required for each combination.

Existing Studies

On account of its multifarious utility, many scholars especially in the field of agricultural geography and agricultural economics have long been engaged in evolving methods to measure crop-combinations in various parts of the world (Bennett 1939; Scott 1957; Johnson 1958; Dot 1959; Refrnllah 1965; Singh 1965; Athawale 1966; Ahmad & Siddiqui 1967; Siddiqui 1967, 1975; Coppock 1967; Tripathi & Aggarwal 1968; Ayyar 1969; Husain 1972; Khan 1973; Mohammad 1975; Singh 1977; Majeed 1981). Geographers have applied a number of simple and sophisticated statistical techniques from arbitrary choice method to the deviation approach. The arbitrary choice method is not rational as by its application other crops grown are excluded, disregarding their percentage weightage in the total cropped area.

A more reliable and rational approach was adopted by Weaver. In his study of crop-combination regions in the Middle West, Weaver demarcated crop associations developed in terms of variables based on certain differences which are relative and not absolute. This method, being statistical, is more scientific. It has attracted the attention of many geographers. Besides this, other methods have been used which have their own limitations.

The Study Area

The South Bihar Plain, which is a part of the Indo-Gangetic Plain, lies between latitudes 24° 30'N and 25° 46'N and longitudes 83° 20'E and 87° 45'E. It is bounded by the river Ganga in the north, the 150 metres Contour line of the scarp of Chota Nagpur Plateau in the south, Rajmahal hills in the east and Uttar Pradesh in the west. It covers an area of 36,192 sq km which constitutes 20.7 per cent of the total area of Bihar. The region has a population of 20.48 million with a density of 566 persons per sq km (1991). This is more than the average density of population in Bihar (497 persons per sq km) and India (267 persons per sq km). The region may be divided into two main physiographic units—the hilly areas consisting of Kharagpur and Rajmahal hills in the east, and the vast plain of the river Ganga and the river Son in the west. It experiences a sub-humid climate with a hot, dry summer from March to May, the rainy season from June to October, and the cold dry winter season from November to February. Annual rainfall varies from 800 mm to 1300 mm and is highly seasonal, variable and erratic. This, considerably, affects agriculture. The soil is, by and large, fertile alluvium which can be divided into Khadar and Bhangar groups. Khadar covers the flood plain in the vicinity of rivers, while the Bhangar is the older alluvium which covers the upland tracts beyond the flood limit. In general, the soil of the region is heavy and fine in texture. About 65 per cent of the total area is under cultivation, 6 per cent is covered by forests, groves and pastures, and the remaining 29 per cent is cultivable waste. The percentage of cultivated land varies greatly. The principal Kharif crops are rice, maize, sugarcane, ragi, tur, moong and sesamum. The major rabi crops are wheat, barley, gram khesari, urad, lentil (Masoor), tisi, rapseed and mustard, potato and onion.

Data Source and Methodology

The study is based on secondary data which have been obtained from government and quasi-government publications. For the measurement of crop association, ranking of crops and crop-combination regions at anchal (block) level, the average data for the agricultrual year 1998-99 has been selected because the technological revolution in Indian agricultrual had made a large impact in the area of this time. Average data for the agriculutral years 1997-2000 has been taken in order to make allowance for fluctuation in area due to natural and human factors. Altogether sixteen crops, (foodgrains and non-foodgrains) which account for more than 80 per cent of the total cropped land of the region are selected. The anchal (block) is used as unit of a study. 146 anchals are identified for the study.

In the present study an attempt has been made to delineate crop-combination regions by using two methods, viz., ranking method and Doi's method. In the ranking method, the first three crops have been included in the combination. A close look at the percentage strength of the crops indicates that by and large the first three ranking crops occupy a substantial proportion of land in the anchals barring a few anchals where crop combination is more complex and heterogeneous. On the basis of 16 crops, association regions have been identified and delineated (Fig. 25.2). The ranking method gives a very simple and generalised picture. Therefore, Doi's method, which perhaps shows an improvement over Weaver's method has been applied. Doi has modified Weaver's formula by substituting $\Sigma \frac{d^2}{n}$ with Σd^2 or the sum of squared differences. Thus, the combination having the smallest Σd^2 will be the combination formed by the major crops only. Σd^2 value may then be referred to in Doi's table of critical values. To plot the results standard cartographic techniques have been adopted which enable the reader to understand the crop-combinations and the constituents crops at a glance. This type of cartography, with extended legends, is unique and original.

Crop-Combination Analysis

The study of crop-combination reflects the variable position of individual crops among themselves. It is helpful in interpreting some aspects of economic and social geography. Such studies provide an adequate understanding of individual crop geography, an integrated reality that demands definition, and distributional analysis of crop combination and the more complex structure of valid agricultural regions.

The cropping structure, cropping strength and crop concentration is determined by the fertility, texture and structure of soil, and by the temperature and moisture components of climate. The socio-economic variables and availability of modem inputs also have a close bearing on the cropping mosaic. Most of the farmers, on the basis of their empirical experiences, are aware of land fertility and the climatic setting, and, therefore cultivate different crops not only in the course of a year but also from one year to another. The change follows a rhythm connected

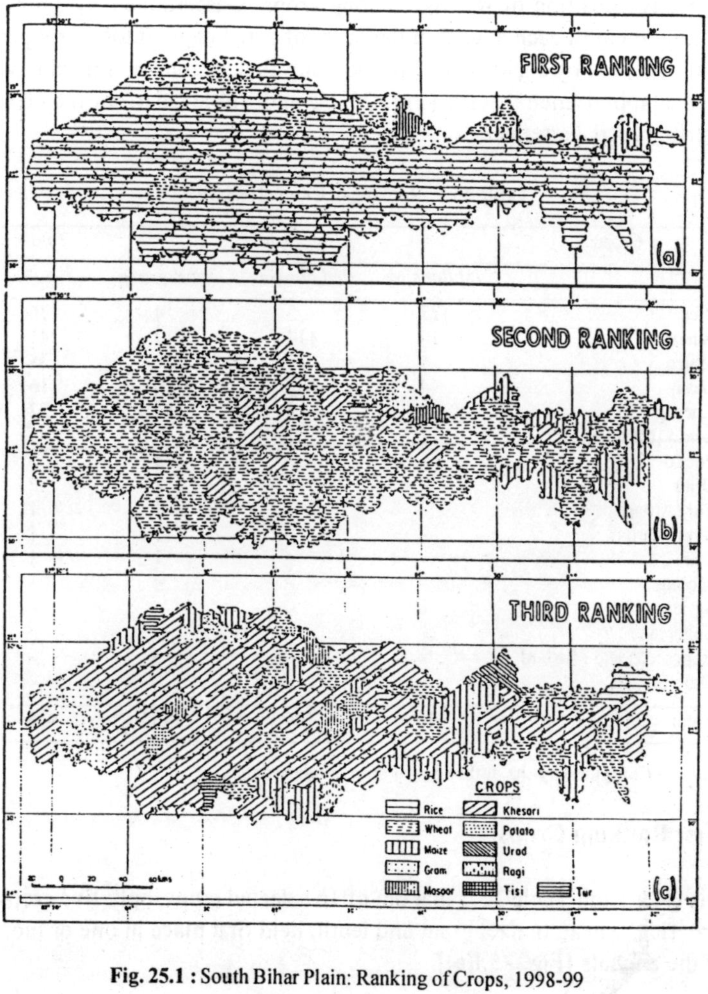

Fig. 25.1 : South Bihar Plain: Ranking of Crops, 1998-99

with the composition of the soil and with sowing, hoeing, weeding and harvesting. Unless the major crops of a region are studied in their ranking order appropriate associations of soil exhaustive and soil enriching crops for each situation cannot be ascertained. For this purpose, a comparison of various crops seems to be essential. The first three leading crops in each of the anchals have, therefore, been ranked for the present study.

Ranking of Crops

A relative position of strength among crops is ascertained by simply ranking them in each anchal in the order of percentage of total cropped land occupied by each crop. Crops ranking first, second and third have been mapped anchal-wise (Fig. 25.1), and Table 25.1 shows clear distributional patterns.

Table 25.1 : Ranking of Crops: 1998-99

Crops	*No. of Anchals*			*Total*
	1st Ranking	*2nd Ranking*	*3rd Ranking*	
Rice	127	5	4	136
Wheat	10	114	17	14!
Maize	4	11	20	35
Gram	4	2	10	16
Khesari	–	13	84	97
Lentil (Masoor)	I	1	3	5
Potato	–	–	3	3
Urad	–	–	2	2
Tur (Arhar)	–	–	1	1
Ragi(Marua)	–	–	1	1
Tisi	–	–	1	1
Moong	–	–	–	–
Sesamum(Til)	–	–	–	–
Sugarcane	–	–	–	–
Rapeseeds and Mustard	–	–	–	–
Onion	–	–	–	–
Total	146	146	146	438

Source: Computed by the author based on secondary data.

First Ranking Crops

It is clear from Table 25.1 that out of 16 selected crops, only five crops, viz., rice, wheat, maize, gram and lentil, held first place in one or more of the anchals [Fig. 25.l(a)].

Rice, spreading over 127 out of 146 anchals, occupies the first position in most of them. Generalising broadly, rice can be said to hold the first rank almost uniformly in the region except in the upper 'levee' region of the Ganga, where there is water logging during heavy floods or the soil is a little more sandy and, hence cannot be profitably cultivated. The soil in the rice producing area varies from new alluvium-calcareous and non-calcareous to older alluvium with heavy cracks. In all the rice-dominated ahchals, the average annual rainfall is 1200 mm. The fairly reliable rain falls mostly in the monsoon season. The average temperature is 26°C in the growing period.

Wheat, the second most important staple cereal, holds the first rank in only 10 anchals and was confined to diara or semi-diara land (river banks of the Ganga and the Son). The soil in the wheat-dominated anchals, is, by and large, alluvium deposited by these rivers and their tributaries. In fact, the fertility is increased every year by these deposits. Apart from that, dany type of loam is good for its cultivation in canal irrigated areas because of the deficiency of moisture is the controlling factor in the South Bihar Plain. Moreover, the development and extension of tube-well and pumping set irrigation has also helped in the diffusion of high yielding varieties of wheat. It is well known that wheat performs well if the crop is provided water and manure at the right time and in the right proportion.

Other first ranking crops are maize, gram and lentil (masoor). Maize and gram rank first in four anchals each of the diara lands on the bank of the Ganga. Maize grows on 'bhith' or upland, which is completely protected from early floods and thrives well on light and sandy loam soil. It is concentrated in Barh anchal in Patna district. Jamalpur anchal in Munger district and Kahalgao and Pirpathi anchals in Bhagalpur district. Among pulses, gram is the most important crop concentrated in 'Tal' region of Ganga in Barhara and Shahpur anchals of Bhojpur district, Pandarak in Patna district and Barahia in Munger district. The chief controlling factor for gram cultivation is perfect soil aeration. Moisture is less important than air in the soil and, therefore, open sandy and well drained loam is particularly suited to this crop. Lentil ranks first only in Mokama anchal of Patna district which is otherwise more suitable for the cultivation of rice. The cultivation of lentil in large areas in the rice region may perhaps due to water logging during floods in the Ganga in the Kharif season.

Second Ranking Crops

The spatial pattern seems to change little in the case of second ranking crops [Fig. 25.l(b)]. Only a total of six crops, viz., wheat, rice, maize, gram, khesari, and lentil, hold second rank in one or more ahchals. Wheat dominates the scene in this case by ranking second an as many as 114 anchals. Rice, maize, gram, khesari and lentil rank second in 5, 11, 2, 13 and 1 ahchals respectively. The dominance of wheat as second ranking crop is clear evidence of the fact that the geographical conditions have favoured its cultivation in the rabi season. Other important reasons are that high yielding varieties of wheat have been diffused in the relatively wet areas of the region. These short duration varieties grow well under controlled irrigation and mature early to spare the land for the sowing and transplantation of paddy.

Khesari is cultivated as the second crop in thirteen anchals of different districts. Rice holds second rank mostly in these anchals where it could not rank first and is cultivated in irrigated areas and along river banks. Maize is cultivated in eleven anchals in the eastern part of the region, particularly in Bhagalpur and Santhal Pargana districts. Two other pulses rank second in two and one anchals respectively. The rabi crops (wheat, khesari, gram and lentil) dominate the agricultural landscape of this region as second ranking crops in 128 anchals.

Third Ranking Crops

The spatial pattern of distribution of third ranking crops is, as expected, somewhat more diversified [Fig. 25.l(c)]. The third ranking crops are rice, wheat, maize, gram, khesari, lentil, potato, urad, tur, ragi and tisi. These crops present in intricate and complex cropping pattern. Khesari, maize and wheat are, however, the main third-ranking crops covering 84, 21 and 17 anchals respectively. There is one compact region of about 70 anchals in the central part of South Bihar Plain where khesari dominates as the third crop. The compactness of this region is somewhat disturbed by several anchals of Munger district where maize and wheat rank third and fourth. It is interesting to note that rice, the major cereal grown in most parts of the region, ranks third in only four anchals. Anchals where rice ranks third are Barbigha in Munger district and Nathnagar, Kahalgaon and Pirpaithi in Bhagalpur district. The areal distribution of wheat as the third ranking crop is scatterec between the Son valley in the west and Rajmahal range in the east. The emergence of wheat as a third ranking crop in Patna, Munger and Bhagalpur districts shows that the traditional varieties of wheat are performing well in areas of humid rice cultivation. Gram is the third ranking crop in 10 anchals, of which 6 anchals are in the south-western part of Rohtas district and the others in two small areas in the north-west and north-east corner of Bhojpur and Santhal Parrgana districts. Lentil and potato rank third in three anchals in the central and northern parts of the region. It may, however, be mentioned that lentil and potato cover considerable areas as fourth ranking crops. These crops do not form any continuous region so far urad, one of the important pulses grown in the region, also occupies two continuous anchals, Munger and Jamalpur in Munger district near the 'terai area along the Ganga. Tur, ragi and tisi are also important third ranking crops occuping one anchal each in different parts of the region. These crops are generally cultivated in the uplands where water availability is low. The spatial pattern of the third ranking crops is in the form of small non-contiguous zones.

The third ranking crops show a notable diversity and occur in non-contiguous zones of appreciable sizes. The diversity in third ranking crops indicates that their selection is governed largely by family requirements and socio-economic conditions.

Crop-combination Regions

In order to increase productivity and to save soils from fertility depletion careful and judicious utilization of land by selecting an appropriate crop combination is essential. It is, therefore, advisable to identify, for each agricultural set-up, a crop-combination which would give optimum agricultural returns and provide employment to farmers and their dependents. By paying more attention to the major constituent crops of a region, farmers can increase the production of food and raw materials. While doing so, the less important crops can be excluded from the combination and the land thus spared could be given to crops which perform well at a reasonably low level of inputs.

Many statistical techniques have been applied for delimitation of crop-combination regions. This paper uses Doi's method. Accordingly, the percentage strength of each crop in each anchal has been arranged in descending order, and with the help of the critical value table evolved by Doi, six crop-combinations have been identified. Figure 25.2 shows all the six crop association regions that have been derived from 16 major crops (rice, wheat, maize, gram, khesari, lentil, urad, tisi, ragi, sugarcane, moong, seasmum, tur, rapeseeds and mustard, potato and onion).

The six crop-association regions, shown in Table 25.2 indicates the variety of crops in each region. These regions emerge as clusters of anchals. The compact areas having the largest number of similar anchals is the 2-crop and 3-crop association regions. It will be quite interesting to analyst the six crop-combinations and the geographical background of each.

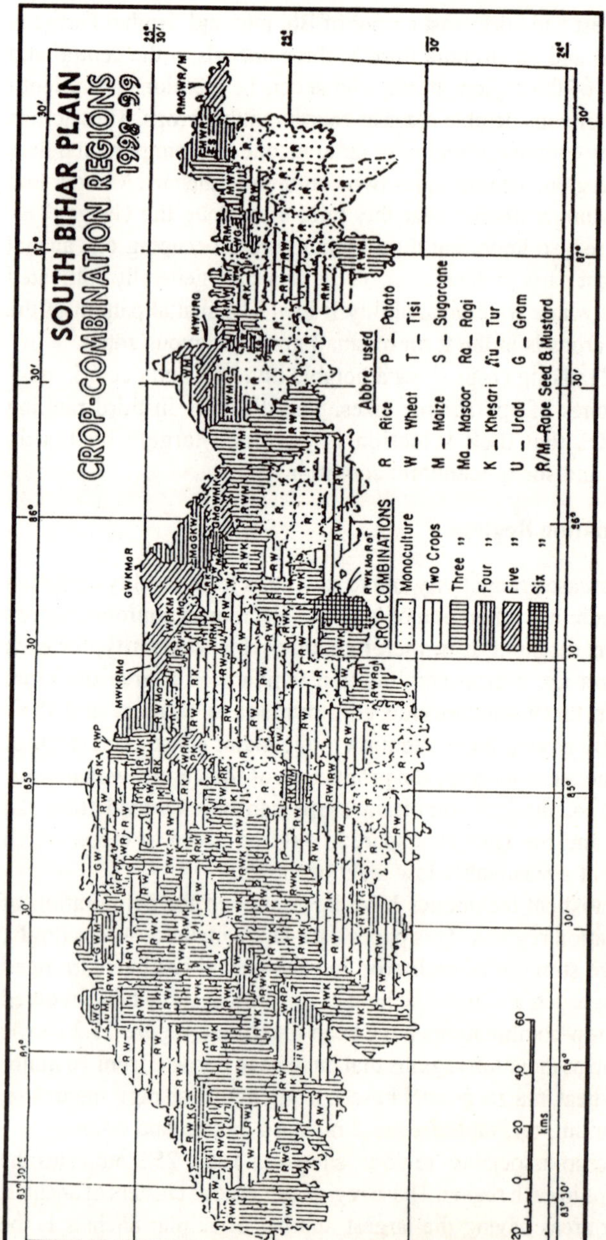

Fig. 25.2 : South Bihar Plain Crop-Combination Regions 1998-99

Table 25.2 : Crop-Combination Regions: 1998-99

	Crop-Combination Regions	*No. of Anchals*	*No. of Regions*
1.	Monoculture regions	24	8
2.	Crop-combination regions	56	14
3.	Crop-combination regions	45	12
4.	Crop-combination regions	13	12
5.	Crop-combination regions	7	5
6.	Crop-combination regions	1	1
	Total	146	52

Source: Computed by the author based on Secondary data.

Monoculture Regions

In the study region, monoculture or single crop dominance is found in 24 out of 146 anchals. Rice has emerged as the dominant crop in these regions. It covers twenty-three anchals in Bhagalpur, Gaya, Nalanda, Munger and Santhal Pargana districts. A major group of eight anchals lies in the extreme north-eastern part of the region and covers the largest area. The second important pocket of four anchals lies in two areas, one located in the western part of Bhagalpur district and other in the southern part of Gaya district. The next pocket of three anchals lies in the central part of Munger district and the remaining four anchals are scattered in different districts. Rice is grown under widely differing climatic and pedological conditions in the region. Moreover, water requirements for this crop are such that cultivation tends to be concentrated in regions where there are flat lowlands, river basins and abundant rainfall. In most of the monoculture anchals, rice is almost entirely dependent on monsoon rains. The high variability of rainfall renders the success of rice cultivation uncertain in areas where the major problem is drainage. Apart from these conditions, rice is well adapted to regions of high temperature and prolonged sunshine. The average temperature throughout the time of cultivation ranges from 20° to 37.7°C.

The geographical conditions described above are suitably found in the northeastern parts of the region, especially in the fertile alluvial plains of the Chandan river in Bhagalpur district, Rajmahal hills and Kharagpur hills. Here rice occupies over 70 per cent of the total cropped area and thus appears in the crop combination map as a mono-crop (Fig. 25.2).

Crop-combination Regions

Two crop-combination are found in fifty-six anchals (Fig. 25.2). Rice, wheat, khesari, gram and maize are combined in different associations to form these combinations. Rice with wheat is the single most important two crop-combination which spreads over forty-five anchals. Rice, owing to alluvial soil and favourable climatic conditions, ranks first. Seven anchals in different districts form a two crop-combination of rice and khesari. Rice and wheat combination is largely found in the central and western parts of the region where land is almost flat and soil is alluvial and loamy. Both these staple crops are, however, soil exhaustive and, therefore, higher returns without soil depletion can be obtained only if a leguminous crop is brought into the crop rotation. Apart from that, there are four other regions of two crop combinations: gram-wheat, rice-maize, wheat-rice and wheat-maize covering one anchal each in different parts of the region.

Three Crop-combination Regions

Three crop-combinations exist in forty-six anchals (Fig. 25.2). The constituent crops of the combination are rice, wheat, gram, khesari, maize, lentil, potato and ragi. Rice-wheat-khesari is the major combination covering twenty-nine anchals in different district. Other important combinations are rice-wheat-maize in four anchals which join a contiguous region office-wheat-khesari everywhere. Twelve more anchals have three crop-combinations, but the constituent crops in each anchal are different from the others. Rice-wheat-gram and rice-khesari-wheat include two anchals each, and the remaining eight anchals have different combinations, viz., wheat-rice-gram, rice-wheat-potato, wheat-rice-maize, rice-wheat-ragi, rice-wheat-lentil, rice-maize-wheat, wheat-maize- rice and maize-wheat-rice.

Number of Four Crop-combination Regions

With the increase in the number of crops in combination, the diversity of crops also increases. There are thirteen anchals scattered all over the region having 4 crop-combinations. Rice dominates the scene in seven anchals out of thirteen. This associations of crops appears dominant in the transition zone of wheat and rice in which farmers prefer to grow rice in the kharif and wheat in the rabi season. Legumes are sown in rotation with rice and wheat to maintain the fertility of the soil.

Five Crop-Combination Regions

In 5 crop-combination regions, the diversity of crops further increases and there is not even a single set of anchals where similarity in crops occurs. Almost all the major food crops are included in this combination. Seven anchals come under the 5 crop-combination, the constituent crops being rice, wheat, maize, gram, khesari, lentil, urad, potato, ragi, rapeseed and mustard. All these 5 crop-combination regions are found along the bank of the Ganga from west to east except Dhanura anchal. Here most of the crops are grown in the rabi season because in the Kharif season the land is covered by river water.

Six Crop-Combination Regions

The 6 crop-combination comes out only in the Gobindpur anchal of Nawada district. It includes rice, wheat, khesari, lentil, ragi and tisi. Once again, rice dominates while wheat and khesari rank second. Owing to high variability of rainfall the farmers in this area cultivate many less moisture requiring crops.

Conclusion and Suggestions

Less diverse combinations are found in the central part as well as in the Son valley where the soil is comparatively fertile and productive. Very diverse crop associations are found in other parts, including the hilly terrain. Here the soil is too poor and infertile to raise cash crops or important cereals. Another important feature is that khesari, one of the leading crops after rice and wheat in almost all crop association regions in central and western parts, decreases in importance towards the north-eastern part of the area. Here, khesari is replaced either by maize, gram or lentil. The main geographical factors causing this replacement are the quality of soil, seasonal distribution of rainfall and the annual temperature.

Trial and adoption of new crop-combinations is essential for increasing production to meet the growing requirements of the ever-increasing population. Factors which hinder uniform adoption of new crop-combinations within a given agro-climatic situation need to be removed. To this end, better adoption models suitable for each meso and micro region have to be evolved. It is necessary for planners and administrators to work for social justice, redistribution of consumption norms and balanced spatial development and pay more attention to a comprehensive development of total rural life as well as to remove the spatial inequalities and imbalances. The farmers, on the other hand, should try and increase their income by concentrating on a few crops, developing a suitable combination of crops within their individual constraints of finance and labour.

References

Ahmad, A. and Siddiqui, M.F., (1967), "Crop Association Patterns in the Luni Basin", *Geographer*, Vol. 14, pp. 71-80.

Athawale, A.G., (1966), 'Some New Methods of Crop-Combination", *Geographical Review of India*, Vol. 28, No. 4, pp. 29-33.

Ayyar, N.P., (1969), "Crop Regions of Madhya Pradesh: A Study in Methodology", *Geographical Review of India*, Vol. 31, No. 1, p. 17.

Bennett, H.H., (1939), *Elements of soil conservation*, (New York: McGraw, Book Comp.)

Coppock, J.T., (1964), "Livestock and enterprise combination in England and wales," *Economic Geography*, Vol. 40, pp. 153-75.

Doi, K., (1959), "The Industrial Structure of Japanese Prefectures", *Proceedings of International Geographical Union*, Regional Conference in Japan, 1957, pp. 310-16.

Husain, M., (1972), "Crop-Combination Regions of Uttar Pradesh: A Study in Methodology", *Geographical Review of India*, Vol. 34, No 2, pp. 143-147.

Johnson, B.L.C., (1958), "Crop Association Regions in East Pakistan", *Geography*, Vol. 52, pp. 86-103.

Khan, A.H., (1973), "Crop-Combinations in Rohilkhand". *Geographer*, Vol. 20, No. 2, pp. 153-162.

Majeed, A., (1981), "Crop-Combinational Analysis: A Review of Methodology," in Mohammad, N. (ed) *Perspectives in Agriculture Geography*, Vol. 4, New Delhi: Concept Publishing Company, pp. 61-76.

Mohammad, N., (1975), "Crop Association Regions in Ghaghara-Rapti Doab", *The North Eastern Geographer*, Vol. 7, Nos. 1 & 2, pp. 3-9.

Rafiullah, S.M., (1965), "A New Approach to Functional Classification of Towns", *Geographer*, Vol. 12, pp. 40-53.

Scott, P., (1957), "The Agricultural Region of Tasmania", *Economic Geography*, Vol. 33, pp. 3-14 & 109-121.

Siddiqui, M.F., (1967), "Combinational Analysis: A Review of Methodology", *Geographer*, Vol. 14, pp. 83-92.

Siddiqui, M.F., (1975), "Crop-Combinations and Specializations in India", *Geographer*, Vol. 21, No. 1, pp. 78-84.

Singh, H., (1965), "Crop-Combination Regions in the Malwa Tract of Punjab", *Deccan Geographer*, Vol. 3, No. 1, pp. 21-30.

Singh, T., (1977), "Bihar: A Study of Crop-Combination Regions", *Indian Journal of Regional Science*, Vol. 9, No. 2, pp. 147-152.

Weaver, J.C., (1954), "Crop-Combination Regions in the Middle West", *Geographical Review*, Vol. 54, No. 2, p. 176.

26

PROGRESS OF AGRICULTURAL MARKETING COOPERATIVES OF U.P. STATE

RAIS AHMAD & ALI GHUFRAN

Marketing cooperatives in Uttar Pradesh are next to agricultural credit. The main objective of promoting marketing cooperatives in the state was to support the primary agricultural credit societies and in turn help the small and medium farmers by providing timely marketing facilities.

The organizational structure of marketing cooperatives in Uttar Pradesh is of three tiers in nature:

- At apex level state cooperative marketing federation;
- Central/District federations at district level; and
- Primary marketing cooperative societies at block/taluka level.

Organization of cooperative marketing societies in each market was taken up on the basis of rural credit survey recommendation in the second five year plan to eliminate malpractices and ensure reasonable price to the agriculturists. However, because of formation of marketing committee and improvement in the means of transportation, the business of marketing societies has been adversely affected because of the competition of private traders. As apex of the marketing societies, there is Uttar Pradesh Cooperative Federation, which markets agricultural produce by market intervention as and when needed.

Coming to the state cooperative marketing federation it is found that in the year 1960-61, the business share of state cooperative marketing federation of Uttar Pradesh to that of total country was 23.5 per cent, which decreased to 10.2 per cent in 1965-66. This figure increased to 14 per cent in 1973-74 and came down to 13.4 per cent in 1997-98. The figure further moved to 16.3 per cent in 1984-85 and remained the same in the year 1989-90.

Similarly in the year 1965-66, the share of district cooperative federation of Uttar Pradesh to that of total country was 7.92 per cent, which decreased to 7 per cent in the year 1973-74 and further fell to 6.6 per cent in 1997-98. This figure further rose to 8 per cent in 1984-85 but again slumped to 4.4 per cent in 1989-90.

Finally coming to the primary cooperative marketing societies, it is observed that in the year 1960-61, the business share of primary cooperative marketing societies of Uttar Pradesh to that of total country was 6 per cent, which came down to 4 per cent in the year 1965-66 and further decreased to 3 per cent in the year 1989-90.

The overall progress and performance of primary cooperative marketing societies, district cooperative marketing federation and state cooperative marketing federation of Uttar Pradesh has been illustrated in Tables 26.1(a) & (b), 26.2, 26.3 respectively.

During the year 1991-92, the membership of district cooperative federation and primary cooperative marketing societies reached 24769 and 918513 respectively with a paid up share capital of Rs. 478.12 lakh and 1235.64 lakh, and working capital of Rs. 2932.97 lakh and 4308.90 lakh.

Table 26.1(a) : Progress and Performance of Primary Cooperative Marketing Societies (All) of Uttar Pradesh

Particulars	*1960-61*	*1973-74*	*1984-85*	*1989-90*
Number of Societies	453	241	276	314
Membership	478054	884501	921000	936000
Paid Up Share Capital (Rs. Thousand)	7925	22762	52208	60400
Working Capital (Rs. Thousand)	20816	96315	232000	290700
Value of Agricultural Produce Marketed (Rs. Thousand)	74469	118839	155778	NA
Total Business Turnover (Rs. Thousand)	74767	151550	407181	835100

Source: *Analytical Study Of Marketing Cooperatives in India (1960-61 to 1990-91), Data Series, xi-xvi*, National Resource Centre, National Cooperative Union of India, New Delhi, pp. 47-59.

Perusal of the Table 26.1(a) shows that during the period 1960-61 to 1989-90, the number of primary cooperative marketing societies increase from 453 to 314, due to which the membership of these societies also increase from 478054 to 936000 for the same period. Paid up share capital and working capital also increased from Rs. 7925 thousand to Rs. 60400 thousand, and from Rs. 20816 thousand to Rs. 290700 thousand for the above period. Due to result of this, the turnover of all primary cooperative marketing societies shows a growth of more than 11 times in the year 1989-90.

Table 26.1(b) : Progress and Performance of Primary Cooperative Marketing Societies (General Purpose) of Uttar Pradesh

Particulars	*1960-61*	*1973-74*	*1984-85*	*1989-90*
Number of Societies	220	230	256	257
Membership	789073	827000	918000	93000
Paid Up Share Capital (Rs. Thousand)	17723	30760	53218	59900
Working Capital (Rs. Thousand)	48856	136853	NA	288100
Value of Agricultural Produce Marketed (Rs. Thousand)	86947	201506	NA	NA
Total Business Turnover (Rs. Thousand)	102626	334168	0	827300

Source: *Analytical Study of Marketing Cooperatives in India (1960-61 to 1990-91), Data Series, xi-xvi*, National Resource Centre, National Cooperative Union of India, New Delhi, pp. 60-70.
NA—Not Available

Perusal of the above Table 26.1(b) shows that during the period 1960-61 to 1989-90, the number of primary cooperative marketing societies (general purpose) increase from 220 to 257, due to which the membership of these societies decrease from 789073 to 93000 for the same period. Paid up share capital and working capital also increased from Rs. 17723 thousand to Rs. 59900 thousand, and from Rs. 48856 thousand to Rs. 288100 thousand for the above period. As of this, the turnover of all primary cooperative marketing societies (general purpose) shows a growth of around 11 times in the year 1989-90.

Table 26.2 : Progress and Performance of District Cooperative Marketing Federation (All) of Uttar Pradesh

Particulars	*1960-61*	*1973-74*	*1984-85*	*1989-90*
Number of Societies	84	51	53	64
Membership	12877	4408	10528	21000
Paid Up Share Capital (Rs. Thousand)	2143	4121	17900	24800
Working Capital (Rs. Thousand)	25900	122394	218902	215400
Value of Agricultural Produce Marketed (Rs. Thousand)	NA	NA	223800	254200
Total Business Turnover (Rs. thousand)	45493	127744	385161	254200

Source: *Analytical Study of Marketing Cooperatives in India (1960-61 to 1990-91), Data Series, xi-xvi*, National Resource Centre, National Cooperative Union of India, New Delhi, pp. 73-83.
NA—Not Available

Perusal of the Table 26.2 shows that during the period 1960-61 to 1989-90, the number of district cooperative marketing federation decrease from 84 to 64, despite this the membership of these societies increase from 12877 to 21000 for the same period. Paid up share capital and working capital also increased from Rs. 2143 thousand to Rs. 24800 thousand, and from Rs. 25900 thousand to Rs. 215400 thousand for the above period. Due to result of this, the turnover of district cooperative marketing federation shows a growth of around 6 times in the year 1989-90.

Table 26.3 : Progress and Performance of State Cooperative Marketing Federation (All) of Uttar Pradesh

Particulars	*1960-61*	*1973-74*	*1984-85*	*1989-90*
Number of Societies	1	2	1	1
Membership	125	478	310	310
Paid Up Share Capital (Rs. Thousand)	3256	6854	138504	215208
Working Capital (Rs. Thousand)	41407	675021	2262997	829719
Value of Agricultural Produce Marketed (Rs. Thousand)	74041	255334	1667000	792800
Total Business Turnover (Rs. Thousand)	143621	807724	5341000	8259100

Source: *Analytical Study of Marketing Cooperatives in India (1960-61 to 1990-91), Data Series, xi-xvi*, National Resource Centre, National Cooperative Union of India, New Delhi, pp. 86-96.

Perusal of the Table 26.3 shows that during the period 1960-61 to 1989-90, the number of state cooperative marketing federation remains the same, but the membership increase from 125 to 310 for the same period. Paid up share capital and working capital made a remarkable growth from Rs. 41407 thousand to Rs. 215208 thousand, and from Rs. 41407 thousand to Rs. 829719 thousand for the above period. Due to result of this. the turnover of state cooperative marketing federation shows a huge growth of around 57 times in the year 1989-90.

As on March, 1994, there were 266 Marketing Societies in Uttar Pradesh having a membership of 918513 members. The overall progress and performance of cooperative marketing societies in Uttar Pradesh from 1982-83 to 1993-94 has been illustrated in Table 26.4.

Table 26.4 : Progress and Performance of Uttar Pradesh Cooperative Marketing Societies from 198 2-83 to 1993-94

(Rs. in Lakh)

Year	*Membership*	*Paid-Up Share Capital*	*Deposits*	*Working Capital*	*Borrowing*	*Sales*
1982-83	901326	502.02	461.36	2252.03	755.02	4194.24
1985-86	912661	800.20	490.36	2918.24	1090.13	3514.59
1989-90	918513	1183.90	646.01	4074.88	1578.81	3254.18
1990-91	918513	1218.27	668.48	4201.08	1667.97	4892.21
1991-92	918513	1235.64	700.38	4308.90	1746.09	3997.07
1992-93	918513	1264.98	750.94	4649.35	1966.70	4429.93
1993-94	918513	1284.92	730.44	4696.19	1969.65	4188.27

Source: *Cooperatives in Uttar Pradesh, Statistical Profile*, 1998, Uttar Pradesh Cooperative Union, Lucknow, Uttar Pradesh, p. 82.

During 1991-92, cooperatives in Uttar Pradesh marketed agricultural produce approximately of Rs. 1958.11 crore, which rose to Rs. 3331.63 crore in the year 1997-98. The overall progress of cooperative marketing in the state from the year 1991-92 to 1997-98 is given in Table 26.5.

On comparing this data of Uttar Pradesh with the data of India, which is Rs. 6502.20 crore in 1991-92 and Rs. 12007.80 crore in 1997-98, it is found that the percentage of agricultural produce marketed by Uttar Pradesh marketing cooperatives to that of India is 30.12 per cent in 1991-92 and 27.75 per cent in 1997-98, which is the highest among the other state's percentage to that of India.

Table 26.5 : Agricultural Produce Marketed by Cooperatives in Uttar Pradesh from 1991-92 to 1997-98

Year	*Value of Agricultural Produce Marketed (Rs. Crore)*
1991-92	1958.11
1992-93	1411.14
1993-94	1986.57
1994-95	2712.34
1995-96	3937.97
1996-97	3300.13
1997-98	3331.63

Source: National Cooperative Development Corporation, Annual Reports, 1992-93 to 1999-2000.

Uttar Pradesh State Horticultural Cooperative Marketing Federation

Fruits and vegetables play an important role both in terms of economic and social values for improving income and nutritional standards of rural masses. The major task is to increase their productivity, contain post harvest loss and create marketing infrastructure and also processing facilities.

National Cooperative Development Corporation is supporting these activities in cooperative sector and encouraging establishment of large fruits & vegetables marketing and export projects involving modern technology. In tune with the policy of Government of India, National Cooperative Development Corporation is according high priority to the development of horticulture in the cooperative sector of the country. It is continuing to assist cooperatives for marketing and processing of fruits & vegetables under its various schemes. Assistance is also extended in collaboration with the National Horticulture Board for post harvest management aspects of horticulture crops to cooperatives for marketing and retailing of fruits & vegetables.

As far as the marketing of fruit & vegetables through cooperatives in Uttar Pradesh is concerned, it is described in Table 26.6, which shows that in Uttar Pradesh the marketing of fruits & vegetables amounts to Rs. 0.17 lakh for the last ten years except Rs. 5.06 lakh in the year 1997-98.

Uttar Pradesh State Horticultural Cooperative Marketing Federation, which comes under the supervision of National Horticultural Board, is an organization of producers and exporters of fruits and vegetables. The federation was established in 1992 with a paid up capital of US$1 million, is situated in the North Indian state of Uttar Pradesh—the largest producer of fruits & vegetables in India.

Table 26.6: Marketing of Fruits and Vegetables by Cooperatives in Uttar Pradesh from 1991-92 to 1999-2000

Year	*Amount (Rs. in Lakh)*
1991-92	0.17
1992-93	0.17
1993-94	0.17
1994-95	0.17
1995-96	0.17
1996-97	0.17
1997-98	5.06
1998-99	0.17
1999-2000	0.17

Source: National Cooperative Development Corporation, Annual Reports from 1991-92 to 1999-2000.

Objectives

The main objectives of the Uttar Pradesh State Horticultural Cooperative Marketing Federation are as listed below:

- Facilitate and promote cooperative marketing of fresh and processed horticultural products to benefit the producer.
- Enhance production & procurement of fresh and processed horticultural products and promotion of horticultural cooperative societies for the benefit of producers.
- Extend necessary help in technical, administrative, financial and other areas to member societies.

Membership and Activities

According to the latest data of 2000-2001, there are 250 primary horticultural cooperative marketing societies in Uttar Pradesh, operating at the village level consisting of over 5000 members. For these societies, Uttar Pradesh State Horticultural Cooperative Marketing Federation has assigned the following activities:

1. Strengthening primary horticultural cooperative marketing societies and cooperative marketing network;
2. Provide technical guidance/inputs to producer member;
3. Promotion of infrastructure development;
4. Pre & post harvest management training for producer members;
5. Study tours for producer members;
6. Market Information dissemination;
7. Logistic support for distant marketing;
8. Domestic trade of horticultural products;
9. Export promotion of main horticultural products of the state;
10. Participation in National & International fairs and buyer-seller meets.

Organizational Structure of Uttar Pradesh State Horticultural Cooperative Marketing Federation

As far as the organizational structure of Uttar Pradesh State Horticultural Cooperative Marketing Federation is concerned, it is of two tier in nature i.e. Uttar Pradesh State Horticultural Cooperative Marketing Federation on the apex and primary horticultural cooperative marketing society at the base level. The organizational structure of Uttar Pradesh State Horticultural Cooperative Marketing Federation is depicted in Figure 26.1.

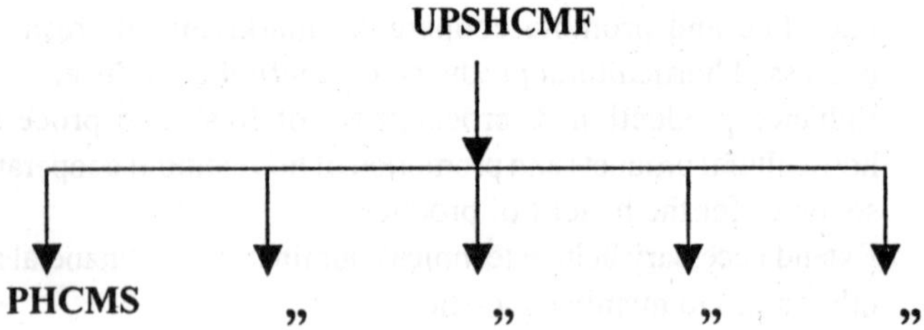

Fig. 26.1: Organizational Structure of Uttar Pradesh State Horticultural Cooperative Marketing Federation

Out of total number of 250 primary horticultural cooperative marketing societies in the state of Uttar Pradesh, there are 119 Primary Horticulture Marketing Societies in Eastern Uttar Pradesh. Lists of these societies in Eastern Uttar Pradesh (division wise) are listed below in Table 26.7.

Though Uttar Pradesh State Horticultural Cooperative Marketing Federation started its operation in the year 1992, it has membership of 119 societies (Eastern Uttar Pradesh), but most of these societies are working only on paper and only a few societies which are situated in Lucknow or Western area of the state are engaged in the cooperative marketing of horticultural produce, particularly fruits.

Table 26.7 : Number of Primary Horticultural Marketing Societies in Eastern Uttar Pradesh

District/Division	*Number of Societies*
Allahabad	38
Fatehpur	19
Pratapgarh	03
Allahabad Division	**60**
Azamgarh	01
Ballia	01
Maunathbhanjan	02
Azamgarh Division	**05**
Basti	01

(Contd.)

(Contd.)

District/Division	*Number of Societies*
Siddarthnagar	03
Basti Division	**04**
Baharaich	15
Gonda	01
Shrawasti	01
Devipatan Division	**17**
Ambedkarnagar	01
Faizabad	01
Sultanpur	02
Faizabad Division	**04**
Gorakhpur	02
Kushinagar	05
Maharajganj	03
Gorakhpur Division	**10**
Mirzapur	02
Mirzapur Division	**02**
Ghazipur	12
Jaunpur	02
Varanasi	03
Varanasi Division	**17**
Total	119

Source: Through Personal Investigation and Discussion with the Officials of the District Cooperative Societies.

Conclusion

In the state of Uttar Pradesh, there was previously no marked tendency towards the cooperative marketing of agricultural commodities. Solitary institutions existed here and there and worked independently.

Actually, the development of cooperative marketing in the state commenced in the late 30s, with the constitution of the Directorate of Marketing and Inspection at the Centre, and on the recommendations of the Royal Commission for Agriculture.

The state government neglected the cooperative marketing institutions upto the first five year plan, as no specific targets were laid down for the betterment of this section of the Cooperative Movement. In the State Ministers Conference, 1955, special attention was given to Marketing Cooperatives and it was recommended that within next 15 years, 50 per cent of the total agricultural business; credit, marketing and processing should be on cooperative lines.

With the introduction of Pilot Project Scheme in the state, the area of operation of the marketing society extends and the main activities of the society were the marketing of member's produce and the provision of warehousing facilities.

For the farmers of the state, a cooperative society was merely a loan society which serves their credit needs. In order to bring desired socio-economic change, it was needed to link credit with non credit activities, which serves the total needs of the farmers and to increase their earning capacity and solvency. For this, during second plan it was recommended to link credit with marketing, in order to make the marketing societies a viable unit.

In the third five year plan, an important place was given to cooperation as a major form of organization in many branches of economic activity especially in the cooperative marketing, and to rebuild an efficient structure for the conjunction with cooperative credit.

During the fourth and fifth plan emphasis was laid on the consolidation and strengthening of agricultural marketing societies, especially of the primary societies.

It is seen that the share of Uttar Pradesh to that of total country regarding turnover of marketing cooperatives, which was 7.92 per cent during the third plan decreased to 4.4 per cent at the end of the seventh plan. Similarly, the business share of primary cooperative marketing societies, decrease to 3 per cent in seventh plan from the mark of 6°|b of second plan. In the year 1990-91, the Uttar Pradesh share regarding the marketing of agricultural produce was 29 per cent to that of total country, which decreased to around 27 per cent at the end of year 1997-98.

The above figure shows that the performance of marketing cooperatives in the state of Uttar Pradesh is not upto a satisfactory level. The reason for this is the less attention is paid towards the primary marketing cooperatives which are the backbone of marketing cooperative organization.

Since the liberalization of the economy has changed the economic structure of the country and withdrawing of protective support from the government, it is admitted that the role and vision of marketing cooperatives in the present economic situation be guide by the global socio-economic trends.

The marketing cooperatives have to work in the interest of the member farmers by:

- Providing better prices for the produce of members,
- Obtaining fast and accurate market information,

- Maximizing sales and procurement operation,
- Effectively utilizing collective purchasing, etc.

But before achieving all these, they have to remove all obstacles coming in their way by properly restructuring their business activities. Unless until, these obstacles are removed, there is very little hope for the marketing cooperatives of the state, to survive and prosper in this new economic environment.

INDEX